Spinoza on Philosophy, Religion, and Politics

Spinoza on Philosophy, Religion, and Politics

The *Theologico-Political Treatise*

Susan James

OXFORD
UNIVERSITY PRESS

OXFORD
UNIVERSITY PRESS

Great Clarendon Street, Oxford OX2 6DP

Oxford University Press is a department of the University of Oxford.
It furthers the University's objective of excellence in research, scholarship,
and education by publishing worldwide in

Oxford New York

Auckland Cape Town Dar es Salaam Hong Kong Karachi
Kuala Lumpur Madrid Melbourne Mexico City Nairobi
New Delhi Shanghai Taipei Toronto

With offices in

Argentina Austria Brazil Chile Czech Republic France Greece
Guatemala Hungary Italy Japan Poland Portugal Singapore
South Korea Switzerland Thailand Turkey Ukraine Vietnam

Oxford is a registered trade mark of Oxford University Press
in the UK and in certain other countries

Published in the United States
by Oxford University Press Inc., New York

British Library Cataloguing in Publication Data

Data available

Library of Congress Cataloging in Publication Data

Data available

Typeset by SPI Publisher Services, Pondicherry, India
Printed and bound by CPI Group (UK) Ltd, Croydon, CR0 4YY

ISBN 978-0-19-969812-7

3 5 7 9 10 8 6 4 2

Acknowledgements

I would not have been able to write this book without the support of Birkbeck College London, and am deeply grateful both to the College, and to my colleagues and students in the Department of Philosophy. It's a particular pleasure to acknowledge my intellectual debts to Alan Coffee, Alexander Douglas, Gabriella Lamonica, Benedict Rumbold, and Stephanie Marston, whose outstanding work on Spinoza and related topics has no doubt influenced me more than I know.

I first began to try to write about the *Theologico-Political Treatise* in the calm surroundings of the Wissenschaftskolleg zu Berlin, where I was a Fellow in 2003–4. It is hard to imagine a more sustaining or comfortable environment for academic work and I am grateful to the then Rector, Dieter Grimm, and to Joachim Nettelbeck, Gesine Bottomley, Reinhart Meyer-Kalkus, Christine von Arnim, Katarzyna Speder, and the rest of the staff for their professionalism and kindness. At the Wissenschaftskolleg I encountered a remarkable community of scholars, whose seminars, workshops, and discussions were a continual source of argument and pleasure. Ronit Chacham, Peter Hall, Pascal Grosse, Stephen Greenblatt, Bernhard Jussen, Dominique Pestre, Robert Pippin, Nono Raz-Krakotzkin, Beate Rossler, and Ramie Targoff: thank you for your companionship and conversation throughout a memorable year.

In 2008 I was fortunate enough to be able to present an earlier draft of this book to a graduate seminar in the Department of Philosophy at Boston University. I should like to express my gratitude to the Department for inviting me to be the John Findlay Visiting Professor and give the Findlay Lecture, and to the members of the seminar for their searching questions. I also have particularly happy recollections of discussions with Aaron Garrett, Charles Griswold, Amelie Rorty, Suzanne Sreedhar, and Daniel Star, who were outstandingly generous with their time and thoughts in the midst of a busy term.

A number of universities and conference organizers have invited me to give talks about aspects of the *Theologico-Political Treatise*, and I have continually revised my ideas about it as a result of discussions with philosophical audiences at the University of Cambridge, Columbia University, the Universities of North Carolina, Dalhousie, Durham, Frankfurt, and Groningen, the Humboldt University, the Universities of Helsinki, Hull, Leeds, Manchester, Michigan, Middlesex, Pennsylvania, Princeton, Saint Andrews, Sussex, Sydney, Toronto,

Texas A and M University, the University of Utrecht, and the European University Institute. I am equally indebted to the comments and suggestions I have received at meetings held by the American Philosophical Association, the British Society for the History of Philosophy, the Forum for European Philosophy, the Humanist Society, the Political Studies Association, the Royal Belgian Academy, and the Vereniging het Spinozahuis.

I also have some more practical debts to acknowledge. Alexander Douglas has generously taken time off from his own research to help me prepare the footnotes of this book, and has compiled the bibliography. I am truly grateful for his learned and indefatigable assistance. At the Oxford University Press, Peter Momtchiloff has as always been an ideal editor, invariably acute, calm, decisive, and encouraging. Sarah Parker, Jenny Lunsford, Eleanor Collins, and Subramaniam Vengatakrishnan have overseen aspects of the book's production with great friendliness and efficiency; and the manuscript has been copy-edited by Barbara Ball and Joy Mellor who prompted me to correct some nasty errors. I feel extremely fortunate to have had the benefit of their wide-ranging expertise.

Although it has a single name on the cover, this book is really a collective product—the fruit of work by a long tradition of experts on Spinoza and seventeenth-century philosophy, on which I have drawn, and to which I have tried to contribute. Among contemporary Spinozists, I am particularly conscious of having learned from Lilli Alanen, Étienne Balibar, Aaron Garrett, Michael Rosenthal, Piet Steenbakkers, and Martin Saar, as well as from a number of scholars who have given me particular kinds of help along the way. With characteristic generosity, Ed Curley has shared his great store of knowledge and allowed me to use his unpublished translation of the *Theologico-Political Treatise*. Stephen Nadler kindly agreed to read this book for the Oxford University Press and relayed suggestions and encouragement; a second, anonymous referee worked through the text with extraordinary care and made many valuable suggestions; Amelie Rorty's grasp of the cheerfulness inherent in Spinoza's philosophical system remains inspiring; and Theo Verbeek's combination of learning and scepticism is a tonic. My greatest debt is, however, to my friend Moira Gatens, with whom I have discussed Spinoza over many years. Her outstanding and politically probing work on his conception of imagination is for me an exemplar, and is integral to the argument of this book.

Among friends and colleagues, philosophical and otherwise, Mark Goldie and Kinch Hoekstra have given me valuable and time-saving advice, Martin Van Gelderen has helped me to understand the history of the Dutch Republic, and Diana Lipton offered me a glimpse of the tradition of biblical interpretation with which Spinoza would have grown up. Invaluable combinations of support, encouragement, and ideas have come from Kum Kum Bhavnani, Judy Davies, Cynthia Farrar, Miranda Fricker, Cheri Frith, Raymond Geuss, Jen Guttenplan, Sam Guttenplan, Jen Hornsby, Melissa Lane, Michael Moriarty, Lyvia Morgan, Tori McGreer, Sarah Patterson, Philip Pettit, Jim Tully, Michelle Spring, and Catherine Wilson. My deep and lasting gratitude to them all.

Life without these friends would be unimaginably poorer, and life without my family would not be worth living. This book is dedicated to the memory of my mother, Elisabeth James, who died as it was conceived. While working on it, I have been sustained through better and worse times alike by Olivia Skinner, Marcus Skinner, and above all Quentin Skinner, whose confidence in the project never failed. He has discussed the book at every stage, commented on several drafts, and probably now knows more about Spinoza than he would wish. My debt to him is immeasurable.

Contents

Meeting the Demands of a Religious Life

The Politics of True Religion

Introduction

One of the cultural images of Spinoza that has come down to us is of an unworldly philosopher who shunned society and devoted his life to the articulation of a highly abstract metaphysical system.[1] Spinoza was indeed an ascetic person, who lived simply amidst the burgeoning luxury of seventeenth-century Holland, so that this picture of him is not altogether wrong; but it is a partial representation, or what he would call an inadequate idea. To appreciate the scope and fecundity of his thought, we need to supplement it with a more sociable image of a man who was neither solitary nor isolated, but was deeply concerned about the condition of the society in which he lived. This Spinoza had many friends who shared his intellectual interests, and was connected to a number of outstandingly original scientists and philosophers. He was a close follower of Dutch theological and political debates, and his interventions in them made him a famous, and in some quarters a notorious, figure. By the end of his life he had become something of a celebrity, a philosopher known as much for his radical views about the organization of a good society as for his metaphysical account of God or nature.

Of the six major works that Spinoza produced, only two were published during his lifetime. One of these was the *Theologico-Political Treatise* of 1670, in which he discussed some of the most divisive and contentious problems then being debated in the Dutch Republic. The book confirmed his reputation as a radical, and according to some people as an atheist, and excited the opposition of religious and secular authorities alike. However, his readers were only able to appreciate his philosophy as a whole when, after his death, his friends published a complete edition of his *oeuvre*. This contained his most comprehensive

---

[1] One influential source for this picture is Pierre Bayle's article on Spinoza in his *Dictionnaire historique et critique* (1697). Bayle says that when Spinoza had retired to the countryside he would sometimes not leave the house for three months at a time. See Pierre Bayle, *Écrits sur Spinoza*, ed. Pierre-François Moreau and Françoise Charles-Daubert (Paris: Berg international, 1983), p. 22.

philosophical text, the *Ethics*, on which he was working when he broke off to compose the *Theologico-Political Treatise*, and to which he returned once the *Treatise* was finished. Although these two works vary enormously in style and scope, they are intimately connected. In the *Ethics* Spinoza offers a long philosophical defence of a particular conception of the good life. By cultivating and sharing our capacity for philosophical understanding, he claims, we can learn how to live in ways that avoid the psychological and social conflicts that are usually so prevalent, and approach an ideal of maximal harmony and empowerment. Achieving this ideal is a difficult process, which always remains incomplete, but its rewards are such that we have every reason to work towards it and get as far as we can.

Couched in the abstract terms that dominate the *Ethics*, the good life is liable to seem a distant goal, attainable, if at all, by only a small number of philosophers in circumstances far removed from the hurly burly of everyday political life. But this is not how Spinoza conceives it. For him, striving to create ways of life that are genuinely empowering and rewarding is an immediate and practical project, to which he and as many as possible of his fellow Dutch citizens can, and should, commit themselves. If they are to make any headway, however, they will first have to foster conditions in which their efforts have a chance of flourishing; and in order to create such conditions they will have to overcome a number of obstacles. This programme drives the *Theologico-Political Treatise*, which is in effect an analysis of the conditions in which the Dutch Republic will be able to sustain a way of life informed by Spinoza's philosophical ideal. It brings his comparatively abstract goal down to earth by spelling out some of its main political and theological implications, by identifying the most important barriers that currently stand in its way, and by showing that they can safely be removed. The *Treatise* translates a philosophical sketch of the good life into a reform plan for a particular community, designed to enable it to cultivate a more harmonious way of life, and to strengthen its capacity to deal with conflict and stress.

The main obstacles that impede the capacity of the Dutch to work constructively towards a more satisfying existence revolve, in Spinoza's view, around the relations between philosophy, politics, and religion. Individuals are best placed to co-operate when they are as free as possible to live as their own ideas dictate. They need to be free to philosophize, as Spinoza puts it, and free to worship in their own fashion. As things stand, these capacities are suppressed by established religions, above all the Dutch Reformed Church and its political allies, who take it upon themselves to dictate what philosophical claims are acceptable and what dogmas the faithful must accept. A large part of Spinoza's task is therefore to overturn this religious outlook. By showing where it goes wrong, he aims to discredit its authority and make way for a form of religious life orientated towards his own harmonious ideal.

Religious and philosophical pluralism are, therefore, preconditions of a peaceful community that can dedicate itself to learning how to improve its way of life by understanding its own situation and potential. But these conditions also need to be sustained by a political system with the same aims, and can easily be thwarted by an oppressive form of rule. Focusing again on the United Provinces, Spinoza defends its republican form of government and speaks up against the supporters of a mixed constitution. The best way for the Dutch to promote increasingly harmonious ways of life is to live in a republic that encourages freedom of worship and the freedom to philosophize.

This bare outline of Spinoza's programme provides a sense of the overall argument of the *Treatise*, and indicates how it complements the philosophical argument of the *Ethics*. But it cannot begin to do justice to the depth and subtlety of his discussion of theologico-politics, or to the determination with which he defends his views against a wide range of opponents. It is this more detailed level of argument, as much as its overarching theme, that philosophical commentators have found so stimulating and have put to many kinds of use. Some have mined it as a source of insight into contemporary problems, exploring Spinoza's work for pertinent themes and arguments.[2] Others have read his work teleologically, interpreting him as an early advocate of contemporary values such as free speech and democracy.[3] A third group has explored the relationship between Spinoza's treatment of theologico-politics and that of other individual philosophers such as Hobbes.[4] A fourth has concerned itself with his debts to particular traditions, such as Judaism.[5] And a fifth has placed

---

[2] See for example Louis Althusser, 'On Spinoza', in *Essays in Self-Criticism* (London: New Left Books, 1976); Moira Gatens and Genevieve Lloyd, *Collective Imaginings: Spinoza, Past and Present* (London: Routledge, 1999); Antonio Negri, *The Savage Anomaly: The Power of Spinoza's Metaphysics and Politics*, trans. Michael Hardt (Minneapolis: University of Minnesota Press, 1991).

[3] The most celebrated current exponent of this approach is Jonathan Israel. See his *Radical Enlightenment. Philosophy and the Making of Modernity* (Oxford: Oxford University Press, 2001).

[4] See, for example, Edwin Curley, '"I Durst Not Write So Boldly" or How to Read Hobbes' Theologico-Political Treatise', in *Studi su Hobbes e Spinoza*, ed. Emilia Giancotti (Naples: Bibliopolis, 1996); Theo Verbeek, *Spinoza's Theologico-Political Treatise: Exploring 'the Will of God'* (Aldershot: Ashgate, 2003).

[5] For example, Steven M. Nadler, *Spinoza's Heresy: Immortality and the Jewish Mind* (Oxford: Clarendon Press, 2001); Heidi M. Ravven and Lenn E. Goodman, eds., *Jewish Themes in*

Spinoza's *Treatise* within some canon, whether of rationalists, Cartesians, or Dutch philosophers.[6]

Each of these approaches has illuminated aspects of Spinoza's work, and this book is deeply indebted to all of them. Nevertheless, it aims to do something different. Works of philosophy are best understood as contributions to ongoing conversations or debates. They question or support, challenge or defend, and even ridicule or dismiss. In some cases, such as Spinoza's *Ethics*, this is not immediately obvious: the geometrical style in which the work is presented is designed to make it appear self-sufficient, and largely removes traces of the conversational partners whose claims are implicitly contested. But in the case of the *Treatise*, where Spinoza argues furiously against a sequence of theological and philosophical opponents, these motivations are impossible to miss. Here philosophy is not so much a conversation as a struggle—a fight against a powerful and deeply entrenched outlook, over issues that both sides regard as utterly fundamental.

Because Spinoza is not only advocating a position of his own, but trying to persuade his readers that his opponents' views are irretrievably flawed, the *Treatise* is shaped by the positions it is contesting. To vindicate his programme, Spinoza has to discredit the theological and political positions that stand in its way; and in order to appreciate both what he is saying and why he is saying it one needs to understand what views he is attacking. For seventeenth-century readers, familiar with the milieu in which the *Treatise* was written and the debates in which it intervened, this would have been relatively straightforward. But it is much more difficult for us. Spinoza addresses himself to problems from which we are estranged and factions that have long ceased to exist, and does not pause to set out their positions in a way that nowadays makes the force of his own arguments perspicuous. To follow him, and to grasp the significance of his claims, it is not enough to explicate his text: one must also set it in the context of the sequence of theological and political debates to which he is contributing.

A great deal of illuminating research has been done on Spinoza's various allies and opponents: on the group of Dutch Cartesians to which he both does and

Spinoza's Philosophy (Albany, NY: SUNY Press, 2002); Yirmiyahu Yovel, *Spinoza and Other Heretics*, 2 vols. (Princeton: Princeton University Press, 1989).

[6] See, for example, Jonathan Bennett, *Learning from Six Philosophers: Descartes, Spinoza, Leibniz, Locke, Berkeley, Hume* (Oxford: Clarendon Press, 2001); Wiep van Bunge, *From Stevin to Spinoza: An Essay on Philosophy in the Seventeenth-Century Dutch Republic* (Leiden: Brill, 2001); Theo Verbeek, *Descartes and the Dutch: Early Reactions to Cartesian Philosophy, 1637–1650* (Carbondale, Ill. Southern Illinois University Press, 1992).

does not belong; on the conservative Calvinists who opposed them; on more moderate strands of Calvinism with which he sometimes allies himself; and so on. These groups and their convictions form landmarks, some clearer than others, in the intellectual landscape through which Spinoza is journeying, and he relies on them to pinpoint his own position. In what follows, I draw extensively on this impressive body of research. But whereas it has largely been used to cast light on Spinoza's treatment of particular themes, I use it to interpret a particular text. I try to reconstruct the variety of interconnecting polemics that organize the *Treatise*, and offer a systematic account of the argument that Spinoza builds up by opposing them. Rather than focusing on a specific aspect of the text—for example its theory of biblical interpretation, its construal of revelation, its defence of religious pluralism, or its analysis of the state—I trace the course of the struggle on which Spinoza is engaged and follow him as he develops his case, addressing first one set of opponents and then another. If one were to take any single section of his polemic, it would of course be possible to reconstruct the debates to which he is contributing in more detail, and to recover a richer set of allusions and controversies than those I have discussed. But the benefits of detailed argument have to be weighed against the pleasures of an overall picture, and I have mainly opted for the latter.

Although attempts to examine the *Treatise* as a unity have not been common, there are, I think, a number of reasons in favour of this approach. The habit of moving easily from one of Spinoza's texts to another, implicitly assuming that his works cohere, is deeply entrenched among commentators and sometimes justified. As it happens, Spinoza is the kind of systematic philosopher who gradually extended his grasp of a set of core problems by approaching them from different angles, steadily building up the structure and implications of a distinctive philosophical outlook. In many cases, then, one text functions as a mirror in which one can get a fresh view of arguments contained in another, and it would be foolish to deny oneself the insights that this mode of interpretation yields. Nevertheless, Spinoza's texts are far from forming a seamless whole. Written for various audiences and diverse purposes, they operate on a number of levels and use different methods to win the agreement of their readers. The context in which a point is made alters its valency, so that it can be dangerous to uproot an argument from one text and plant it in another.

To appreciate what Spinoza is trying to achieve in the *Treatise*, one needs to be sensitive to the levels at which he is arguing in its different sections, and to the way that each level contributes to the overall goal of this particular text. The best way to observe this rule, so it seems to me, is to follow the development of the *Treatise's* polemic from beginning to end, concentrating both on what it advocates and on what it rejects. The benefits of this approach are partly historical. It enables one to reconstruct, at least in part, the ground-clearing aspect of Spinoza's enterprise, by revealing what he regards as the main obstacles to an empowering way of life, and what he takes to be wrong with them. It allows us to see the *Treatise* not just as a set of more or less appealing claims, frozen in the past, but as an active theologico-political intervention in the politics of its time and a bid to redirect the course of power. Perhaps this should be enough; but in the case of such a wild and suggestive work as the *Treatise*, approaching it systematically and contextually also yields insights of general philosophical interest, which bear on our own predicament as much as on that of the Dutch state in the second half of the seventeenth century. These will emerge as we go along, but they include Spinoza's analysis of superstition; his account of the relationship between theological and philosophical thinking; and his analysis of the affinities between religion, politics, and philosophy, each of which contributes in its own way to the creation of a harmonious and empowering way of life. What we do with these conclusions is up to us. But the better we understand the interlocking set of positions that Spinoza defends in the *Treatise*, the more clearly shall we be able to hear them.

Chapter 1

Spinoza's Project

During the 1640s René Descartes became embroiled in a series of disputes with a group of Dutch professors at the Universities of Utrecht and Leiden who attacked the theological orthodoxy of his philosophical method and conclusions.[1] In the spring of 1647, immediately after composing a letter of protest to the curators of Leiden University, Descartes complained to one of his regular correspondents, Princess Elisabeth of Bohemia, that his difficulties with the Dutch were exacerbated by the form of their political organization. In Holland, he wrote, 'as is ordinarily the case in all states run by the people', the theologians who are most insolent and shout the loudest have the most power.[2] This being the case, it was hardly surprising that Gijsbertus Voetius, Rector of the University of Utrecht and one of the Dutch Reformed Church's most combative and vocal theologians, had launched a campaign to get the teaching of Cartesian philosophy banned, and with the help of allies at Leiden had pursued it for the past six years.[3] Elisabeth responded sympathetically but calmly. Disagreements

---

[1] For a full account of this dispute, see Wiep van Bunge, *From Stevin to Spinoza: An Essay on Philosophy in the Seventeenth-Century Dutch Republic* (Leiden: Brill, 2001); Theo Verbeek, *Descartes and the Dutch: Early Reactions to Cartesian Philosophy, 1637–1650* (Carbondale: Southern Illinois University Press, 1992), pp. 13–33; Theo Verbeek, 'Tradition and Novelty: Descartes and Some Cartesians', in *The Rise of Modern Philosophy: The Tension between the New and Traditional Philosophies from Machiavelli to Leibniz*, ed. Tom Sorell (Oxford: Clarendon Press, 1993).

[2] Descartes to Elisabeth, 10 May 1647, in René Descartes, *Oeuvres de Descartes*, ed. Charles Adam and Paul Tannery (Paris: Vrin, 1974) vol. V. p. 17. References to this edition of Descartes' works will be abbreviated as 'AT' below. Translation from *The Correspondence between Princess Elisabeth of Bohemia and René Descartes* ed. and trans. Lisa Shapiro (Chicago: University of Chicago Press, 2007), p. 161.

[3] Gijsbert Voet, or Gisbertus Voetius (1589–1676), was the primary professor of theology and the Rector of the University of Utrecht during and after Descartes' final residence in the Netherlands. A staunch defender of orthodox Calvinism, he became one of the most powerful critics of Cartesian philosophy, which had come to the attention of the theological faculty at Utrecht by way of Descartes' friend, the professor of medicine Henricus Regius (1598–1679).

of this kind were, she explained, just part of the price that the Dutch pay for their liberty. Although theologians can speak their mind in all societies, their liberty knows no restraint in democratic states such as Holland, where conflict is consequently prone to arise.[4]

Descartes and Elisabeth were both beneficiaries of the freedoms that the Dutch prized so highly. He had moved to Holland in 1628 and had remained there for many years, pursuing his philosophical and scientific work without interference from the authorities. Her family had taken refuge in The Hague after her father, the Elector Palatine, had been ousted from power and driven from his territory.[5] However, in this exchange of views they dwell on the limitations of the state that had made them welcome. Republics or democracies such as the United Provinces tend to privilege liberty; but by allowing freedom of judgement and thus of worship, such states not only permit theologians to uphold their theological opinions, but also give them power to oppose views of which they disapprove. As a republic, then, the United Provinces is vulnerable to theologically driven conflicts, of which the Voetian attack on Cartesianism is just one example.

Judging from the long drawn out history of this particular dispute, Elisabeth and Descartes had a point. What began as a local disagreement about the Utrecht university curriculum turned in the course of the 1640s into a highly politicized split, which extended far beyond academia and shaped Dutch political life for several decades. On the one side, orthodox Calvinist theologians led by the tirelessly polemical Voetius defended the teaching of Aristotelianism as the only philosophy consonant with Scripture and thus with true religion. Cartesianism, they argued, represented a heterodox threat to faith and did not belong in Christian universities, where philosophy should be subordinated to theology. On the other side, Descartes' advocates defended his novel philosophical approach to the investigation of nature, despite the fact that some of its results conflicted with claims made in the Bible. Cartesian philosophy was in their view independent of theology and did not threaten the essential teachings of Scripture. There was therefore no reason why it should not be taught.

As this conflict developed, each side became roughly aligned with a broader political party on which it relied for support. The Cartesians looked to the

Descartes complained of Voetius' abusive and threatening remarks in the *Letter to Father Dinet*, appended to the second edition of his *Meditations*, published in 1642.

[4] Elisabeth to Descartes, May 1647, AT V.47, Shapiro ed., *Correspondence*, p. 162.
[5] Shapiro ed., *Correspondence*, pp. 7–8.

republicans who dominated the States of Holland and were led from 1653 by the Grand Pensionary, Johann de Witt. While De Witt sometimes ruled in the Voetians' favour, he created an environment in which their demands were held in check and the Cartesians remained, as they put it, free to philosophize.[6] More generally, he upheld an unusual level of intellectual and religious freedom. The Voetian theologians, by contrast, made common cause with those of de Witt's opponents who were hostile to his republican government and favoured a mixed constitution, in which the power of the States was offset by that of a quasi-monarchical Stadtholder.[7] One of De Witt's most dramatic innovations had been to abolish this traditional office in the province of Holland and diminish its power elsewhere, but many people still longed for a more hierarchical system, and hoped for the return of a Stadtholder who would impose greater uniformity on religious and intellectual life.

The controversy between Voetians and Cartesians went on by fits and starts, lurching from one compromise to another. As late as 1656, for example, the States of Holland found it necessary to issue a decree ordering the two groups of university professors to refrain from trespassing on each other's domains and avoid provoking one another. (They were to abstain from invectives and odious insinuations, present the truth simply, and avoid pointing out hateful consequences that could be expected to give offence to others.[8]) As far as their teaching was concerned, the two parties gradually established a reasonably effective division of labour. But the broader tensions that they had come to represent did not disappear, and supporters of each side remained suspicious of the other. Any attempt to limit or suppress philosophical discussion or publication tended to stir up an old fear that the theologians were trying to extend their authority, and philosophers who overstepped the official boundary around their subject could expect to arouse a comparably anxious response on the part of the theologians.

Spinoza, who embarked on his philosophical career sometime in the early 1650s, belonged firmly on the Cartesian side of this divide. After his excommunication from the Amsterdam synagogue in 1656 he became part of an

---

[6] Herbert H. Rowen, *John De Witt, Grand Pensionary of Holland, 1625–1672* (Princeton: Princeton University Press, 1978), ch. 20.

[7] Ibid. ch. 19.

[8] The final draft of the edict was released on 30 September 1656. While it stipulated that 'the 'philosophemata' drawn from the philosophy of D. Cartesius, which now gives some offence, shall cease to be set forth', it also required both sides of the conflict to 'refrain from all invectives and all direct or indirect labelling of one or the other side, being satisfied to present the truth simply'. Ibid. p. 407.

intellectual circle whose members were interested in Descartes' work, and is thought to have attended lectures at Leiden University where Cartesianism was being taught.[9] A letter from Henry Oldenburg, Secretary of the Royal Society in London, records that in 1661 he and Spinoza had a conversation 'about the principles of the Cartesian philosophy, and of the Baconian',[10] and two years later, Spinoza was giving instruction on Descartes' *Principles of Philosophy* to a young student, Johannes Caesarius.[11] From the point of view of the teacher, the lessons were disappointing: Spinoza confided to a friend, Simon De Vries, that Caesarius was nothing but trouble, and was too boyish and unstable to appreciate the truth.[12] Nevertheless, the exercise prompted him to work up the course he had written for his unworthy pupil into an exposition of Parts I and II of the *Principles*, set out in geometrical order. The result was published in 1663 by the radical Mennonite publisher Jan Rieuwertsz with an introduction by Lodewijk Meijer—both members of Spinoza's circle—and was translated from Latin into Dutch by a third friend, Peter Balling.[13]

The Principles of Philosophy Demonstrated in the Geometrical Manner cannot but have consolidated Spinoza's reputation as a philosopher sympathetic to Descartes. It placed him alongside the Dutch Cartesians and against the Voetian Calvinists who continued to regard the new philosophy as dangerously heterodox. At the same time, its *Appendix concerning Metaphysical Thoughts* put into circulation some of Spinoza's own philosophical views, which, as De Vries indicates in a letter of 1663, were already being studied in a fuller form by friends and sympathizers. As De Vries writes, 'Our group is arranged this way: one of us (each in turn) reads through, explains according to his own conceptions, and then proves everything, following the sequence and order of your propositions. Then, if it happens that one cannot satisfy the other on some

[9] Steven M. Nadler, *Spinoza: A Life* (Cambridge: Cambridge University Press, 1999), pp. 191ff.

[10] Letter 1; Spinoza, *Epistolæ*, ed. Carl Gebhardt, vol. IV, *Opera* (Heidelberg: Carl Winter, 1924), p. 5: English translation: *Letter: August 1661–August 1663*, in *The Collected Works of Spinoza*, vol. I, ed. and trans. Edwin Curley (Princeton: Princeton University Press), pp. 163–4.

[11] Theo Verbeek, 'Spinoza and Cartesianism', in *Judaeo-Christian Intellectual Culture in the Seventeenth Century: A Celebration of the Library of Narcissus Marsh (1638–1713)*, ed. Allison Coudert (Dordrecht: Kluwer, 1999), p. 175.

[12] Letter 9; Spinoza, *Letters: August 1661–August 1663*, in *The Collected Works of Spinoza*, vol. I, pp. 193–6. Simon de Vries (1633–67) was an Amsterdam merchant who at various points tried and failed to give Spinoza financial assistance.

[13] Pieter Balling (dates unknown) was a Mennonite merchant who participated in a group to discuss Spinoza's philosophy. In 1662 he published a pamphlet, *The Light upon the Candlestick* (*Het licht op den kandelaer*), which argued for a non-confessional, personal form of religion that was mistaken by many for a tract by the Quaker William Ames.

point, we make a note of it and write to you, so that you can if possible make it clearer to us. Under your guidance we may be able to defend the truth against those who are superstitiously religious and Christian, and to stand against the attacks of the whole world'.[14]

The work to which this letter refers seems to have been a version of the *Short Treatise*, Spinoza's first extant attempt to set out the lineaments of the radical philosophical system he would later develop in the *Ethics*.[15] It is therefore not surprising that De Vries should take it for granted that its claims will run into opposition from 'superstitious' Christians. Spinoza expresses the same worry himself, and when Oldenburg urged him to publish the work he hung back: 'I fear, of course, that the theologians of our time may be offended and with their usual hatred attack me, who absolutely dread quarrels'.[16] Oldenburg responded with some light-hearted encouragement. 'Let it be published, whatever rumblings there may be among the foolish theologians. Your Republic is very free, and gives great freedom for philosophizing.... Come, then, excellent Sir, banish all fear of arousing the pygmies of our time. Long enough have we appeased ignorant triflers. Let us set full sail for knowledge and penetrate more deeply into Nature's mysteries than anyone has done before us'.[17] But Spinoza was not convinced.

Since criticism by Calvinist theologians could be extremely harsh, it is easy to understand why Spinoza might have preferred to avoid their mixture of philosophical and personal abuse. However, by the 1660s Cartesianism had become an established feature of Dutch intellectual life, and it seems possible that his anxieties about the Reformed Church were excessive. What did he really have to fear? The answer is difficult to gauge, but at least two factors need to be taken into account. Both in his *Appendix containing Metaphysical Thoughts*, and in the *Short Treatise*, Spinoza makes claims about God that are, from a Calvinist point of view, more heterodox than any expressed by Descartes.[18] He

---

[14] Letter 8. *Letters: August 1661–August 1663*, in *The Collected Works of Spinoza*. (Princeton: Princeton University Press, 1985) p. 190, modified. On Spinoza's philosophical associates, see K. O. Meinsma, *Spinoza et son cercle: Étude critique historique sur les hétérodoxes hollandais*, trans. S. Roosenberg and J.-P. Osier (Paris: Vrin, 1983); Nadler, *Spinoza*, ch. 8.

[15] Nadler, *Spinoza*, p. 202.

[16] Letter 6. *Letters: August 1661–August 1663*, in *The Collected Works of Spinoza*, vol. I, p. 188.

[17] Letter 7. *Letters: August 1661–August 1663*, in *The Collected Works of Spinoza*, vol. I, p. 189.

[18] Probably the most significant of these was the suggestion that all things exist necessarily, which would entail that God did not create the world by freely choosing something contingent. Spinoza, *Korte Verhandeling Van God, Den Mensch, En Deszelfs Welstand*, ed. Carl Gebhardt, vol. I, *Opera* (Heidelberg: Carl Winter, 1924). English translation: *Short Treatise on God, Man and his Well-Being*, in *The Collected Works of Spinoza*, vol. I, pp. 59–156. I. iv; Spinoza, *Renati Des Cartes Principiorum Philosophiæ Pars I. Et Ii., More Geometrico Demonstratæ Per Benedictum De Spinoza. Accesserunt Ejusdem Cogitata Metaphysica*, ed. Carl Gebhardt, vol. I, *Opera* (Heidelberg: Carl

could therefore expect to be challenged. In addition, the political situation was becoming more dangerous. De Witt's authority was waning, and the United Provinces found itself without effective political or military leadership at a point when longstanding international disputes over fishing, trade, and colonial territory were coming to a head. In 1664 war broke out, and in the following year the Dutch navy was badly defeated. But even during the prelude to this crisis, old fissures reopened. The supporters of the Stadtholder gathered strength, and the Republican party increasingly began to be viewed as libertine. In these circumstances De Witt's government could no longer be counted on to protect Cartesians and religious nonconformists from the theologians, so that people such as Spinoza and his friends were more vulnerable than before.[19]

At such a juncture, Spinoza might have been expected to keep quiet; but in fact he did quite the opposite. Leaving his *Short Treatise* unpublished, and setting aside the draft of his *Ethics*, he began to work in earnest on a *Theologico-Political Treatise*, directly confronting the outlook on which the theological opponents of Cartesianism had built their case. In the autumn of 1665 he explained to Oldenburg that his reason for writing about the interpretation of Scripture was threefold: to speak out against the prejudices of the theologians, which prevent people from turning their minds to philosophy; to disabuse the populace of their opinion that he is an atheist; and to defend the freedom to philosophize in the face of the preachers' attempts to suppress it.[20] The space for philosophizing that had been carved out during the struggles of the 1640s and 1650s was evidently not secure enough to prevent theologians, preachers, and populace from invading it.[21]

Establishing that philosophy and theology can safely cohabit is one of the central aims of the *Theologico-Political Treatise*; but rather than dealing with this issue in

Winter, 1924). English translation: *Appendix Containing Metaphysical Thoughts*, in *The Collected Works of Spinoza*, vol. I, pp. 299–346, Appendix II, chs. 8 and 9. This was a suggestion that had been made by Jacobus Arminius and was rejected by orthodox Calvinists. Jacobus Arminius, *The Works of James Arminius*, trans. James Nichols and William Nichols (Grand Rapids, Mich.: Baker Academic, 1986), II. 33–5. Voetius's strongly opposing, orthodox Calvinist view is presented in Andreas J. Beck, 'Gisbertus Voetius (1589–1676): Basic Features of His Doctrine of God', in *Reformation and Scholasticism: Texts and Studies in Reformation and Post-Reformation Thought*, ed. W. J. van Asselt and E. Dekker (Grand Rapids, Mich.: Baker Academic, 2001).

[19] Maarten Roy Prak, *The Dutch Republic in the Seventeenth Century: The Golden Age*, trans. Diane Webb (Cambridge: Cambridge University Press, 2005), ch. 3.

[20] Letter 30; Spinoza, *Epistolæ*, p. 166.

[21] See Piet Steenbakkers, 'The Text of Spinoza's Tractatus Theologico-Politicus', in *Spinoza's 'Theologico-Political Treatise'*, ed. Yitzhak Y. Melamed and Michael A. Rosenthal (Cambridge: Cambridge University Press, 2010).

isolation, Spinoza addresses the broader set of disagreements with which it had become associated. Directly contesting the pessimistic assessment of republics on which Descartes and Elisabeth had agreed twenty or so years earlier, he sets out to show that theologically inspired discord of the sort that had plagued the United Provinces is not an unavoidable consequence of a republican constitution. On the contrary, it can and should be resolved, and the goal of the *Treatise* is to show how this can be done. As its title page explains, the work is made up of several dissertations, 'wherein it is shown not only that freedom to philosophise can be granted without injuring piety or the peace of the republic, but that peace and piety are endangered by the suppression of this liberty'.[22] Despite the conviction of the Voetians and their allies, the freedom to philosophize is not, so Spinoza aims to show, incompatible with piety. There need be no tension between the requirements imposed by religion and the practice of philosophizing, and no struggle between philosophers and theologians. In fact, *unless* the freedom to philosophize is respected, piety is threatened; and so, too, is the peace of the republic.

As Spinoza presents the *Treatise*, it is an explicit intervention in the political debates by which he is surrounded, and an offer to resolve a longstanding struggle without compromising freedom, that most central of all republican values. 'Since we happen to have the rare good fortune of living in a republic where everyone is granted complete freedom of judgment and is permitted to worship God according to his understanding, and where nothing is thought to be dearer or sweeter than freedom, I believed that I should be doing something that is neither unwelcome nor useless if I showed not only that this freedom can be granted without harm to the piety and the peace of the Republic, but also that it cannot be abolished unless piety and the peace of the Republic are abolished with it'.[23] The task of the *Treatise* is thus to reconcile three values: the freedom to philosophize, piety, and peace. By interpreting each in the light of the others, and by setting them in the context of his broader philosophical commitments, Spinoza will outline a form of political life in which they are not only compatible, but mutually dependent. Without the freedom to philosophize, piety cannot be fully achieved and peace is fragile; without stable peace there can be no piety or freedom to philosophize; and so on.

---

[22] Benedictus de Spinoza, *Tractatus Theologico-Politicus*, ed. Carl Gebhardt, vol. III, *Opera* (Heidelberg: Carl Winter, 1924), Preface, p. 3. All translations of this text are by Edwin Curley whose edition is forthcoming with Princeton University Press.

[23] Ibid. Preface, p. 7. On the complex notion of Dutch freedom, see Martin van Gelderen, *The Political Thought of the Dutch Revolt, 1555–1590* (Cambridge: Cambridge University Press, 1992), ch. 6, Raia Prokhovnik, *Spinoza and Republicanism* (Basingstoke: Palgrave Macmillan, 2004), chs. 3 and 5.

Spinoza was not alone in desiring such a harmonious way of life, but because the tensions and conflicts standing in its way had proved so intractable, the possibility of achieving it seemed remote. Needless to say, he is alive to the ambitiousness of his project, and its complexity is reflected in the structure of his work. The path traced by the text is a tortuous one, and before he can set out along it, Spinoza needs to win his readers' trust. To gather them around him, he presents the position he is going to defend as an antidote to a corrosive and degraded way of life dominated by superstition. At first glance, this may seem a strange place to start, but it is carefully calculated to direct attention to what will prove to be two of Spinoza's deepest preoccupations. Superstition's status as the opposite of true religion alerts us to the fact that, of all the values the *Treatise* is aiming to uphold, the nature of piety will prove to be the most controversial. The question of what constitutes true religion and what is merely superstition will run through much of his text. Still more fundamentally, superstition is a phenomenon in which theological and political issues are inextricably bound up. The problems that it raises set the scene for a theologico-political treatise, and illuminate the nature of the difficulties with which Spinoza is going to grapple.[24]

Superstition

Like the majority of his contemporaries, Spinoza views superstition as a deformation of religion, a pathology that arises when religion goes wrong. This disturbing relationship had been forcefully characterized by Francis Bacon, one of the philosophers whose work Spinoza had discussed with Oldenburg. 'For as it addeth deformity to an ape to be so like a man', Bacon comments, 'so the similitude of superstition to religion makes it the more deformed. And as wholesome meat corrupteth to little worms, so good forms and order corrupt into a number of petty observances'.[25] These petty observances are indeed numerous, and take a plethora of forms. In a wilfully eclectic catalogue of follies, Spinoza's contemporary Thomas Hobbes notes that superstition encompasses pretended experience, pretended revelation, false prophecy, oracles, the leaves of the Sybils, enthusiasm, theomancy or the prediction of events, horoscopy, judiciary astrology, thumomancy or presage, necromancy, conjuring,

---

[24] Nancy Levene, *Spinoza's Revelation: Religion, Democracy, and Reason* (Cambridge: Cambridge University Press, 2004); André Tosel, 'Superstition and Reading', in *The New Spinoza*, ed. Warren Montag and Ted Stolze (Minneapolis: University of Minnesota Press, 1997).

[25] Francis Bacon, 'Of Superstition', in *Francis Bacon*, ed. Brian Vickers, *The Oxford Authors* (Oxford: Oxford University Press, 1996), p. 374.

witchcraft, augury, palmistry, monsters, portents such as inundations, comets, earthquakes, or meteors, 'and innumerable other such vaine conceipts'.[26] However, although superstition can be made to look merely ridiculous, it is in fact dangerous. As Bacon again explains, it dismounts sense, philosophy, natural law, piety, law, and reputation, and 'erecteth an absolute monarchy in the minds of men'. So much so, that it 'hath been the confusion of many states, and bringeth a new *primum mobile* that ravisheth all the spheres of government'.[27]

The phenomenon Bacon describes is an extremely powerful one. Superstition cuts us off from the material and immaterial worlds by obstructing crucial and elementary forms of response such as sight, hearing, and touch. At the same time, it threatens accepted standards of probity by destroying our susceptibility to natural piety and blunting our concern for reputation. As the disciplining hold of social norms loosens, the threats embodied in the law cease to carry weight, and even the universally valid inferences of philosophy can get no purchase on the distempered self. By degrees superstition creates an 'absolute monarchy' in the mind, a rule verging on tyranny both in its inability to control itself and in its adamant refusal to be checked.

One of the most striking features of this account is the marginal position that it allots to the epistemological critique of superstitious practices. While nothing in Bacon's analysis undermines the likelihood that the claims made by witches, diviners, or sorcerers are false, this in itself does not make them more threatening than any other kind of error. What makes superstition so ominous is not its epistemological status, but rather something about the psychic condition of its victims, namely the rigidity with which they adhere to a particular affective outlook, and the intransigence with which they cling to the various beliefs and feelings that it sustains. Viewed like this, superstition is worlds away from the ignorant misconstrual of nature, or from the cynical manipulation of popular passions for political gain. It is a form of obsession that disempowers the self by shutting down its capacity to modify its own beliefs and affects and making it resistant to external remedies.

What sustains these unfortunate dispositions? In the writings of a range of classical authors and their humanist descendants, superstition is said to be rooted in a kind of fear, and is in its most naked form a species of terror. Perhaps the most vivid and influential exposition of this view is to be found in an essay

---

[26] Thomas Hobbes, *Leviathan*, ed. Richard Tuck. (Cambridge: Cambridge University Press, 1996), pp. 81–2.
[27] Bacon, 'Of Superstition', p. 373.

written by Plutarch, which draws a distinction between two kinds of error. Although error is always to some degree harmful, certain mistakes such as the belief that atoms are the principal elements of material things, do not cause 'any pricking and troublesome pain'.[28] By contrast, other false judgements should arouse our pity, 'because they engender many maladies and passions, like unto worms and such filthy vermin'.[29] Among the latter class of errors are the errors surrounding superstition, an excessive and torturing fear of the gods that 'humbles a man down to the very ground'.[30]

As Plutarch portrays it, superstitious fear of the gods is painful in itself; but the suffering it causes is aggravated by its tendency to reinforce the mistaken beliefs and inappropriate feelings around which it is organized. Because it generates a kind of passionate constancy that lies at the other end of the spectrum from the steady critical outlook delivered by reasoning, superstition gives rise to a cognitive and psychological rigidity that can damage even the everyday capacity to relate means to ends.[31] In most circumstances, our passions generate corresponding desires, such as the desire of the proud for esteem or of the angry for vengeance, and someone in the grip of an affect will be motivated to try to achieve whatever goal it dictates. But this is not the case with fear, which 'carries with it a certain blockishness or stupidity, destitute of action, perplexed, idle, dead, without any exploit or effect whatsoever'.[32] To varying degrees, fear undermines our capacity to engage with the world.

In the case of superstition, this passivity is exacerbated by the fact that the fear in question lacks a determinate object, so that the desires to which it gives rise are not sufficiently specific for practical reason to get to work on them. The superstitious man 'that stands in fear of the gods, feareth all things, the land, the sea, the air, the sky, darkness, light, silence and his very dreams'.[33] Fearing everything might in principle make one want to flee from everything, but since it is not clear how one would go about satisfying such a desire, there is something peculiarly paradoxical and self-defeating about superstition.[34] Of all types of fear, Plutarch concludes, 'there is none so full of perplexitie and unfit for action'.[35] To compound their suffering, the victims of superstition are vulnerable to a range of typical afflictions, including insomnia and terrifying fantasies and dreams. In an effort to deal with these symptoms, they resort to

---

[28] Plutarch, *Moralia*, trans. Frank Cole Babbit (Cambridge: Harvard University Press), 164E. Quoted from Plutarch, *The Philosophie, Commonly Called, the Morals Written by the Learned Philosopher, Plutarch of Chæronea*, trans. Philemon Holland (London, 1603), p. 260.
[29] Ibid.   [30] Ibid.   [31] Plutarch, *The Morals*, p. 261.
[32] Ibid.   [33] Ibid.   [34] Ibid.   [35] Ibid.

ceremonies and rituals, and when these devices fail to cure them of their anxiety, are liable to spiral down into a state of abject desperation,[36] intensified by the fact that superstition weakens their capacity to resist it. 'Thus, unhappy and wretched superstition, by fearing overmuch and without reason . . . never taketh heed how it submitteth itself to all miseries'.[37] Once a person is in this state of mind, circumstances that would not otherwise be particularly danger-ous come to pose a serious threat. Superstitious rulers and military leaders, for example, become unable to deal effectively with their responsibilities, and are liable to embark on destructive courses of action. Some commit suicide; some become incapable of making necessary decisions; and some act out their frustrations in displays of cruelty and barbarism. Superstition is therefore not just a cause of individual misery. It can also constitute a political problem against which states need to be on their guard.

Plutarch's account is reiterated in a wide range of early modern writings, some of them political, others medical or philosophical, and is also explored in the drama of the period.[38] Spinoza clearly has this general conception of superstition in mind, both in the *Ethics*—where the dangers of obsessive anxiety and mental vacillation run through his reflections on human psychology—and also in the Preface to the *Treatise*. It is common knowledge, he there remarks, that fear encourages and preserves superstition, and that people only suffer from it when they are afraid. 'If men could manage all their affairs in accordance with a definite plan, or if fortune were always favourable to them, they would never be possessed by superstition'.[39] As things are, however, our desires for ends that we cannot be sure of attaining expose us to the interdependent passions of fear and hope, so that we are not only inclined to shift from one affect to the other as our perception of our prospects changes, but also tend to swing between exaggerated states of confidence and anxiety.[40] When things go well, we become over-optimistic and blind to the limits of our knowledge and power (though, even then, our satisfaction is often tinged with fear of loss). When things go badly, our efforts to alleviate our anxiety drive us to grasp at straws

---

[36] Ibid.

[37] Plutarch, *The Morals*, pp. 262–3.

[38] Evan Cameron, *Enchanted Europe: Superstition, Reason and Religion, 1250–1750* (Oxford: Oxford University Press, 2010); Susan James, 'Shakespeare and the Politics of Superstition', in *Shakespeare and Early Modern Political Thought*, ed. David Armitage, Conal Condren, and Andrew Fitzmaurice (Cambridge: Cambridge University Press, 2009).

[39] Spinoza, *Tractatus Theologico-Politicus*, Preface, pp. 5–6.

[40] Ibid. Preface, p. 5. On Spinoza's conception of vacillation, see Minna Koivuniemi, 'L'imagination et les affects chez Spinoza', *Documents Archives de Travail et Arguments*, 52: *Spinoza. L'esprit, les passions, la politique* (2010).

and take refuge in all sorts of fanciful hypotheses. To relieve the fear to which uncertainty exposes them, people construct and cling to beliefs and practices that they find comforting, and this is how superstition gets a hold. For instance, Spinoza elaborates, if an event reminds an individual of some past happiness, they will take it to be a lucky omen, and are liable to stick to this belief even if it 'deceives them a hundred times'.[41] Again, when a person is struck with wonder at some strange occurrence, they will often treat it as an indication of divine anger. 'Prey to superstition and contrary to religion, they will consider it a sacrilege not to avert disaster by sacrifices and prayers', and will recklessly invent things 'as if the whole of nature were as insane as they are'.[42]

Since hope and fear are in Spinoza's view normal responses to uncertainty, superstition is a pervasive feature of human existence. The more people strive for ends that are beyond their control, the more they expose themselves to anxiety; and the more anxious they become, the more they are liable to console themselves with superstitious beliefs and practices, to the point where there is 'no advice so foolish, absurd or groundless that they will not follow it'.[43] Moreover, superstition is quick to spread: once an individual or group has acquired an emotional investment in a superstitious practice, they will try to bolster their confidence by persuading other people to share their outlook, even at the cost of making them 'as wretched as themselves'.[44] Rehearsing the standard account of the sufferings to which superstition gives rise, the *Treatise* also enumerates its cognitive deficiencies. As the superstitious become fixated on their delusions they become impervious to reasoning, and cling to whatever practices they favour, regardless of their irrationality.[45] 'Indeed', Spinoza observes, 'they believe that God rejects the wise, and writes his decrees not in the mind, but in the entrails of animals, and that fools, madmen and birds predict his decrees by divine inspiration and prompting. Thus does fear make men insane'.[46]

Superstition, as it is portrayed here, is both a theological and a political phenomenon. In its theological dimension it springs from a misunderstanding of God that arises when individuals and communities deal with their anxieties

---

[41] Spinoza, *Tractatus Theologico-Politicus* Preface, p. 5. See also Spinoza, *Ethica*, ed. Carl Gebhardt, vol. II., *Opera* (Heidelberg Carl Winter, 1924). English translation: *Ethics*, in Curley ed., *The Collected Works of Spinoza*, vol. I, pp. 407–617, 3p50.

[42] Spinoza, *Tractatus Theologico-Politicus*, Preface, p. 5.

[43] Ibid.

[44] Spinoza, *Ethics*, 4p63s.

[45] Spinoza, *Ethics*, 4p44, 5p9.

[46] Spinoza, *Tractatus Theologico-Politicus*, Preface, p. 5.

by turning in an uncritical vein to imaginary conceptions of the deity and making them the basis of pseudo-religious forms of worship. But superstition also has political features. Both because it tends to take diverse forms, and because the loyalty aroused by any single superstition tends to be shortlived, it introduces a source of endemic instability and division into the life of a community. Equally, it creates risks when it afflicts particularly powerful individuals, and can do enormous damage to the smooth running of the state. Superstition therefore needs to be seen as a theologico-political phenomenon. It intertwines the political and theological implications of fear, and simultaneously opposes piety and peace. Since it represents such a grave danger to the values of a republic, taking steps to control it is bound to be one of the essential tasks of government.[47]

Dwelling on this theme, Spinoza spells out the forms of political and theological corruption to which superstition leads. Starting with its political aspect, he reiterates a judgement voiced by Plutarch and numerous Roman moralists and historians, and echoed by their humanist successors;[48] although the psychological need for reassurance to which superstition answers is always present, it is particularly strong at moments of political or military crisis, when even leaders are liable to succumb to it. To illustrate this point, Spinoza appeals to the Roman text that he cites most frequently in the *Treatise*, Quintus Curtius Rufus's life of Alexander the Great. Curtius Rufus's work had been widely admired within the humanist tradition as a model of eloquence. It had been praised by Lipsius for its language and style, Erasmus had produced an edition of it,[49] and it had been put into Dutch by Jan Glazemaker who would later become the translator of part of Spinoza's *Ethics*.[50] Mining its insights, Spinoza now focuses on Quintus Curtius's claim that even the boldest rulers are liable to become superstitious when they confront great danger and uncertainty.

---

[47] Steven B. Smith, *Spinoza, Liberalism, and the Question of Jewish Identity* (New Haven: Yale University Press, 1997), pp. 29–34. On this theory of superstition and government, and its relation to Althusser's theory of 'Ideological State Apparatuses', see Warren Montag and Ted Stolze, 'Preface', in *The New Spinoza*, ed. Warren Montag and Ted Stolze (Minneapolis: University of Minnesota Press, 1997), p. xviii.

[48] See, for example, Marcus Tullius Cicero, *De Natura Deorum*, ed. Joseph B. Mayor (Oxford: Oxford University Press, 1880), II. 70–2.

[49] Anthony Grafton, *What Was History? The Art of History in Early Modern Europe* (Cambridge: Cambridge University Press, 2007), pp. 3–6.

[50] Jan Hendriksz Glazemaker (1619–82) was probably the translator of Spinoza's works into Dutch, and is also likely to have translated much of Descartes' work for Jan Rieuwertsz.

For example, it was only when Alexander feared military defeat at the hand of Darius that genuine superstition drove him to employ seers. Once he emerged victorious he stopped consulting them until he and his army were again in trouble, at which point he 'lapsed again into superstition, that mocker of men's minds', and ordered Aristander 'to enquire into the outcomes of things through sacrifices'.[51]

As well as corrupting the judgement of political leaders, superstition undermines their power. On the one hand, it creates a niche for agents who claim to be able to allay fear, and thus for augurs, seers, or prophets who may challenge the authority of a sovereign or general. On the other hand, since the relief that such figures offer is usually only temporary, people who rely on it tend to shift restlessly from one form of consolation to another, and are in Spinoza's judgement 'best pleased with what is new and has not yet deceived them'.[52] Because, as Curtius Rufus again summarizes, 'nothing sways the multitude more effectively than superstition', leaders need to be wary of it.[53] However, as Spinoza points out, it is difficult to heed this advice. One way of coping with superstition is to impose a religion so grandiose that it will win and sustain popular loyalty, which is why such immense efforts have been made to 'embellish religion, whether true or false, with such ceremony and pomp' that everyone will adhere to it with the deepest reverence'.[54] The most systematic advocates of this approach are the Ottomans, but as their case illustrates, it carries prohibitive costs. To uphold religious uniformity, 'the Turks consider it a sacrilege even to debate religion, and fill everyone's judgment with so many prejudices that they leave no room in the mind for sound reason, and no room even to be in doubt'.[55] The outcome is a counterproductive form of irrationality: 'the greatest secret of monarchical regimes is to deceive men, by cloaking the fear by which they are held in check with the specious name of religion. They will then fight for slavery as if for freedom, and

---

[51] Spinoza, *Tractatus Theologico-Politicus*, Preface, p. 6.

[52] Ibid.

[53] Quintus Curtius Rufus, *Historiae*, ed. C. M. Lucarini, *Bibliotheca Scriptorum Graecorum et Romanorum Teubneriana* (Berlin: Walter de Gruyter, 2009), IV.x.7; Spinoza, *Tractatus Theologico-Politicus*, Preface, p. 6.

[54] Spinoza, *Tractatus Theologico-Politicus*, Preface, pp. 6–7.

[55] Ibid. Preface, p. 7.

count it no shame, but the highest honour, to give their blood and lives so that one man may have grounds for boasting'.[56]

The Ottoman strategy for suppressing the political dangers of superstition therefore amounts to tyranny. In order to create absolute political loyalty, monarchical regimes such as theirs are sometimes willing to quash their subjects' critical capacities, described here in recognizably Cartesian terms as rooted in the freedom to doubt. People who have been thus indoctrinated are indeed submissive, but they are also slaves; and for the Dutch, 'who have the rare good fortune to live in a state where nothing is held to be dearer than freedom', such a policy would be disastrous.[57] Here Spinoza encourages his readers to reflect on the destruction that absolute government would wreak in their own case. But it is striking that his illustrations of the *political* dangers posed by superstition appeal to two relatively distant examples, Alexander the Great and the Ottoman Empire, neither of which speaks directly to the situation of the United Provinces. This is quite deliberate. Spinoza's aim is not to suggest that the existing government of the Dutch Republic relies on superstition to maintain the loyalty of its citizens; on the contrary, he commends it for upholding political liberty. Nevertheless, his critique of Turkish absolutism is intended to alert his readers to the risks inherent in monarchical regimes, and implicitly evokes two potential dangers. It serves first of all as a reminder of the Spanish, who had been driven from the United Provinces at the beginning of the seventeenth century and remained hostile to the republic. By winning their independence, the Dutch had thrown off a regime that, as Amsterdam Jews were all too aware, used its Inquisition to impose religious uniformity, and continued to persecute dissidents, including *conversos* accused of secret Judaizing.[58] In addition, Spinoza's critique functions as a warning against the party of people within the republic who regretted the loss of the

---

[56] As Curley points out, this is an allusion to Quintus Curtius Rufus, one of several in this section of the Preface. Quintus Curtius Rufus, *History of Alexander*, trans. John C. Rolfe, 2 vols., *Loeb Classical Library* (Cambridge: Harvard University Press, 1946), I.iv.10.

[57] Spinoza, *Tractatus Theologico-Politicus*, Preface, p. 7.

[58] On the Dutch Revolt, see Martin van Gelderen, *The Dutch Revolt* (Cambridge: Cambridge University Press, 1993), ix–xlviii; Pieter Geyl, *A History of the Dutch Speaking Peoples 1555–1648* (London: Phoenix Press, 2001), ch. 4; Prokhovnik, *Spinoza and Republicanism*, ch. 1. On the Amsterdam Jewish community, see Chaya Brasz and Yosef Kaplan eds., *Dutch Jews as Perceived by Themselves and by Others: Proceedings of the Eighth International Symposium on the History of the Jews in the Netherlands*, (Leiden: Brill, 2001); Yosef Kaplan, *An Alternative Path to Modernity: The Sephardi Diaspora in Western Europe* (Leiden: Brill, 2000). On the relation between Jewish tradition and the Inquisition, see Amnon Raz-Krakotzkin *The Censor, the Editor and the Text: The Catholic Church and the Shaping of the Jewish Canon in the Sixteenth Century* (Philadelphia: University of Pennsylvania Press, 2007).

Stadtholder, and favoured a return to a mixed constitution. As friends of a quasi-monarchical system that might degenerate into the kind of tyranny exemplified in popular imagination by Spain and the Ottoman Empire, they pose an indirect but internal threat to an existing way of life in which political stability is not obtained by superstitious means.

When Spinoza moves to discuss superstition's *theological* dimension, his analysis comes still closer to home and criticizes a state of affairs that is implicitly but recognizably that of the United Provinces. In a deeply unflattering sketch, he portrays a pluralist society where superstition rules, and where religious authorities use the pretext of religion to undermine the political loyalty of the populace. 'With shameless licence', these figures 'turn the heart of the multitude (who are still liable to pagan superstition) away from the sovereign powers, so that everything may again collapse into slavery'.[59] Alongside the relatively distant threat of state-imposed slavery, we now come to the more immediate threat of a form of slavery that may ensue if the political powers of the republic are taken over by the church. Getting into his stride, Spinoza bluntly condemns what currently passes for religion. People who claim to be Christians committed to love and peace devote themselves to ferocious and corrupting conflict. Individual denominations require their members to adhere to faiths that amount to the unquestioning acceptance of dogmas antithetical to reason and, by punishing anyone who fails to conform, stunt the capacity for free and rational judgement. Furthermore, by applying this policy quite generally and condemning rationality as irreligious, churches do their best to suppress the freedom to philosophize, not only within their own congregations but outside them as well.[60]

This malaise is not confined to Christianity, but extends to pagans, Turks, and Jews. The members of a religion are distinguished by their dress, their place of worship, the particular beliefs they profess, and the master whose words they swear by, but they all lead the same kind of life, in which 'their faith is known more easily from their hatred and contentiousness than from their love'.[61] However, although corruption is universal, what chiefly concerns Spinoza is not the state of religion in general, but the mores of the most powerful Christian denomination in Holland, the Dutch Reformed Church.[62] By playing on the

---

[59] Spinoza, *Tractatus Theologico-Politicus*, Preface, p. 7.

[60] Ibid. Preface, p. 8.

[61] Ibid.

[62] The Dutch Reformed Church (*Nederlandse Hervormde Kerk*), founded in the late sixteenth century, was prevented from becoming an officially established church by Article 13 of the Union of Utrecht (1579). Nevertheless, it enjoyed a unique level of public influence: it provided

fears of the populace, the Church encourages superstitious beliefs and practices, and where necessary uses coercive methods to impose them.[63] This in turn undermines its members' capacity to reflect on the limitations of a superstitious way of life, and to distinguish truth from falsehood. Furthermore, since no single faction within the Church possesses enough power to impose its outlook on the whole community, conflict is endemic, and containing it consequently becomes one of the burdens of government.[64]

How has this lamentable situation arisen? According to the *Preface*, it has been precipitated by the fact that religious officials view themselves, and are viewed by others, as eminent dignitaries deserving of substantial rewards. The social status and financial benefits attaching to their positions make the ministry attractive to men who lack any religious vocation and are motivated solely by ambition and greed. In consequence, 'the temple itself has degenerated into a theatre where one hears, not the Doctors of the Church, but orators who have no desire to teach the people, and are possessed by a longing to win popular admiration for themselves, to censure those who disagree with them, and to teach only those new and unfamiliar doctrines that the people most admire'.[65] The least spark of the divine light has been extinguished, and dissension, envy, and hate are the order of the day.

At one level, this analysis is straightforward. Ministers who are engaged in a competitive quest for followers and prestige feel no compunction about exploiting the anxieties of their supporters, and holding out fanciful remedies in the name of religion.[66] This policy has a detrimental effect on the rationality and freedom of ordinary people and, as we have seen, tends to be politically destabilizing. However, Spinoza's account also draws attention to a further dimension of the instability that superstition engenders, and thus of the knot of problems he is addressing. Religious corruption, as he has so far portrayed it, is fuelled by the longing of ministers to be admired above the rest, and each of them will typically feel some combination of envy, hatred, and resentment for those who outstrip them. But because these officials are competing for ends

---

pastoral care to the republic's soldiers and sailors as well as owning or at least controlling many of its public, charitable, and educational institutions. It was common for the Dutch to refer to the NHK as 'the public church'. Benjamin J. Kaplan, *Divided by Faith: Religious Conflict and the Practice of Toleration in Early Modern Europe* (Cambridge, Mass.: Harvard University Press, 2007), pp. 177–8. See also Israel, *The Dutch Republic: Its Rise, Greatness and Fall, 1477–1806*, pp. 367–71.

[63] Spinoza, *Tractatus Theologico-Politicus*, Preface, p. 7.
[64] Ibid. Preface, p. 8.   [65] Ibid. Preface, p. 16.   [66] Spinoza, *Ethics*, 4p63s.

over which they have little control, they are particularly vulnerable to superstition. 'The men who are most thoroughly enslaved to every kind of superstition are the ones who immoderately desire uncertain goods'.[67] When churchmen bent on gaining ephemeral forms of prestige expose themselves to hope and fear, they are liable to become superstitious and to display the credulity and inconstancy that this condition brings with it. Like the populace they seek to control, their vulnerability will incline them to seek solace in doubtful beliefs and practices, adapted in each case to their own particular psychic needs; and when this is combined with their competitive desire for popular support it will fuel religious conflict.

Spinoza's contempt for the majority of the religious class is shared by many of his fellow-philosophers. His friend, Lodewijk Meijer, for example, had compared the Church's dogmatic philosophers to oracles, unfitted for discussion or debate;[68] and in his *Ethics*, Spinoza would again explain that, when self-esteem depends on the good opinion of the populace, it lasts only as long as the admiration on which it is based. 'That is why he who exults at being esteemed by the multitude is daily made anxious, and strives, sacrifices and schemes in order to preserve his reputation. For the multitude is fickle and inconstant; unless one's reputation is guarded, it is quickly destroyed. Indeed, because everyone desires to secure the multitude's applause, each one willingly puts down the reputation of the other. And since the struggle is over a good thought to be the highest, this gives rise to a monstrous lust of each to crush the other in any way possible'.[69]

In the *Treatise*, this attack is no doubt partly directed at the Reformed Church's preachers, who were often poorly educated and are, as we have seen, picked out by Spinoza as opponents of the freedom to philosophize. But it is significant that he nowhere suggests that superstition is an affliction of the ignorant alone. The assumption that education can protect people against superstition is implicit in the widely held seventeenth-century view that superstition arises from false beliefs about the relations between cause and effect. This opinion is voiced, for example, by Thomas Hobbes, who remarks that a superstitious person is someone who hopes 'for good or evill luck... from things that have no part at all in the causing of it'.[70] It is also present within the Protestant theological tradition, for instance in a commentary on the

---

[67] Spinoza, *Tractatus Theologico-Politicus*, Preface, p. 5.

[68] Louis Meyer, *La philosophie interprète de l'écriture sainte*, trans. Jacqueline Lagrée and Pierre-François Moreau (Paris: Intertextes, 1988), Prologue, p. 21.

[69] Spinoza, *Ethics*, 4p58s.   [70] Hobbes, *Leviathan*, p. 78.

Heidelberg Catechism written by the prominent theologian Zacharias Ursinus (1534–83). Ursinus describes superstition as a matter of attributing effects 'to certine things, or observations of gestures or words, as depend not either on natural, or moral reason, or on the word of god, and either doe not at al follow and fal out, or are wrought by the divels'.[71] Attributing events to forces that cannot be explained by appeal either to reason or to the word of God contained in Scripture therefore qualifies as superstition. And even if the forces are in fact inefficacious, it is still impious to appeal to them, because this is a way of failing to obey the divine word and worship God alone.[72] On this basis, the Reformed Church did its best to outlaw a wide range of ordinary practices that were held to be incompatible with natural reason and the religion commanded in Scripture. Some, such as witchcraft and fortune telling, were mentioned in the homilies used to drum the catechism into church congregations.[73] Others were explicitly ruled out by the catechism itself, which specified that members of the church must eschew all idolatry, sorcery, and enchantments.[74] Interpreting these exclusions, the Church at various times appealed to them to condemn devotional images and religious music, and to police popular habits such as the use of talismans, diviners, and healers.[75] By drawing on a classical understanding of superstitious practices, Spinoza stands back from the assumption that they are solely to be understood in epistemological terms, as ignorant and mistaken beliefs about causes. While he concedes that hard-headed authorities can appeal to superstition to dupe the uneducated, and that when they do so they exploit an ignorance of causal connections that does indeed make people vulnerable to superstition, the effectiveness of their strategy depends on superstition's passionate aspect, and in particular on the capacity of the powerful to play on the hopes and fears of the populace.[76] Quoting a remark attributed to Alexander the Great, who is reported to have said that, during war, 'prestige is an

---

[71] Quoted in Stuart Clark, *Thinking with Demons: The Idea of Witchcraft in Early Modern Europe* (Oxford: Clarendon Press, 1997), p. 484.

[72] Ibid. pp. 489–508.

[73] Ibid. pp. 493, 506.

[74] 'The Heidelberg Catechism,' in *The Creeds of Christendom: The Evangelical Protestant Creeds*, ed. Philip Schaff (New York: Cosimo Books, 2007), Q.94.

[75] On the view that attempts to define and control superstition were part of a broader attempt by all churches to regulate lay behaviour, see Jean Delumeau, *Catholicism between Luther and Voltaire: A New View of the Counter-Reformation*, trans. Jeremy Moiser (London: Burns and Oates, 1977), pp. 175–202.

[76] 'For example, Augustus persuaded the Romans that he was descended from Aeneas, who was believed to be the son of Venus and among the Gods; he wanted to be worshipped with temples and sacred images, by flamens and priests'. Spinoza, *Tractatus Theologico-Politicus*, ch. 17, p. 204. This passage draws on Tacitus, *Annals*, I.10.

important factor, and a false belief has often done duty for the truth',[77] Spinoza acknowledges the obvious fact that many superstitious beliefs are mistaken. But as Alexander indicates, what makes these false beliefs efficacious is a commander's prestige, which enables him to sway his soldiers when they are particularly vulnerable to fear.

Since superstition arises 'not from reason, but from the strongest passions' including hope and fear, hatred and anger, and since all human beings are susceptible to these passions, almost anyone may in principle become superstitious, the educated along with the ignorant and the great along with the multitude. Spinoza is convinced that an understanding of the philosophical principles he sets out in the *Ethics* can conquer superstition, by simultaneously transforming our knowledge of causal laws and our affective responses to events;[78] but the same cannot be said for other kinds of education. There is therefore no reason to assume that the training received, for example, by theologians or political leaders will necessarily protect them against superstition. All ranks and classes are subject to this kind of deformation, and when it afflicts them, conflict will inevitably arise. Thus, in the case of the Reformed Church, as Spinoza portrays it, the anxieties of the populace are sometimes coolly exploited by preachers bent on gaining power and prestige.[79] And as he points out in the *Ethics*, nothing but 'a savage and sad superstition' legitimates the suppression of pleasure on which the Church tends to insist.[80] But superstition also affects the Church's officials, and enters into the competing positions that are passionately defended by opposing theological factions. Much as the preachers struggle amongst themselves for followers, so Calvinist theologians engage in ferocious disputes in order to gain or uphold their authority. Superstition and its consequences extend right up the church hierarchy, infecting its disputes about the nature of Christian doctrine and the practice of true religion.

Cultivating true religion and political freedom

The predicament to which Spinoza aims to offer a solution is, therefore, a delicate and pervasive one. In order to contain the damaging effects of superstition, the Dutch must find a way to reform a powerful religious class that is doubly implicated in a superstitious way of life, both because its members are

---

[77] Quintus Curtius Rufus, viii.8.   [78] Spinoza, *Ethics* 1 Appendix.
[79] Spinoza, *Tractatus Theologico-Politicus*, Preface, p. 6.
[80] Spinoza, *Ethics*, 4p45s.

themselves to varying degrees superstitious, and because its status to some extent depends on encouraging superstition in the population at large. However, for the reasons already sketched, any such reform will be a difficult undertaking. The use of coercion is dangerous, because it reduces freedom and tends to produce its opposite, slavery. The fluidity of superstition suggests that attempts to contain one form may have the effect of creating others. And the streak of cognitive rigidity to which superstition gives rise makes it particularly difficult to shake.[81]

Spinoza is nevertheless undaunted. His contempt for the religious milieu in which he finds himself is palpable, and as he explains in the Preface, it is a sense of outrage that has impelled him to write.[82] Religion has become a battlefield in which what is called faith is nothing but a set of prejudices and mysteries that turns men from rational beings into beasts, prevents them from using their judgement to distinguish truth from falsehood, and seems designed to put out the light of the intellect. Theologians have grossly distorted the Scriptures by accommodating them to Platonic and Aristotelian speculations until the prophets rave with the Greeks; and out of fear for their own positions, religious officials persecute anyone who disagrees with them.[83] In summary, 'the natural light is not only disdained but condemned by many as a source of impiety, human inventions are treated as divine teachings, credulity is taken for faith, the controversies of the philosophers are debated with the utmost passion in Church and State, and in consequence, the most savage hatreds and disagreements arise, by which men are easily turned to rebellions'.[84]

By unmasking the flawed assumptions on which the theologians ground their conclusions, Spinoza aims to discredit their conception of piety and undermine the superstitious practices that feed on it; and since they derive their account of the beliefs and behaviour that a religious life requires from the Bible, the way to reveal their errors is to adopt their own method of enquiry and find out what Scripture teaches us. This is why, as Spinoza explains, he has resolved to examine Scripture afresh, 'with an unprejudiced and free spirit, affirming nothing concerning it, and admitting nothing as its teaching, that it did not very clearly teach me'.[85]

But how persuasive can Spinoza expect his investigation to be? As he is quick to acknowledge, once people become emotionally invested in a purportedly pious doctrine that is in fact grounded on prejudice, nothing he can say is likely to shift their opinions. Equally, since he cannot hope to free the common

---

[81] Spinoza, *Tractatus Theologico-Politicus*, Preface, p. 7.   [82] Ibid. Preface, p. 9.
[83] Ibid. Preface, pp. 7–9.   [84] Ibid. Preface, p. 9.   [85] Ibid.

people from fear, he cannot hope to free them from superstition. Their constancy, Spinoza claims, lies in their obstinate adherence to impulse rather than reason, and they are inured to any arguments he can offer. So, given that there is virtually no chance of persuading people like these, it would be pointless and even counterproductive for them to read the *Treatise*. 'I do not ask the common people, or anyone who suffers from the same passions as the common people, to read these pages; indeed, I would prefer them to neglect this book entirely rather than making trouble by interpreting it perversely, as is their custom with everything. They will do themselves no good, but will harm others who would philosophise more freely if they were not prevented by this one thought: that reason must be the handmaid (*ancilla*) of theology. For the latter, I am confident that this work will be extremely useful'.[86]

It is unlikely that the common people would have had much opportunity to read the *Treatise*, which was written in Latin. But what about the other group Spinoza mentions who, though not themselves of the common people or *vulgus*, suffer from its passions? This body surely includes the more intransigent theologians of the Reformed Church, but as Spinoza knew from experience, it also contains some of their secular supporters. In the December of 1664 Spinoza had embarked on a correspondence with a Dordrecht grain merchant, William Van Blyenbergh, who had read his exposition of Descartes' *Principles* and wrote asking him to resolve a metaphysical problem with a bearing on providence.[87] If God not only creates the soul but maintains it in existence, is he not the immediate cause of all its volitions? But if so, is he not the immediate cause of evil volitions, and thus the cause of evil? 'Be assured, Worthy Sir, that I ask these things only from a desire for the truth, not from any other interest. I am a free person, not dependent on any profession, supporting myself by honest trade and devoting my spare time to these [metaphysical] matters'.[88] Spinoza's candid reply produced a string of further objections, and as letters flew back and forth the intellectual differences between the two men became increasingly evident. At the end of a month Spinoza wrote to Blyenbergh in

---

[86] Ibid. Preface, p. 14.

[87] Willem van Blyenbergh (?–1696) was a grain broker with an avid interest in philosophy and theology. In 1663 he published a small book entitled *Theology and Religion defended against the views of Atheists, wherein it is shown by natural and clear arguments that God has implanted and revealed a Religion, that God wants to be worshipped in accordance with it, and that the Christian Religion not only agrees with the Religion revealed by God but also with the Reason which is implanted in us.* See Spinoza, *The Correspondence of Spinoza*, ed. and trans. Abraham Wolf (London: Frank Cass, 1966), p. 54.

[88] Letter 18. *Spinoza: Letters: July 1664–September 1665*, in *The Collected Works of Spinoza*, vol. I, pp. 349–97, 357.

exasperation. 'I hardly believe that we can instruct one another with our letters. For I see that no demonstration, however solid it may be according to the laws of demonstration, has weight with you unless it agrees with that explanation which you, or theologians known to you, attribute to sacred Scripture'.[89] What aligned the likes of Blyenbergh with the *vulgus* and made them unable to benefit from Spinoza's work was their obstinate adherence to the view that rational enquiry must not contradict the Bible.

While the *Treatise* is *about* these people's attitudes, it is not written *for* them. Who, then, is it for? Who is meant to read it?[90] Like Descartes, who had conceded in the Preface to his *Meditations* that few people were capable of getting much out of his text,[91] Spinoza warns that he is writing for a limited audience. His book is addressed to 'philosophical readers',[92] and particularly to those whose willingness to philosophize freely is hindered by their belief that philosophical enquiry must submit to the conclusions reached by theologians. While these people are not so deeply sunk in superstitious forms of thought and action as to be beyond persuasion, some of them are nevertheless held back by the worry that philosophizing may lead them into an impious way of life and jeopardize their salvation. One aim of the *Treatise* is to liberate them by showing that piety or true religion does not conflict with the freedom to philosophize.

Since he is writing for an audience versed in philosophical reasoning, Spinoza is free to address its members in philosophical terms. As we shall see, he assumes that some of the readers he has in mind are already familiar with his own philosophical position, whether because they have read the Appendix to his published *Principles*, or because they have come into closer contact with him.[93] They include, one can assume, the group of friends mentioned by Simon De

[89] Letter 21. *Letters: July 1664–September 1665*, in *The Collected Works of Spinoza*, vol. I, p. 375.

[90] Daniel Garber, 'Should Spinoza Have Published His Philosophy?', in *Interpreting Spinoza: Critical Essays*, ed. Charlie Huenemann (Cambridge: Cambridge University Press, 2008).

[91] 'I would not urge anyone to read this book except those who are able and willing to meditate seriously with me.... Such readers, I know, are few and far between. Those who do not bother to grasp the proper order of my arguments and the connections between them, but merely try to carp at individual sentences, as is the fashion, will not get much benefit from reading this book'. René Descartes, *The Philosophical Writings of Descartes* (3 vols), trans. John Cottingham, Robert Stoothoff, and Dugald Murdoch (Cambridge: Cambridge University Press, 1985), II.8. References to this translation of Descartes' works will henceforth be abbreviated 'CSM'. AT VII.10.

[92] Spinoza, *Tractatus Theologico-Politicus*, Preface, p. 12.

[93] Edwin Curley, 'Notes on a Neglected Masterpiece: The *Tractatus Theologico Politicus* as Prolegomenon to the *Ethics*', in *Central Themes in Modern Philosophy*, ed. M. Kulstad and J. Cover (Indianapolis: Hackett, 1990).

Vries who had discussed Spinoza's ideas and were ready to defend them. In fact, small as this group may have been, it is possible that the *Treatise* was written primarily for them. Just as they had used his earlier manuscript to learn how 'to defend the truth against those who are superstitiously religious and Christian',[94] Spinoza may have thought that the *Treatise* would show them how to defend the autonomy of philosophy against opponents who thought it should be subordinated to theology. Treating them as a sort of Leninist vanguard, he may have been trying to equip them with a forensic manual that would enable them to concede as much as possible to the theologians, yet trip them up when necessary.

If so, the individuals who made up Spinoza's cadre held a range of unorthodox religious views. Several of his closest philosophical associates came from Mennonite backgrounds, and a number of these were members of the Collegiant movement, a nonconformist sect which adhered to a minimal set of doctrines and practices, and was viewed with deep suspicion by the Reformed Church.[95] Already non-Calvinist, and already committed to Spinozist philosophy, they were primed to find the arguments of the *Treatise* persuasive. However, judging from his own account, Spinoza also seems to be writing for people who are not part of this inner circle and still need to be persuaded that philosophizing is compatible with piety; and if this aspect of his project is to succeed, it must be couched in terms that this group of readers will find convincing.

In the *Treatise* Spinoza draws a standard distinction between two ways of thinking. Each depends on and is manifested in individual and collective ways of life, and each incorporates a form of reasoning that can be used more or less effectively.[96] The first way of thinking, imagining, is grounded on our everyday experience, and its basic materials can be roughly divided into three classes:

[94] Letter 8. *Letters: August 1661–August 1663*, in *The Collected Works of Spinoza*, vol. I, p. 190.

[95] The Collegiants, a movement of radical Protestants who had no ministers but met to discuss and interpret the Bible, broke away from the Arminian Remonstrants in the 1620s. Theologically eclectic, they took on elements of Arminianism, Anabaptism, and Socinianism, as well as spiritualism. Their first college was founded at Rijnsberg, where Spinoza lived from around 1661 to 1663, and their members included a number of his friends, including Balling and Jelles. Andrew C. Fix, *Prophecy and Reason: The Dutch Collegiants in the Early Enlightenment* (Princeton: Princeton University Press, 1991).

[96] The distinction between imagining and reasoning to which he is appealing was a familiar one, which went back to Aristotle and continued to be used by both Aristotelians and their opponents. We find versions of it in several of the authors whose work Spinoza had studied most carefully, including Maimonides, Descartes, and Hobbes; but as this suggests, it was part of an accepted framework on which normal philosophical discussion relied.

our ideas of particular things together with the signs by which we organize and communicate them; the desires and other passions that shape both the nature of our experience and the way we act on it; and the informal modes of reasoning that we bring to bear on our passions and ideas.[97] It is mainly on the basis of imagining that we construct conceptions of ourselves and the world, and take part in collective forms of life. However, because imagining works with what Spinoza describes as the inadequate or incomplete ideas yielded by our limited experience, and because the passions integral to it have their own dynamics and effects, the actions and social practices to which it gives rise are not always advantageous to us. At worst, they may be destructive, as for example when an individual routinely becomes enraged and violent but cannot break the habit, or when a community is unable to find a way out of endemic internal conflict. But imagining can also be productive, and in many circumstances people use their experience to build comparatively if imperfectly harmonious ways of life.

In addition, communities and individuals can use the resources of imagination in a critical spirit: they may, for instance, modify the classificatory assumptions underlying a system of signs, bring their experience to bear on their current passions, or revise the means–ends inferences on which they base particular patterns of action. In doing so, they engage in an informal kind of reasoning that is part and parcel of imagining; but their capacity to reason well or badly will be largely determined by their passions. For example, someone whose strong affective investment in a belief undermines their capacity to assess it will be disadvantaged as a reasoner (at least in this particular case), while someone who has a broader ability to exercise what Spinoza calls free judgement will be better placed to reason well. As we have seen, superstition is one of the affective phenomena that puts one at a disadvantage; but even the most accomplished imaginative reasoning will always be limited by the fact that it works with ideas that are grounded on our limited experience, and embodies an incomplete understanding of nature. While the actions to which imagination guides us may satisfy our desires, and the conclusions to which they lead may enable us to achieve many of our ends, the knowledge that we gain through it will only possess what Spinoza calls moral certainty and, however compelling it may seem, remains fallible.[98]

---

[97] Spinoza, *Ethics*, 2p40s2, Spinoza, *Short Treatise*, in *The Collected Works of Spinoza*, vol. I, p. 98ff. Benedictus de Spinoza, *Tractatus De Intellectus Emendatione*, ed. Carl Gebhardt, vol. II, *Opera* (Heidelberg: Carl Winter, 1924). English translation: *Treatise on the Emendation of the Intellect*, in *The Collected Works of Spinoza*, vol. I, pp. 3–45, §19.

[98] On the distinction between moral and mathematical certainty, see Rosalie Colie, *Light and Enlightenment: A Study of the Cambridge Platonists and the Dutch Arminians* (Cambridge: Cambridge

Different qualities of imaginative thinking can therefore have vastly different effects, and a community such as the Dutch Reformed Church which lacks the capacity to imagine well can do a huge amount of damage. Part of Spinoza's project is to show his readers how to use the resources of imaginative thinking to examine their attitudes to particular things such as the Bible, and to criticize the dogmas and practices of the Reformed Church. Cultivating the capacity to use one's imaginative capacities fruitfully, for example by making reliable inferences about the nature and relationships of natural objects, is part of what is involved in using what Spinoza calls the natural light of reason. As individuals and members of communities we may be better or worse at it; and our skills are reflected in our ways of life.

Contrasted with imagining is a more specialized way of thinking, practised by people who can rightly be described as philosophers. Whereas imagining focuses on particulars, deals in incomplete or inadequate ideas, and arrives at fallible conclusions, philosophical reasoning transcends these limitations. It concerns itself with general notions of types of things, strives to articulate adequate or accurate ideas, and demonstrates its conclusions with absolute certainty. Unlike imagining, it provides a true account of the most general ontological categories, and of the general laws that govern types of things. In principle it can offer us a true understanding of ourselves, and in doing so can open up the possibility of a profoundly empowering common form of life.[99]

This latter way of thinking constitutes reasoning in the fullest sense. But because it makes use of specialized skills that have to be learned and is at least in part the fruit of a particular type of education, only some people are equipped for it. Like everyone else, philosophers bring the natural light of reason to bear on their deliberations about particular things and actions, and exercise this capacity throughout their lives. However, they also aim for something more: to cultivate a further kind of rational understanding that Spinoza sets apart from the everyday business of imagining and portrays as transformative. Rational understanding enables us to overcome the inadequacy of our ordinary beliefs and outlooks, and gives us a new and unified conception of ourselves, nature, God, and how to live. As we learn to philosophize we come to see things very differently, and this in turn alters what we can do.

University Press, 1957); Henry G. Van Leeuwen, *The Problem of Certainty in English Thought, 1630–1690* (The Hague: Nijhoff, 1963).

[99] On the relation between imagining and reasoning, see Spinoza, *Ethics* 2p40–4, 4p35, 4p59–73.

Philosophy's power to change us makes it attractive, but also alarming. If reasoning of the kind that philosophers engage in can eclipse the deliberations that underpin our everyday ways of life and threaten what we take to be the most fundamental pieties of religion, is the freedom to pursue it desirable? Or would it be safer not to cultivate it? The more philosophically advanced of Spinoza's readers who are thoroughly committed to the project of acquiring philosophical knowledge will already have resolved this dilemma. But others who are still hovering on the brink may be held back by the fear that further philosophical study will jeopardize their religion and way of life. In order to take the plunge, they need to be reassured that it is safe to do so; and in this state of mind they will probably not be willing to put their trust in philosophical reasoning, since its power is what is in question. To bring them round to his view, Spinoza will therefore need to draw on the resources of imagination in order to show that philosophizing does not threaten salvation.

This diversity of Spinoza's audience helps to explain why the argument of the *Treatise* proceeds on two interconnected levels. Sometimes it is conducted in an abstract vein that presupposes a familiarity, not just with the tools of philosophy in general, but more specifically with the doctrines of Cartesianism and with Spinoza's own position. At other times it appeals to the everyday forms of evidence and probabilistic inference that belong to the realm of imagination, and is consequently accessible to readers who do not have, or need to have, much philosophical knowledge. While Spinoza's reasons for arguing at these two levels are partly explained by his intended audience, he also acknowledges that the problems he is dealing with are not all susceptible to a single form of investigation. Some can only be fully resolved in philosophical terms, while others arise out of, and depend on, imagination. For example, questions about the history of particular individuals such as Adam or Moses can only be settled by means of imaginative, historical reasoning, whereas questions about the true nature of God are—so Spinoza will claim—the preserve of philosophy. The way that he presents and defends a specific point is therefore shaped by two cross-cutting concerns—type of audience and type of problem—and the four resulting categories interweave as he shifts from one to another.

During the five years in which the *Treatise* was written, 1665–70, the Dutch Reformed Church gave notice of its willingness to prosecute authors who contested its doctrines. Among the people who suffered from this policy were two of Spinoza's friends: Lodewijk Meijer, the author of the Introduction to Spinoza's exposition of Descartes' *Principles*, and Adriaan Koerbagh. In 1666, Meijer published *Philosophy, the Interpreter of Holy Scripture*, in which he boldly argued that Cartesian philosophy provided the only sure way to determine the meaning of the divine law revealed in Scripture.[100] This attempt to show that Cartesianism could resolve theological problems confirmed the Voetians' worst fears, and Meijer was investigated by the Church. Two years later, Koerbagh's *A Flowerbed Containing All Sorts of Delights* appeared.[101] Ranging in satirical vein over a number of risky subjects, it challenged the Church's conception of superstition, questioned its interpretations of the Bible, contested its account of the status of Scripture, and proposed that the power of religious institutions should be strictly limited. Koerbagh was arrested and taken chained in an open cart to Amsterdam, where he was questioned by the city's magistrates. Sentenced to ten years' imprisonment, he died in jail in 1669.

With these warnings before him, it is not obvious why Spinoza went ahead and published the *Treatise*. While he presumably calculated that he would avoid prosecution, he must have known that his book would not be received quietly and have prepared himself for the attacks launched against it by individuals and authorities alike. Perhaps after Koerbagh's death he felt a responsibility to stand up for the views he shared with him, by exposing the errors of the Reformed theologians. Perhaps he was also trying to overcome the anxieties about which Oldenburg had gently teased him, and act courageously in the manner that Oldenburg had recommended. (In this sense, too, we might read the *Treatise* as a struggle against the passions that are conducive to superstition.) Perhaps he was moved by his avowed sense of outrage. Whatever his reasons, publishing the *Treatise* was the second great confrontation of Spinoza's life. Just as he had refused to bend to the rabbis of the Amsterdam synagogue and had accepted the costs of excommunication, so he now refused to compromise with the theologians and their supporters.[102] The *Treatise* sets out to undermine the outlook on which they based their claim to authority, and thus to challenge their power.

---

[100] Lodewijk Meijer, *Philosophia S. Scripturæ Interpres* (Amsterdam: 1666).

[101] Adriaan Koerbagh, *Een Bloemhof von allerley lieflykheyd sonder vedriet geplant* (Amsterdam, 1668).

[102] In July 1656, Spinoza was excommunicated from his Synagogue and symbolically cast out of the people of Israel, for his 'evil opinions and acts'. No member of the Jewish community was allowed to communicate with him in writing or in person, nor even to come within four cubits of him, nor to read any treatise composed by him. Detailed examinations of Spinoza's excommunication can be found in Lewis Feuer, *Spinoza and the Rise of Liberalism* (Brunswick: Transaction, Inc., 1987), ch. 1; Asa Kasher and Shlomo Biderman, 'Why Was Baruch De Spinoza Excommunicated?', in *Skeptics, Millenarians and Jews*, ed. David S. Katz and Jonathan Israel (Leiden: Brill, 1990); Nadler, *Spinoza*, ch. 6.

Revelation

Chapter 2

The Meaning of Prophecy

Spinoza's aim is to unmask practices that sustain fear and repress the capacity to reason. But where should his critique begin? According to the corrupted form of Calvinism that he aims to discredit, the two testaments of the Bible are our only public source of religious knowledge. Scripture contains the word of God communicated to the prophets, and the teachings of the Church are justified by the fact that they are based on nothing less than divine revelation. This conception of biblical authority purportedly sustains the hesitations of would-be philosophers, who believe that obeying the divine law set out in Scripture is necessary to their salvation and are afraid that philosophically grounded convictions may conflict with the requirements of true religion. Part of the task of the *Treatise* is to reassure them, by showing that the fruits of natural reasoning do not contradict revelation, so that philosophizing will not threaten their hope of eternal life. If Spinoza can convince them of his own view that 'Scripture leaves reason absolutely free', he will have removed a major obstacle to the growth of understanding and liberty.[1]

The interpretation of the Bible with which Spinoza now begins to engage focuses on prophecy. 'The prophets', Calvin had explained, 'did not speak of themselves, but, as organs of the Holy Spirit, uttered only that which they had been commissioned from heaven to declare. . . . the Law and the prophecies are not teachings handed on at the pleasure of men or produced by men's minds as their source, but are dictated by the Holy Spirit'.[2] 'God commanded his servants, prophets and apostles to commit his revealed word to writing', the Dutch Reformed Church's *Belgic Confession* reaffirmed, 'and he himself wrote

---

[1] Benedictus de Spinoza, *Tractatus Theologico-Politicus*, ed. Carl Gebhardt, vol. III, *Opera* (Heidelberg: Carl Winter, 1924), Preface, p. 10.

[2] David Puckett, *John Calvin's Exegesis of the Old Testament* (Louisville: Westminster John Knox Press, 1995), p. 26. See also *Calvin and the Bible*, ed. Donald E. McKim (Cambridge: Cambridge University Press, 2006); R. Ward Hodder, *John Calvin and the Grounding of Interpretation* (Leiden: Brill, 2006).

with his own finger the two tables of the law.'[3] Biblical revelation communicates laws that God has decreed for us and enables us to discern how he requires us to live.[4] 'Whatsoever man ought to believe unto salvation is sufficiently taught' in Scripture, and the doctrine it contains is 'most perfect and complete in all respects'.[5]

At the same time, the Bible reveals God's plan for humanity. Since 'nothing happens by chance, but every event in the world depends on God's secret purpose', prophecy enables us to discern that the course of historical events is providentially determined.[6] Together, the Old and New Testaments form a unified narrative organized around a sequence of covenants between God and man, culminating in the promise of Christ's kingdom on earth. (The covenant made with the patriarchs is so like ours in substance and reality, Calvin had proclaimed, that the two are actually one and the same.[7]) 'Christ promises his followers today no other Kingdom of Heaven than that in which they may sit at the table with Abraham, Isaac and Jacob', and on the basis of Scripture we can be absolutely confident that the kingdom of heaven will come about.[8] 'For the very blind are able to perceive that the things foretold in [the canonical books of Scripture] are fulfilling'.[9]

In Spinoza's own generation, this providentialist reading of Scripture was elaborated by Johannes Cocceius, professor of theology at the University of Leiden and an influential though controversial voice within Reformed theology. God's original covenant with Adam was an unequal one, Cocceius argued, resembling that between a master and a slave. As long as Adam obeyed the law that God had set out for his benefit, he won God's approval and sustained a form of *amicitia* or friendship with him; but as soon as he broke the law by eating the fruit of the tree of knowledge, God withdrew his friendship. While the covenant was not altogether nullified, it became impossible for human

---

[3] 'The Belgic Confession', in *The Creeds of Christendom: The Evangelical Protestant Creeds*, ed. Philip Schaff (New York: Cosimo Books, 2007), Article 3.

[4] See Calvin's commentary on 2 Timothy 3:16 ('All Scripture is inspired by God and is profitable for doctrine, for reproof, for correction, for instruction and for righteousness') for the view that one can only benefit from Scripture if one concentrates on the prophecies it contains. John Calvin, *Commentaries on the Epistles to Timothy, Titus, and Philemon*, trans. Rev. William Pringle (Edinburgh: Calvin Translation Society, 1856), pp. 248–50.

[5] 'The Belgic Confession', Article 3. See also Calvin's commentary on 2 Timothy 3:16: '...he who knows how to use the Scriptures properly, is in want of nothing for salvation, or for a holy life.' Calvin, *Commentaries on the Epistles to Timothy, Titus, and Philemon*, p. 250.

[6] Puckett, *Calvin's Exegesis*, p. 30; 'The Belgic Confession', Article 13.

[7] Puckett, *Calvin's Exegesis*, p. 37.

[8] Ibid. p. 39.

[9] 'The Belgic Confession', Article 5.

beings to abide by it, and put them in a condition of *servitudo* or bondage characterized by fear of the deity. Fear prompted them to obey, whilst their inability to fully obey fed their fear. In his mercy, God then instituted the so-called covenant of grace with believers, enabling them to acquire a grounded faith that the effect of Adam's sin will at some point be reversed and friendly relations with God restored. Faith therefore coexisted with a fear that was only mitigated when Christ engraved the law on the heart. Liberated by his inter-vention, the faithful no longer have any reason to fear God; but they must still struggle with their passions—fear included—as they await Christ's kingdom on Earth and the renewal of an unqualified friendship between God and man.[10]

Cocceius's interpretation of the covenants illustrates how deeply Dutch Calvinist theology was informed by an interpretation of Scripture which located the Reformed Church and its members at a particular stage of history. In their current state, human beings have to contend with anxieties that originated in Adam's first disobedience and are plagued by fears that expose them to the threat of superstition. As we shall see, Spinoza will adamantly reject any such narrative, along with the conception of God on which it depends. But he nonetheless reworks some of its most central themes in his own idiom, and retains the theological contrast between human imperfection and salvation around which Calvinism is organized. For Cocceius and other Calvinist theo-logians, fear and the superstition to which it gives rise stand in the way of a form of freedom and salvation that will only be realized in the kingdom of Christ, and until this kingdom arrives human beings will have to struggle against their passions. In Spinoza's philosophy, too, superstition and enslavement to the passions are obstacles to salvation. But the means to overcome them, insofar as it can be realized, lies in our understanding. Philosophy rather than the pre-destined will of God or the intervention of the Holy Spirit is the route to blessedness.[11]

These affinities can help us to appreciate some of the ways in which Spinoza's own intellectual concerns overlap with those of his Calvinist contemporaries. Despite his hostility to the Reformed Church's dogmatism, he finds resonant ideas in the work of some of its theologians, and uses them to create a bridge between his own position and theirs. The complex interplay between the two

[10] W. J. van Asselt, *The Federal Theology of Johannes Cocceius (1603–1669)* (Leiden: Brill, 2001), pp. 39–47, 127, 249–75; Ernest Bizer, 'Reformed Orthodoxy and Cartesianism', *Journal for Theology and the Church*, 2 (1965), p. 20.

[11] Spinoza, *Ethics*, in Curley ed. *The Collected Works of Spinoza*, vol. I, 5p31c, 5p33c, 5p42.

outlooks is one of many indications that Spinoza's engagement with Calvinism is an authentic one. He is bitterly critical of what he regards as the deformed conceptions of piety sponsored by the churches, and does all he can to discredit them. But he does not straightforwardly reject the Church's religious outlook. Instead, he approaches it as a distorted and imperfect attempt to capture the moral teaching of Scripture, which, he contends, can correctly be regarded as divine.[12] The Bible is, therefore, the medium or common ground through which he both criticizes his opponents and articulates his own position, so that when he challenges the Church's interpretations of Scripture, his objections are not merely strategic or instrumental. On the contrary, he is disputing a reading of a text that, like the theologians of the Reformed Church, he views as a source of profound insight into the nature of true religion. His hostility to Calvinism, and indeed to other biblically based confessions, is therefore by no means unqualified. What makes them so destructive is that, by defending a distorted account of the meaning and status of biblical doctrine, they deprive their adherents of insights that could and should contribute to their freedom and blessedness. Instead of liberating its followers from disempowering ways of life, the Reformed Church promotes superstition and locks individuals into a form of slavery.

To unmask the Church's misuses of Scripture, Spinoza begins by critically examining a sequence of received claims about what the Bible teaches; and since the core doctrines of the text are held to have been revealed to the prophets, he focuses first of all on prophecy. What is prophecy, how does it work, and what does it teach us? Spinoza will have much to say about these issues, but before taking up the main strand of his argument he pauses to situate his discussion within a sequence of contemporary debates. Prophecy or revelation, he boldly announces, 'is the certain knowledge of a thing revealed to men by God, and a prophet is one who interprets God's revelation'.[13] It remains to ask, however, what range of phenomena this definition applies to. When we discuss prophecy, what are we talking about? Spinoza is on safe ground in assuming that the prophecies recorded in the Bible are indeed cases of revelation, and does not expect anyone to disagree with him. But he treads more carefully when canvassing the possibility that there may also be living prophets, whose direct knowledge of the divine word could in principle challenge established doctrines.[14]

---

[12] Spinoza, *Tractatus Theologico-Politicus*, ch. 7, p. 99.
[13] Ibid. ch. 1, p. 15.   [14] Ibid. ch. 1, p. 16.

Not surprisingly, the Reformed Church resisted this hypothesis; but within the nonconformist sects, where 'free prophesying' was a widespread practice, opinion was divided. Prophecy, in this sense of the term, occurred when a person felt spiritually moved to speak in a religious meeting, and the history of the Collegiant movement to which many of Spinoza's closest friends belonged illustrates the range of meanings commonly attributed to it. Initially, the Collegiants had regarded free prophesying as a form of inspiration due to the Holy Spirit, but in the middle years of the century they had abandoned this conviction. Under the influence of Galenus Abrahamsz, a leading member of the Amsterdam college, they adopted the view that, although Christ had endowed the members of the apostolic church with a special power to know and proclaim God's truth, this capacity had atrophied when the purity of the church was corrupted by Constantine. There are thus no longer any living prophets.[15]

The contrary opinion continued to be held by sects such as the Anabaptists, whose anti-Trinitarian theology set them at odds with the Calvinist church. Prophecy, they claimed, was alive and well, and in a sense they were undoubtedly right. As Spinoza was well aware, self-proclaimed prophets regularly appeared, and sometimes contested the power of existing religious institutions.[16] To take a particularly florid example, a charismatic Ashkenazi Jew from Smyrna called Shabbatai Zevi had arrived in Amsterdam in 1666 announcing himself to be the Messiah. Under his influence a section of the Jewish community gave up work in order to spend its time in celebration and prayer, while a number of individuals, both Christians and Jews, sold their property and made plans to decamp to Jerusalem.[17] A sense of the international stir that Zevi aroused is conveyed in a letter to Spinoza from Henry Oldenburg who reports

---

[15] Andrew C. Fix, *Prophecy and Reason: The Dutch Collegiants in the Early Enlightenment* (Princeton: Princeton University Press, 1991), pp. 94–109.

[16] In Holland there was an important distinction between radical Anabaptists and Mennonites, a fissiparous, breakaway sect led by Menno Simmons. More than 200 radical Anabaptists were executed in Holland between 1534 and 1536 in the wake of a plot to seize Amsterdam, and during the first half of the sixteenth century they continued to be persecuted as heretics, libertines, and schismatics. Menno Simmons rejected many aspects of their theology, including their anti-Trinitarianism, and the use of violence. Jonathan Israel, *The Dutch Republic: Its Rise, Greatness and Fall, 1477–1806* (Oxford: Clarendon Press, 1995), pp. 87–94.

[17] Michael Heyd, 'The "Jewish Quaker": Christian Perceptions of Sabbatai Zevi as an Enthusiast', in *Hebraica Veritas? Christian Hebraists and the Study of Judaism in Early Modern Europe*, ed. Alison Coudert and Jeffrey Shoulson (Philadelphia: University of Pennsylvania Press, 2004); 'Shabbatai Zevi', in *Encyclopaedia Judaica* (Farmington Hills: Macmillan Reference, 2007).

a rumour that the Jews 'having been dispersed for two thousand years, are to return to their country'. What have the Jews of Amsterdam heard about the matter, he asks, and 'how they are affected by such an important announcement, which if it were true would seem to bring a crisis on the whole world?'[18] As matters turned out, Zevi did not live up to his followers' expectations, and they were rudely disillusioned when, captured by the Ottomans, he converted to Islam. But other self-proclaimed prophets arose to take his place.

Abiding by his personal motto, '*Caute*' or 'Caution',[19] Spinoza treats the phenomenon of living prophecy with circumspection. 'As far as we know', he writes, 'there are no prophets nowadays'.[20] This careful formulation offers guarded support for the Reformed Church's view that knowledge of prophecy can only be derived from the Bible. At the same time, it leaves open the possibility that there may have been prophets whose insights are not recorded in Scripture, a point for which the *Treatise* will in due course allow. For now, however, Spinoza is content to assume that Scripture is our only source of information about prophetic revelation, and to base his discussion on the divine word as interpreted by the prophets of the Bible.[21]

At the same time, he is emphatic that prophecy is not the only means by which God reveals himself to man, so that revelation as he conceives it has a far wider scope than his Calvinist opponents were willing to acknowledge. The opening paragraphs of the *Treatise* contain a vigorous defence of the claim that philosophical understanding qualifies as a form of revelation, because it depends on our idea of God and the natural laws that he determines.[22] When we acquire knowledge by natural reasoning, God reveals it to us. Elaborating this striking claim, Spinoza concedes that there are significant epistemological differences between prophetic and natural revelation. While anyone can in principle acquire and appreciate the certainty of the knowledge that reasoning reveals, the insights that prophetic revelation vouchsafes are only accessible to individual prophets.[23] Furthermore, while biblical revelation is conveyed

---

[18]   Letter 33. Spinoza, *The Correspondence of Spinoza*, ed. and trans. Abraham Wolf (London: Frank Cass, 1966), p. 217.

[19]   Steven M. Nadler, *Spinoza: A Life* (Cambridge: Cambridge University Press, 1999), p. 244.

[20]   Spinoza, *Tractatus Theologico-Politicus*, ch. 1, p. 16.

[21]   The view that there are no longer any prophets was also defended by Johannes Hoornbeek in *Summa Contraversiarum Religionis* (Utrecht, 1653). See Michael Heyd, *'Be Sober and Reasonable': The Critique of Enthusiasm in the Seventeenth and Early Eighteenth Centuries* (Leiden: Brill, 1995), pp. 34–5.

[22]   Spinoza, *Tractatus Theologico-Politicus*, ch. 1, p. 15.

[23]   Ibid. ch. 1, p. 22.

through words and images, its philosophical counterpart is 'dictated to us . . . in a far more excellent way that agrees most satisfactorily with the nature of the mind, as everyone who has tasted the certainty of the intellect has doubtless experienced for himself'.[24] The brevity and premises of Spinoza's argument for these conclusions indicate that it is primarily addressed to readers who are familiar both with Cartesian metaphysics and also with Spinoza's own philosophical position.[25] For this audience, he sets himself against a Calvinist conception of reason as a frail and corrupted instrument and extols the pleasures of understanding as revealed by God.

In one form, then, prophecy encompasses the natural knowledge that philosophizing yields, and in the more familiar form known from the Bible it may have been practised by prophets whose insights have been lost to us. Revelation, it seems, is not always mysterious and extends into the familiar reaches of current life. Nevertheless, as Spinoza now goes on to observe, common or uneducated people are prone to be fascinated by prophecy of the biblical kind, and often fail to recognize natural revelation for what it is.[26] Thirsting for things that are 'rare and foreign to their nature', they 'spurn their natural gifts' and prefer to dwell on spectacular events that defy explanation.[27] The full extent of revelation is widely misunderstood, and its more flamboyant manifestations are given a disproportionate amount of attention.

Embedded in this critical analysis is the tacit implication that, when authorities such as the Reformed Church go along with the popular conception of revelation, they reinforce the disposition of ordinary people to turn their backs on reasoning and encourage them to take refuge in ignorant wonder. In doing so, they foster conditions in which superstition can take hold, and lend support to the superstitious practices on which corrupt religion thrives. To counteract these tendencies, one might expect Spinoza to develop his conception of the revelatory dimension of reasoning, as he will later go on to do in the *Ethics*. But here in the *Treatise*, where he has set himself to win over readers who are half in

---

[24] Ibid. ch. 1, p. 16.

[25] It appeals, for instance, to Descartes' claim that all our knowledge depends on knowledge of God, and draws on the traditional distinction between the formal and objective reality of ideas that he uses in the *Meditations*. (AT VII.40ff/CSM II.28ff.) If the philosophers for whom Spinoza was writing were predominantly Cartesian in their sympathies, he could safely assume that they would be familiar with these ideas, and would find his argument accessible. In addition, any readers acquainted with his own philosophical position would have seen in the argument his distinctive conception of a God in whom we participate (ibid.). To this extent, then, the demonstration is aimed at a philosophically informed audience of people who are equipped to understand it.

[26] Ibid. ch. 1, p. 15.   [27] Ibid.

sympathy with his opponents' anti-philosophical reading of Scripture, this would be a counterproductive course to take. Having given them a glimpse of a more inclusive conception of revelation, he now draws back and settles down to work within the bounds set by the Church's view that the only way to understand prophetic revelation is to study the Bible. 'Whatever can be said about these matters', he allows, 'can be sought only from Scripture. For what can we say about things exceeding the limits of intellect, beyond what has been passed down to us from the prophets themselves, either orally or in writing? Our only alternative is to expound the sacred books. . . . But with this precaution: we should not maintain anything about such matters, or attribute anything to the prophets themselves, that they did not clearly say'.[28]

This passage contains two important concessions to orthodoxy. In promising to base his conclusions solely on biblical evidence, Spinoza is announcing that he will use the standard interpretative method adhered to by the Reformed Church's theologians and summed up in the adage '*Scriptura interpretes sui*', Scripture must be interpreted by Scripture.[29] At the same time, his reiteration of this phrase signals that there is something he is not going to do, namely to treat the natural light of reason as an independent standard that can be used to judge between competing interpretations of the Bible. While the *Tractatus* was being written, this heterodox approach had been advocated in Loedwijk Meijer's *Interpretation of Holy Scripture* and, during the scandal that the book aroused, fiercely repudiated by Calvinists of all stamps.[30] So when Spinoza aligns himself with the mode of interpretation favoured by the Church, he is letting his readers know that he is not going to follow Meijer's example.

Interpreting Scripture by Scripture

In due course Spinoza will provide a full account of the interpretative method he favours. At the start, however, he simply employs two standard hermeneutic techniques. Like the Jewish commentators whose works he had studied at school, and the Christian theologians with whom he is now engaging, he first assembles and compares biblical passages that are relevant to his chosen theme. When their meaning is less than transparent, a second technique comes into

---

[28] Ibid.

[29] Jean Calvin, *Institutes of the Christian Religion*, ed. and trans. John Thomas McNeill and Ford Lewis Battles, *The Library of Christian Classics* (Philadelphia: Westminster Press, 1960–1), I.10.1.

[30] Theo Verbeek, *Spinoza's Theologico-Political Treatise: Exploring 'the Will of God'* (Aldershot: Ashgate, 2003), p. 99.

play—that of examining the original Hebrew meanings of problematic words or phrases. Here Spinoza aligns himself with a Dutch Protestant heritage that was itself to some extent indebted to Jewish textual scholarship.[31] The earliest Christian Reformers had brought the fruits of a classical humanist tradition to bear on Scripture, and in the opening decades of the seventeenth century leading figures such as Joseph Scaliger, together with his pupils, Daniel Heinsius and Hugo Grotius, had made the University of Leiden a major centre of humanist studies.[32] As they and their students learned the languages in which the earliest available versions of biblical manuscripts were written, theologians began to use Hebrew sources as a matter of course On the whole, then, Calvinists would have regarded Spinoza's approach to decoding the Scriptures as entirely natural, and indeed unavoidable.[33]

Putting his method to work, Spinoza's first aim is to arrive at a clear account of what Scripture says about the way God communicates with his prophets, and to undermine the supposition that the process is a supernatural one. Surveying the relevant passages, and engaging with a discussion of the same topic by the twelfth-century rabbi Moses Maimonides, he notes that revelations are invariably described as consisting of words or images.[34] These are usually imagined, in the sense that they take the form of dreams or visions, but there are two striking exceptions to the rule. Moses and the Israelites heard God speak with a real voice, and Moses saw God's back on Mount Sinai. This is made clear, for instance, in Numbers 12.6: 'If there be a prophet among you, I the Lord will make myself known unto him in a vision, and will speak to him in a dream. My servant Moses is not so... With him will I speak mouth to mouth, even apparently, and not in dark speeches; and the similitude of the Lord shall he behold'.

The observation that revelations take the form of words and images allows Spinoza to defend a claim that is absolutely vital to his argument: that prophecy occurs by means of capacities that belong to what philosophers

---

[31] For example, to Maimonides's discussions of equivocal terms in his *Guide for the Perplexed.* See Sara Kelin-Braslavy, 'Bible Commentary', in *The Cambridge Companion to Maimonides,* ed. Kenneth Seeskin (Cambridge: Cambridge University Press, 2005).

[32] Anthony Grafton, *Joseph Scaliger: A Study in the History of Classical Scholarship* (Oxford: Clarendon, 1983–93), Vol. 1, *Textual Criticism and Exegesis;* H. J. de Jonge, 'The Study of the New Testament', in *Leiden University in the Seventeenth Century: An Exchange of Learning,* ed. Th H. Lunsingh Scheurleer and G. H. M. Posthumus Meyjes (Leiden: Brill, 1975).

[33] Calvin had studied Hebrew at Basel and Strassburg, and appeals in his commentaries on Scripture to etymology, usage, and context. He uses, and criticizes, rabbinical sources in order to clarify the meaning of the Old Testament. See Puckett, *Calvin's Exegesis,* pp. 57–67.

[34] Spinoza, *Tractatus Theologico-Politicus,* ch. 1, p. 20.

call imagination.[35] As we saw in Chapter 1, one of the points on which Aristotelians and Cartesians were able to agree was that our interconnected abilities to sense, feel passion, fantasize, and remember can all be grouped together as aspects of imagining. With this analysis in hand, and despite the fact that the term 'imagination' does not occur in Scripture, Spinoza takes it that we are in a position to see that imagining is the means by which revelation works. To be sure, we cannot give a full account of all the antecedent causes of particular revelations; 'if you ask by what laws of nature this revelations was made, I confess I do not know'.[36] But we can safely infer the general conclusion that what made the prophets exceptional was their imaginative power, and that this was what enabled them to arrive at insights denied to ordinary people.

To illuminate the full range of biblical prophecy, imagining must be able to account not only for dreams and visions, but also for Moses' 'real' encounters with God. Accepting this challenge, Spinoza rejects a view that he attributes to Maimonides, that because no one can see an angel with his eyes open, revelation can only occur in dreams,[37] and argues instead that revelations can sometimes be phenomenologically indistinguishable from ordinary perception. 'Some men, with open eyes, imagine certain things so vividly that it is as if they had those things before them',[38] so that Moses' encounter with God may have been as vivid as one with his brother Aaron. Spinoza elaborates this view in a letter to his friend Pieter Balling, who had written to him about the death of his child, asking for advice. Shortly before his son became ill, Balling recounts, he had woken in the night and heard the sound of sobs like those the dying boy would utter. Was this, he now wondered, a premonition or omen? Spinoza replies that the sobs were the fruit of Balling's imagination. When a father loves his son with such intensity that it is as if they are one and the same being, he

---

[35] Maimondes is the rabbinical writer to whom Spinoza refers most frequently in the *Treatise*. See Catherine Chalier, *Spinoza lecteur de Maïmonide: La question théologico-politique* (Paris: Cerf, 2006); Harry Austryn Wolfson, *The Philosophy of Spinoza* (New York: Meridian Books, 1958). Here he breaks with Maimonides's view that prophets are distinguished both for their intellects and for their imagination. Moses Maimonides, *The Guide for the Perplexed*, trans. Michael Friedländer, 2nd ed. (London: Routledge, 1928), II.32. See Howard T. Kreisel, *Prophecy: The History of an Idea in Medieval Jewish Philosophy* (Dordrecht: Kluwer, 2001); Steven B. Smith, *Spinoza, Liberalism, and the Question of Jewish Identity* (New Haven: Yale University Press, 1997), pp. 92–7.

[36] Spinoza, *Tractatus Theologico-Politicus*, ch. 1, p. 27.

[37] This underrates Spinoza's indebtedness to Maimonides's discussion. See Maimonides, *Guide*, II.41.

[38] Spinoza, *Tractatus Theologico-Politicus*, ch. 1, p. 28fn.

may be exceptionally sensitive to the child's condition. Balling's loving attention enabled him to apprehend that his son was sickening, though he expressed
this knowledge not in an idea of an impending illness, but rather by association,
in an idea of the child's cries.[39]

To reassure Balling that intimations of this kind lie within normal human
bounds, Spinoza recounts an experience of his own. 'When I awoke one
morning, when the sky was already growing light, from a very heavy dream,
the images which had come to me in my dream remained as vividly before my
eyes as if they had been real things, especially the image of a certain black and
scabby Brazilian whom I had never seen before. This image for the most part
disappeared when, in order to divert myself with something else, I fixed my
eyes on a book or some other object; but as soon as I again turned my eyes
away . . ., the image of the black man (*Aethiopis*) again reappeared as vividly as
before, and again and again until it gradually disappeared. What happened to
me with my inner sense of sight happened also with your sense of hearing. But
since the cause was very different, your case was an omen and mine was not'.[40]

Balling's premonition can be seen as a lesser instance of the imaginative
insight attained by the prophets and attested to in Scripture. Where his
attentiveness made him aware of his son's impending illness, the prophets'
outstanding sensitivity allowed them to grasp what the Bible calls the word of
God. And where Spinoza's image of the Brazilian was vivid and lingering
enough to make him doubt that he had dreamed it, something similar explains
Moses' waking image of God. Since imagination can account for all forms of
prophecy, 'we can affirm without any reservation that the prophets perceived
God's revelations only with the aid of imagination, i.e. by the mediation of
words or images, the latter of which might be either true or imaginary. For
since we find no other means in Scripture except these, we are not permitted to
feign any others, as we have already shown'.[41]

This is a significant step in Spinoza's argument on which much of his
subsequent discussion will rely, but it is not yet sufficient to discredit the
view he is trying to overturn–that revelation is caused by supernatural as
opposed to natural means. As he acknowledges, exponents of this position

---

[39] Moira Gatens and Genevieve Lloyd, *Collective Imaginings: Spinoza, Past and Present*
(London: Routledge, 1999), pp. 19–23; Genevieve Lloyd, *Routledge Philosophy Guidebook to
Spinoza and the Ethics* (London: Routledge, 1996), p. 64.

[40] Letter 17. *Letters: July 1664–September 1665*, in *The Collected Works of Spinoza*, vol. I,
pp. 352–3. Translation modified.

[41] Spinoza, *Tractatus Theologico-Politicus* ch. 1, p. 28. Spinoza explains why the mind's knowledge of the existence of external bodies via imagination is inadequate in *Ethics*, 2p26c.

are bound to retort that the Bible repeatedly describes the prophets not simply as people of exceptional imaginative power, but as instilled with the spirit of God.[42] His next task is therefore to consider what this means. Embarking on a close textual analysis, and examining individual passages with an almost gleeful attention to diversity, Spinoza notes that 'spirit' translates the Hebrew word *ruagh*, which can mean wind, breath or breathing, courage and strength, power and ability; it can mean intention, will, mind, decision or appetite, and serves to express all the passions of the heart. Finally, it can mean the regions of the world.[43] If these are the available meanings of 'spirit', what does it mean to speak of the spirit of God? Again, Scripture sustains many different interpretations. Things attributed to God can belong to his nature or be parts of him, as in the eyes of God; they can be within his power, as in the heavens of God; they can be imparted by him to the prophets as in the law of God; they can be of superlative degree, as when men of exceptional strength are called sons of God, or exceptionally large trees are called the trees of God; they can be beyond ordinary human understanding and therefore sources of wonder, as when miracles are called works of God; they can exceptional of their kind, as when Pharaoh tells Daniel that he possesses the mind of God.

This is Spinoza's first foray into linguistic analysis, and one might be forgiven for concluding that such a cornucopia of possibilities would make it impossible to arrive at a compelling conclusion about the meaning of 'spirit of God'. However, he is confident that particular occurrences of the phrase can be disambiguated by taking account of the contexts in which they occur, and provides a string of examples to illustrate his point. Sometimes, he wryly observes, 'the spirit of God' simply means a strong, dry wind.[44] Sometimes it means the mind of man.[45] But if we focus on the context of phrases such as 'the spirit of God was in the prophet' or 'men were filled with the spirit of God and with the Holy Spirit', it emerges that they have four distinct meanings: first, that the prophets were endowed with more than ordinary virtue; second, that they cultivated piety with exceptional constancy of heart; and third that they perceived God's mind or judgement. Finally, the causes of prophecy were referred to God because they were not understood, and were viewed with wonder.[46]

This compressed survey of biblical usage gives a flavour of one of the argumentative devices on which the *Treatise* will rely. Rather than providing detailed defences of the scriptural interpretations at which he arrives, Spinoza

---

[42] Spinoza, *Tractatus Theologico-Politicus*, ch. 1, p. 21.   [43] Ibid. ch. 1, pp. 22–3.
[44] Ibid. ch. 1, p. 24.   [45] Ibid. ch. 1, p. 25.   [46] Ibid. ch. 1, p. 27.

adopts the tone of an authority whose assumptions and inferences successfully cut through centuries of hermeneutic uncertainty and yield readings that are beyond reasonable doubt. As we shall see, some of the analyses he defends are radical; but in this case his conclusion was widely accepted and even taken for granted. Yes, prophets receive God's word and in this sense perceive his thoughts. Yes, the prophets were people of exceptional virtue and piety. And yes, we do not fully understand the process that results in revealed knowledge. None of this would have excited particular comment. Nonetheless, Spinoza's position is deliberately deflationary, because it implies that this is *all* that is meant when the Bible talks about prophets being filled with the spirit of God. Scripture therefore does not commit us to the view that prophecy is the fruit of supernatural powers bestowed by the Holy Spirit, and to think otherwise, Spinoza contemptuously remarks, would be to dream that the prophets had human bodies but not human minds, 'and thus that their sensations and consciousness were of an entirely different nature from our own'.[47] Instead, it indicates that the way to understand revelation is to view it as the outcome of an imaginative capacity that all human beings possess to some degree. The prophets were indeed extraordinary; but what made them so was the unusual quality of their imaginations, which gave them access to insights that lay beyond the reach of more ordinary people.

The limits of revealed knowledge

By characterizing revelation as an exercise of imagination, Spinoza has already implicitly distinguished the kind of knowledge that it provides from the intellectual knowledge supplied by philosophical reasoning. The latter, as any reader versed in Cartesianism would have appreciated, guarantees that its conclusions are beyond doubt or, as Spinoza puts it, mathematically certain. There is consequently no need to check them against any other standard, or to adjust them in the light of claims made in Scripture, since nothing except further natural reasoning can strengthen them. However, while reasoning of this sort yields speculative truths about the essences of things, it cannot tell us about the non-essential properties of individuals, and in order to gain knowledge of particular entities and states of affairs we have to rely on imagination. The knowledge that we derive from imagination is grounded on limited experience and lacks mathematical certainty; but it is nevertheless sufficient for many of our purposes. To take Spinoza's own example, a merchant who has

---

[47] Ibid. ch. 1, p. 15.

learned a reliable method for working out how to calculate proportions may not understand the mathematics on which the method is based, but still knows the right answers.[48] Or to take a different case, my expectation that a friend will keep her promise to meet me is based on my limited experience of her, but I nonetheless know that she will come.

Prophets who possess extraordinary powers of imagination are therefore well placed to acquire knowledge about individual things; but is there any reason to expect that they are capable of revealing philosophical truths? According to Spinoza, imaginative gifts are not generally accompanied by exceptional skill in reasoning. Our experience and reason both show us that 'those who have the most powerful imaginations are less able to grasp things by pure intellect. And conversely, those who are more capable in their intellect, and who cultivate it most, have a more moderate power of imagining, and have it more under their control. They keep it, as it were, in check, lest it be confused with intellect'.[49] This observation is borne out by Scripture, where figures of exceptional wisdom, such as Solomon, do not possess the gift of prophecy, while prophets are often uneducated, and sometimes, as in the case of the unfortunate Hagar, are even uneducated women.[50]

The view that imagination and reason do not sit easily together, and that individuals who excel in one rarely shine in the other, had its roots in the classical tradition and was often reiterated by seventeenth-century authors. For example, in *The Advancement of Learning*, a work that Spinoza knew, Francis Bacon quotes Tacitus's remark that people who invent fictions are inclined to believe them and are thus by implication poorly suited to concentrating on general truths,[51] an opinion that Spinoza echoes in his early work, *On the*

---

[48] Spinoza, *Ethics*, 2p40c2. Spinoza, *Treatise on the Emendation of the Intellect,* in *The Collected Works of Spinoza*, vol. I, §23.

[49] Spinoza, *Tractatus Theologico-Politicus*, ch. 1, p. 29.

[50] Hagar was an Egyptian slave belonging to Abraham. When Abraham's wife Sarah failed to become pregnant, Hagar became Abraham's concubine and gave birth to Ishmael. Late in her life, Sarah bore Isaac and wanted Ishmael out of the way. He and Hagar were sent into the desert. When Ishmael was about to die of thirst, God sent an angel to tell his distraught mother that he would become a great king, at which point she found a well and gave Ishmael water to drink (Genesis 16 and 21).

[51] '. . . an inquisitive man is a prattler; so upon the like reason a credulous man is a deceiver: as we see it in same, that he that will easily believe rumours will as easily augment rumours and add somewhat to them of his own; which Tacitus wisely noteth, when he saith, *Fingunt simul creduntque*: so great an affinity hath fiction and belief'. Francis Bacon, *The Advancement of Learning*, ed. James Spedding, Robert Ellis, and Douglas Heath, vol. IV, *The Works of Francis Bacon* (London: Longmans, 1858), I.iv.9.

Emendation of the Intellect.[52] Thus, although the Bible does not directly tell us what kind of knowledge the prophets possessed, it gives us information from which we can infer that they were less than exceptional as philosophical reasoners, so that we should not expect their revelations to contain speculative insights of the sort that only philosophy can yield. 'Therefore', Spinoza concludes, 'those who look to the books of the prophets for wisdom and knowledge of natural and spiritual matters go entirely astray'.[53]

Debate about the scope of prophetic insight was far from new, and Spinoza is here engaging with a range of opponents, living and dead. Among them is Maimonides, who had argued in his *Guide for the Perplexed* that, although the capacity to prophesy does indeed depend on a prophet's imagination, prophets also possessed astonishing intellects.[54] They were exceptional in both departments of knowledge, and are therefore to be trusted on philosophical as well as practical subjects. The same view was held by some of Spinoza's contemporaries. Because the prophets possessed exceptional intellectual gifts, they claimed, we can not only appeal to revelation or the word of God to gain an intellectual understanding of 'natural and spiritual matters', but can use the results of this exercise to test knowledge that we acquire by other means. Rather than trusting to our own rational capacities, we should subject any conclusions they yield to higher prophetic authority.

Spinoza's contention that revelation is the fruit of imaginative rather than intellectual powers challenges this view by implying that prophecy is incapable of yielding knowledge of natural philosophy. If revelation is the fruit of imagination it can only be morally certain and is in this respect inferior to philosophical knowledge.[55] Theologians who want to appeal to Scripture to test knowledge grounded on natural reason are therefore proposing to test conclusions arrived at by a method that guarantees mathematical certainty against claims of a lesser degree of certainty, derived from the imagination of the prophets by a process that we do not fully understand. This makes no sense. Yet there exist brazen advocates of this approach who elevate revelation over reasoning. They 'openly confess that they . . . know God only through created

---

[52] Spinoza, *Treatise on the Emendation of the Intellect* §58.

[53] Spinoza, *Tractatus Theologico-Politicus*, ch. 1, p. 29.

[54] Maimonides, *Guide*, II.36–8. Maimonides allows that the capacity to prophesy also depends on a prophet's imagination and bodily state (II.36) but claims that prophets are able to grasp speculative matters, which Spinoza will deny (II.38).

[55] Spinoza, *Tractatus Theologico-Politicus*, ch. 2, p. 30. According to Spinoza, '[philosophical] truth requires no sign' in order to be known with certainty. Spinoza, *Treatise on the Emendation of the Intellect* §36.

things (of whose causes they are ignorant), and do not blush to accuse philo-sophers of atheism'.[56]

The immediate opponents against whom this barb is aimed are the anti-Cartesian followers of Voetius within the Reformed Church. As we saw in Chapter 1, this powerful and conservative group objected to Descartes' claim that natural or philosophical reasoning yields an incontrovertible understand-ing of the physical world. In the first place, they argued, the Cartesian position misunderstands the proper role of natural philosophy, which is to support rather than challenge theology. As Voetius himself expressed it, 'If a student of physics examines many things in such a science and aims to become experienced in it, what else is he doing but admiring and consider-ing the works of almighty God, and at the same time lending a helping hand to the theologians, and indeed to all lovers and readers of Holy Writ . . . in order to understand even better so many of its chapters and proverbs'.[57] Since the aim of physics is to explicate and supplement the Bible,[58] physical questions are simultaneously theological ones, and philosophy and theology are mutually implicated. A further deficiency of Cartesianism was that it licensed a range of specific conclusions which ran counter to biblical testi-mony. For example, Descartes' support for the Copernican hypothesis con-flicted with a number of texts, which clearly indicate that the sun moves round the Earth.[59] Once again, the Voetians insisted that Scripture should be given priority.

The clash between biblical physics and Copernicanism had a long history and was not confined to the Netherlands. In Italy, for instance, it had played a part in the Catholic Church's condemnation of Galileo.[60] The United Provinces was nevertheless one of the arenas in which the struggle between the two cosmological theories was played out, and here as elsewhere the quarrel tended to focus on the interpretation of a small number of scriptural passages. Foremost among these was the Old Testament account of Joshua's battle against the

---

[56] Spinoza, *Tractatus Theologico-Politicus*, ch. 2, p. 29.

[57] Quoted by J. A. van Ruler, *The Crisis of Causality: Voetius and Descartes on God, Nature, and Change* (Leiden: Brill, 1995), pp. 26–7. See also Verbeek, *Spinoza's Theologico-Political Treatise*, pp. 94–5.

[58] Ruler, *Crisis of Causality*, p. 318.

[59] Rienk Vermij, *The Calvinist Copernicans: The Reception of the New Astronomy in the Dutch Republic, 1575–1750* (Amsterdam: Koninklijke Nederlandse Akademie van Wetenschappen, 2002), Part IV.

[60] Maurice A. Finocchiaro, *The Galileo Affair: A Documentary History*, California Studies in the History of Science (Berkeley: University of California Press, 1989).

Ammonites, during which the sun is said to have 'stood still in the midst of heaven, and hasted not to go down about a whole day'.[61]

Many commentators agreed that the author of this passage believed that the sun moves round the Earth. To put the point in terms of seventeenth-century debate, the author was not a Copernican, thus not a Cartesian, and did not accept the heliocentric hypothesis of which natural philosophers were increasingly persuaded. But for the Voetians, the text contributed to the overall evidence in favour of the pre-Copernican position. The view that the Earth is stationary is confirmed by Scripture, by Aristotelian philosophy, and by our experience of the fact that the ground we stand on does not move. We therefore have no reason to deviate from it.[62] As Voetius insisted, the conclusion 'that the heavens stand still and the earth turns round each day cannot be proved from Scripture. Scripture clearly denies this. . . . The objections that some people put forward are vain and absurd'.[63]

No philosopher who had studied and been persuaded by Descartes' physics could possibly accept this claim. Joshua's and Descartes' accounts of planetary motion are mutually contradictory, and since the latter was supported by the superior power of natural reasoning it was not in serious doubt. Along with all Dutch Cartesians, Spinoza is a Copernican.[64] However, he recognizes that in order to successfully undermine the Voetian position, he will need to engage with another of Voetius' objections—that to reject Joshua's testimony is in effect to accuse the Holy Spirit of uttering falsehoods. To put the point another way, if the sun does not move around the Earth, why does revelation suggest otherwise?[65]

At stake here is the central issue of how the Bible should be read. Whilst a small number of Calvinist theologians tended to the extreme view that it must always be interpreted literally (Du Bois, for example, was prepared to assert that the Bible teaches and dogmatizes in every word and expression[66]), such an unmodulated approach to the problem of interpretation was extremely unusual, and in fact unsustainable. (Spinoza remarks in a letter to Blyenbergh that he has 'never seen a theologian so dense that he did not perceive that sacred scripture often speaks of God in a human way and expresses its meaning in

---

[61] Joshua 10:13. Debate about this goes back to Augustine: Augustine, *Confessions*, trans. R. S. Pine-Coffin (Harmondsworth: Penguin Books, 1961), pp. 271–2.

[62] Ruler, *Crisis of Causality*, p. 19.

[63] Quoted in Vermij, *Calvinist Copernicans*, p. 163.

[64] Spinoza, *Tractatus Theologico-Politicus*, ch. 2, p. 36.

[65] Vermij, *Calvinist Copernicans*, p. 261; and see his discussion of Schoock on p. 51.

[66] Ibid. pp. 2, 83.

parables'.[67]) Almost all contributors to the debate about the relation between revelation and philosophy agreed that at least some biblical passages reflect the attitudes and beliefs of comparatively uneducated people and are, as the point was usually expressed, accommodated to their understanding. To interpret the Scriptures correctly, we need to take this aspect of their historical context into account.

The role of accommodation in the process of interpreting divine communications had been debated since antiquity. Plutarch, for example, had explored the issue from a pagan point of view in a dialogue about the Delphic oracle, during which one of his characters proposes that the literary style of prophecy (whether poetry or prose) is accommodated to the education of the priestess and her audience.[68] Jews and Christians continued to reflect deeply on the hermeneutic issues that accommodation raises,[69] and when Calvin took up this heritage, he conceded that certain revelations are not literally true, but reflect the personalities and understanding of individual prophets and their audiences.[70] Prophets 'borrow their similitudes from an earthly kingdom, because our ignorance would make it almost impossible for us to comprehend in any other way the unspeakable treasure of blessings'.[71]

For all their disagreements, the Voetians and their Cartesian opponents were united in the view that the prophets sometimes speak with the vulgar. The questions that divided them were not about *whether* biblical prophecy is sometimes accommodated to the understanding of ordinary people, but about where in the text such accommodations occur, and this is the issue that Spinoza next addresses. As he protests with barely suppressed frustration, 'those who indiscriminately accept as the universal and unconditional teachings of God everything contained in Scripture, and who do not know accurately what is accommodated to the grasp of the multitude, are bound to confuse the opinions of the multitude with divine doctrine, to hawk human inventions and beliefs as divine teachings, and to abuse the authority of Scripture'. This is 'the principal reason why the followers of the sects teach as doctrines of the faith so

---

[67] Letter 21. *Letters: July 1664–September 1665*, in *The Collected Works of Spinoza*, vol. I, pp. 380–1.

[68] 'The Oracles at Delphi no longer given in verse', in Plutarch, *Moralia*, trans. Frank Cole Babbitt, *Loeb Classical Library* (Cambridge: Harvard University Press, 1928), V.320–9.

[69] Discussion about the question of accommodation can be found in Amos Funkenstein, *Theology and the Scientific Imagination: From the Middle Ages to the Seventeenth Century* (Princeton: Princeton University Press, 1986), pp. 213–71; J. Samuel Preus, *Spinoza and the Irrelevance of Biblical Authority* (Cambridge: Cambridge University Press, 2001), pp. 187–90 and *passim*.

[70] Puckett, *Calvin's Exegesis*, pp. 28, 35.

[71] Calvin, Commentary on Isaiah 32:19. Quoted in Puckett, *Calvin's Exegesis*, p. 112.

many and such contrary opinions, and confirm them by many examples from Scripture, with the result that it long ago became a proverb among the Dutch: *geen ketter sonder letter*—no heretic without a text'.[72]

Spinoza's analysis of prophecy is intended to provide a solution to these problems.[73] By illuminating the process through which prophecy works, it offers a working principle for distinguishing the true meaning of revelation from prophetic utterances that are accommodated to the minds of the prophets and consequently do not have to be taken at face value. This approach had already been pursued by two prominent Dutch Cartesians in the early 1650s. Lambert van Velthuysen had contested the Voetians' anti-Copernicanism on the grounds that Scripture has to be read in context, while Christopher Wittich had argued that the Scriptures speak with the vulgar when discussing natural phenomena. Following their lead, Spinoza appeals to our knowledge of imaginative thinking in order to explain the character of prophecy. Our imaginative capacities, and thus the way we interpret and engage with our environment, are shaped by our bodily constitution and history. However, the skills we bring to bear on this project vary from one person to the next. Some of us are better attuned than others to the likely effects of passions such as envy, fear, or love. Some of us are more observant when faced with a particular phenomenon such as the mood of a crowd, the ripeness of a crop, or the beauty of a building. Furthermore, variables such as these shape the meanings we are able to discover in the world, and determine the scope and limits of our imaginative knowledge.

Once we realize that the prophets were neither passive recipients of information conveyed to them by some supernatural means, nor brilliant intellects capable of understanding the essences of things, but rather individuals whose exceptional insights derived from their imaginations, various features of the revelations described in Scripture fall into place. First, it ceases to be surprising that prophecy often takes the form of the narratives and parables that Bacon

---

[72] Spinoza, *Tractatus Theologico-Politicus*, ch. 14, p. 173.

[73] See Bizer, 'Reformed Orthodoxy and Cartesianism', pp. 52, 54; The Heidelberg Catechism, Q84, 85. Wittich, drawing from 2 Timothy 13, claims that the ends of Scripture fall under four headings: to teach the principles of Christian religion; to refute errors of faith; to correct wickedness in life and death; to discipline, showing what is just and unjust. Christophoros Wittichius, *Consensus Veritatis in Scriptura Divina . . . Revelatæ cum Veritate Philosophica a R. Descartes Detecta* (Nijmegen, 1659), pp. 19–21. His point is that Scripture therefore doesn't teach us anything about natural philosophy. See Verbeek, *Spinoza's Theologico-Political Treatise*, pp. 95–7.

describes as divine poesy.[74] Since imagination deals in individual things and events, one would expect the truths it arrives at to reflect this fact, and images and narratives answer to the purpose.[75] Second, since we know from experience that our imaginative capacities come and go depending on the state of our bodies and other circumstances, we should not be taken aback by the discovery that the exceptional powers of the prophets were inconstant. They could only prophesy when conditions were right.[76] Third, since revelations are invariably the fruit of a particular prophet's imagination, we should expect them to be consonant with that individual's beliefs, temperament, and education, as the Bible in fact confirms.[77] For example, domestic animals figure in the revelations of prophets who are countrymen, battles in those of soldiers, and thrones in those of courtiers. Dispirited or angry prophets foretell calamities, while the feminine character of women prophets fits them to receive revelations of God's mercy.[78] The style and clarity of a prophecy, be it cultured, compressed, stern, or prolix, varies with the learning and temperament of the prophet in question.[79] And finally, revelation reflects a prophet's beliefs about God. Taking examples discussed in both the rabbinical and Christian traditions, Spinoza reminds his readers that 'Isaiah saw seraphim with six wings, Ezekiel beasts with four wings; Isaiah saw God clothed and sitting on a royal throne, Ezekiel saw him in the likeness of a fire'.[80] Doubtless, he comments, each saw God as he was accustomed to imagine him.[81]

A grasp of the dimensions of imaginative thought provides us, in Spinoza's view, with an understanding of the forms that accommodation can be expected to take. Once we acknowledge that talk about the manner in which God accommodates himself to the mind of a prophet just is talk about the way a prophet's imaginative resources shape the meaning with which he or she endows a particular event, we are better placed to identify accommodated passages and to deal with the problems they pose. Returning to the disputed text about Joshua's battle against the Ammonites, Spinoza emphasizes that, if we are to respect the rule that Scripture should be read in terms of Scripture, we have to face the fact that Joshua's beliefs are pre-Copernican. 'Nothing in Scripture could be clearer than that Joshua, and perhaps the writer who

---

[74] Bacon, *Advancement*, II.i.1. Vermij notes that in a work of 1653 Wittichius discusses the sympathetic (to him) accounts of accommodation given by all sorts of people, including Maimonides and Bacon. Vermij, *Calvinist Copernicans*, p. 258. See Christophoros Wittichius, *Dissertationes Duæ* (Amsterdam, 1653), esp. Preface and I.ii.

[75] Spinoza, *Tractatus Theologico-Politicus*, ch. 1, p. 28.

[76] Ibid.   [77] Ibid. ch. 2, p. 32.   [78] Ibid. ch. 2, p. 33.

[79] Ibid. ch. 1, p. 28.   [80] Ibid.   [81] Ibid. ch. 2, p. 34.

THE MEANING OF PROPHECY 57

composed the history, thought that the sun goes round the earth, but that the earth is at rest, and that the sun stood still for some time'.[82] Commentators who deny this distort the meaning of the text, in a fashion that allows anything at all to be read into it and spells the end of biblical criticism.[83] Some of them, Spinoza complains, have twisted the passage to make it conform to the view that the heavens are immutable.[84] Others have implausibly claimed that it is consistent with Copernicanism.[85] And yet others, finding that it upholds a view they regard as false, have pretended to be unable to understand it.[86]

There is, however, no need to tie oneself in hermeneutic knots; for although the Voetians are adamant that the prophets must be treated as a reliable source of information about natural philosophy, this is a misapprehension. Since the men and women to whom God revealed his word were exceptional for their imaginative rather than their intellectual abilities, there is no reason to suppose that they possessed more than ordinary understanding of the laws of nature, or indeed of other philosophical matters. The Bible itself, therefore, provides us with a warrant to disagree with their opinions about the causes of natural phenomena. While we can safely assume that Joshua faithfully recorded his experience of the day of battle, we do not have to accept that he was an accurate observer.[87] Nor do we have to accept his interpretation of events. He and his army believed that the sun stood still in the sky; but we know independently that this was not the case, and Scripture confirms that Joshua was not well placed to make an authoritative judgement on the matter. While we cannot be sure what caused the phenomenon he observed, we can speculate that it may have been due to the unusually cold atmosphere.[88] And while we cannot know precisely what Joshua meant by his revelation, we can at least determine what he did not mean. We can confidently infer that it was not about astronomy, and that the Bible, when properly read, does not suggest otherwise.

Part of the purpose of Spinoza's argument is, as he points out, to further his goal of showing how theology can be separated from philosophy.[89] If prophets are distinguished by their imaginative rather than their rational capacities, the revealed knowledge studied by theologians must deal with matters that can be grasped by imaginative means, and does not extend to the philosophical realm.

---

[82] Ibid. ch. 2, pp. 35–6.   [83] Ibid. ch. 2, p. 37.
[84] See Maimonides, *Guide*, I.72, II. 35.
[85] Spinoza, *Tractatus Theologico-Politicus*, ch. 2, p. 36.
[86] Ibid. ch. 2, pp. 36–7.   [87] Ibid. ch. 6, p. 92.
[88] Ibid. ch. 2, p. 36.   [89] Ibid. ch. 2, p. 44.

Revelation therefore does not undermine or cast doubt on philosophically grounded conclusions. Applied to natural philosophy, this was not a novel conclusion. Spinoza is reiterating an objection to the Voetian conception of biblical physics with which he could expect many of his readers to be familiar. But this is not all that he does. In a deceptively offhand discussion, he also applies his analysis of accommodation to a range of scriptural pronouncements on other topics, thus further reducing the area in which revelation is epistemically authoritative.

This phase of Spinoza's argument focuses on an apparently assorted sequence of biblical narratives, the first of which concerns Solomon's account of the dimensions of the Temple. During the middle years of the seventeenth century, a number of authors attempted to reconstruct the architecture of the ancient temple, despite the fact that Solomon's account of its measurements appeared to be inaccurate. Spinoza owned a book by Rabbi Jacob Jehuda Leon containing a detailed description of the Temple supplemented by etchings and models, and Cocceius's 1666 commentary on Ezekiel was also illustrated with figures of the building, drawn by Karl Kechel, the curator of astronomical instruments at the University of Leiden.[90] For all their fascination, Spinoza now suggests, these works are bound to be inconclusive. Although we know that Solomon was exceptionally wise about moral matters, we have no evidence that he was a learned mathematician. We can therefore legitimately assume that his account of the measurements of the Temple was accommodated to his limited mathematical knowledge, and should not be surprised that the dimensions he gives are based on an approximate grasp of the relation between the diameter and circumference of a circle.[91] Mathematics is therefore one of the subjects on which the Bible does not speak with authority.

Moving on to the historical information contained in Scripture, Spinoza takes up another controversial case, namely Noah's assertion that the whole human race apart from his own family was destroyed by the Flood. Following

---

[90] Jacob Judah Leon, *Retrato del Templo de Selomoh* (Middelburg, 1642). See no. 82 of the list of Spinoza's books in J. Freudenthal, *Die Lebensgeschichte Spinozas in Quellenschriften, Urkunden und Nichtamtlichen Nachrichten*, 2 vols. (Leipzig: Verlag von Veit & Comp., 1899), vol. 1, p. 356. Johannes Cocceius, 'Prophetia Ezechielis: Commentario Illustrata (1668)', in *Opera Omnia Theologica Exegetica Didactica Polemica Philologica* (Amsterdam, 1673–5). See Vermij, *Calvinist Copernicans*, p. 253. Spinoza touches on this puzzle in a letter to Simon De Vries (Letter 9).
[91] Isaac La Peyrère, *A Theological Systeme* (London, 1665), p. 239; Spinoza, *Tractatus Theologico-Politicus*, ch. 2, p. 36. See also Richard H. Popkin, *Isaac La Peyrère (1596–1676): His Life, Work, and Influence* (Leiden: Brill, 1987); Richard H. Popkin, *The Third Force in Seventeenth Century Thought* (Leiden: Brill, 1992), p. 34.

the lead of Isaac La Peyrère, who had argued that the Old Testament does not provide an accurate account of the age of the Earth or the history of the human race, and had dismissed the story of the Flood, Spinoza concludes that we are not constrained to share Noah's opinion.[92] He believed that the world beyond Palestine was uninhabited, but this was a mistake and we are free to disagree with him.

As these examples indicate, Spinoza is beginning to carve out a broad area of enquiry in which the writ of revelation does not run. His discussion of Solomon underscores his view that, because prophets do not possess exceptional intellects, they cannot be expected to possess knowledge of the principles of mathematics, any more than they can be expected to understand natural philosophy. But his interpretation of the story of Noah draws attention to a different point. As we have seen, working out whether a prophecy is accommodated to the understanding of a prophet is a matter of working out whether the content of the prophecy is the kind of thing that the particular prophet could have known. Sometimes, the claim in question is a philosophical one. However, as this case illustrates, biblical utterances can also contain claims about historical processes, which can only be investigated by imaginative means. Noah's mistake was not a philosophical one. He simply had some false empirical beliefs. However, since the point of Scripture is not to teach us about empirically grounded subjects such as the history of the world, we do not have to take such beliefs seriously.

Turning now to our knowledge of ourselves, Spinoza considers the case of Cain, who clearly thought that his will was free when he reports God as saying to him, 'If thou doest well, shalt thou not be accepted? And if thou doest not well, sin lieth at the door'. Once again, though, Cain's revelation was accommodated to his understanding. 'To those prophets who believe that men act from free choice and from their own power, God was revealed as indifferent, and as unaware of future human actions'.[93] And once again, the usual conclusion follows. 'Even though the freedom of the will is contained very clearly in the words and reasoning of [God's warning to Cain], we are permitted to think the contrary'.[94]

Spinoza has steadily chipped away at the domain in which prophecies are authoritative. Prophetic utterances about natural philosophy, mathematics, human nature, or history do not have to be believed. Nor, as he now emphatically reminds us, do claims about the supernatural, divine or otherwise.

---

[92] Spinoza, *Tractatus Theologico-Politicus*, ch. 2, p. 37.
[93] Ibid. ch. 2, p. 32.   [94] Ibid. ch. 2, pp. 33, 43.

References to the Devil are not to be taken literally.[95] (Here the *Treatise* contradicts the Reformed Church's doctrine that devils exist and are 'as murderers watching to ruin the Church and every member thereof'.[96]) Nor are anthropomorphic representations of God. For example, if Moses has recognized that God is omnipresent he would not have thought that he could only communicate with him on Mount Sinai. And if Adam had realized that God is omniscient, he would not have tried to hide from him.[97] We therefore have no reason to look to revelation as a source of natural or speculative knowledge about the deity.[98]

By offering a systematic explanation of how accommodation works, Spinoza aims to give his readers something to chew on. To challenge his conclusions about the authority of revelation, he implies, they will have to take issue with his analysis of prophecy as a purely imaginative capability and show, in a manner consistent with the biblical evidence, how the prophets could have possessed a knowledge of philosophical truths. He himself is confident that this cannot be done. No persuasive reading of Scripture will sustain the claim that the prophets were exceptional philosophers, and to contend that revelation works in some special way that is too mysterious for us to comprehend is just to give up the attempt to understand it. Worse still, it is to pander to the ignorance and anxiety that are the fertile soil of superstition. There is, however, no need to take refuge in the unintelligible. Once we see that what we call revelation is the fruit of rare but nonetheless natural imaginative powers, and appreciate that it is not a means to speculative knowledge, we do not need to worry if our philosophical conclusions diverge from the beliefs of the prophets. Revelation has its own authority; but its writ does not extend to philosophical matters, which include both nature and God. Nor is it invariably a reliable guide to the morally certain truths that we learn through imagination.

Prophecy and moral knowledge

On what subjects, then, *is* revelation authoritative? Spinoza's discussion of this crucial question is surprisingly cursory. The common theme of biblical

---

[95] Ibid. ch. 2, p. 42.

[96] 'The Belgic Confession', Article 12.

[97] On Spinoza's discussion of Adam, see Paolo Grassi, 'Adam and the Serpent', in *Feminist Interpretations of Benedict Spinoza*, ed. Moira Gatens (University Park, Pa.: Pennsylvania State University Press, 2009). See also Paolo Grassi, *L'interpretazione del'imaginario: Uno studio di Spinoza* (Pisa: Edizioni ETS, 2002).

[98] Spinoza, *Tractatus Theologico-Politicus*, ch. 2, p. 42.

prophecies, he announces, is that they are concerned with 'love and how to conduct our lives', and yield knowledge of 'matters of integrity and morals'.[99] Scripture makes it clear that revelation is not the only source of moral knowledge; Solomon, for example, was not a prophet, but evidently understood a number of important moral truths. Nevertheless, the prophets provide an entirely trustworthy account of the way of life we should follow. While Spinoza's readers would have been comfortable with his claim that the Bible's fundamental message is about how to live religiously or well, they might nevertheless have wondered how he could be so confident that the prophets' pronouncements about the good life were not accommodated to their individual minds. What ensured that their *moral* insights were reliable, although their grasp of God, nature, and history was not? The answer to this worry emerges indirectly from Spinoza's analysis of prophecy's epistemological basis.

Any method for acquiring knowledge must provide standards for distinguishing trustworthy from untrustworthy claims, and in the case of prophecy the first step in this process consists in separating genuine revelations from the utterances of false prophets. Sticking closely to Calvinist orthodoxy, Spinoza reiterates three biblically grounded features of authentic revelation: the experience must be vivid, the revelation must be accompanied by a sign, and the heart of the prophet must be inclined only towards the right and good.[100] By itself, he explains, the first of these conditions is not a sufficient test of genuine revelation, since prophecy depends on imagination and therefore carries no guarantee of certainty.[101] Whereas a philosopher's clear and distinct ideas are self-affirming, a prophet can be convinced that he has heard the word of God and yet be wrong. Prophets therefore needed further evidence before they could conclude that their revelations were genuine, and the first test they applied was to ask for a sign. For example, when Gideon was told by God that he would liberate the Israelites, he replied, 'If now I have found grace in thy sight, then show me a sign that thou talkest with me'. After he had laid out meat and unleavened cakes on a rock, 'the angel of the Lord put forth the end of his staff that was in his hand, and touched the flesh and the unleavened cakes; and there rose up fire out of the rock and consumed the flesh and unleaved cakes'.[102] An accompanying miracle could therefore confirm a prophecy, but even this was not sufficient to guarantee it because, as Moses warns, 'the Lord also worketh miracles and signs to try his people'.[103] Like

---

[99] Ibid. ch. 2, pp. 42, 35.   [100] Ibid. ch. 2, p. 31.
[101] Ibid. ch. 2, p. 30.   [102] Judges 6:11–22.
[103] Spinoza, *Tractatus Theologico-Politicus*, ch. 2, p. 30; ch. 6, p. 87. Cf. Deut. 13:2.

revelations, signs can be deceptive, and in order to determine whether they are authentic it is necessary to consider what Scripture has to say about a prophet's character. Judging from the biblical record, 'God never deceives the pious and the elect... [He] uses them as the instruments of his piety, but the impious as executors of his anger'.[104] So if a prophet whose revelations are confirmed by signs is also virtuous, their testimony can be trusted.

At first glance, it is difficult to see how Spinoza can reconcile this means of assessing prophecies with his account of accommodation. If a prophet's experience of revelation is the fruit of imagination and therefore needs to be tested against further evidence, surely the same will be true of prophetic signs. But if signs are no more trustworthy than the revelations they are supposed to vindicate, how can they be used to distinguish authentic from inauthentic prophecy? Elaborating, Spinoza takes it that signs are indeed part of a prophet's imaginative experience, accommodated, like revelation itself, to his or her individual personality. For example, when Gideon's meat and bread bust into flame, he took this to be a sign from God; but another prophet, for instance one who knew more about cooking in the desert, might have been less impressed.[105] However, because signs unlike revelations are public, their interpretation is not always entirely up to the prophet. Part of their function is to persuade the prophet's audience that his revelation is genuine, and in order to succeed they must answer to that particular audience's knowledge and expectations. When Isaiah struck a rock with his staff and water flowed out of it, his followers were satisfied; but again, another group might have remained sceptical. An aspect of the prophet's imaginative genius therefore lies in the ability to recognize and interpret signs that both they and their audiences find compelling.[106]

Viewed like this, signs belong to a practice in which prophets test their experience of revelation against conventional criteria. They provide a standard to which both prophets and others can appeal, and indicate whether an individual is undergoing the kind of experience that is agreed to constitute genuine revelation. In addition, they serve to exclude the claims of prophets who fail to receive a sign or cannot persuade other people that a sign has been given. But this is not the end of the matter. Since signs can be used by false

---

[104] Ibid. ch. 2, p. 31.

[105] Ibid. ch. 2, p. 32.

[106] See Stuart Clark, *Thinking with Demons: The Idea of Witchcraft in Early Modern Europe* (Oxford: Clarendon Press, 1997), ch. 18; Lorenzo Vinciguerra, *Spinoza et le signe: La Genèse de l'imagination* (Paris: Vrin, 2005).

prophets to deceive their audiences, the presence of a sign is not enough to distinguish genuine from merely apparent prophecies. Some additional test is needed, and here the prophet's character comes into play. When all the evidence indicates that a prophet is honest and attuned to the good, the possibility that he is deliberately deceiving his audience can be ruled out. The combination of revelation and sign then provides grounds for concluding that a genuine revelation has occurred.

To say that a prophecy is genuine in the sense just described does not, however, imply that it is true, and it remains to ask whether or how revelation can qualify as a source of knowledge. As we have seen, Spinoza is emphatic that it does not meet the criteria for philosophical knowledge. The question is therefore whether it can qualify as a species of imaginatively grounded knowledge that should command acceptance. Where topics such as God, nature, and history are concerned, Spinoza has already established that the answer is negative. The prophets are often wrong about these things, and there is no reason to treat their views with special respect. But in moral matters the situation is different. Scripture attests that the prophets were men and women of virtue and integrity, and were therefore the kind of people to whom moral authority is rightly accorded. This constitutes a compelling ground for accepting their moral insights, or at least for accepting that the moral content of genuine revelation is true.[107]

On Spinoza's reading, the biblical record belies Cicero's much-quoted adage that the best prophet is simply the best guesser,[108] and vindicates Hobbes's suggestive comment that the best guesser is he who 'hath most *Signes* to guesse by'.[109] The imaginative powers of the prophets made them sensitive to signs that other people could not read, and enabled them to articulate a class of moral truths that are difficult to come by. By reasoning about the character of revealed knowledge (or adding reasoning to imagination),[110] we can come to appreciate why we ought to accept the prophets' moral claims and count them among the things we know. To be sure, such knowledge is not indubitable or mathematically certain. But, Spinoza asserts, it has a high degree of moral certainty. It would be absurd to reject it simply because it falls short of the standards of

---

[107] See Theo Verbeek, *Descartes and the Dutch: Early Reactions to Cartesian Philosophy, 1637–1650* (Carbondale: Southern Illinois University Press, 1992), pp. 72–3.

[108] Marcus Tullius Cicero, *De Divinatione*, ed. Arthur Stanley Pease (Urbana: University of Illinois Press, 1920–3), II.5.

[109] Thomas Hobbes, *Leviathan*, ed. Richard Tuck (Cambridge: Cambridge University Press, 1996), p. 22.

[110] Spinoza, *Tractatus Theologico-Politicus*, ch. 2, p. 30.

philosophical reasoning,[111] as if 'to organise our lives wisely, we should admit nothing that can be called in doubt as true'.[112] We accept the testimony of people who are well informed about navigation, childcare, or history. Why, then, should we not also accept the testimony of the prophets, whose imaginative capacities give them exceptional insight into the demands of a moral way of life?

Understanding what prophecy is and how it works shapes our attitude to revelation, and gives us a means of assessing the claims made by individual prophets. But as Spinoza's analysis has illustrated, this process is a complex one, and relies on several interconnected forms of reasoning. To find out what a prophet actually said we must restrict our gaze to the Bible and interpret Scripture by Scripture. By examining the text we may be able to elucidate the prophet's figures of speech, or confirm that his words are to be taken in a literal sense. Two other kinds of reasoning then come into play to determine whether the revelation in question is accommodated. A further look at the biblical evidence indicates whether the prophet was an authority on the topic in question. (For instance, the Bible does not give us any reason to believe that Joshua was knowledgeable about astronomy.) And our independent grasp of the limits of imaginatively based knowledge provides another way to answer the same question. (Although imagination can teach us many things about the planets, it will not give us a mathematically certain grasp of planetary motion.) These enquiries will yield one of two possibilities. On the one hand, they may lead us to the conclusion that a revelation is not accommodated, in which case the interpretative quest that Spinoza has so far described is over. On the other hand, they may indicate that a revelation is accommodated to the mind of the prophet, and in doing so open up a wider vista. We are free to disagree with the content of the revelation (for example by rejecting Joshua's account of the motion of the sun); but the issue of whether it has a deeper meaning, and whether that meaning is recoverable, remains unresolved.

So far, Spinoza has mainly been concerned to show that, because many of the claims made in the Bible are accommodated to the minds of particular speakers or their audiences, we do not need to treat Scripture as a source of natural or spiritual knowledge. This fact about it gives us a sufficient reason to set aside a revealed opinion, and allows us to hold beliefs that diverge from prophetic utterances. For readers who are worried that their philosophical commitments may conflict with biblical doctrine, this is an enormously encouraging result.

---

[111] Ibid. ch. 2, pp. 30–1.   [112] Ibid. ch. 15, p. 187.

Using the technique Spinoza has outlined, they can identify and cleave to prophecies that reveal the Bible's divine teaching, whilst otherwise following their philosophical inclinations. A grasp of the limits of revealed knowledge can quell the anxiety that studying philosophy may endanger their salvation, and release them to enjoy the pleasures of intellectual enquiry.

As well as defending philosophy against an inflated conception of the reach of theological understanding, this perspective is also designed to dampen the pretensions of superstition. By giving individuals the means to arrive at judgements of their own about the meaning and force of revelation, it aims to increase their confidence in their capacity to reason about theological issues, and counteract the fears that encourage subservience to religious authority. Prophecy, it insists, is not a supernatural phenomenon that only an ecclesiastical elite are fit to interpret. Instead, it is an aspect of the capacity to imagine that all humans possess, and can be explained on the same principles as more commonplace forms of imaginative thought and action. There is therefore no need to conceive of prophecy as a thing apart, or to imaginatively endow prophets with threatening powers that lie entirely beyond our ordinary understanding. We should approach revelation calmly and rationally, distancing ourselves from the purveyors of superstition 'whose greatest hatred is directed against those who cultivate true knowledge and true life'.[113]

---

[113] Ibid. ch. 2, pp. 29–30.

Chapter 3

What Divine Law Is Not

Through his discussion of revelation, Spinoza has defended the view that the prophets were only authoritative on moral issues, and that their teaching only concerned the nature of a good life. His next step is to consider what this teaching recommends. In the Bible, living in the virtuous fashion that merits salvation is presented as a matter of obeying laws made by God and communicated to his prophets. Scripture posits a divine lawmaker whose commands specify how one must relate both to him and to one's fellow human beings. To understand the moral teaching of the Bible one must therefore pay attention to the nature of divine law, whilst also taking account of the ways in which the biblical account of it is accommodated to the minds of the common people. What sort of law is it? What does it require of us? What is it meant to achieve? And who is bound by it? In Chapters 3 and 4 of the *Treatise* Spinoza offers a radical set of responses to these questions, and in doing so challenges many of the Reformed Church's most deeply held tenets. Divine law, he argues, is not at all what the Church thinks it is. Moreover, this fact has far-reaching implications for the nature of true religion.

The question of what is involved in obeying the divine law and the separate question of what is achieved by doing so are central both to Calvinist theology and to Spinoza's criticism of it. By resolving these issues, they agree, one determines what a truly religious life is like, and how obedience to the law relates to salvation. On both these crucial points, the *Treatise* directly challenges Church doctrine, arguing first that the epistemological commitments of a truly religious life are far more minimal than Calvinists assert, and second that salvation is simply a matter of living in accordance with the divine law. Contrary to the Reformed Church's teaching, God has not predestined some individuals to be saved and others lost; nor does our ability to follow the law depend on a supernatural process commonly described as the intervention of the Holy Spirit. The heterodox interpretation of the divine law that Spinoza now goes on to construct also has immediate implications for the relation of theology and philosophy. Unless his analysis of the divine law and the ways in which it can be known can be adequately defended, he will not be able to show that philosophy and theology need not clash, but can harmoniously contribute to a peaceful form of political life. So although his preoccupations may seem rather arcane to twenty-first century eyes, they will turn out to be vital to his case.

God and his chosen people

The *Heidelberg Catechism* used by the Dutch Reformed Church identifies the law of God with the Ten Commandments given to Moses.[1] However, as Calvin had explained, the Commandments need to be interpreted with care, because God's covenant with the Jews was a way of training an unsophisticated and childlike people who could not be counted on to obey the law. To help them, the law was presented in vivid terms and required them to follow various ritual practices; but these figures and ceremonies were subsequently abolished when Christ taught the divine law in its universal form, extending it from a single people to the boundaries of the Earth.[2] However, even in this new version, the truth and substance of the original law remains.[3] Interpreted as to their spirit rather than their letter, the Ten Commandments are indeed the law of God, and remain a fundamental part of Christian teaching.

Spinoza does not challenge the view that the Commandments identify valuable moral rules, and can—in a sense to be specified—be described as divine laws. However, he also takes it for granted that the divine law, properly so called, is eternal. It does not change, nor does God ordain it sometimes for one group of people, sometimes for another. The view that aspects of the Mosaic Law were abrogated or abolished in a new covenant must therefore rest on a profoundly mistaken conception of divine law itself.

In Chapter 4 of the *Treatise*, Spinoza will discuss his reasons for holding this view. Here, however, he announces it indirectly by focusing on a biblical narrative that seems flatly to contradict it. On one natural reading of the Pentateuch, God favoured the Jewish people above all other nations by

---

[1] 'The Heidelberg Catechism', in *The Creeds of Christendom: The Evangelical Protestant Creeds*, ed. Philip Schaff (New York: Cosimo Books, 2007), Q92.

[2] Jean Calvin, *Institutes of the Christian Religion*, ed. and trans. John Thomas McNeill and Ford Lewis Battles, *The Library of Christian Classics* (Philadelphia: Westminster Press, 1960–1), II.V.ii.1.

[3] 'The Belgic Confession', in *The Creeds of Christendom: The Evangelical Protestant Creeds*, ed. Philip Schaff (New York: Cosimo Books, 2007), Article 25.

revealing his law to them alone, and promising to give them an exclusive reward for obedience.[4] But if the divine law is universal and eternal, this story will have to be explained away as an accommodated account of the law that we are not obliged to accept. Taking up the challenge, Spinoza now goes on to offer a thoroughly deflationary account of it. When the Bible says that God promised to reward the Jews, it does not mean that he ordained the divine law for them alone.[5] Nor does it mean that he promised to reward them by endowing them with capacities that set them apart from other human beings, or by guaranteeing them some special form of salvation. All it means is that God determined that the ancient state of Israel would flourish for a comparatively long time.[6] Moreover, since this state collapsed many centuries ago, the election of the Jews is a historical phenomenon and has no implications for the present or future.[7] Jews have nothing more to look forward to than anyone else.

Modern scholars have puzzled over the hostility that this view seems to embody. Why, they have asked, does Spinoza turn against his own people? Why does he try to crush the hopes of Jewish communities for whom the assurance that they belonged to a people chosen by God remained a palpable source of optimism? Why does he dismiss an interpretation of Scripture that helped to hold Jewish communities together? And what conscious or unconscious aggression is he expressing towards the synagogue from which he had been excommunicated?[8] There is indeed something harsh about Spinoza's

---

[4] Benedictus de Spinoza, *Tractatus Theologico-Politicus*, ed. Carl Gebhardt, vol. III, *Opera* (Heidelberg: Carl Winter, 1924), ch. 2, p. 39.

[5] Ibid. ch. 3, p. 54.

[6] Ibid. ch. 3, pp. 47–8.

[7] Ibid. ch. 3, p. 54.

[8] Commentators who have taken up the topic of Spinoza's relationship with the Jewish community include Geneviève Brykman, *La Judéité de Spinoza* (Paris: Vrin, 1972); Hermann Cohen, 'Spinoza über Staat und Religion, Judentum und Chistendum', in *Jüdische Schriften*, ed. Bruno Strauss (Berlin: Schwetschke, 1924); Emmanuel Levinas, 'Le Cas Spinoza', in *Difficile liberté: Essais sur le Judaisme* (Paris: Albin Michel, 1963); Shlomo Pines, 'Spinoza's "Tractatus Theologico-Politicus" and the Jewish Philosophical Tradition', in *Jewish Thought in the Seventeenth Century*, ed. Isadore Twersky and Bernard Septimus (Cambridge, Mass.: Harvard University Press, 1987); Michael Rosenthal, 'Spinoza, History, and Jewish Modernity', in *Philosophers and the Hebrew Bible*, ed. Charles H. Manekin and Robert Eisen (Bethseda: University of Maryland Press, 2008); Steven B. Smith, *Spinoza, Liberalism, and the Question of Jewish Identity* (New Haven: Yale University Press, 1997); Leo Strauss, 'How to Study Spinoza's "Theologico-Political Treatise"', in *Jewish History and the Crisis of Modernity* (Albany NY: SUNY Press, 1997); Leo Strauss, *Persecution and the Art of Writing* (Glencoe Ill.: Free Press, 1952); Leo Strauss, *Spinoza's Critique of Religion* (New York: Schocken Books, 1965); Yirmiyahu Yovel, *Spinoza and Other Heretics*, 2 vols. (Princeton: Princeton University Press, 1989).

description of the Jews as a people whose hearts have been emasculated by their religion,[9] and these questions have been the source of rich and suggestive speculations about Spinoza's own passions. However, while he clearly aims to undercut a certain image of what it means to be a Jew, his position has broader implications that are arguably more relevant to explaining what he is trying to achieve in the *Treatise*. To appreciate the force of his discussion, we need to place it in the context of Calvinist theology, and examine its implications for messianism and millenarianism.

How should we interpret Moses' claim that God chose the Hebrews for himself before all other nations, prescribed just laws exclusively for them, and revealed these facts to them alone? Should we take them at face value, or do they express some implicit insight in a style that is accommodated to the understanding and situation of the ancient Hebrews and their prophets? Drawing on his analysis of revelation, Spinoza opts unhesitatingly for the latter alternative. Echoing Calvin, he asserts that Moses was speaking to a people who 'did not know true blessedness' in terms that accorded with their 'childish power of understanding' in order to persuade them to obey the laws he had made.[10] His account of the divine law served a theologico-political purpose, and will not stand up to philosophical scrutiny. So far, this argument follows a familiar pattern and, like its predecessors, arrives at a negative conclusion. We do not have to accept the biblical claim that God ordained a moral law specifically for the Jews, complete with rewards and punishments. Now, however, Spinoza takes a further argumentative step and sets out to explain the sense in which the Jews *were* chosen by God. Thinking back to his analysis of prophecy, one might expect him to appeal to a mixture of biblical and philosophical evidence; but in this case the balance is sharply tipped in a philosophical direction. While he looks briefly to Scripture for support, his case rests principally on a condensed and abstract philosophical argument, which presupposes a good deal of philosophical knowledge on the part of his readers. In addition, as we shall subsequently see, it embodies several controversial claims.

As Spinoza presents the matter, the Mosaic prophecies essentially claim that God decided or chose to give the Hebrews some benefit that he did not bestow on other nations. To understand what it amounted to, we therefore need to analyse this proposition, first by examining what Scripture refers to as a choice or decision made by God. We know that all natural events are determined by

---

[9] Spinoza, *Tractatus Theologico-Politicus*, ch. 3, p. 57.   [10] Ibid. ch. 3, pp. 45, 53.

universal laws of nature, which are simultaneously God's eternal decrees, and that these laws govern all human actions. 'No one does anything except according to the predetermined order of nature'.[11] Furthermore, since this order consists of divine decrees, we can describe the entire course of events, human and otherwise, as 'elected' or 'chosen' by God. For example, 'no one chooses any manner of living for himself, nor does anything, except by the special calling of God, who has chosen him before others . . . for this manner of living'.[12] So, returning to the election of the Jews, the sense in which God 'chose' to benefit them is no different from the sense in which he 'chose' that Joshua should defeat the Ammonites, or 'chose' that you should be reading this page. Whatever their election amounts to, it is just one state of affairs among others, explicable as an outcome of God's natural laws or decrees.

Turning now to the benefit that the Jews were promised, we need to consider how it might have been acquired and what it might have been. In general, benefits can be gained in two ways. One class, which lie within human power in the sense that we ourselves cause them, can be said to come about with God's internal help. (For example, when Spinoza relies on reason to understand an argument, the process is determined by God; but God acts through Spinoza's natural capacities or gives him internal help.) A second class of benefits, which can be said to depend on God's external help, are caused by things other than ourselves, and do not lie within our own power. (For example, when the wind blows Spinoza along in the direction he wants to go, he is the beneficiary of God's external help.)[13] The benefit awarded to the Jews will therefore be one of these kinds. But before we can decide which, we need to work out what sort of benefit it was; and in order to determine this, we need to consider what types of benefit exist. Here we can distinguish benefits of three kinds: coming to understand things by their first causes, that is to say coming to understand them in relation to God; controlling one's passions, that is to say possessing the knowledge of the good that enables one to live virtuously; and living in health and security. The benefit enjoyed by the Hebrews must therefore have consisted in one or a combination of these possibilities.[14]

---

[11] Ibid. ch. 3, p. 46. See Spinoza, *Ethics*, in Curley ed., *The Collected Works of Spinoza*, vol. I: 'God's intellect is the only cause of things' (1p17s); 'we act only from God's command' (2p49s); 'all things follow from the necessity of the divine nature, and happen according to the eternal laws and rules of Nature' (4p50s); 'the laws of Nature concern the common order of Nature, of which man is a part' (4p57s).

[12] Spinoza, *Tractatus Theologico-Politicus*, ch. 3, p. 46.   [13] Ibid.   [14] Ibid.

What we are looking for is a benefit that can be exclusively enjoyed by one group of people and denied to others. But, according to Spinoza, neither of the first two types satisfies this condition. Understanding things by their first causes and controlling one's passions ultimately depend on natural reasoning, an aptitude that all human beings possess to some degree. To put the point differently, these benefits are the fruit of a form of internal help that God makes available to everyone through universal laws of nature. The capacity to achieve them therefore cannot belong specifically to the Jews. God cannot have benefited one nation by giving them exclusive access to wisdom or understanding and thus to the further benefits that flow from them, because this would be inconsistent with the universal laws of nature that he decrees.[15]

In addition (and here Spinoza makes a separate though related point), God cannot have given the Jews exceptional knowledge of the true good that enables one to control one's passions and live virtuously, and thus cannot have given them exceptional access to the salvation that it produces. The reason for this is that the happiness which arises from knowing the true good is not enhanced by the fact that other people do not possess the same knowledge. (If you know what the true good for human beings amounts to, the fact that I am ignorant of it will not benefit you.)[16] So if God had tried to benefit the Jews by giving them knowledge of the true good, he would not have given them a genuine advantage over other nations. It is obvious, Spinoza urges, that they 'would have been no less blessed if God had called everyone to salvation'.[17] Equally, God would have been no less close to the Jews if he had been as close to others, the law would have been no less just if it had been prescribed for everyone, and miracles would have been equally revealing of God's power if they had been performed among other nations.[18] Since it is inconceivable that God could have made a mistake about this, we can conclude that the Jews are not exceptional as to their knowledge of the good, and thus as to their ability to achieve salvation.

This leaves the last of Spinoza's three kinds of benefit—living in health and security. It is evident that achieving and sustaining this goal is a precarious

---

[15]   Ibid. ch. 3, pp. 47–8.

[16]   Ibid. ch. 3, p. 44. See also Spinoza, *Ethics* 4p18s. 'All men who are governed by reason—that is, men who, from the guidance of reason, seek their own advantage—want nothing for themselves that they do not desire for other men'; Spinoza, *Treatise on the Emendation of the Intellect*, §14.

[17]   Spinoza, *Tractatus Theologico-Politicus*, ch. 3, p. 45.

[18]   Ibid.

business, and does not lie entirely within the power either of individuals or communities. No matter how knowledgeable individuals become, they remain vulnerable to external forces beyond their control, so that a prudent man and a fool have a more or less equal chance of leading healthy and secure lives.[19] And even when societies have effective laws and vigilant leaders, they remain exposed to the uncontrollable events that Spinoza describes as goods of fortune. When, therefore, a society manages to endure peacefully for a long time, its survival must at least in part be due to God's external help, that is to say, to external causes.[20]

Applying this conclusion to the case of the Jews, Spinoza reaches the culmination of his argument. The Hebrew people were chosen or elected by God in the sense that his laws or decrees enabled them to create a secure state which lasted for an unusually long time. 'The Hebrew nation was chosen by God before all others not by virtue of anything to do with rational understanding or the tranquillity of the mind, but by virtue of its social organisation, and the fortune through which it became a state and survived for so many years'.[21] It 'excelled the other nations only in that it conducted those affairs which pertain to the security of life auspiciously and overcame great dangers, and all this mainly by God's external aid alone'.[22] This is all that the benefit of election amounted to, and it is, furthermore, a thing of the past. 'Since God is equally well-disposed to all and chose the Hebrews only with respect to their social order and state, we conclude that each Jew, considered outside that social order and state, possesses no gift of God which would place him above other men, and there is no difference between him and a gentile'.[23]

This levelling conclusion rests on a number of premises and distinctions that—in the *Treatise*—Spinoza does little if anything to defend. To be persuaded of it, readers must be willing to accept a metaphysical premise about determinism, a claim about the nature of the true good, and the exhaustiveness of two sets of distinctions about the kinds of benefits that humans can enjoy and the ways in which they are caused. Nevertheless—and presumably expecting to carry his readers along with him—Spinoza uses these assumptions to reach a more incisive type of conclusion that any he has so far defended. As well as indicating that a prophecy is accommodated to the mind of the prophet in question and his audience, reasoning can in this case determine the meaning of the prophecy by establishing that only one interpretation of it is compatible with our philosophical knowledge of God and nature. Spinoza pauses as usual to note that the biblical evidence does not contradict anything he has said. For

---

[19] Ibid. p. 47, ch. 3. [20] Ibid. [21] Ibid.
[22] Ibid. ch. 3, pp. 48–9. [23] Ibid. ch. 3, p. 50.

example, we can infer from the fact that Moses only offered temporal rewards and punishments in return for obedience that the laws he imposed on the Jews were a civil code rather than a moral one. 'For as God chose them only for the establishing of a special kind of society and state, they must have had laws of a special kind'.[24] But his case is predominantly philosophical. By bringing reason to bear on revelation, we can arrive at well-founded conclusions about the meaning of the prophecies surrounding the law revealed to Moses.

This is a bold strategy, made bolder by the fact that Spinoza relies on some controversial assumptions. His central premise asserts that God's decrees take the form of universal laws of nature, and while Calvinists would not have doubted that natural laws are one of the means by which God determines the course of events, Spinoza advances the much more contentious claim that God's decrees and universal laws of nature are one and the same thing. 'The universal laws of nature, according to which all thing happen and are determined, are nothing but the eternal decrees of God'.[25] The view that laws of nature are decreed by God was familiar within Calvinist theology. We find it, for example, in the Arminian testament, where Episcopius writes that God's fore-ordained works 'are wont in one word to be called his decrees'.[26] So Spinoza's appeal to it would not immediately have excited any surprise. In fact, however, the version that he espouses (that divine decrees and laws of nature are the same thing) was unorthodox, and as Van Velthuysen would point out once the *Treatise* had been published, implies an extremely strong necessitarianism which leaves no room for God to be able to conceive things which differ from those that exist.[27] By the time he wrote the *Treatise*, Spinoza had explicated this view for public consumption in his *Appendix Containing Metaphysical Thoughts*,[28] and defended it in the more private context of his correspondence with Blyenbergh.[29] Members of his intellectual circle and readers of

---

[24] Ibid. ch. 3, p. 48.

[25] Ibid. ch. 3, p. 46.

[26] Simon Episcopius, *The Confession or Declaration of the Ministers or Pastors Which in the United Provinces Are Called Remonstrants, Concerning the Chief Points of Christian Religion*, trans. Thomas Taylor (London, 1676), p. 97.

[27] See *The Correspondence of Spinoza*, ed. and trans. Abraham Wolf (London: Frank Cass, 1966), p. 295. See also Wiep van Bunge, 'On the Early Dutch Reception of the *Tractatus Theologico-Politicus*', *Studia Spinozana*, 5 (1989).

[28] Spinoza, *Appendix Containing Metaphysical Thoughts*, in *The Collected Works of Spinoza*, vol. I, pp. 307, 309.

[29] Letters, 18–24. *Letters: July 1664–September 1669*, in *The Collected Works of Spinoza*, vol. I, pp. 354–92.

his work could therefore have grasped his own particular reasons for holding it. At this stage, however, Spinoza does not need his readers to accept the full force of his position. He only needs them to agree to some version of the claims that capacities such as our ability to gain philosophical understanding and live virtuously are determined by universal laws that can be understood as divine decrees, and that these laws or decrees apply equally to all human beings. This will be enough to rule out the possibility that the Jews might have been given a special share of what Spinoza regards as genuine benefits, namely philosophical knowledge of God and the good, and to support the conclusion that these advantages are available to all peoples.

A further premise—that the happiness an individual gains from a knowledge of the true good is not increased by the fact that others do not share it—points in the same direction. At first glance, the premise seems questionable. For example, in the competitive conditions of a university disputation, a theologian's happiness might well be enhanced by knowing something of which their opponent was ignorant, because the knowledge in question might enable him to win the debate. In his *Ethics*, Spinoza explains in more detail why this view is mistaken, and 'arises only from envy and a bad heart'.[30] True happiness, he argues, derives from philosophical understanding, and is not threatened or made less valuable by the fact that other people possess it. Your knowledge of the true good does not diminish mine; on the contrary, since it enables us to work together to empower ourselves, the commonality of our knowledge is overwhelmingly in each of our interests.[31] Viewed from this perspective, the belief that one can enhance one's true happiness by capitalizing on other people's ignorance is the result of a failure to appreciate where one's true good lies.

Spinoza proceeds on the assumption that his readers' thinking has advanced to a point where they can recognize the kinds of benefit he is talking about, and see that God cannot consistently have bestowed them on the Jews alone. However, as often in the *Treatise*, there is something equivocal about the claims on which Spinoza's argument is grounded. On the one hand, readers versed in Calvinism might have found them open to orthodox interpretation. On the other hand, they usher in unorthodox conclusions that shake the foundations of Calvinist theology and send tremors through other confessions. It is to these implications that we now need to turn.

---

[30] Spinoza, *Tractatus Theologico-Politicus*, ch. 3, p. 44.
[31] Spinoza, *Ethics*, 4p36–7.

The means to salvation

The *Treatise's* claim that God does not give anyone special access to the benefits that yield blessedness or salvation is superficially directed against the Jews. It is they who are brought down to earth and deprived, so to speak, of any lasting privilege over other nations. But Spinoza's argument also has critical implications for Calvinist theology, although he does not make this point explicit. If salvation is available to everyone, because God's decrees ensure that no one entirely lacks the ability to work out what a good life involves and live accordingly, how can God predestine some people to be saved and others lost? Picking up something of the *Belgic Confession's* conception of the true Church as the 'assemblage of those who are saved', and out of which there is no salvation',[32] Spinoza allows that 'if the prophets foretold a new and eternal covenant of the knowledge, love and grace of God' this was promised to the pious of all nations.[33] But everything hangs here on the question of who can be pious. According to Spinoza, anyone can. For the Reformed Church, by contrast, salvation is reserved for the Elect.

Spinoza's philosophical deconstruction of the divine election of the Jews therefore puts pressure on Calvinism's exclusiveness, and challenges the doctrine of predestination over which the Reformed Church had held out against the Arminians at the Synod of Dort.[34] From a doctrinal point of view, this is grave enough. At the same time, however, and perhaps still more damagingly, Spinoza questions and rejects the conception of divine providence to which both the Church and the Arminians remained committed. In the words of the *Belgic Confession*, 'nothing can befall us by chance, but by the direction of our most gracious and heavenly father, who watches over us with a paternal care ... so that not a hair of our head, nor a sparrow, can fall to the ground without his will'.[35] Included in God's plan for humanity are, of course, Adam's sin, the coming of Christ, and last but not least, the Day of Judgement, when 'the secrets and hypocrisy of men shall be disclosed and laid open before all', the wicked shall be plunged into the eternal fire, and the elect shall be crowned with honour and glory. 'Therefore', the Article concludes, 'we expect the great

---

[32] 'The Belgic Confession', Article 28.

[33] Spinoza, *Tractatus Theologico-Politicus*, ch. 3, pp. 55–6.

[34] 'The Canons of the Synod of Dort', in *The Creeds of Christendom: The Evangelical Protestant Creeds*, ed. Philip Schaff (New York: Cosimo Books, 2007), First point, Articles 7–13. On Dutch theological debates about predestination, see Karl Bangs, *Arminius: A Study in the Dutch Reformation* (Nashville: Abingdon Press, 1971).

[35] 'The Belgic Confession', Article 13.

day with a most ardent desire'.[36] An ardent desire to hasten God's kingdom on earth was far from uncommon in seventeenth-century Holland. Among both Christians and Jews, groups of believers lived in the conviction that the Messiah was (depending on the religion in question) about to arrive or return. Moreover, it was for many of these people an item of faith that the Messiah would only rule once God's promise to re-establish a Jewish kingdom had been fulfilled.[37] The project of either literally or metaphorically returning the Jews to Jerusalem was therefore one of a number of factors that sustained a complex set of connections between the two communities.

By the time Spinoza came to write the *Treatise*, scholarly links between Dutch Christians and Jews had been established for more than a generation. It was not uncommon for Christians to turn to Jews for instruction in biblical Hebrew, and sometimes in the Torah and Kabbalah as well.[38] Christians of various kinds wrote commentaries on Jewish texts.[39] And there are records of a few cases where Christians and Jews held private conversations on theological topics. During the early 1660s, for example, Isaac Orobio da Castro, a Jewish doctor who had been a victim of the Spanish Inquisition, joined a group of Christians to consider whether Jews who live as Christians can be saved, and whether Christians are obliged to observe the seven divine commandments given to the sons of Noah and transmitted to Moses.[40]

Although these exchanges were no doubt comparatively rare, they generated enough mutual interest to produce counter-reactions. On one side, orthodox Calvinists became anxious that the activities of Jewish scholars threatened the

[36] Ibid. Article 37.

[37] Amos Funkenstein, *Theology and the Scientific Imagination: From the Middle Ages to the Seventeenth Century* (Princeton: Princeton University Press, 1986).

[38] For example, Voetius's son was taught by Menasseh Ben Israel. See Aaron L. Katchen, *Christian Hebraists and Dutch Rabbis: Seventeenth Century Apologetics and the Study of Maimonides' Mishneh Torah* (Cambridge Mass.: Harvard University Press, 1984), pp. 92–3, 98. Grotius is also reported to have consulted Menasseh. See Menasseh ben Israel, *The Hope of Israel*, ed. Henry Méchoulan and Gérard Nahon, trans. Moses Wall, 1652 (Oxford: Oxford University Press, 1987), p. 28. Menasseh wrote 300 letters to scholars on theological and other topics. See Yosef Kaplan, *An Alternative Path to Modernity: The Sephardi Diaspora in Western Europe* (Leiden: Brill, 2000), p. 23.

[39] Cocceius, for example, wrote a commentary on Mishnais tractates published in 1629. See Katchen, *Christian Hebraists*. Adam Boreel, a Hebraist who settled in Amsterdam in 1645, published a Hebrew edition of the Mishna. See Ernestine van der Wall, 'Petrus Serrarius and Menasseh Ben Isarel: Christian and Millenarian Messianism in Seventeenth-Century Amsterdam', in *Menasseh Ben Israel and His World*, ed. Yosef Kaplan, Henry Méchoulan, and Richard H. Popkin (Leiden: Brill, 1989).

[40] Yosef Kaplan, *From Christianity to Judaism: The Story of Isaac Orobio De Castro* (Oxford: Oxford University Press, 1989), pp. 116ff.

purity of the Church. Voetius, for instance, argued that Jewish texts should only be published with an accompanying Calvinist commentary to guide the unwary reader. He also opposed the publication of Menasseh Ben Israel's *Conciliator*, in which Menasseh appealed to a mixture of rabbinical and Christian commentators to show that both religions were bent on the same project of arriving at a consistent reading of Scripture.[41] On the other side, some rabbis worried that the *converso* community had already dissipated its identity by taking too much of its learning from Gentile sources, and needed to concentrate on restoring its heritage by studying the oral Torah and practising the Law.

Despite these doubts and hesitations, one of the strands of belief that existed in both traditions and formed a basis for co-operation was millenarianism or messianism. During the 1640s and 1650s, the project of creating the right conditions for the Jews' return to Jerusalem had been energetically pursued by Menasseh Ben Israel, whose publishing house, prolific writings, and vast correspondence made him one of the most influential of Amsterdam's rabbis. The coming of the Messiah, he claimed, would bring about the moral and political transformation of the Jewish people, who would reinhabit their original territory and be governed in security and peace.[42] However, before this blessed state could come about, a number of problems had to be solved.

A first difficulty concerned the fate of the ten lost tribes of Israel who had been captured and enslaved when their nation was overrun by the Assyrians. According to one view, the lost tribes had to be found before the Jews could be reunited, and their whereabouts consequently became the subject of much speculation. Around 1645, a Portuguese *converso* named Antonio de Montezinos arrived in Amsterdam, claiming to have discovered the tribes' descendants in a remote part of Spanish New Granada. Interviewed under oath by a panel of which Menasseh was a member, he recounted the story of a journey to the banks of the River Cauca, where he had met a secluded group of 'Indians' who recited the Jewish profession of faith in Hebrew.[43]

Montezinos's narrative was among the factors that prompted Menasseh to write *Esperanza de Israel* (*The Hope of Israel*), a messianic work dedicated to the parnassim of the Amsterdam synagogue, who at that time included Spinoza's father.[44] The book was published in Spanish and Latin in 1650, and appeared in English later in the same year. After surveying the evidence, it concludes that

---

[41] Katchen, *Christian Hebraists*, pp. 147–8.

[42] Menasseh ben Israel, *The Hope of Israel*, p. 45.

[43] Ibid. pp. 69–72.

[44] Steven M. Nadler, *Spinoza: A Life* (Cambridge: Cambridge University Press, 1999), p. 100.

the tribes are scattered in several parts of the world, but will converge on Egypt and Assyria before the return to Jerusalem. Moreover, although the date of this redemptive moment is uncertain, it is not far off. The struggles revealed to Daniel are past, and before long 'the twelve tribes shall be joined under one prince, that is under Messiah son of David'.[45]

The Hope of Israel caught the attention of a broad audience of Christian millenarians, stretching far beyond the boundaries of the United Provinces, who shared Menasseh's conviction that redemption was at hand.[46] But in other respects, their hopes and expectations diverged. In particular, many millenarians were convinced that Christ would not return until the Jewish people had been converted to Christianity,[47] and therefore viewed the question of how to bring about such a mass conversion as pressing. One proposed method, an early form of ecumenicism, sought to bring Christians and Jews together by articulating a shared core of religious doctrine. On the Christian side, for example, Isaac de la Peyrère formulated what he presented as an inclusive version of Roman Catholicism, to which Jews could in his view readily sign up. His *Du Rappel des Juifs*, published in 1643, urged the King of France to unite the Jewish people by conquering Palestine and ensuring safe passage to Jews from all over Europe, so that their conversion to his religious tenets could be brought about. Perhaps partly by way of response, the Amsterdam rabbi Saul Levi Morteira articulated a minimalist faith based on the Old Testament, which appeared in 1659 in his final work, *Tratado de la Verdad de la Ley de Moseh*.[48]

---

[45] Menasseh ben Israel, *The Hope of Israel*, p. 159.

[46] Menasseh ben Israel, *The Hope of Israel*, p. 46.

[47] See J. Van den Berg, 'Eschatological Expectations Concerning the Conversion of the Jews in the Netherlands During the Seventeenth Century', in *Puritans, the Millennium and the Future of Israel: Puritan Eschatology from 1600–1660*, ed. P. Toom (London: James Clark, 1970). This view seems to have been held, for example, by Petrus Serrarius (1600–69), a Collegiant theologian and follower of Shabbatai Zevi, with whom Spinoza was acquainted, and also by Cocceius. Menasseh ben Israel, *The Hope of Israel*, p. 50; van der Wall, 'Petrus Serrarius and Menasseh Ben Isarel: Christian and Millenarian Messianism in Seventeenth-Century Amsterdam', pp. 164–9.

[48] Adam Sutcliffe, *Judaism and Enlightenment* (Cambridge: Cambridge University Press, 2003), pp. 107–8. Menasseh was also responding to Dutch Calvinist attempts to convert the Jews. For example, Voetius's colleague Hoornbeek had produced an elaborate conversion manual, dedicated to the States of Holland, criticized by Menasseh in his *Vindiciae Judaeorum* (1656). See van den Berg, 'Eschatological Expectations Concerning the Conversion of the Jews in the Netherlands During the Seventeenth Century', p. 142; Lucien Wolf, *Menasseh Ben Israel's Mission to Oliver Cromwell* (London, 1901), p. 114. Both Menasseh Ben Israel and Serrarius urge that, as the kingdom of God approaches, the two faiths should abandon their historical animosity towards one another and co-operate in bringing about the days of judgement and salvation. See van der Wall, 'Petrus Serrarius and Menasseh Ben Isarel. Christian and

Taking a less ambitious route, other Christian millenarians concentrated their attention on the biblical claim that, before their return to Zion, the Jews would be scattered throughout the world.[49] One could help to realize this prophecy, they reasoned, by enabling Jews to live peacefully in Christian states, whilst simultaneously placing them in environments where it would be easier to convert them. This plan was among the motivations for a meeting in 1651, at which the members of an English mission in Holland assured Menasseh Ben Israel that Oliver Cromwell would welcome the return of the Jews to a country from which they had been expelled nearly five hundred years earlier. Cromwell's aspirations were not purely eschatological, for he also had his eye on the economic advantages of admitting Jews to England; but this did not trouble Menasseh, who was alive to the financial benefits to be gained from trade based in London. Undeterred, he addressed a pamphlet to Cromwell under the title *How Profitable the Nation of the Jewes are*, and in 1655 travelled to England to seek permission for the foundation of a new Jewish community.[50] Despite long negotiations, Menasseh's request was rejected; but the story nevertheless illustrates the importance that both Christian and Jewish communities attached to prophecies about the election of the Jews. The expectations that these created gave the Jewish community a reason for explaining its theology to Christians and for negotiating with Christian rulers in the hope that they would take steps towards restoring the nation. At the same time, they gave Christian millenarians a reason for negotiating with Jews and identifying common ground between the two faiths.

As the century went on, the conviction that salvation would occur in historical time grew stronger within both religions, and by the time Spinoza came to write the *Treatise*, Christian and Jewish authorities in the Netherlands had become anxious to rein in its more enthusiastic manifestations. The arrival of the false Messiah, Shabbatai Zevi, had caused a shudder in church and synagogue, and in each institution the profound sense of shock and disillusionment administered by his apostasy was not entirely unwelcome.[51]

Millenarian Messianism in Seventeenth-Century Amsterdam' in *Menasseh Ben Israel and His World*, ed. Kaplan, Méchoulan, and Popkin (Leiden: Brill, 1989).

[49] See Harold Fisch, 'The Messianic Politics of Menasseh Ben Israel', in *Menasseh Ben Israel and His World*.

[50] Wolf, *Menasseh Ben Israel's Mission to Oliver Cromwell* (London, 1901).

[51] Michael Heyd, 'Menasseh Ben Israel as a Meeting Point of Jewish and European History: Some Summary Comments', in *Menasseh Ben Israel and His World*. In 1667, Serrarius produced a Latin translation of a work about conversion by De Labadie: *Jugement Charitable sur l'État Présent des Juifs*. See van den Berg, 'Eschatological Expectations in *Menasseh Ben Israel and His World*,

In these circumstances, anti-millenarian Calvinists, and for that matter non-millenarian Jews, might have found Spinoza's downbeat interpretation of divine election a congenial one. Nor is this accidental. One of Spinoza's aims is surely to undermine a set of debates that had surrounded him all his life, by discrediting the belief that salvation hinges on the fortunes of the Jewish people. If God's promise to the Jews does not bear on their future, there is no reason for messianists to believe that it is their fate to return to Jerusalem, or indeed that God has any particular plan for the Jewish people. All such hopes are misguided. Equally, Christian millenarians have no grounds for appealing to revelations about the special role of the Jews in support of their interpretations of the Second Coming, and have no good reason for trying to convert Jews to their faith. When the prophets talk about rebuilding the Temple and returning to Jerusalem they are not foretelling future events, but speaking figuratively.[52]

By removing a single brick from the wall of scriptural prophecies dealing with the coming of the Day of Judgement, Spinoza makes the entirety of the Reformed Church's providentialist narrative less stable. Prophecy, as Dutch Calvinists saw the matter, is the ground of faith, and gives us an insight into the divine plan on which our fates depend. By deflating the meaning of one of the revelations around which this plan is organized and claiming that it has no bearing on the future, Spinoza implicitly raises the question of whether this may not also be true of other prophecies as well. If the divine law through which we can attain blessedness or salvation was never ordained for a single nation, but has always been equally accessible to all, Calvinism's commitment to a sequence of covenants between God and man cannot be more than an accommodated version of the truth. In that case, however, our salvation does not depend on accepting it, any more than it depends on accepting a pre-Copernican view of the relation between the sun and Earth. We can safely agree that God did not ordain the divine law especially for the Jews, or promise them benefits that are not available to other people in exchange for obedience.

Taking up his interpretation of the Jews' election and pressing ahead with his levelling argument, Spinoza goes on to consider whether God revealed laws to other communities as well. It is perfectly clear, he points out, that God has given laws to many communities by means of the natural processes that

---

p. 150; van der Wall, 'Petrus Serrarius and Menasseh Ben Israel, in *Menasseh ben Israel and his world*, p. 167.

[52] Spinoza, *Tractatus Theologico-Politicus*, ch. 3, p. 56.

constitute his external help. For instance, 'God established kings and priests in Jerusalem, and prescribed rites and laws for them, before he founded the nation of Israel'.[53] The benefit of living in a society that protects the health and security of its people can be acquired by ordinary means and is not unique to the Jews. There remains, however, the lurking question of whether God *revealed* laws to nations other than the Jews, or whether their election may have consisted in the fact that they alone had true prophets. Again, Spinoza answers in the negative. We can establish on the basis of both sacred and profane histories that the gift of prophecy did not belong solely to the Jews, and that, as well as revealing things about the Hebrew nation, it dealt with the fates of other peoples as well.[54] For example, the Old Testament records that uncircumcised Gentiles such as Noah were prophets, and that Jews prophesied to and about other nations such as the Egyptians. In addition, Gentile communities had prophets of their own. '[T]hose whom the gentiles were accustomed to call augurs and divines were true prophets.... So we conclude that the gift of prophecy was not peculiar to the Jews, but common to all the nations'.[55]

Here again, Spinoza clears the way for a conception of blessedness that does not depend on formal religious allegiance or membership of a nation. For Jews who identified salvation with the restoration of their state, this ideal would inevitably have been unsatisfying; but it might at the same time have held an appeal for *conversos* who had lived for part of their lives as Christians, far from the influence of the Old Testament law. Within the Amsterdam community there were many such people, some of whom worried that they might have forfeited salvation. For them Spinoza's message is a comforting one because, although Jews are not especially favoured by God, they are not especially unfavoured either. Furthermore, the same applies to Christians and peoples of other faiths. In this respect, Spinoza's view transcends both a strand of Christian anti-Semitism that remains present in the work of seventeenth-century Christian theologians, and a continued hostility to Christians on the part of separatist Jews. But its lesson would not have been easy to accept. One of the implications of his argument is that a prevalent misunderstanding of the election of the Jews is fundamental to an eschatology that fuels false hopes in

---

[53] Ibid. ch. 3, p. 49.   [54] Ibid. ch. 3, p. 50.

[55] Ibid. ch. 3, p. 53. In his *Epistola Invective contra Prado*, Orobio de Castro claims that Juan de Prado also held this view. Israël S. Révah, *Spinoza et le Dr. Juan De Prado* (Paris: La Haye, 1959), p. 114.

people of various faiths. Rather than asking themselves how they can better their own condition, its adherents yearn for a messiah who will take this responsibility from them, and their hope of imminent salvation is irretrievably mixed with fears of disappointment and damnation. Their unstable combination of anxiety and desire are the ingredients of superstition, and play into the hands of unscrupulous religious officials and false prophets, who promote superstitious attitudes and practices. In the hands of flamboyant characters such as Shabbatai Zevi, superstitions such as messianism and millenarianism can rock the social fabric; but even in their more mundane guises, they hold out hopes that are harmful and corrupting. To show that there is no longer any sense in which the Jews, or indeed the Calvinist elect, are God's chosen people, is therefore to discredit an outlook that feeds superstition. In Spinoza's harsh phrase, it 'emasculates the heart' by generating fantastical hopes and fears that distort one's understanding of one's circumstances, and stand in the way of the ability to pursue courses of action that are truly beneficial. By contrast, his own interpretation of divine election is potentially liberating. Instead of false hope, it offers well-grounded confidence.

Chapter 4

What Divine Law Is

Spinoza's assumption that any law attributable to God must apply to all people, regardless of time and place, has enabled him to argue his way to a negative conclusion about divine law: if we want to understand it, we should not concentrate on legislation devised for specific communities such as the Jews, however counter-intuitive this may seem in the light of Scripture. However, it remains to provide a positive account. No doubt many everyday conceptions of divine law are mistaken. But when these are put aside, what is left standing? What is the law of God, and how can we come to know it? As we saw at the beginning of the previous chapter, these are vital questions for Spinoza and his opponents, and many of their differences hang on them. The time has come to address them directly.

For the Reformed Church's theologians it was beyond doubt that the substance of divine law can be learned from Scripture. But the question of whether the Bible is our only means to come by this knowledge was more contentious. Conservative theologians tended to insist that we can only gain adequate insight into the way of life that God has decreed for us through revelation, so that without the Bible we cannot hope to be saved.[1] But others, such as Cocceius, were less strict. Scripture, they argued, is undoubtedly the easiest and clearest way to discover what the divine law commands. But it is also possible to arrive at the same knowledge by natural reasoning. Because God has made his law doubly accessible to us, prophecy can confirm conclusions reached by other means.[2]

Spinoza's analysis of divine law falls broadly into the latter camp. In his view, one can come to know the law through a process of reasoning that does not

---

[1] Jean Calvin, *Institutes of the Christian Religion*, ed. and trans. John Thomas McNeill and Ford Lewis Battles, *The Library of Christian Classics* (Philadelphia: Westminster Press, 1960–1), III.ii.5.

[2] W. J. van Asselt, *The Federal Theology of Johannes Cocceius (1603–1669)* (Leiden: Brill, 2001).

rely on Scripture, and the conception one arrives at by this method coincides with the account given by the prophets. At this level, his view contradicts the adamant position held by the Voetians, but does not take issue with more concessive forms of Calvinism. However, as soon as one examines Spinoza's conception of divine law in detail, it becomes obvious that it is far more radical than its overall place in this debate suggests. By entirely extinguishing any conception of God as a legislator who imposes commands on human beings, Spinoza not only abandons the assumptions of moderate Calvinism, but simultaneously undercuts the theological outlooks of a number of other denominations as well. In a sequence of concentrated arguments, he reshapes the framework of natural law within which Christian commentators had traditionally positioned the moral laws imposed by God. Divine laws, he argues, are either necessary and eternal, so that they cannot be disobeyed, or else they are made by human beings. God does not issue commands, and our salvation or blessedness cannot therefore depend on obeying them.

Whilst radical, this point of view is not entirely original. In defending it, Spinoza draws on strands of thought articulated by other natural law theorists, and in effect contributes to a broad seventeenth-century reconsideration of the habit of conceiving God in juridical terms.[3] Nevertheless, the conclusions reached in the *Treatise* are uniquely daring. Picking up hints and implications from his contemporaries, particularly from Hobbes, Spinoza incorporates them into a joltingly impersonal account of a divine law that is not ordained for humankind.

Spinoza cannot have failed to be aware that his analysis ran counter to the beliefs of many of his readers and, if fully understood, would deeply offend the sensibilities of pious Calvinists. Perhaps this is why he presents it as a minor variant of positions already in play, and concedes as much as possible to his adversaries. Without compromising his convictions, he tends to let the radical character of his position speak for itself, and wherever possible represents it as continuous with the core values of Calvinist theology. One of the main devices on which he relies is to transpose the language of the Bible into a philosophical key. At each stage of his exposition he takes terms that are at home in theological contexts and puts them to more narrowly philosophical use. Natural laws are characterized as

---

[3] The other major contributor to this trend is Thomas Hobbes. See Knud Haakonssen, *Natural Law and Moral Philosophy from Grotius to the Scottish Enlightenment* (Cambridge: Cambridge University Press, 1996); Richard Tuck, 'Grotius and Selden', in *The Cambridge History of Political Thought 1450–1700*, ed. J. H. Burns and Mark Goldie (Cambridge: Cambridge University Press, 1991).

divine decrees, knowledge of nature is identified with knowledge of God, the power of natural things is equated with the power of God, and natural knowledge is seen as a form of divine revelation. These modulations, which are defended within the systematic philosophical position that Spinoza develops elsewhere, allow him to range in a philosophical vein over topics that also concern theologians, and to draw on his own conceptions of God, nature, and law to undermine their beliefs. In due course, he will discuss a number of these transitions at greater length; but his immediate interest lies in the harmonies and dissonances between theological and philosophical conceptions of law.

Defining law

Early modern debates about divine legislation were intricate and confrontational. Ever since antiquity, theorists had argued over the nature of law as an organizing principle of civil, moral, and religious life, and had attempted to provide satisfying answers to a series of basic questions. What types of laws exist? Who makes them? Who is obliged to obey them? Who has the authority to change or challenge them? And how does one set relate to another? By the seventeenth century, the jurists had developed a range of systematic but competing replies, so that any attempt to discuss the status of revealed law could easily get bogged down in controversy. Spinoza's response to this state of affairs is to say as little as possible about the tradition to which he is contributing. Rather than explicitly acknowledging the precise positions of his predecessors or opponents, he initially rests his argument on an accepted and uncontentious distinction between human and divine law. Among early-modern legal theorists, the category of human law was generally understood to encompass the civil laws made by human authorities about sacred or secular matters. Divine law, by contrast, came in two forms, natural and revealed. God has ordained natural laws that are accessible to human reason, but has also set out his revealed or positive law in Scripture. As Hobbes, for example, explains in *De Cive*, 'Natural law is the law which God has revealed to all men through his eternal word which is innate in them, namely natural reason', while positive law is that 'which God has revealed to us through the prophetic word'.[4]

If human beings live under the jurisdiction of the divine law, and will be punished for disobeying it, it is vital that they should know what it requires of them. According to the more pessimistic members of the Reformed Church,

---

[4] Thomas Hobbes, *On the Citizen*, ed. Richard Tuck and Michael Silverthorne (Cambridge: Cambridge University Press, 1998), p. 156.

the human spirit is so corrupted that we cannot rely on reason to discover the tenets of natural law, and must rely on Scripture alone. As Calvin had explained, 'The Lord has provided us with a written law to give us a clearer witness of what was too obscure in the natural law, shake off our listlessness, and strike more vigorously our mind and memory'.[5] While this stance remained orthodox, Calvinists of a more rationalist bent worried that it might encourage an undesirable scepticism about the ability of reason to deliver knowledge. Reiterating a view that goes back at least as far as Thomas Aquinas, they argued that the natural and revealed forms of the divine law are complementary.[6] God has provided us with two distinct ways of learning his fundamental decrees, and because one of these is sometimes more illuminating or accessible than the other, we need to have recourse to both. In the Netherlands, as elsewhere in Europe, this view remained prominent, and both inside and outside the Reformed Church its advocates kept up a robust defence of reason's power to grasp the law of nature.[7] Spinoza is therefore able to assume that the divine law is legislated in two forms, natural and positive, and that neither is worthless as a source of knowledge. The questions that preoccupy him are how each should be understood, and how one relates to the other.

Continuing the practice he has by now established in earlier chapters of the *Treatise*, Spinoza begins his discussion with a definition: 'the word law (*lex*), taken in its absolute sense, means that in conformity with which each individual, or all or some members of the same species, act in one and the same certain and determinate manner'.[8] Laws in the absolute sense of the term therefore

---

[5] Calvin, *Institutes*, II.viii.2.

[6] The notion of natural law is sometimes traced back to Aquinas, according to whom the universe is governed by divine reason, the source of what he describes as the eternal law, and also of the part of the eternal law that applies to man, namely the law of nature (Thomas Aquinas, *Summa Theologica* (Rome: Forzani, 1894) I.ii.Q91.1.3). The law of nature contains moral rules that all human beings are required to follow, and sets a standard for the civil laws of Christian states, which should seek to mirror God's kingdom on earth (Aquinas, *Summa Theologica* I.ii. Q95.2). To ensure that humans are in a position to work out what the law of nature commands, God has made it accessible to natural reason; but because its tenets have also been revealed to the prophets, a second way to learn what it requires us to study the Bible (Aquinas, *Summa Theologica* I.ii.Q94.4, Q106.1).

[7] Lambert van Velthuysen, *De initiis primæ philosophiæ juxta fundamenti clarissimi Cartesii, tradita in ipsis meditationibus, necnon de Deo et mente humana* (Utrecht, 1662). See also Henri Krop, 'Spinoza and the Calvinistic Cartesianism of Lambertus Van Velthuysen', *Studia Spinozana*, 15 (1999).

[8] Benedictus de Spinoza, *Tractatus Theologico-Politicus*, ed. Carl Gebhardt, vol. III, *Opera* (Heidelberg: Carl Winter, 1924), ch. 4, p. 57. On Spinoza's treatment of law, see Gail Belaief, *Spinoza's Philosophy of Law* (The Hague: Mouton, 1971); Moira Gatens and Genevieve Lloyd, *Collective Imaginings: Spinoza, Past and Present* (London: Routledge, 1999), pp. 95–100; Donald

manifest themselves in regular patterns of action, and as Spinoza now goes on to claim, such patterns can be explained in two ways. They may be attributable to the nature or definition of a particular type of thing. For instance, it is in the nature of bodies that, when they collide, each loses as much motion as it imparts. Equally, it is in the nature of human beings that, when a person sees a thing of a particular kind, they are reminded of other things that resemble it. Just as bodies conform to physical laws of motion, human minds conform to psychological laws of association, and in doing so bodies and minds both behave in a lawlike fashion.[9] Alternatively, a pattern of action may result from a human decision. For example, when a group of people agree to live in accordance with a set of rules, they will tend to act in whatever manner the rules specify.

Although the difference between these two types of pattern seems clear enough, Spinoza pauses to defend it. If, as he believes, 'everything is determined by the universal laws of nature to exist and produce an effect in a certain and determinate way',[10] there will be no distinction between regularities that depend on human decision and those that depend on the nature of a particular species of thing. Our decisions, like everything else, must be determined by the laws governing human nature, so that regularities or patterns of action arising from decisions are just instances of the regularities that arise from the natures of

Rutherford, 'Spinoza's Conception of Law: Metaphysics and Ethics', in *Spinoza's 'Theologico-Political Treatise': A Critical Guide*, ed. Yitzhak Y. Melamed and Michael A. Rosenthal (Cambridge: Cambridge University Press, 2010).

[9] Spinoza, *Tractatus Theologico-Politicus*, ch. 4, p. 58. On this 'scientific' conception of natural law, see Edwin Curley, *Spinoza's Metaphysics: An Essay in Interpretation* (Cambridge Mass.: Harvard University Press, 1969); Jon Miller, 'Spinoza and the Law of Nature', *History of Philosophy Quarterly*, 20. 3 (2003); J. R. Milton, 'Laws of Nature', in *The Cambridge History of Seventeenth Century Philosophy*, ed. Daniel Garber and Michael Ayers (Cambridge: Cambridge University Press, 1998); J. R. Milton, 'The Origin and Development of the Concept of the "Law of Nature"', *Archives Européennes de Sociologie*, no. 22 (1981). For a more comprehensive discussion of different conceptions of law in the early modern period, see *Natural Laws and Laws of Nature in Early Modern Europe: Jurisprudence, Theology, Moral and Natural Philosophy*, ed. Lorraine Daston and Michael Stolleis (Aldershot: Ashgate, 2008).

[10] Spinoza, *Tractatus Theologico-Politicus*, ch. 4, p. 58. On Spinoza's determinism, see John Carriero, 'Spinoza's Views on Necessity in Historical Perspective', *Philosophical Topics*, 19 (1991); Edwin Curley and Gregory Walski, 'Spinoza's Necessitarianism Reconsidered', in *New Essays on the Rationalists*, ed. Rocco J. Gennaro and Charles Huenemann (Oxford: Oxford University Press, 1999); Don Garrett, 'Spinoza's Necessitarianism', in *God and Nature: Spinoza's Metaphysics: Papers Presented at the First Jerusalem Conference (Ethica I)*, ed. Yirmiyahu Yovel (Leiden: Brill, 1991); Olli Koistinen, 'Spinoza's Proof of Necessitarianism', *Philosophy and Phenomenological Research* 67 (2003); Christopher Martin, 'A New Challenge to the Necessitarian Reading of Spinoza', in *Oxford Studies in Early Modern Philosophy*, ed. Daniel Garber and Steven Nadler (2010).

things. Spinoza concedes that this is so: we are indeed as much a part of nature as plants or stars, and our decisions are therefore determined by nature's all-encompassing and lawlike power. But he nevertheless maintains that there are compelling reasons for distinguishing the two types of pattern he has picked out. While we know in general that all states of affairs are the effects of law-governed antecedent causes, we often know very little about the causal chains that give rise to specific events. As a result, 'universal considerations concerning fate and the connection of causes cannot help us to form and order our thoughts concerning particular things'.[11] The best way to explain many patterns of action is therefore to cite the human decisions that are their proximate causes, without worrying about the natures from which these proximate causes flow, or the underlying laws to which they conform.

There is, to be sure, a sense in which this mode of explanation is deficient, insofar as it does not show that the patterns of action that we are trying to explain follow necessarily from their antecedents. If, for example, we attribute the Israelites' worship of the golden calf to their decision to throw in their lot with a deity less demanding than Jehovah, we do not rule out the possibility that they might have done something else instead. By citing just one of the antecedent causes of their action, we treat the *explanandum* as a state of affairs that might or might not have occurred, when in fact it is fully determined. Spinoza is aware of the misunderstandings to which this approach can lead, but nevertheless regards it as perfectly legitimate. We have an interest in accounting for the patterns of action that agents create by deciding to do one thing rather than another, and given the limits of our knowledge, appealing to their decisions is the best mode of explanation at our disposal. Since 'we are completely ignorant of . . . how things are ordered and connected, it is better, and indeed necessary, to consider them as possible'.[12]

The distinction between patterns of action that arise from the natures of things and those that arise from human decisions is therefore a significant one, and differentiates two types of law. But there is more to be said about the differences between them. As Spinoza next points out, the second is more deeply embedded in ordinary language. In everyday life, we talk about laws, not just as patterns of action that flow from decisions, but more specifically as patterns that flow from particular kinds of decision. A law is a command (*mandatum*) that someone decides to issue, and that others can decide to follow

---

[11] Spinoza, *Tractatus Theologico-Politicus*, ch. 4, p. 58.

[12] Ibid. ch. 4, p. 57. For Spinoza's definition of possibility see *Ethics*, in Curley ed., *The Collected Works of Spinoza*, vol. I, 1p33s1.

or ignore.[13] Judged by this standard, laws of the other sort, namely patterns of action that flow from the nature of particular kinds of things, do not count as laws at all. Since humans cannot but conform to the necessary laws that govern them, it makes no sense to think of these as commands that can be followed or ignored.[14] So when philosophers or jurists describe the patterns of action they find in nature as laws, they are using the term in what Spinoza characterizes as a figurative sense.[15] They are picking up on the view that laws are regular patterns of action, while abstracting from the claim that they are primarily commands or rules of right.[16]

The view that laws can be characterized as commands was a familiar one, held across the entire theological spectrum. Calvin, for instance, takes the divine commandments revealed in Scripture as exemplary cases of law,[17] while Hobbes emphasizes in more than one of his works that law is 'is not advice (*consilium*) but command (*mandatum*)'.[18] However, rather than simply adopting it, Spinoza introduces two important changes to this argument.[19] The first relaxes the stipulation that laws are commands by redefining them as prescriptions. A law, we are told, 'is a manner of living that man *prescribes* (*praescribit*) to himself and others for some end'.[20] Explaining this shift, Spinoza points out that becoming subject to law is widely assumed to be a matter of submitting to the commands of a legislator who imposes his will regardless of one's own desires.[21] But this is a misapprehension. It is true, of course, that

---

[13] Spinoza, *Tractatus Theologico-Politicus*, ch. 4, p. 57.

[14] Edwin Curley, 'Spinoza's Moral Philosophy', in *Spinoza: A Collection of Critical Essays*, ed. Marjorie Grene (Notre Dame: University of Notre Dame Press, 1973), p. 371.

[15] Spinoza, *Tractatus Theologico-Politicus*, ch. 4, p. 58.

[16] Ibid. ch. 4, p. 57.

[17] Calvin, *Institutes*, II.viii.2.

[18] Hobbes, *On the Citizen*, pp. 153–4. See also Thomas Hobbes, *Leviathan*, ed. Richard Tuck (Cambridge: Cambridge University Press, 1996), pp. 361–2. On the view that Spinoza defends, cf. Suárez's account of an indicative law: Francisco Suárez, *De legibus, ac deo legislatore, 1612*, ed. and trans. Ammi Brown et al. (Oxford: Clarendon Press, 1944), II.vi.

[19] See Edwin Curley, '"I Durst Not Write So Boldly" or How to Read Hobbes' Theologico-Political Treatise', in *Studi su Hobbes e Spinoza*, ed. Emilia Giancotti (Naples: Bibliopolis, 1996).

[20] Spinoza, *Tractatus Theologico-Politicus*, ch. 4, p. 58. On the metaphysical and political implications of this definition, see Michael Rosenthal, 'Miracles, Wonder and the State', in *Spinoza's 'Theologico-Political Treatise'*, ed. Yitzhak Y. Melamed and Michael A. Rosenthal (Cambridge: Cambrdige University Press, 2010).

[21] Spinoza, *Tractatus Theologico-Politicus*, ch. 4, p. 59.

legislators frequently use threats and promises 'to restrain ordinary people (*vulgus*), like a horse with a harness'.[22] Subjects consequently come to think of themselves as enslaved to their legislators, and attribute their condition to the fact of living under law. However, the threat and exercise of punishment are not intrinsic features of legislation, but merely practical devices for enforcing it. The idea of a law that is not backed up by coercive measures of any kind is perfectly coherent, and indeed, law is at its strongest when people obey it because they understand the reasons for doing so, rather than because they fear punishment. In themselves, then, laws are not commands. Rather they are prescriptions that can be obeyed or disobeyed.[23] Disengaging law from the means used to enforce it, and even from an external legislator who imposes it, opens up space for the view that people can prescribe laws for themselves, regardless of whether they are coerced or cajoled into following them. As we shall see, this conception of self-legislation will play a central part in Spinoza's argument, and will allow him to argue that one can follow the divine law in the absence of a legislating God. Equally, it will allow him to defend the view that true followers of the law have internalized its requirements and willingly impose them on themselves. The law, as the New Testament puts it and the Reformed Church reaffirms, is then written on the fleshly tables of the heart.[24]

Moving to a second and equally significant revision, Spinoza shifts the emphasis from the type of speech-act that gives rise to law (Is it a command? Is it a prescription?) to the question of what the speech-act achieves. Departing from the style of definition reiterated, for instance, by Hobbes, he presents law not merely as a prescription, but rather as a manner of living that has been prescribed in order to achieve some end. To live under law is therefore to live in a particular fashion that is fundamentally purposive, and is designed to achieve a specific goal. This claim plays an important part in Spinoza's analysis of the law of God, to which he now turns.

---

[22] Ibid.

[23] According to Calvin, for example, God has instituted promises and threats 'in order to imbue our hearts with love of righteousness and with hatred of wickedness'. (Calvin, *Institutes* II. viii.4). And according to political writers such as Hobbes, law can only be effective if a legislator possesses the power to punish transgressors (Hobbes, *Leviathan*, p. 117).

[24] 2 Corinthians 3:3, Calvin, *Institutes*, I.vii.12, 'The Canons of the Synod of Dort', in *The Creeds of Christendom: The Evangelical Protestant Creeds*, ed. Philip Schaff (New York: Cosimo Books, 2007); 'Rejection of Errors', §6.

Defining divine law

Equipped with a definition of law that reflects his broader philosophical convictions and is adapted to the argument he wants to develop, Spinoza now begins to put it to work by asking what types of law exist. What ways of living *do* men prescribe for themselves or others, and what ends are these ways of living designed to achieve? Still following convention, he begins by distinguishing human from divine law. His characterization of the first is straightforward and familiar. Human laws are the civil ordinances that the members of political communities impose in order to protect their lives and the states in which they live.[25] It is only when he comes to the divine law that Spinoza gives his readers a reason to sit up. It would have been natural to say at this point that divine laws are prescriptions laid down by God; but this line is not available to Spinoza, because his definition stipulates that laws are ways of living laid down by *men*. What distinguishes the divine law from its civil counterpart is not that it is made by the deity, but rather the nature of its goal. While civil law aims at security, the aim of divine law is to realize our highest good, which consists in the knowledge and love of God. The divine law is therefore a way of living directed to this end, and it is on account of its end that we describe it as divine.[26]

We now have a definition of divine law. But so far it is wholly stipulative. How do we know that our supreme good lies in the knowledge and love of God? Even if this turns out to be true, is the fact that a law aims to promote the supreme good enough to qualify it as divine? Is there not more to it, as many readers of the *Tractatus* would have assumed? Responding to the first of these anxieties, Spinoza defends his claim that our highest good consists in the knowledge of God by showing that it is philosophically demonstrable and can be deduced from human nature.[27] (This, he points out, also guarantees that it is 'universal or common to all men'.[28]) As usual, his argument rests on a

---

[25] Spinoza, *Tractatus Theologico-Politicus*, ch. 4, p. 59. On Spinoza's conception of the good, see Charles Jarrett, 'Spinoza on the Relativity of Good and Evil', in *Spinoza: Metaphysical Themes*, ed. Olli I. Koistinen and John I. Biro (Oxford: Oxford University Press, 2002); Jon Miller, 'Spinoza's Axiology', in *Oxford Studies in Early Modern Philosophy*, ed. Daniel Garber and Steven Nadler (2005); Steven Nadler, 'Spinoza in the Garden of Good and Evil', in *The Problem of Evil in Early Modern Philosophy*, ed. Elmar Kremer and Michael Latzer (Toronto: University of Toronto Press, 2001); Andrew Youpa, 'Spinoza's Theory of the Good', in *The Cambridge Companion to Spinoza's Ethics*, ed. Olli Koistinen (Cambridge: Cambridge University Press, 2009).

[26] Spinoza, *Tractatus Theologico-Politicus*, ch. 4, p. 59.

[27] Ibid. ch. 4, p. 61.

[28] Ibid.

number of assumptions that are taken for granted, two of which need to be highlighted.

Since the better part of us is our intellect, our greatest good must consist in perfecting our intellectual powers by cultivating the kind of knowledge that only they can yield.[29] However, we can offer at least two reasons for thinking that this kind of knowledge depends on knowledge of God. The first is that nothing, including our intellectual knowledge, can exist or be conceived without God. (Here Spinoza simply states a claim that he has discussed in his *Appendix containing Metaphysical Thoughts* and will demonstrate in the *Ethics*, meanwhile relying on his readers not to question it.)[30] The second can be extracted from Descartes' *Discourse on Method*, and is designed to appeal to his Cartesians readers. 'The certainty that really removes all doubt' depends on the knowledge of God because, 'as long as we have no clear and distinct idea of God, we can doubt everything'.[31] Unless we have some clear and distinct idea of God, all our claims to knowledge can be doubted, and none of them can possess the certainty characteristic of the clear and distinct ideas that we arrive at through the use of our intellect.[32]

Taking these two conclusions as decisive, the argument now moves on to explain the sense in which our philosophical knowledge is not only dependent on God, but also consists in knowledge of him. To learn about the effect of a thing is, in Spinoza's view, to learn about its cause, the thing itself. God is the cause of everything in nature. So as we come to know more about the natural things of which he is the cause, we come to know more about his nature or essence.[33] All intellectual knowledge is therefore knowledge of God, and on

---

[29] Ibid. ch. 4, p. 60.

[30] Spinoza, *Ethics* 1p15. On the metaphysical principles at work in Spinoza's conception of law, see Yitzhak Y. Melamed, 'The Metaphysics of the *Theologico-Political Treatise*', in *Spinoza's 'Theologico-Political Treatise'*, ed. Yitzhak Y. Melamed and Michael A. Rosenthal (Cambridge: Cambrdige University Press, 2010).

[31] Spinoza, *Tractatus Theologico-Politicus*, ch. 4, pp. 59–60. See also Spinoza, *Parts I and II of Descartes' 'Principles of Philosophy'*, in *The Collected Works of Spinoza*, vol. I, pp. 224–98, 231–8. Moreau links this passage to Descartes' *Discours*, AT IV38; 2nd Rep., AT IX 110; 4th rep. AT IX, pp. 189–90. See Benedictus de Spinoza, *Traité Théologico-Politique*, ed. Fokke Akkerman, Jaqueline Lagrée, and Pierre-François Moreau, vol. 3, *Œuvres de Spinoza* (Paris: Presses Universitaires de France, 1999), p. 723.

[32] In the *Ethics*, Spinoza claims that the mind has an adequate idea of God's essence (*Ethics* 2p47). But it's not clear there that all our other adequate or clear and distinct ideas depend on it. I'm grateful to the Oxford University Press's anonymous reader for drawing my attention to this point.

[33] Spinoza, *Tractatus Theologico-Politicus*, ch. 4, pp. 59–60.

the assumption that our highest good lies in perfecting ourselves by cultivating our intellectual knowledge, it follows that our highest good simultaneously lies in cultivating knowledge of God.

A parallel argument offers a more explicitly normative defence of the same conclusion. The degree of perfection that a person attains is directly proportional to the perfection of the things they love. Since God is the most perfect being, the most perfect people are those who love God. And since our greatest good lies in perfecting ourselves as far as possible, our greatest good lies in loving God. As Spinoza puts it, 'The love of God is man's highest happiness and blessedness, and the ultimate end and object of all human actions'.[34] However, one cannot love God without knowing him, and indeed, the more one truly understands his perfection, the more one loves him. So our greatest good lies not only in loving God, but in knowing him as well, and these are the twin goals of the divine law. 'The highest reward of the divine law is the law itself, viz. to know God and to love him from true freedom and with a whole and constant heart'.[35]

The conclusion that the divine law enjoins us to love God would not have troubled readers of the *Treatise* who accepted the theology of the Reformed Church, and would therefore have shared Calvin's belief that the law demands our souls to be 'entirely filled with the love of God'. But Spinoza's analysis nevertheless challenges the Church's outlook at several key points. Perhaps the most obvious is his insistence that we can come to know the substance of the divine law by philosophical reasoning. Reflection on the notion of law provides us with a schematic understanding of the divine law as a way of life that aims to realize our highest good, and reflection on the nature of the deity leads us to the conclusion that our highest good consists in the knowledge and love of God. The divine law is, 'as it were written in the human mind', and is in principle available to everyone.[36]

For a strict Calvinist, such confidence in our intellectual powers smacked of pride and vanity, and flew in the face of Calvin's insistence that our deeply fallible minds need written proof of holy doctrine, so that 'it should neither perish through forgetfulness, nor vanish through error, nor be corrupted by the audacity of men'.[37] However, this is an outlook with which Spinoza has no patience. To anyone with any experience of philosophical reasoning, he insists, the contention that it is fundamentally untrustworthy is bound to seem absurd.

---

[34] Ibid. ch. 4, p. 60. See also Spinoza, *Ethics* 5p27, 5p36s.
[35] Spinoza, *Tractatus Theologico-Politicus*, ch. 4, p. 62.
[36] Ibid. ch. 5, p. 69.   [37] Calvin, *Institutes*, I.vi.3.

Philosophers are of course capable of making mistakes, but their fallibility is not a warrant for rejecting their method and adopting modes of enquiry that are inferior guides to the truth. In fact, since the truths to which reasoning gives us access follow from God's nature, they are in a sense revealed or dictated to us by him.[38] Rather than turning our backs on the knowledge that he provides, we should rejoice in its power and strive after the blessedness it yields.[39]

Wrapped up in this argument is a challenge to those orthodox theologians who held that we can only understand and follow the divine law with the help of Scripture. Since, as Spinoza has demonstrated, we can only fully love God if we know what he is, and since, as the *Treatise's* discussion of prophecy has established, true and incontrovertible knowledge of God can be attained only by philosophical reasoning, it follows that only philosophical reasoning can yield a full understanding of our highest good. As Spinoza will later go on to emphasize, historical narratives such as those included in the Bible certainly have their uses and can serve the practical function of helping us to live as the divine law dictates. But because they are grounded on imaginative thought and experience, and therefore yield conclusions that are only morally certain, they cannot provide the fullest and most satisfying knowledge of God of which human beings are capable. In short, philosophy can in principle give us an understanding of our highest good that is superior to anything that a narrative can deliver, and for those capable of attaining it can supplant the Scriptures. Furthermore, because rational knowledge is in some sense available to everyone, anyone can use it to understand and prescribe the divine law, whether or not they have access to the Bible.

This assessment of the power and significance of Scripture poses just the kind of challenge that orthodox Dutch Calvinist theologians found most threatening and outrageous. In his earlier chapters, Spinoza has progressively undercut the theological claim that Scripture is an unparalleled source of certain knowledge by arguing that only philosophy can yield incontrovertibly true conclusions about nature and God. Now, pushing further along the same path, he claims that only philosophy can provide incontrovertible knowledge of the divine law, so that even the most central moral teachings of the Bible lie within philosophy's domain. While theologians may uphold their authority in a variety of ways, they cannot legitimately claim that Scripture alone holds the key to the law. In principle, anyone can work out what it prescribes without appealing to the Church.

---

[38] Spinoza, *Tractatus Theologico-Politicus*, ch. 1, pp. 15–16.   [39] Ibid. ch. 4, p. 62.

This, however, is only the first stage of Spinoza's debate with his Calvinist adversaries. So far, the substance of the divine law as he has explicated it can be summarized in a practical conclusion: pursue the greatest human good by cultivating the knowledge and love of God. But if we now return to his definition, it is clear that this conclusion does not yet amount to a law. To turn it into a law, someone must prescribe it as a way of living for themselves and others with the aim of promoting the highest good on which the discussion has so far concentrated. While it is a truth that humans achieve blessedness by devoting themselves to the knowledge and love of God, and while the practical conclusion 'Love God' is consequently one that all humans have strong reasons to take to heart, something else is needed to give this precept the status of divine law.

Many of Spinoza's contemporaries would have found this an extremely surprising claim. For them, a rationally grounded conclusion about how to live was a prototypical instance of a law commanded by God and made accessible through the natural light of reason. The claim that such a precept was *not* a law cast doubt on a deeply embedded conception of nature as a juridical realm governed by divine purposes, and threatened to upset an established and influential tradition of thought. In questioning it, Spinoza takes up a view articulated by Hobbes, who had argued both in *De Cive* and *Leviathan* that there are two ways to think about the laws of nature: as revealed by God or as 'proceeding from nature'. If we concentrate on the second, we find that rational investigations of nature, human and otherwise, do not yield commands, but only 'theorems' or 'dictates of reason'. What we call the laws of nature, Hobbes claims, are 'nothing other than certain conclusions, understood by reason, on what is to be done and not to be done'; whereas 'a law, properly and precisely speaking, is an utterance by one who by right commands others to do or not to do. Hence, properly speaking, the natural laws are not laws, insofar as they proceed from nature'.[40]

Viewed in this way, a law of nature is 'a precept or general rule, found out by reason' about the best means to our conservation and defence.[41] It tells us what it is good for human beings to do, and possesses an authority 'legible to all men that have use of natural reason'; but it only becomes law in the sense of a

---

[40] Hobbes, *On the Citizen*, p. 56. Compare 'These dictates of Reason, men use to call by the name of Lawes, but improperly: for they are but Conclusions or Theoremes concerning what conduceth to the conservation and defence of themselves; wheras Law, properly is the word of him, that, by right hath command over others.' Hobbes, *Leviathan*, p. 111.

[41] Ibid. p. 91.

command when its theorems are legislated or commanded by some suitably authoritative agent.[42] As we have seen, Spinoza does not agree that theorems only become laws when they acquire the force of commands, but the *Treatise* nevertheless takes over Hobbes's view that there is a vital distinction between laws and rationally grounded conclusions. When, for example, a philosophical examination of human nature leads us to the conclusion that our true good lies in the knowledge and love of God, what we arrive at is a precept. 'The sum total and highest precept (*praeceptum*) of the divine law is to love God as the highest good'.[43] For the precept to become a law, some agent must then prescribe a way of life designed to realize our highest good.

How is this transformation to be brought about? Discussing the civil law, Hobbes had argued that only a sovereign legislator is capable of imposing a common way of life that will protect individuals and the state, and as we shall see, Spinoza broadly agrees. But in the case of the divine law the paths of the two philosophers diverge. Backing away from unwanted controversy, Hobbes concedes that, if we consider the laws of nature as they have been legislated by God in the Bible, 'they are very properly called by the name of laws; for Holy Scripture is the utterance of God, who issues commands in all things by the highest right'.[44] This is not a view that Spinoza can accept. The precepts 'know and love God' can only become laws if some human agent prescribes a way of life designed to realize them, and there are at least two ways in which this can be done. Nothing rules out the possibility that a political legislator or some other public authority may impose rules and conventions aimed at the highest good. In addition, rational individuals and communities can set themselves to realize this goal by devoting themselves to knowing and loving God. As Spinoza's definition indicates, one can prescribe the divine law for oneself without subjecting oneself to the commands of another agent.

Much the most striking feature of this view is its quiet insistence that the divine law always takes the form of a prescription laid down by human beings. Here Spinoza pointedly fails to engage with a predominant and looming assumption—that divine laws are not made by humans, but by God. Because the biblical conception of God as a legislator formed part of the bedrock of Protestant theology and played an essential role in underpinning the provi-

---

[42] Ibid. pp. 191, 268, *passim*.

[43] Spinoza, *Tractatus Theologico-Politicus*, ch. 4, p. 60.

[44] Hobbes, *On the Citizen*, pp. 66–7. Compare 'But yet if we consider the same Theoremes, as delivered in the word of God, that by right commandeth all things; then are they properly called Lawes'. Hobbes, *Leviathan*, p. 111.

dentialist outlook of Calvinism and other Protestant confessions, any attempt to sidestep it was bound to leave a great many readers shocked and unsatisfied. The juridical character of the relation between God and man could not be ignored, and certainly could not be ruled out by mere definition. Acknowledging the lacuna in his analysis, Spinoza concedes that there is a further question to consider. We need to discover 'whether, by the natural light, we can conceive God as a lawgiver or prince, who prescribes laws to men'.[45] But the answer he gives in both the *Treatise* and the *Ethics* would in some ways have been a troubling one.

Philosophical reasoning, Spinoza argues, shows us that God is not an anthropomorphic being who makes laws in the sense of prescribing ways of living for humanity. Despite the descriptions to be found in the Bible, any laws that he lays down are of a quite different kind from those made by human rulers.[46] The great majority of the Calvinist theologians whose outlook Spinoza is contesting would have agreed that the anthropomorphic God of the Bible is at least to some extent a figurative representation of the deity, adapted to the needs and understandings of ordinary people. Nevertheless, the doctrines of the Reformed Church unequivocally committed them to the idea of a legislating God who created everything in the world, 'and doth still uphold and govern them by his eternal providence and infinite power'.[47] While they shared Spinoza's view that the deity does not impose the divine law as a prince imposes civil decrees, this was not the issue that preoccupied them. The vital question on which claims to orthodoxy rested concerned the sense in which God *is* a lawmaker, and it is at this point that the *Treatise* offers a radically heterodox view. As we have seen, Spinoza's definition of a law assumes that lawmakers aim to realize a goal, so that if God is to legislate the divine law he too must act for ends. Rejecting Calvinism's providentialism, Spinoza now denies that this is something God can do. Instead, he develops an impersonal analysis of a divine law in which the concerns of human beings play no part.

'When he would have Jonah cast into the sea', Calvin writes, 'God sent a wind by stirring up a whirlwind . . . From [this] I infer that no wind ever arises or increases except by God's express command. . . . His general providence not only flourishes among creatures so as to continue the order of nature, but is by

[45] Spinoza, *Tractatus Theologico-Politicus*, ch. 4, p. 62.
[46] Ibid. ch. 4, p. 65.
[47] 'The Belgic Confession', in *The Creeds of Christendom: The Evangelical Protestant Creeds*, ed. Philip Schaff (New York: Cosimo Books, 2007), Article 12.

his wonderful plan adapted to a definite and proper end'.[48] According to Calvin, the natural order commanded by God is adapted to definite human ends. The deity has a plan, which determines the fates of individual human beings such as the unfortunate Jonah, and uses natural phenomena to bring about these fates. These two claims play a central role in Calvinist theology; but Spinoza dispenses with both of them. As he will argue in the *Ethics*, God does not in fact act for ends. If he did, there would be something he lacked and needed to achieve; but in that case he would be imperfect. Since we know independently that he is perfect, it follows that this would render his nature inconsistent.[49] And since God's nature cannot be both inconsistent and perfect, we can conclude that he is not a purposive being.

This brief argument is not intended to stand alone. In the *Ethics* it will form part of a broader critique of the teleological mode of explanation traditionally favoured by advocates of Aristotelianism, who included the Voetian theologians within the Dutch Reformed Church. These philosophers, as Spinoza represents them, share Calvin's assumptions. For example, if a tile has fallen from a roof onto a man's head and killed him, they will say that the tile fell in order to bring about his death. If you point out that the wind was blowing hard at the time they will ask why or for what end the wind was blowing.[50] Ultimately they will claim, as Calvin does, that the wind, the falling tile, and the man's death are all part of God's wonderful plan.

Spinoza argues that this approach gets things back to front. It explains natural events in terms of their effects (the tile fell in order to kill the man) when we should be following Descartes' lead and explaining effects in terms of their causes (the man died because the tile fell on his head). The *Ethics* offers a number of reasons for preferring the latter approach, but one of the most audacious is its claim that God is not the sort of being who makes plans, and is therefore not the sort of being who can prescribe ways of living that are designed to achieve particular ends. If this is so, it follows immediately that he cannot make laws in the manner of a legislator or prince. More drastically still, it follows that 'God directs nature as its universal laws require, but not as the particular laws of human nature require, and that God takes account not just of the human race, but of the whole of nature'.[51]

---

[48] Calvin, *Institutes*, I.xvi.7.
[49] Spinoza, *Ethics*, 1app.
[50] Ibid. 1app.
[51] Ibid. 1app. See also Spinoza, *Tractatus Theologico-Politicus*, ch. 16, p. 199. 'The divine laws seem to us to be laws *or* things instituted just as long as we do not know their cause. But when this

By ruling out Calvin's conception of divine providence, Spinoza at the same time puts himself at loggerheads with the theologians of the Dutch Reformed Church. Philosophical reasoning, so he claims, demonstrates that some of their most fundamental doctrines are not only mistaken, but complicit with forms of enquiry that block the natural light and stand in the way of true understanding. To put themselves on a genuinely illuminating track, philosophers need to abandon this Aristotelian and Calvinist outlook and adopt a Spinozist one instead. But this is not a light or easy transition. Those who make it will find themselves giving up a conception of a legislating deity, together with the notion of salvation that flows from it, in favour of a God who is indifferent to the fates of human beings and does not impose a legal order on them.

If this were all that Spinoza had to say, his position would by seventeenth-century standards be very stark indeed. In place of a world ruled by a deity who demands obedience from human beings, he would be offering one in which juridical language does not apply to God. However, whether or not such a clean break with the natural law tradition was conceivable during Spinoza's lifetime, he certainly does not make it. Although he holds that God cannot legislate in the manner of a prince and does not determine ends for human beings, he next goes on to argue that there is nevertheless a sense in which philosophical reasoning enables us to understand God as a lawmaker.

Defining natural divine law

At the beginning of his discussion of divine law, Spinoza has distinguished two senses of law 'taken absolutely': patterns of action attributable to the necessity of nature, and those attributable to human decisions. His investigation of the latter category has established that it does not offer a credible model for laws made by God. But what about the former? So far, such a possibility has been set aside on the grounds that patterns of action flowing from the laws of nature are only figuratively to be described as laws.[52] Now, however, Spinoza returns to it, arguing that these laws can after all legitimately be viewed as divine decrees (*decreta*).

The discussion that follows rests implicitly on the assumption that natural events are governed by universal laws which determine everything that happens, and that these laws, together with the chains of events that follow from

---

is known, they thereby cease to be laws, and we embrace them not as laws, but as eternal truths'. Spinoza, *Tractatus Theologico-Politicus*, ch. 16, p. 198n.

[52] Spinoza, *Tractatus Theologico-Politicus*, ch. 4, p. 58.

them, are manifestations of God's nature. It is consequently not too much of a jump to say, as Spinoza has repeatedly done, that all events are determined by God. Individual events follow necessarily from laws of nature, and because the laws themselves are manifestations of God's perfect essence, they too are necessary. (For them to have been different, God would have to have had another essence; but such an essence would have been imperfect, in which case God would not have been God.)[53] Events are therefore determined by God's nature.

Spinoza takes it for granted that the relationships between one event and another, and between a law and the events that flow from it, can be described in causal terms. We can say, for instance, that a falling tile played a role in causing a man's death, or that a law of motion causes bodies to interact in a particular way. Equally, we can say that God is the immanent cause of all bodily motions. However, these causal relations can also be expressed in psychological terms as manifestations of God's understanding and will. Since God's will and intellect are one and the same (God always understands what he wills and wills what he understands), 'we affirm the same thing when we say that God wills something as when we say that he understands it'.[54]

We may thus say that God's will and intellect are interchangeable. There remains, however, what might be described as a conceptual distinction between them. When we think about the states of affairs of which God is the ultimate cause, we can think of them in two ways: either as ideas that God understands or as ideas that he wills.[55] To illustrate the point, Spinoza takes the necessary truth that the internal angles of a triangle add up to one hundred and eighty degrees. Focusing on the fact that the nature of the triangle is contained from eternity in the divine nature, we may say that this is a truth God understands. Alternatively, adopting a different point of view, we may concentrate on the fact that its necessity depends on the divine nature, and say that God wills it. The same applies to other truths, for example the truth that our highest good consists in the love and knowledge of God. This, too, can be conceived either as something that God understands or as something that he wills. Generalizing, then, we arrive at a rather abstract sense in which we can think of God as decreeing natural laws and the truths that flow from them.

The point of this argument is to vindicate a sense in which God operates as a kind of legislator, while rejecting any suggestion that his decrees resemble laws made by human beings. One crucial difference is that, whereas 'God's

---

[53] Spinoza, *Ethics*, 1p33s2.   [54] Spinoza, *Tractatus Theologico-Politicus*, ch. 6, p. 82.
[55] Ibid. ch. 4, p. 62.

affirmations and negations always involve eternal necessity' human laws can be ignored.[56] As Spinoza had put the point earlier in the *Short Treatise*, 'All laws that cannot be transgressed are divine laws...All laws that can be transgressed are human laws. For everything that man decides for his own well-being is not necessarily for the well-being of the whole of nature. On the contrary, it may be destructive of many other things'.[57] For example, it is impossible for us to bring it about that the angles of a triangle do not add up to one hundred and eighty degrees; but breaking the civil or divine laws that human beings prescribe is often within our power.[58] A second and equally vital difference concerns the issue of ends. As we have seen, human laws are inherently purposive: they prescribe ways of life in order to achieve specific goals. By contrast, God's decrees are simply expressions of his perfection and do not aim at anything. Nor are they designed with humanity in mind. Although the laws of nature determine what happens to each one of us, they are not made *for* us, and we read too much into them if we interpret the deity in Calvinist vein as a being who uses nature to shape our fates.

Although Spinoza's conception of God as the immanent cause of the laws of nature is by most Christian and Jewish standards shockingly unorthodox, the view that the laws of nature are divine decrees is not. In advocating it, Spinoza adopts a familiar stance and holds out an olive branch to his more anxious or unpersuaded readers. God is not a lawmaker; but he does exercise his will by issuing all-encompassing decrees to which we are subject. He 'acts and guides all things only from the necessity of his own nature and perfection'.[59] There is, then, a 'natural divine law' not made by human legislators alongside the human version of the divine law that aims to realize our highest good.[60] This conclusion would not have satisfied strict Calvinists, but it brings the argument of the *Treatise* back into the fold of natural law. Juridical language, it allows, can properly be applied to God and used to explain the natural world, and there is after all a sense in which we are bound by divine commands.

The claim that natural laws can be understood as decrees is put forward several times in the *Treatise*, and since it plays an important role in the argument of the text there is no reason to suspect that Spinoza was in any doubt about it.

---

[56] Ibid. ch. 4, p. 63.

[57] Spinoza, *Short Treatise on God, Man, and His Well-Being*, in *The Collected Works of Spinoza*, vol. I, ch. xxiv.

[58] To mark this point, Spinoza largely reserves the term 'law' for human prescriptions and commands, but describes divine volitions as 'decrees'.

[59] Spinoza, *Tractatus Theologico-Politicus*, ch. 4, p. 66.

[60] Ibid. ch. 4, p. 61.

All the same, it is difficult to tell how deeply he is committed to it and whether he regards it as a more than provisional conclusion. The suspicion that it may be less than final is fuelled by the *Ethics*, in which Spinoza stares into an impenetrable chasm separating divine will and intellect from their human counterparts. 'If will and intellect do pertain to the eternal essence of God', he writes, 'we must of course understand by each of these attributes something other than what men commonly understand. For the intellect and will which would constitute God's essence would have to differ entirely from our intellect and will, and could not agree with them in anything except the name. They would not agree with one another any more than do the dog that is a heavenly constellation and the dog that is the barking animal'.[61] If we had a fuller understanding of God's essence, this passage seems to suggest, we would appreciate that it makes no more sense to try to understand the divine will by analogy with human will than to try to understand a dog by analogy with a constellation of stars. Because they have only a name in common, the one cannot teach us anything about the other, and we go wrong when we attempt to grasp the character of God's volitions by extrapolating from our own experience of willing. Spinoza does, of course, chart some of the differences between divine and human will: where our volitions are informed by a fragmentary grasp of the causal order, God's are not; where our volitions can fail to be realized, God's cannot; and so on. To some extent, then, we are capable of understanding the differences between the two, and avoiding the errors that arise from interpreting the first in the light of the second. But if they are really as divergent as Spinoza's analogy implies, his own conception of divine volition must be incomplete. Along with other seventeenth-century philosophers, he does not conceive it in a fashion that shares only a name with the kind of willing we ourselves are capable of, and continues to model it on its human counterpart.

If we can know that the two types of volition are as different as Spinoza says, and also know that a full understanding of the difference between them lies as yet beyond our grasp, it is hard to be sure that we are justified in describing natural laws as divine volitions and decrees. Perhaps this view successfully captures the true nature of God. But perhaps it is a distorting projection—an attempt to stretch our knowledge of the role of volition in the creation of human law to make it cover the natural divine law. It may be that, in mapping the juridical notion of decree onto the causal workings of nature, we are importing a notion that ultimately has no place. This moment of hesitation

---

[61] Spinoza, *Ethics*, 1p17s.

bears immediately on Spinoza's analysis. If the view that God issues decrees reflects an incomplete understanding of his nature, it is possible that a fuller philosophical grasp of his essence will lead us to abandon the attempt to characterize God in legal terms. (We might even stop describing the patterns of action that types of things display as laws.) The conciliatory conception of divine decrees that Spinoza has taken over from the tradition of natural law may drop out, thereby widening the gulf between human lawmaking and whatever it is that the deity can be said to do. This shadowy possibility is not avowed in the *Treatise*; but it nevertheless hovers behind the argument, holding out the possibility of a still less juridical idea of God than the one Spinoza explicitly upholds.

The suggestion that our understanding of the divine will may be incomplete also offers a moment of insight into Spinoza's conception of philosophical reasoning. In the *Treatise*, this kind of reasoning is often presented as a process in which clear and distinct ideas, shorn of all imaginative content, are pellucidly inferred from one another. Starting out from common notions whose truth is beyond doubt, philosophers use deductive rules of inference to demonstrate new claims, thus guaranteeing the mathematical certainty of their conclusions.[62] However, as we can now see more clearly, this model is an ideal, or perhaps even a caricature. Where the natural light is exceptionally strong, as in some areas of geometry, we may be able to demonstrate results that qualify as mathematically certain; but much of the time our reasoning will be far less final and clearcut. Spinoza's discussion of divine will is a case in point. Philosophical reasoning about the way in which we form our ideas has placed him at a considerable critical distance from our everyday habits of thought, and made him aware of the dangers of extrapolating from human experience. Proceeding cautiously, he has identified several respects in which God's will is unlike our own, and contemplates the prospect that divine and human volition may be still more different than he can currently show.

Viewed in this light, reasoning is messier and more recognizable than an idealized account of philosophical method implies. Rather than proceeding tidily from one certainty to another, it has enabled Spinoza to recognize that his idea of a divine decree is not clear and distinct, and has given him grounds for wondering how fully he understands it. But this does not immediately imply that the idea is unfit for philosophical use. Philosophers are bound to work with ideas that fall short of the ideal, and need to continue to take a critical attitude

---

[62] Spinoza, *Tractatus Theologico-Politicus*, p. 84fn. See Meijer's Preface to Spinoza, *Parts I and II of Descartes' 'Principles of Philosophy'*, in *The Collected Works of Spinoza*, vol. I, pp. 224–30.

to the ideas they have, in the expectation that their strengths and limitations will gradually become evident. Furthermore, as Spinoza's discussion of divine volition also indicates, the boundary between philosophical reasoning and the imaginative thinking on which we depend in other areas of our lives is less sharp than his more programmatic statements seem to imply. The question mark hanging over the idea that God's volitions are decrees arises from the suspicion that it may be based on a projection. It may impose an aspect of our own imaginative experience of willing on to a God who actually operates quite differently, in a way that we have not comprehensively understood. Yet, in the absence of an argument to validate this suspicion, the idea is good enough to reason with. While philosophers do their best to arrive at universal truths that are not compromised by the vagaries of human experience, they often cannot rule out the possibility that the ideas they are reasoning with continue to carry traces of imagination.

Reasoning is thus a process in which our understanding is gradually clarified, and must start from whatever ideas a particular individual or community can muster. Whilst Spinoza is persuaded that everyone is in principle capable of forming some clear and distinct ideas,[63] this is not to say that everyone can articulate or make use of more than a very few of them. In practice, human reasoning is often a fumbling affair, in which truths are only partially grasped and their implications only partially worked through. Spinoza does not spell out this comfortably Cartesian conception of the natural light, perhaps because he assumes that many of his readers will already be familiar with, and sympathetic to, Descartes' method. However, there are some points in the *Treatise* at which his own commitment to it becomes clear and the suggestion that a conclusion may not be final swims into view. The claim that God is a lawmaker only insofar as he decrees the natural divine law is already, by seventeenth-century standards, a radical one. The tentativeness surrounding it opens up possibilities that are more radical still.

In the course of an elaborate argument, Spinoza has identified two senses of divine law: the natural divine laws that are God's decrees, and the ways of life that human agents prescribe in order to foster knowledge and love of God. There is, however, an obvious connection between them. By learning about divine law in the first sense, we can gain an understanding of our highest good. Although God's decrees or the laws of nature are not adapted to human ends, humans are nonetheless governed by them, and one of the truths that they

---

[63] Spinoza, *Tractatus Theologico-Politicus*, ch. 7, p. 113. See also Spinoza, *Ethics*, 2p38c, 2p39, 2p40, 2p46.

determine is the character of our highest good. It follows necessarily from the laws of human nature that our true blessedness lies in loving and knowing God. The aim of divine law in the second sense is to prescribe a way of life that will realize this goal, and we can only undertake this task if we have some conception of what our highest good consists in. As we have seen, a reliable way to acquire this knowledge is to study the natural divine law, in particular the laws of human nature. By grasping the most general formulation of our highest good and working out what it implies, we can develop a fuller conception of what ways of life will foster it. (What forms of social organization are most conducive to loving God? How are people best motivated to pursue this goal? And so on.) This enterprise, Spinoza tells us, is the task of ethics;[64] and natural reasoning of this kind is the most widely available way to discover what the divine law requires of us, thus putting ourselves in a position to prescribe it.

Anyone who arrives at these insights has travelled a long way from the theologians who ground their view of a legislating God on the Bible. As we have seen, Spinoza is fully aware of the distance he has created between his own outlook and that of the Reformed Church. Even for its more moderate theologians, there was much that was discordant in his position. If God does not prescribe laws that humans can obey or disobey, what is the difference between salvation and damnation? What will motivate us to love him? And above all, what are we to make of the law revealed to the prophets? In due course Spinoza will address all these questions, but his most immediate concern is with the last. How is he to reconcile his view with the scriptural narrative of the law?

Defining revealed law

Having set out his understanding of the divine law in its full depth and complexity, Spinoza now follows his usual practice and goes on to argue that his conclusions accord with Scripture. 'When Scripture says that this or that has been done by God...it really understands nothing but that it has been done according to the laws or order of nature, and not, as the common people thinks, that for some period nature has ceased to act'.[65] To get this stage of his discussion under way, Spinoza returns to the law of Moses. As he has already explained, this law is not to be interpreted as a divine law ordained for the Jews alone; but as he now goes on to add, it can 'be called the Law of God or the divine law. For we

---

[64] Spinoza, *Tractatus Theologico-Politicus*, ch. 4, p. 60.   [65] Ibid. ch. 6, p. 89.

believe it was enacted by the light of prophecy'.[66] Prophets can articulate laws that qualify as divine. But in what sense? Spinoza's first task is to explain.

It is clear from the narratives of the Old Testament that when God revealed laws to prophets such as Adam and Moses he did not reveal himself as the cause of the natural divine law, but rather as an anthropomorphic legislator. Adam, for example, failed to recognize that the divine decrees which constitute the natural divine law are necessary. He imagined a God who forbade him to eat of the tree of knowledge, but left him free to obey or disobey.[67] Equally, he did not realize that 'the highest reward of the law is the law itself' and lies in satisfactions intrinsic to realizing the highest good by knowing and loving God.[68] Rather, Adam's God threatened him with expulsion, 'as if he were a lawgiver or a prince'.[69] Moses, likewise, failed to perceive that God's decrees are eternal and therefore apply to all human beings.[70] This is reflected, for instance, in the fact that he represented the existence of God not as an eternal truth, but as the substance of a divine commandment issued to the Israelites, by which they alone were bound.

The explanation for these features of prophetic revelation, as we saw in Chapter 2, is that the prophets' insights were accommodated both to their own understanding and to the 'defective knowledge of the common people'.[71] Prophecy does not reveal the natural divine law and is not adapted to do so. Rather, it appeals to imagination in order to arouse wonder and devotion by representing causes as laws.[72] Viewed from the perspective of a philosophical understanding of God, prophetic revelation is bound to appear insufficient as a form of knowledge, and philosophers may consequently feel inclined to dismiss it. However, this is an attitude that Spinoza strongly resists. The prophets were in their different ways striving to formulate and convey the content of natural divine law; but because they could only grasp it in a form accommodated to their understanding and that of their peoples, they introduced local elements that vitiated its necessity and universality. Their revelations fell short of truths that philosophical reasoning can capture more fully, but they nevertheless gestured towards these truths in imaginative terms. As Calvin had expressed it, the Old Testament law 'contained the shadow of good things to come, not the living likeness of the things themselves'.[73]

---

[66] Ibid. ch. 4, p. 61.   [67] Ibid. ch. 4, p. 63.   [68] Ibid. ch. 4, p. 62.
[69] Ibid. ch. 4, p. 63.   [70] Ibid. ch. 4, p. 58.   [71] Ibid. ch. 4, p. 65.
[72] Ibid. ch. 6, pp. 90, 93.
[73] David Puckett, *John Calvin's Exegesis of the Old Testament* (Louisville: Westminster John Knox Press, 1995), ch. 2, p. 40.

The prophets' shadowy understanding of natural divine law gave them imaginative insight into aspects of the highest human good and enabled them to enact the divine law in Spinoza's other sense of the term. They prescribed ways of life that directly or indirectly encouraged the knowledge and love of God. In this sense, the laws they revealed are divine. Through revelation, for example, Moses 'perceived the way the people of Israel could best be united in a certain region of the world, and could form a whole society or set up a state, as well as the way that the people could best be compelled to obedience'.[74] The result was a secure and peaceful community in which the Jews were able, as both Calvin and Spinoza would put it, to grow up. However, Moses 'did not perceive, nor was it revealed to him, that this was the best way, nor even that the goal they were aiming at would necessarily follow from the general obedience of the people in that region of the world. Hence he did not perceive these things as eternal truths, but as precepts and things instituted, and he prescribed them as laws of God'.[75]

Interpreted in this way, the Bible supports Spinoza's conception of what it is to enact the divine law: it must be prescribed by human agents who have a sense of the highest human good, and one way to acquire such a sense is through prophetic revelation. This analysis is, however, set against the backdrop of the natural divine law. Whilst Scripture makes it plain that the moral precepts embedded in the laws of nature are not complicated, and can be made appealing by prophets, the only way to gain a full understanding of the sense in which they are decreed by God is through natural reasoning. The weight of Spinoza's argument therefore rests on the power and validity of natural reasoning as a means of decoding the natural divine law.

Searching for particular passages of Scripture that 'commend the natural light and the divine law', Spinoza first fixes on God's command to Adam.[76] This, he concedes, is difficult to interpret; but as far as he can see, the law that Adam was not to eat the fruit of the tree of knowledge amounts to an injunction to seek the good from love of the good and not from fear of evil, and 'contains the whole divine natural law and agrees absolutely with the dictate of the natural light'.[77] Clearer evidence can be found in Proverbs, where Solomon describes the human intellect as the fountain of true life.[78] Putting this passage together with others, we find that Solomon's teaching is familiar: 'our intellect and knowledge depend only on the idea or knowledge of God, arise from it, and

---

[74] Spinoza, *Tractatus Theologico-Politicus*, ch. 4, p. 64.   [75] Ibid.
[76] Ibid. ch. 4, p. 68.   [77] Ibid. ch. 4, p. 66.   [78] Proverbs 16:22.

are perfected by it alone'.[79] The Old Testament therefore confirms the position that Spinoza has already reached independently.

In the New Testament the point is made still clearer. According to the *Treatise*, the only biblical character who fully comprehended the natural divine law was Jesus Christ, who occupies a unique place in human history.[80] Despite the fact that the Scriptures sometimes represent him as a prophet who prescribed laws in the name of God, Christ's revelations were in fact of a quite different kind; for whereas the prophets' conceptions derived from their imaginations, his knowledge of God was unmediated by words or images. He understood God adequately and truly.[81] In fact, God's nature and decrees were so fully revealed to his mind that there is a sense in which 'we can say that God's wisdom . . . assumed a human nature in Christ'[82] and can conceive of him as the mouth of God.[83] Equipped with such perfect understanding, Christ was able to teach the divine law in its universal form. By contrast with the prophets, his mind 'was accommodated to the opinions and teachings universal to the human race, i.e. to common and true notions'.[84]

The theologians of the Reformed Church were fully committed to the doctrine that Christ taught the divine law in its universal form. But they would have been startled by the gloss Spinoza puts on it. His interpretation of Christ's teaching implies first of all that prophetic revelation is not the only way to come to know the divine law. By seeing past the local, imaginative contributions of the prophets, Christ was able to articulate the law as it applies to everyone. Because our imaginative ideas alone are inherently limited, he cannot have achieved this feat by imaginative means; and on the basis of what Spinoza has so far said, it seems that the only other available method is natural reasoning. Through the example of Christ, the New Testament makes it clear that reasoning can yield an understanding of the divine law.

There is, however, an interpretative puzzle to overcome. There is no biblical evidence that Christ steadily worked out the relations between one thing and another in the manner of a philosopher. If anything, he seems to have grasped the moral truths that follow from God's nature all at once. So rather than confirming the position that Spinoza has been at pains to expound, this aspect of Scripture seems to introduce yet another way of acquiring knowledge of God's decrees. In his *Short Treatise* Spinoza had described a form of 'clear

---

[79] Spinoza, *Tractatus Theologico-Politicus*, ch. 4, p. 67.   [80] Ibid. ch. 1, p. 21.
[81] Ibid. ch. 4, p. 64.   [82] Ibid. ch. 1, p. 21.   [83] Ibid. ch. 4, p. 64.
[84] Ibid. See Alexandre Matheron, *Le Christ et le salut des ignorants chez Spinoza* (Paris: Aubier Montaigne, 1971).

knowledge' that does not depend on testimony, on experience or even on reasoning, but is rather an immediate manifestation to the intellect of the object itself.[85] If the object of knowledge is good, he had added, it produces love. 'So if we come to know God in this way we must necessarily unite with him'.[86] Later on, writing in the *Ethics*, Spinoza characterizes what he calls *intuitive* knowledge as proceeding 'from an adequate idea of the formal essence of certain attributes of God to the adequate knowledge of the essences of things'.[87] Arguably, this is the superior kind of knowledge that Spinoza believes Christ to have possessed. Through intuition, Spinoza was able to articulate the tenets of the divine law that show us how to pursue our greatest good.

From the fact that someone is equipped with an intuitive grasp of the conclusions at which a philosophical reasoner can arrive by a more laborious route, it does not follow that they are incapable of spelling out the relationships they perceive, or teaching the truths they have attained. In the *Treatise*, Spinoza claims that the divine law was revealed to the Apostles through Christ's mind:[88] that is to say, Christ taught it to them. Here the *Treatise* tacitly rejects the *Belgic Confession*'s claim that the Apostles gained their knowledge from the Holy Spirit; but it remains to establish whether Christ taught them that the law can be understood by natural reasoning. Quoting Paul's *Letter to the Romans*, Spinoza argues that he did. When Paul remarks that 'God's hidden things, from the foundations of the world, are visible in his creatures through the intellect, and his power and divinity, which are to eternity', he indicates 'sufficiently clearly that everyone, by the natural light, clearly understands God's power and eternal divinity, from which he can know and deduce what he ought to pursue and what he ought to flee'.[89] By implication, then, Paul affirms that the natural light is capable of showing us what we ought above all to pursue, namely the knowledge and love of God.

According to Spinoza, a study of the Bible therefore supports the view that there are three different ways of coming to know what the divine law prescribes. You can either rely on the imaginative perceptions of the prophets, or else use natural reason to work out what the law aims at, or else grasp it by intuition. Although imagination on the one hand, and reason and intuition on the other, yield two different conceptions of the law, one local and the other

---

[85] Spinoza, *Short Treatise on God, Man, and His Well-Being* in *The Collected Works of Spinoza*, vol I, pt II, ch. 1.

[86] Ibid. Part II, ch. 22.

[87] Spinoza, *Ethics*, 2p40s2.

[88] Spinoza, *Tractatus Theologico-Politicus*, ch. 1, p. 21.

[89] Ibid. ch. 4, p. 68.

universal, each is directed to the same end, and captures our highest good as it is determined by the natural divine law. In each case God reveals himself, once through imagination, again through reason, and yet again through intuition. And because the results of all three methods of enquiry coincide, the imaginative sources that theologians study can be reconciled with the fruits of philosophical reasoning.

Defences of this type of view were not uncommon in seventeenth-century Holland;[90] but Spinoza's is deeply ambivalent in that it holds out concessions to Calvinist theology with one hand while snatching them away with the other. As we have seen, its insistence that philosophers can understand the law without appeal to Scripture was deeply problematic for Calvinists, who would not have found Spinoza's selective readings of Scripture compelling. Equally, his interpretation of the figure of Christ was from their point of view unsatisfactory. Although the *Treatise* contains an echo of Calvin's view that the Old Testament law is a shadow of things to come, Spinoza explicitly distances himself from 'the things that certain churches maintain about Christ'; and when read from a Calvinist perspective there is a disturbing amount that the *Treatise* fails to say.[91] Spinoza's Socinian Christ, for example, is not the son of God, nor does he intercede for human beings. In fact, beneath the concessive surface, Spinoza incorporates the figure of Christ into a conception of the divine law that brings it down to earth. When the prophets take themselves to be imposing laws made by God, it is they who make them in God's name. Christ's extraordinary mind enables him to articulate the universal law, but there is no indication that he is himself divine. And God himself does not make law in the manner of a legislator or prince. Insofar as divine laws can be broken, they are made by human beings, and the responsibility for them is entirely ours.

---

[90] Asselt, *Federal Theology*, ch. 3, Johannes Cocceius, *Summa theologiae ex scripturis repetita* (Amsterdam, 1669), ch. 46, §6.

[91] Spinoza, *Tractatus Theologico-Politicus*, ch. 1, p. 21.

Chapter 5

Worship

To follow the divine law we must live in a way that promotes our highest good, the knowledge and love of God. But what does that mean in practice? Should we devote ourselves to the project of extending our understanding of God by reasoning philosophically about the natural world, ourselves, or the deity? Should we take our lead from Scripture and enter into a religion organized around rites and ceremonies? Or are these only two of many ways of life that can meet the requirements of the divine law?

Within the United Provinces these questions were highly charged, and in setting out to answer them Spinoza cannot avoid the controversies they had aroused. As he begins to spell out the practical implications of his analysis of law, he enters into two debates: one about whether the divine law requires us to observe ceremonies, and thus whether doing so is necessary for salvation; the other about the role of biblical narratives in a pious way of life. Having discussed these issues, Spinoza announces that he has said everything he wants to say about the divine law; but it seems that he has not after all quite finished. With a further flourish, he seeks to destroy one more dogma by showing that the divine law is not affirmed by miracles as these are generally understood.

Ceremonies, narratives, and miracles are disparate themes, and each raises problems of its own. However, they are linked in Spinoza's mind by the fact that all three have given rise to controversies which threaten the proper understanding of the way of life that the divine law prescribes. In the debates surrounding them, an imaginative conception of God gets out of hand and creates a distorted picture of the law, which is then used, whether self-consciously or not, for nefarious religious or political ends. Needless to say, superstition enters into this process, so that in criticizing its manifestations Spinoza is simultaneously identifying practices that purport to be pious, but are in fact ways of displacing and manipulating fear. Having rejected the notion of a God who imposes his laws on human beings with the help of threats and promises, the *Treatise* now begins to examine the consequences of this move for everyday religious practice.

Ceremonies: their character

Within the Dutch Reformed Church, and indeed many other Protestant confessions where the Bible was regarded as the single key to true religion, ceremonies were a fraught issue.[1] Everyone agreed that they could sometimes be harmful. For example, it is obvious from the Old Testament that they become idolatrous and lead people into sin when they divert the devotion that should be reserved for God to some undeserving object, such as the golden calf worshipped by the ancient Jews.[2] One can catch a sense of the horror with which the Reformers viewed this danger from Calvin's condemnation of animal sacrifice. 'What is more vain and absurd', he had asked, 'than for men to offer a loathsome stench from the fat of cattle in order to reconcile themselves to God?... The whole *cultus* of the law, taken literally and not as shadows and figures corresponding to the truth, will be utterly ridiculous'.[3] Worship must not be ridiculous. So it is vital to distinguish the forms and ceremonies of the ancient law that were adapted to the particular needs of the Jews from the true demands of the divine law that are concealed within them. And there's the rub. How does one separate these genuine demands from their outward forms? In Calvin's view, Roman Catholics who think that music is conducive to piety and use it in church services are 'behaving like apes', implementing a law made not for them but for the Levites of the ancient Hebrew state.[4] Everything depends on where one draws the line between ceremonies that the divine law requires or condones, and ceremonies that are detrimental to religious life.

In some cases, the Dutch Reformed Church found the distinction easy to make. The Second Commandment, it claimed, clearly rules out the use of images in worship and ritual.[5] Equally, there were good reasons for observing

---

[1] Benjamin J. Kaplan, *Calvinists and Libertines: Confession and Community in Utrecht, 1578–1620* (Oxford: Clarendon Press, 1995).

[2] Exodus 32.

[3] Jean Calvin, *Institutes of the Christian Religion*, ed. and trans. John Thomas McNeill and Ford Lewis Battles, *The Library of Christian Classics* (Philadelphia, Pa.: Westminster Press, 1960–1), II. vii.1.

[4] David Puckett, *John Calvin's Exegesis of the Old Testament* (Louisville: Westminster John Knox Press, 1995), p. 41.

[5] Simon Episcopius, *The Confession or Declaration of the Ministers or Pastors Which in the United Provinces Are Called Remonstrants, Concerning the Chief Points of Christian Religion*, trans. Thomas Taylor (London, 1676), p. 158; 'The Heidelberg Catechism', in *The Creeds of Christendom: The Evangelical Protestant Creeds*, ed. Philip Schaff (New York: Cosimo Books, 2007), Q98.

the Fourth Commandment, 'Remember the Sabbath Day and keep it holy'. As Calvin had explained, the original purpose of the Sabbath was to nominate a time when the Jews could be trained in piety and obedience to the law, and at the same time to provide a day of rest from worldly work, symbolizing the spiritual rest that the Messiah would bring. But once Christ had taught that believers are bound to devote themselves to God not just one day in seven but the whole time, the commandment's significance altered. The Sabbath still continues to provide an occasion for believers to gather together and take part in various salutary rites. Equally, it continues to provide servants and workmen with a day of rest.[6] But the attention of Calvinist congregations is not meant to stop at these observances, which are intended to help them live in accordance with the universal law by committing them, internally as well as externally, to knowing and loving God. Ceremonies, then, can be 'ladders by which the faithful might ascend to heaven'.[7] Their value and significance is also affirmed in the New Testament, where Christ himself instituted two ritual practices, baptism and the Lord's Supper. These sacraments of the Reformed Church are 'visible signs and seals of an inward and invisible thing, by means whereof God worketh in us by the power of the Holy Ghost', and administering these 'ceremonies' is one of the marks by which the true Church is known.[8] In addition, there are a number of other practices such as public Bible reading and prayer which, though not instituted by Christ, nevertheless contribute to order and decency within the Church.[9]

Unfortunately, the conviction that the primary function of ceremonies is to encourage piety and to unite believers in the Church left plenty of room for disagreement about which particular practices were adapted to these ends, and by the middle of the seventeenth century this uncertainty had crystallized into a range of specific disputes. The more moderate theologians took a comparatively relaxed attitude to ceremonies, including the Sabbath. As Cocceius and his followers argued, going to church on Sundays is one of the ways in which Christian communities habitually testify to their own unity and their friendship with God, but one can be a true believer without doing so.[10] However, in the

---

[6]   Calvin, *Institutes*, II.viii.32.

[7]   Puckett, *Calvin's Exegesis*, pp. 38–40.

[8]   'The Belgic Confession', in *The Creeds of Christendom: The Evangelical Protestant Creeds*, ed. Philip Schaff (New York: Cosimo Books, 2007), Articles 33, 29.

[9]   Episcopius, *Confession*, pp. 243–4.

[10]   Wiep van Bunge, *From Stevin to Spinoza: An Essay on Philosophy in the Seventeenth-Century Dutch Republic* (Leiden: Brill, 2001), p. 54. See, for instance, Abraham Heidanus, *Eenige Stellingen Aengaende den Rust-Dagh en den Dagh des Heeren . . . uyt het Latijn Vertaelt* (Utrecht, 1658).

eyes of stricter theologians such as Voetius this was a deeply irresponsible position. It implicitly denied that the substance of the Old Law survives in the New, thus amounting to a form of antinomianism. Still worse, it drastically underrated the Church's responsibility to encourage and admonish its members. Since the law taught by Christ demands obedience in every aspect of our lives, the Church has a duty to ensure that its members practise it exactly 'as taught by God, and genuinely accepted, intended, and desired by believers'.[11] To achieve this, however, it must impose a much more rigorous disciplinary regime than the one proposed by Cocceius and his followers.

This outlook was known in the United Provinces as precisionism. While its advocates held the standard view that the divine law is written on the fleshly tables of the heart,[12] they were profoundly impressed by the concupiscence of fallen man and convinced that, unless people were reminded of their religious duties at every turn, they would fall into sin. To avert this fate, the Church needed to set out the precise demands of a godly life and ensure that they were strictly imposed, by requiring salutary practices and banning any that might encourage superstition and idolatry. From the 1640s, precisionism had a strong hold over orthodox theologians, who duly opposed what they regarded as a range of impious activities, including gambling, drinking, going to the theatre, dancing, cock-fighting, and lending money at interest. They tried to enforce observation of the Sabbath, to outlaw organ music in church, and to ban the use of incense and candles at funerals. And they did their best to impose a range of further restrictions, such as requiring men to cut their hair above the ears and to wear long collars.[13]

---

[11] Gisbertus Voetius, 'Concerning "Precision" in Interpretation of Questions 94, 113, and 115 of the [Heidelberg] Catechism', in *Reformed Dogmatics: J. Wollebius, G. Voetius, F. Turretin*, ed. John Walter Beardslee (Oxford: Oxford University Press, 1965), p. 317. This and others of Voetius' works in this selection by Beardslee come from Volume III of Gisbertus Voetius, *Disputationes Theologicae Selectae*, 5 vols. (Utrecht, 1648–69).

[12] II Corinthians 3:3.

[13] The question of hair length became fraught when the Voetian supporter Jacob Borstius delivered sermons in the 1640s about the dangers of wearing long hair (Bunge, *From Stevin to Spinoza*, p. 74.) According to Voetius, such apparently trivial matters can very quickly add up to something very important: 'If there is any little thing, with the smallest evil, in anyone's life; for example the vanity of hairdressing, or of religious syncretism, or superstitious worship, or some other 'little thing', as it is called, straightway it becomes a great concern for mind and conscience. If [its significance] is denied, then someone asks about adding a second 'little thing', a third person a third matter, a fourth a fourth, and so on, and one learns to carry this burden of conscience, just as Milo went on carrying his calf after it had become a bull'. Gisbert Voetius, 'Concerning Practical Theology', in *Reformed Dogmatics: J. Wollebius, G. Voetius, F. Turretin*, ed. John Walter Beardslee (Oxford: Oxford University Press, 1965), pp. 278–9.

These efforts renewed and intensified a set of longstanding feuds both within the Church and between Church and state. The leniency of some influential theologians such as Cocceius gave the Voetians a fresh position to argue against, and added urgency to their efforts to impose precisionism. At the same time, it fuelled their political disputes with the States of Holland. As we saw in Chapter 1, religious and political factions in the United Provinces were closely aligned. Broadly speaking, theologians who were keen to reconcile Calvinist theology with Cartesian philosophy favoured and were protected by the republican States party, while the supporters of the Voetians looked for support to the party of the Stadtholder. During the early 1650s, when the Stadtholder's party had been temporarily worsted and the States were led by De Witt, the Church's orthodox faction became a centre of opposition to the government. Threatened by what it regarded as De Witt's excessively tolerant attitude to religious diversity, and by the arrival of a wave of Polish Socinian immigrants, it again began to demand that the state should provide greater support for its policies, and marshalled its preachers to uphold this claim in their sermons.[14] De Witt's negotiations with these critics ranged over a number of issues, some of which concerned the Church's authority to ban, shape, or impose religious ceremonies.[15] On the whole he kept the precisionists at bay and maintained an environment in which people were comparatively free to worship as they wished. But by the time the *Treatise* came to be written, De Witt's power was in decline. Spinoza addresses a situation in which the Church's efforts to police the use of ceremonies had ceased to be a joke and needed to be rigorously disputed.

Spinoza is a stern critic of precisionism, and sets out to defend a point of view that has strong affinities with that of Cocceius and his followers: while ceremonies can promote unity and piety, they are not essential to religious life. Pressing this attitude to its limit, Spinoza argues that the way of life prescribed by the divine law does not require any ceremonial practices at all. 'They cannot be counted among the actions which are, as it were, the offspring or fruits of the intellect and of a healthy mind'.[16] To see that the divine law is indifferent to

---

[14] Herbert H. Rowen, *John De Witt, Grand Pensionary of Holland, 1625–1672* (Princeton: Princeton University Press, 1978), p. 439.

[15] For instance, towards the end of 1659 the Voetians began publicly attacking the right of the Cocceians to conduct church services in a way that was, from the Voetian point of view, unorthodox. Soon the States of Holland, led by De Witt, ordered the synods and the Theology Faculty of Leiden to stop writing about this topic. Ibid. p. 425.

[16] Benedictus de Spinoza, *Tractatus Theologico-Politicus*, ed. Carl Gebhardt, vol. III, *Opera* (Heidelberg: Carl Winter, 1924), ch. 4, p. 62.

rites and rituals, it is enough to remind ourselves that we can come to understand its precepts by means of a capacity for reasoning that is, 'as it were, written in our minds'.[17] Since all human beings have the ability to reason, and thus in principle possess the means to arrive at a correct grasp of the divine law by a method in which ceremonies play no part, it must be possible to follow the law without their help. Furthermore, since we know through reasoning exactly what the law recommends (namely that we should devote ourselves to knowing and loving God), it is clear that the law itself does not impose any ceremonial observances on us, or represent them as essential conditions of blessedness.

It remains true, of course, that most of us need to be encouraged to understand and follow the law, and that ceremonies can play a part in this process. But while Spinoza agrees that this is so, he denies that it has any bearing on his immediate argument. Because ceremonies appeal to the imagination, they need to be adapted to the imaginative habits and experience of individual communities.[18] The natural light, by contrast, enables us to transcend this localized variety of thought and feeling, and to arrive at universal insights applicable to everyone.[19] By this means, we can come to understand what constitutes the supreme good of all human beings.[20] If the divine law were to require us to observe particular ceremonies, these would inevitably be suited to some communities rather than others, and would compromise its universality. Ceremonies therefore cannot be part of the divine law.

If this philosophical argument fails to convince, the same conclusion can be derived from the Bible.[21] Careful examination of the text reveals that the prophets drew a clear distinction between divine and civil law. Because civil laws are designed for people whose obedience cannot be counted on, they have to be backed up by sanctions; and because civil laws aim to secure various worldly benefits, these sanctions are temporal. Civil legislators get people to obey the civil law by threatening them with external punishments and offering them external benefits. By contrast, sanctions play no part in the divine law, and the only benefits it brings are the internal ones that contribute to blessedness. The fact that the prophets often dwell on the internal satisfaction of blessedness when teaching the divine law makes it clear that they grasp this fact. They appreciate that this is the only benefit that divine law yields, and that temporal penalties and advantages relate to civil laws alone. Hence, we find

---

[17] Ibid. ch. 5, p. 69. [18] Ibid. ch. 5, p. 73.
[19] Ibid. ch. 4, p. 61. [20] Ibid.
[21] Ibid. ch. 5, p. 70.

Moses treating the observation of ceremonies as part of the civil code and imposing external penalties on people who break laws about ritual. If he had wanted to teach his people that observing ceremonies was relevant to true blessedness, he would have condemned 'not only the external action, but also the consenting of the mind, as Christ did'.[22] The same applies to the other prophets. So, at least in the Old Testament, there is no textual evidence for the view that practising ceremonies is necessary in order to attain blessedness.

Like Cocceius, and for that matter like the precisionists, Spinoza does not deny that ceremonies and rites can serve a variety of useful ends. They can promote a way of life that accords with the divine law by fostering conditions in which people are better placed to know and love God, and can help to bind communities together.[23] Against the precisionists, however, he insists that these are social functions, which have no direct bearing on the practice of true religion. Spinoza's clearest articulation of this point comes in his discussion of circumcision and its relation to the survival of the Jewish people. As we have seen, he has rejected the view that the Jews survived because God chose them to eternity. He now goes on to argue that the explanation of their continuing unity as a people lies partly in the purely social practice of circumcision. 'I think the sign of circumcision is so important in this matter that I am persuaded that it will preserve the Nation to eternity'.[24] It exerts such a binding force on Jews that it is comparable, so Spinoza claims, to the Chinese pigtail, which both identifies individuals as members of a particular nation and separates them from everyone else. The social convention of wearing a pigtail has enabled the Chinese to 'preserve themselves for so many thousands of years that they surpass all other nations in antiquity'.[25] And on account of circumcision, it remains possible that the Jews will one day re-establish their state (*imperium*).[26] Spinoza's grasp of Chinese history leaves something to be desired, but what matters here is his insistence that ceremonies can exert great power in holding people together while being completely independent of true religion. They can reinforce the imagined identities of particular communities, but are irrelevant to the way of life prescribed by the divine law. Giving up circumcision would

---

[22] Ibid.   [23] Ibid. ch. 5, p. 73.

[24] Ibid. ch. 3, p. 57.

[25] Ibid. Moreau's commentary on this section states that this was an error, and that the pigtail was imposed on the Chinese by the Manchurian dynasty in 1644. Benedictus de Spinoza, *Traité Théologico-Politique*, ed. Fokke Akkerman, Jacqueline Lagrée, and Pierre-François Moreau, vol. 3, *Œuvres de Spinoza* (Paris: Presses Universitaires de France, 1999), p. 722.

[26] Spinoza, *Tractatus Theologico-Politicus*, ch. 3, p. 57.

probably have a profound sociological effect on the Jews and damage their unity as a people; but it would not be irreligious in the sense of contravening the divine law.

Spinoza is genuinely interested in exploring a range of factors that have either enabled Jews to merge with other communities or kept them apart, and contrasts the experiences of Sephardic Jews in Spain and Portugal. Although the historical evidence he cites is decidedly odd, the issue would undoubtedly have been much debated by the *marranos* among whom he grew up.[27] However, his remarks about circumcision have a further significance. According to both the Reformed Church and the Arminian creed, Christ abolished circumcision and replaced it with the sacrament of baptism.[28] 'By a certain analogy (i.e. proportion or likeness) [baptism] doth not unaptly answer unto the sign of circumcision, which under the Old Testament was a sign of sacred initiation (i.e. entrance) . . . into the people of God'.[29] By arguing that circumcision is not essential to a religious way of life, Spinoza allows his readers to draw the same conclusion about baptism, and indeed about both the Calvinist sacraments. As he elsewhere explains more explicitly, 'As for the ceremonies of the Christians, viz., baptism, the lord's supper, festivals, public prayers, and whatever others there may be in addition which are and always have been common to all Christianity, if Christ or the Apostles instituted these (which so far I do not find to be sufficiently established) they were instituted only as external signs of the universal church, and not as things which contribute to blessedness'.[30] Despite the Reformed Church's view that all its doctrine is derived from Scripture, there need be nothing irreligious about a life entirely devoid of ceremonies, sacraments included, and in order to assess the value of ceremonial practices we need to consider their consequences.

Taking up this point, Spinoza now expounds some of the damaging effects that ceremonies can have, not only on the integrity of religion but also on the

---

[27] Ibid. ch. 3, p. 56. Spinoza suggests that Jews assimilated more readily in Spain than in Portugal because 'all the privileges of native Spaniards were granted to those who accepted that religion' whereas 'just the opposite happened to those whom the King of Portugal compelled to accept the religion of his state'. This analysis is generally thought to be incorrect. For a more reliable analysis of the history of the *Marranos*, see Renée Levine Melammed, *A Question of Identity: Iberian Conversos in Historical Perspective* (Oxford: Oxford University Press, 2004), 76ff. and *passim*. On discussions of this question by *Marranos* among Spinoza's contemporaries, Moreau cites Philippus van Limborch and Baltasar Oróbio De Castro, *De veritate religionis Christianæ, amica collatio cum erudito Judæo* (Gouda, 1687), p. 89.

[28] 'The Belgic Confession', Article 33.

[29] Episcopius, *Confession*, p. 238.

[30] Spinoza, *Tractatus Theologico-Politicus*, ch. 5, p. 76.

state. Developing this view, he allows his readers to infer that, if religious ceremonies were to be imposed in the way that precisionists recommend, the republican form of liberty for which the Dutch had fought would be bound to suffer. Rather than making this case outright, Spinoza draws a series of analogies between the Hebrew state under Moses, the Ottoman Empire, and the Dutch Republic of his own day. This step marks a crucial transition in the overall argument of the *Treatise*. Until now, the text has been concerned with a sequence of theological disputes, each of which bears on the connected problems from which Spinoza began: the need to resist the corrupting force of superstition, and the need to show that theology does not cramp the style of philosophical investigation or vice versa. Although the debates so far discussed have a range of political implications, these have not yet risen to the surface. Now, for the first time, Spinoza attacks the religious commitments of his opponents on overtly political grounds, arguing that they have destructive political consequences. In doing so, he begins to connect the freedom to philosophize with political liberty, and to open up the political dimension of superstition. These themes, like the historical resources on which he begins to draw, will occupy him throughout the rest of his work.

Ceremonies: their use and abuse

To delve more deeply into the political use and abuse of ceremonies, Spinoza sets out to examine the role they played in preserving and stabilizing the Hebrew state. For Calvinists this was familiar territory; but before launching into a detailed analysis of the role of ritual, Spinoza sets the scene by providing a general account of the purposes that states are meant to serve and the benefits that should flow from them. How better to focus his readers' attention on this issue than to start with Hobbes's account of a state-less condition, a state of nature in which life is, as the Latin version of *Leviathan* puts it, *indigna* as well as *bruta*?[31] Echoing this memorable description, Spinoza identifies two conditions that must be met if humans are to avoid an existence that is *paene brutali* (almost brutish).[32] They must live in societies where labour is divided; and they must submit to rule (*imperium*) and consequently to law.[33] If, *per impossibile*, people

---

[31] Thomas Hobbes, *Thomæ Hobbes Malmesburiensis opera philosophica quæ Latine scripsit, omnia . . .* (Amsterdam, 1668), VIII.65, ch. 13.

[32] Spinoza, *Tractatus Theologico-Politicus*, ch. 5, p. 73.

[33] Ibid. ch. 5, p. 74.

were entirely rational, they would voluntarily obey the law for their own good; but as things are, legislation needs to be backed up by the threat of punishment.

While we know from experience that coercive government can be moderately effective, it also carries risks. When people obey the law only out of fear, they will do everything they can to thwart their rulers,[34] so that sovereigns who terrorize their subjects into submission cannot be altogether secure, and live under permanent threat of rebellion. There are, however, better ways to govern. One is to form the kind of state that Spinoza will later describe as a democracy, in which the community as a whole holds sovereignty, and each citizen plays a part in making the law. In a democratic community where laws are enacted by common consent, a citizen who obeys them follows rules that he himself has made, and therefore does not subject himself to the will of anyone else. This in turn guarantees a form of political liberty. In circumstances where everyone acts on their own authority, the notion of obeying the law has no application, and however many laws the community makes, each citizen remains, as Spinoza puts it, 'equally free'.[35] A further option is to award sovereignty to an individual or group whose extraordinary qualities enable them to win the loyalty of the people. This form of government also overcomes the disadvantages that arise when a sovereign rules by fear. Under such governments, however, the freedom of citizens to act as their own will dictates is reduced. And because this is something they are liable to resent, even exceptionally charismatic leaders may find it difficult to retain their authority.[36]

With this constitutional typology in hand, Spinoza turns to consider the ancient Hebrew state. This focus on what may seem an arbitrarily chosen case is partly explained and justified by his concern to show that his conclusions accord with Scripture. However, as we shall see, comparisons between the divinely ordained state of the Jews and the modern states in which Spinoza and his contemporaries lived were a staple of political debate.[37] In the Dutch case, a number of writers had exploited the analogy in order to cast an aura of divinity over the United Provinces, and in his own way Spinoza is about to follow suit.

---

[34] Ibid.

[35] Ibid. This conception of liberty is important to Spinoza's overall position and will be discussed at greater length later in the *Treatise*. On the republican tradition to which it belongs, see Martin van Gelderen, *The Political Thought of the Dutch Revolt, 1555–1590* (Cambridge: Cambridge University Press, 1992); Quentin Skinner, *Liberty before Liberalism* (Cambridge: Cambridge University Press, 1998).

[36] Spinoza, *Tractatus Theologico-Politicus*, ch. 5, p. 74.

[37] See Chapter 11.

To appreciate the character of the Hebrew state, we need to remember that it was founded by a people who had just escaped from slavery and had no experience of government. 'Almost all of them were crude in their understanding (*ingenium*) and weakened by wretched bondage'.[38] Since they lacked the capacity to hold sovereignty collectively, and as Spinoza puts it were unable to exercise collective right (*jus*),[39] their only option was to invest sovereignty in a group or individual who possessed the ability to make and enforce the law. Moses' prophetic power equipped him for this task, but like any other ruler, he needed to find an effective way to make the Jewish people obey the laws he ordained, the more so because they would not allow themselves to be coerced by force alone, and were also under threat of war. Rather than trading on their fears, Moses 'took the greatest care that the people should do its duty spontaneously (*sponte*)' and found several ways of creating willing obedience.[40] By enacting laws in the name of God and thus introducing religion into the state, he ensured that his people's devotion to the deity was extended to the law itself. Religion and politics, along with the passions they evoked, became inseparable. He also made sure that his laws were not too demanding, and promised benefits in return for obedience, once again in the name of God. Finally, he ensured that the law governed every aspect of life, so that people 'were not permitted to eat, dress, shave, rejoice or do anything at all, except in accordance with order and commandments prescribed in the laws'.[41]

As this description makes clear, Moses was the original precisionist, the creator of a regime in which there was a ceremonial way to perform even the most ordinary actions, and in which people were made conscious of their duty to obey the law at each and every moment of their waking lives. Through the medium of ceremony, devotion to God was translated into devotion to law, and thus into willing submission. This strategy succeeded in creating a secure and enduring state. However, as Spinoza goes on to point out, the obedience of the Jewish people was bought at a price. The law guaranteed that the people could not act 'according to their own wills (*decreta*) but only according to the command of someone else, and that, in their actions and reflections, they acknowledged that they were not subject to their own right in anything, but entirely subject to the right of another'.[42] Although Moses achieved his political goal, he was only able to do so by completely depriving his subjects of any part in legislating either the civil or the divine law.

---

[38] Spinoza, *Tractatus Theologico-Politicus*, ch. 5, p. 75.   [39] Ibid.
[40] Ibid.   [41] Ibid.   [42] Ibid.

The kind of political freedom that comes from making rather than submitting to law was vital to the broadly republican conception of political liberty upheld by De Witt and the States party during the 1650s and 1660s. As this view held, and as Spinoza has just explained in his account of collective sovereignty, one can possess the status of a free man only if one imposes the law on oneself.[43] For anyone who values this kind of liberty, the Jews' total subjection to the law will be politically and morally repugnant. Even if Moses' form of government was the best available at the time, his people were unfree. Their devotion to the law ensured that they did not have to be forced to follow it, so that their actions were free in the sense of uncoerced. But by virtue of their submission to a law that they had not determined for themselves, they lacked the status of free men. Furthermore, and here we return to the point at issue, insofar as their devotion was enhanced by ceremonial observances, ceremonies played a central part in creating and maintaining their servitude.

In the Preface to the *Tractatus*, Spinoza associates this form of government with Turkish despotism, and contrasts it with the political life of a free commonwealth. As he there explains, one of the techniques used by despotic regimes is to encourage the people to fear God rather than the sovereign, 'so that they will fight for slavery as they would for freedom'.[44] While Spinoza does not directly compare Moses with the Ottoman Sultan, the analogy is nevertheless implicit, serving as a powerful reminder of the damage that ceremonies can do to freedom once they become enshrined in law. Moses, so Spinoza seems to imply, was a benign despot who did what was best in the circumstances. He did not rule by fear, and is thus exonerated from the charge of resorting to superstition. But he used ceremonies to help arouse devotion to a system of laws that secured temporal benefits at the cost of making his people 'hang on the words of their ruler'.[45] By contrast, the Ottoman sultans are wicked despots who employ religious ceremonies to foster superstition, thereby furthering their own interests at their subjects' expense.

The fact that ceremonies can be used for good or ill embodies a vital political lesson. When Voetian Calvinists urge the Dutch States to enforce religious rituals such as the observance of the Sabbath, their intentions are not necessarily benign. They may be using the dynamics of fear to impose a distorted

---

[43] On this conception of political liberty, see also Chapter 11. On its relation to the conception of personal freedom that Spinoza develops in the *Ethics*, see Susan James, 'Freedom, Slavery and the Passions', in *The Cambridge Companion to Spinoza's Ethics*, ed. Olli Koistinen (Cambridge: Cambridge University Press, 2009).

[44] Spinoza, *Tractatus Theologico-Politicus*, Preface, p. 7.

[45] Ibid. ch. 5, p. 75.

understanding of the divine law, and encouraging the belief that it requires one to observe ceremonies over which the Church exercises control. They may also be trying to bring about a form of sovereignty incompatible with political liberty. (When citizens are made subject to laws that they have not prescribed for themselves, they become unfree.) Finally, if the state were to co-operate with the Church to create a situation in which popular religious devotion enabled the Church to realize its sectarian interests, a free republic might degenerate into a despotism.

Ceremonies therefore need to be treated cautiously. Since they play no part in the divine law, they are not intrinsic to a way of life devoted to the highest good, knowing and loving God. Rather, they are local institutions, sometimes made compulsory by civil legislation as was the case with the Mosaic commandment to observe the Sabbath. In this form they can serve the useful function of encouraging a way of life that promotes a flourishing state, along with the temporal advantages it brings. They can help to generate political loyalty, solidarity, and devotion to the law; and ceremonies authorized by a civil legislator can encourage devotion to God, so that politics becomes a simultaneously theological enterprise. Wise sovereigns will appreciate the harms and benefits to which ceremonies can give rise and will legislate accordingly. But whatever role they play in political or theologico-political life, ceremonies are only imposed by a particular civil jurisdiction, and otherwise exert no claim on us. For example, the Dutch state might decree that men should cut their hair above the ears if its legislators thought that this would somehow have beneficial consequences. But no such measures are required by the divine law.

As Spinoza pauses to point out, this outlook is increasingly reflected in Dutch political practice.[46] At the beginning of the seventeenth century, the Japanese had forbidden members of the Dutch East India Company to practise Christian ceremonies on Japanese territory, and in order to maintain its trading post off Nagasaki, the Company had had to agree that its members would abide by Japanese law. When this came to be known in Holland, at least one Church synod protested; but the Company's decision was upheld, and it was generally accepted that, when in Nagasaki, Dutchmen did not have to publicly practise their religion in order to count as faithful Calvinists.[47] Ceremonies

---

[46] Ibid. ch. 5, p. 76.

[47] Christianity was banned in Japan in 1614. This became an issue for the Dutch in the 1640s, when the Dutch East India Company passed an ordinance against public Christian worship at its trading post on the island of Deshima near Nagasaki. When this news reached the Netherlands, at

were dispensable. The same conclusion was endorsed by religious movements within Holland such as the Collegiants and Quakers, who eschewed all but the most minimal ceremonial practices and devised forms of worship adapted to their own beliefs. Spinoza's argument defends this kind of pluralism in the face of a precisionist desire to impose elaborate and uniform ceremonial practices, and in doing so defends both religious and political liberty.

Biblical narratives

As Spinoza has so far presented it, learning about the divine law is an intellectual project. To act in accordance with the supreme good one must first understand it by coming to know God, and in the process strengthening one's love for him. Whether or not the readers of the *Tractatus* agreed with this analysis, they would have been quick to see that it appears to have two troubling implications. First, since understanding the divine law requires a good deal of philosophical know-how, it seems to be a privilege of the learned. Second, as we have seen, Spinoza's account seems to make the Bible entirely dispensable. Needless to say, these claims could not possibly have been accepted by the Reformed Church, and as Spinoza's argument develops, it emerges that he does not in fact endorse either of them himself. He therefore needs to set the record straight by explaining what role the Bible plays in teaching the divine law. He places this discussion against a background assumption that he and the Reformed Church shared, that whatever the complexities involved in interpreting the Bible's more abstruse claims, it is a fundamentally didactic work whose central doctrines are hard to miss. Moreover, because its message is accommodated to the understanding of ordinary people, more or less anyone can use it to grasp the precepts of the divine law, together with the truths about God and the good life that enable one to follow them. A reliable way to learn about the divine law is therefore to read or listen to the Bible.

Spinoza approaches this assumption obliquely and in a philosophical register by asking how one could in principle persuade someone of the fundamental philosophical truths that Scripture contains. How, for example, could you enable them to understand that there is a God who directs and sustains the world with supreme wisdom?[48] The surest method would be deduce the truths

---

least one synod of the Reformed Church complained, and a debate ensued. See Carl Gebhardt, *Kommentar zum Tractatus Theologico-Politicus*, ed. Carl Gebhardt, vol. V, *Opera* (Heidelberg: Carl Winter, 1987), pp. 24–7; Spinoza, *Traité Théologico-Politique*, p. 728.

[48] Spinoza, *Tractatus Theologico-Politicus*, ch. 5, p. 77.

in question from self-evident axioms; but because following a chain of clear and distinct ideas is a laborious business and requires exceptional circumspection, sensitivity, and self-control, this mode of argument will only convince people who are already comparatively learned.[49] A more widely applicable technique is to appeal to imagination or experience (*experientia*).[50] For although this approach cannot establish conclusions with mathematical certainty, it can provide a level of confirmation quite sufficient for non-philosophical purposes. The best way to teach the divine law to ordinary people is therefore to appeal to their experience. And since the Bible is full of narratives, parables, and imagery that are the stuff of experiential or imaginative thought, it is clearly adapted to this purpose. Revealed as it was for the use of a whole nation, and then for the entire human race, it offers an accessible, figurative account of the divine law which can be used to teach ordinary people what the law consists in and kindle their desire to live in the manner that it recommends. 'If Scripture were to relate the destruction of some state in the way the political historians usually do', Spinoza comments, 'that would not stir up the common people at all. But if it depicts things poetically and refers them to God, as it usually does, it will move them very much'.[51]

The key narratives of Scripture therefore 'teach and enlighten men enough to imprint obedience and devotion on their hearts', and knowledge of them is 'necessary for ordinary people who are not able to perceive things clearly and distinctly'.[52] One of the Bible's central functions is to make the divine law available to communities who would not otherwise have access to it. Furthermore, because the common people are not in a position to pick out the most important biblical narratives for themselves, and may not be able to understand them without help, they need ministers to teach them.[53] So although it is possible to come to understand the divine law by means of natural reason and without the help of Scripture, and although anyone who does so 'is completely blessed, and indeed more blessed than ordinary people, because, in addition to true opinions he has a clear and distinct conception',[54] the Bible and biblical instruction are in practice indispensable.

Spinoza may thus be said to agree with the claim of the *Belgic Confession* that 'there must be ministers or pastors to preach the word of God'.[55] This concession aligns him with at least a part of the Reformed Church's doctrine,

---

[49] Ibid. [50] Ibid. [51] Ibid. ch. 6, p. 91.
[52] Ibid. ch. 5, pp. 77–8. [53] Ibid. ch. 5, p. 79.
[54] Ibid. ch. 5, p. 78.
[55] 'The Belgic Confession', Article 30.

and separates him on one point from the principles of the Collegiant movement to which so many of his friends belonged. The Collegiants had no ministers or pastors, and met as equals to study the Bible. They offered a model of religious life that Spinoza does not discuss, in which the divine law is learned through Scripture without the assistance of experts or hierarchy. To be sure, the members of the movement were not on the whole drawn from the 'common people'; many of them were highly educated, and as a group presumably did not need to be told which biblical narratives to concentrate on. They therefore represent a transitional way of life, somewhere between the official biblical instruction that Spinoza here defends, and philosophical study of the divine law in which authority derives from the clarity and distinctness of one's own ideas.

As we saw in Chapter 4, the question of whether one needs to be familiar with Scripture in order to know the divine law in a manner that will enable one to be saved remained contested in the United Provinces during Spinoza's lifetime, and any discussion of the issue was bound to evoke differences between the Voetians and their various enemies. The position Spinoza has set out is clearly at odds with the Voetian view that one cannot come to know the divine law without the help of Scripture, and also contradicts Cocceius's more moderate claim that the Bible is the best and easiest way to learn the law. However, it would have been rash of Spinoza openly to contradict these authorities, and rather than doing so he directs his criticisms against the twelfth-century rabbi, Moses Maimonides, together with his fifteenth-century successor, Rabbi Joseph. Commentators have rightly objected that Spinoza's interpretation of these authors is misleading,[56] but at this point interpretative

---

[56] A number of scholars have argued that Maimonides' view is in fact much subtler than Spinoza acknowledges, and that Spinoza may well have been aware of this fact. If so, this may lend weight to the suggestion that Maimonides is standing in for Meijer, and Spinoza is not particularly concerned to get him right. See Jacqueline Lagrée, 'Louis Meyer et la *Philosophia S. Scripturae Interpretes*. Projet Cartésien, Horizon Spinoziste', *Revue des sciences philosophiques et théologiques*, 1 (1987); Jacqueline Lagrée, 'Sense et Vérité: Philosophie et théologie chez L. Meyer et Spinoza', *Studia Spinozana*, 4 (1988); Jacqueline Lagrée and Pierre-François Moreau, 'La lecture de la Bible dans le cercle de Spinoza', in *Le grand siècle et la Bible*, ed. Jean-Robert Armogathe (Paris: Beauchesne, 1989); Pierre Macherey, 'Louis Meyer, Interprète de l'écriture', in *Avec Spinoza: Études sur la doctrine et l'histoire du Spinozisme* (Paris: Presses Universitaires de France, 1992); Warren Montag, *Bodies, Masses, Power* (London: Verso, 1999), ch. 1; Pierre-François Moreau, 'Les principes de la lecture de l'écriture sainte dans le *Tractatus Theologico-Politicus*', in *L'écriture sainte au temps de Spinoza dans le Système spinoziste* (Paris: Presses Universitaire de Paris Sorbonne, 1992); Sylvain Zac, *Spinoza et l'interprétation de l'écriture* (Paris: Presses Universitaires de France, 1965), pp. 27–8. For dissenting views, see Wim Klever, 'L'erreur de Lambertus Van Velthuysen (1622–85) et des Velthuysiens', in *The Spinozistic Heresy / L'hérésie*

accuracy may not be his primary concern. Rather, he seems bent on making Maimonides and Joseph stand in for the Calvinists to whom he is opposed. Maimonides is said to hold that, in order to count among the pious and the wise, it is not enough to follow the law under the guidance of reason. One must follow it as the law ordained by God and revealed to Moses. In the same vein, Joseph argues that, even if Aristotle had lived in accordance with the principles set out in his *Ethics*, he would still not have been saved, because he embraced his own teachings as dictates of reason rather than as revealed through prophecy.[57] For Joseph, as for Dante, even so virtuous a philosopher as Aristotle could not be included among the blessed. By the time the *Treatise* was written, the question of whether the heathen could be saved had been extensively debated, notably in colonizing nations such as Spain and Portugal, and a range of authorities had rejected Joseph's position. Perhaps this state of play adds strength to Spinoza's conviction that the Voetians' claim is not only wrong but not worth further consideration. As he has argued at length, it will not stand up and is, as he now puts the point, a mere figment or invention, unsupported either by reason or the authority of Scripture. 'An account of it is sufficient to refute it'.[58]

Natural reason can therefore make the Bible dispensable. But there remains the possibility that Scripture can be marginalized in a different way, if other texts also contain accessible versions of the divine law. In the communities with which Spinoza is most familiar, Jews and Christians used biblical narratives to make the essentials of the law plain and inspire their co-religionists to pursue the knowledge and love of God. As it happens, Scripture is an effective means of promoting the way of life that constitutes blessedness or salvation, and fulfils this function better than other texts such as historical chronicles, poetic dramas, or the Koran. However, if this ceased to be true, Spinoza now contends, there would be no reason to accord the Bible its special status.[59] Its religious value does not derive from the fact that it contains a record of divine revelation, but depends on its ability to change our way of life by helping us to cultivate the

Spinoziste: The Debate on the Tractatus Theologico-Politicus, 1670–1677, ed. Paolo Cristofolini (Amsterdam: APA-Holland University Press, 1995); Theo Verbeek, *Spinoza's Theologico-Political Treatise: Exploring 'the Will of God'* (Aldershot: Ashgate, 2003), p. 108.

[57] Spinoza, *Tractatus Theologico-Politicus*, ch. 5, p. 80.
[58] Ibid.
[59] Ibid. ch. 5, p. 79. On seventeenth-century discussion of the meaning of signs, see Stuart Clark, *Thinking with Demons: The Idea of Witchcraft in Early Modern Europe* (Oxford: Clarendon Press, 1997), ch. 18. See also Lorenzo Vinciguerra, *Spinoza et le signe: La Genèse de l'imagination* (Paris: Vrin, 2005).

law. The latter is what makes it sacred, and if another text fulfilled the same function, it too would acquire religious value.

Developing this line of thought later in the *Treatise*, Spinoza suggests that we should think of the Bible as a material object. In general, objects are not sacred or profane in themselves, but gain these qualities through the way they are used. This is confirmed in Scripture, for example by Jeremiah, who claims that Solomon's temple only deserved to be described as the temple of God as long as it was used to promote piety and religion, but became profane when it was taken over by thieves and murderers. (Like the modern temple condemned in the Preface of the *Treatise*, it ceased to house truly religious people.) Equally, Spinoza adds, the tablets of the law were sacred while they symbolized the Jews' commitment to the covenant they had made with God, but became mere stones once the covenant was broken. The same point applies to the Bible. 'Scripture is sacred and its utterances divine as long as it moves men to devotion towards God. But if they completely neglect it, as the Jews formerly did, it is nothing but paper and ink'.[60]

This account of the significance of Scripture is consonant with the broader theory of meaning on which Spinoza relies to interpret it. The Bible consists of a sequence of books, each made up of a particular arrangement of written words, and the meaning of any given word is largely determined by the way it is used.[61] A word token possesses the meaning it does by virtue of the way it is combined with other word tokens. To put the point another way, a word has no fixed meaning in itself, but acquires meaning through its relationships with other words. By analogy, so Spinoza now suggests, we can understand the properties of the Bible as a whole by conceiving of it as part of a system of signs and asking what agents have done, or are now doing, with it. Its meaning is determined by its relationships with other things, and just as the meaning of a word alters over time as agents combine it with other words in new ways, so the normative properties of Scripture are subject to change. To make Scripture sacred, a community has to use it to move people to devotion; but as soon as they treat it in some other way, say as a stirring tale of military prowess or an anthropologically fascinating Bronze Age epic, it ceases to fulfil this function

---

[60] Spinoza, *Tractatus Theologico-Politicus*, ch. 12, p. 161.

[61] The view that the Bible is made up of words and sentences has already been aired in chapter 1 of the *Treatise*. It is also defended by Meijer: Lodewijk Meijer, *Philosophia S. Scripturæ Interpres* (Amsterdam: 1666), xvi.9, p. 104; Louis Meyer, *La philosophie interprète de l'écriture sainte*, trans. Jacqueline Lagrée and Pierre-François Moreau (Paris: Intertextes, 1988), xvi.9, pp. 230–1.

and becomes profane.[62] It sacredness therefore consists simply in the fact that it is used to promote piety.

Hovering over this discussion is the deeply subversive thought that virtually anything, including for instance the Koran, can be or become sacred. As Lambert Van Velthuysen[63] observed in his attack on the *Treatise*, Spinoza has left himself no means to resist the conclusion that Mahomet was a true prophet, 'since even the Turks cultivate the moral virtues about which all the nations are agreed in accordance with his command'.[64] This argument is offered as a *reductio ad absurdum*; but Spinoza responds that it is exactly right. If, as Velthuysen claims, Mahomet's teachings inspire the Turks to practise the divine law, 'I believe they have the spirit of Christ and are saved, whatever convictions they may in their ignorance hold about Mahomet and the oracles'.[65] By implication, then, the Koran can be used in a fashion that renders it sacred.

This stretch of argument aims to draw attention to the harm that can arise when people turn the Bible into a ceremonial object and treat it as sacred in itself. Those who wrongly believe that the Bible is sacred by virtue of the fact that it is in some literal or quasi-literal sense the word of God often get caught up in other destructive errors. Their conviction that the divine word is only to be found in Scripture not only makes them unduly critical of the heathen, but also encourages them to get bogged down in fruitless controversies about the text. Taking over an insult that his Calvinist opponents were fond of hurling at one another, Spinoza hints that these flaws constitute a form of idolatry and amount to worshipping the Bible rather than God.[66] Idolatry is of course a distraction from the demands and pleasures of true religion. But treating the biblical texts as the sole repository of divine law can also function as a doubtful panacea for the anxieties associated with superstition. Fear and the other passions, so Spinoza will explain in the *Ethics*, are our experience of our interactions with external things, and are therefore inherently relational, and experience of this kind is inherently limited in certain characteristic ways. For

---

[62] Spinoza, *Tractatus Theologico-Politicus*, ch. 12, p. 160.

[63] Lambert van Velthuysen or Lambertus Velthusius (1622–85) was a doctor of medicine who, being independently wealthy, was able to abandon medical practice to be a full-time amateur theologian. He was originally a fairly moderate critic of Spinoza's *Tractatus Theologico-Politicus*; later a friend of Spinoza's, though one who remained critical of his theological attitudes.

[64] Letter 42. *The Correspondence of Spinoza*, ed. and trans. A. Wolf (London: Frank Cass, 1966), pp. 239–54.

[65] Ibid. Letter 43, p. 259.

[66] Spinoza, *Tractatus Theologico-Politicus*, ch. 12, p. 162. Van Velthuysen also argued that the Voetians were idolatrous. See Henri Krop, 'Spinoza and the Calvinistic Cartesianism of Lambertus Van Velthuysen', *Studia Spinozana*, 15 (1999).

example, when in the ordinary course of things we fear God as vengeful or punitive, we fail to take account of the ways in which we ourselves and our other relationships contribute to this affect. What is it about us that makes us susceptible to this anxiety? What other circumstances may be feeding it? Failure to understand our anxieties may in turn prompt us to make some other external object a source of solace by investing it with passion. We may, for instance, represent the Bible as the key to everlasting happiness and the antidote to our fear, once again ignoring the respects in which this image has more to do with us than with the book on which we fix our hopes. As Spinoza indicates here, and as Marx and Freud would later agree, living in the grip of this kind of illusion limits the personal freedom that comes with self-understanding; but such a constrained way of life can also he kept in place by forms of theologico-political servitude that give power to those whose interests the illusion serves. In seventeenth-century Amsterdam, the idolatrous belief that Scripture itself is sacred enhanced the power of officials within the Reformed Church, who built this conviction into religious practices over which they exercised control. By arguing that access to Scripture is neither necessary nor sufficient for piety, Spinoza warns his readers against them, and holds out the prospect of a religion in which the Bible plays no essential part.

Miracles

The Bible is full of miraculous events. The dead are raised, seas part, water gushes from the desert, the sun stands still in the sky, and prophets are drawn up to heaven in fiery chariots. Since Scripture attributes these extraordinary episodes directly to God and implicitly contrasts them with the normal course of the laws of nature, incautious readers are liable to come away with various firm impressions. These will include the belief that the actions of God are distinct from the force of nature, which operates independently of the deity in a regular and lawlike fashion, and that God sometimes interrupts the natural order in order to direct events. It is through these actions, it seems, that he reveals his presence and concern for humanity. Miracles, therefore, provide us with our clearest evidence of his existence and providence, and by attending to them we can come to understand him.

Spinoza attributes precisely this outlook to the *vulgus*—the ordinary or common people—and condemns it as a set of foolish prejudices.[67] Miracles, he now sets out to show, do not teach us anything about God, but contribute

---

[67] Spinoza, *Tractatus Theologico-Politicus*, ch. 6, pp. 81–2.

to a misleading view of the deity that stands in the way of philosophical enquiry and has no bearing on salvation. However, it is surely not only or primarily the *vulgus* whose views Spinoza wishes to condemn. Ordinary people get many of their theological opinions from the teachings of churches, and established churches have an interest in upholding their own doctrines in the face of conflicting philosophical positions. Insofar as the Reformed Church's commitment to divine providence is sustained by the conviction that God performs miracles, it too holds the 'opinions and prejudices' that Spinoza sets out to criticize. Unless this was so, they would not be worth rebutting with such care.

Since miracles have already been discussed in the *Treatise*, it may seem rather surprising that Spinoza should return to them. As we saw in Chapter 2, signs or miracles play a central role in the practice of prophecy, where they indicate that a revelation is genuine. By bringing about an event that a prophet and his audience cannot explain in natural terms, God makes his presence clear and lends his authority to the prophet. Admittedly, miracles do not constitute conclusive proof of authentic revelation because, as Scripture indicates and Spinoza again points out, God tests his people by sending signs to false prophets.[68] Nevertheless, they are a necessary condition of revelation and are integral to prophecy as the Bible describes it.

Prophetic miracles can also be explained in the terms that Spinoza has already rehearsed. The prophets' imaginative gifts enabled them to represent the world in ways that fostered devotion to God, and signs were part of this process. Miracles struck their audiences as events that could only be accounted for as the actions of God, and consequently aroused wonder (*admiratio*), a standard response to events that surprise us and do not fit with our experience.[69] (As Spinoza illustrates in his *Short Treatise*, someone who has only seen sheep with short tails will wonder at the long tails of sheep from Morocco. 'Similarly, they tell of a peasant who deluded himself into thinking that there were no fields beyond his own. One day he missed one of his cows and had to go in search of her, and was astonished to find that there were many small farms like his own'.[70]) Furthermore, when wonder is joined with love it becomes devotion.[71] So, human psychology being what it is, miracles

---

[68] Ibid. ch. 6, p. 87.   [69] Ibid. ch. 6, p. 81.

[70] Spinoza, *Short Treatise on God, Man, and His Well-Being*, in *The Collected Works of Spinoza*, vol. 1, pp. 99–100.

[71] Spinoza, *Ethics*, in *The Collected Works of Spinoza*, vol. 1, 3p52.

can arouse devotion for God, thereby helping to generate and sustain the way of life prescribed by the divine law.

We can allow, however, that biblical accounts of miracles serve this function without accepting that the accounts themselves provide an accurate record of events. As Spinoza pauses to remark, the capacity to perceive and describe events accurately is a rare talent. In general, observers interpret their experience in the light of their existing opinions, particularly when the events they are concerned with are unfamiliar, or when their interests are involved. 'That is why men tell more about their own opinions in chronicles and histories than about the events they describe, and why two men whose opinions differ can give such disparate descriptions of a single event that they seem to be speaking about two different things'.[72] So when, for example, the author of the book of Joshua reports that the sun stood still, he is recording, like other chroniclers, the testimony of a particular group of observers. But there is no reason to assume that he gives an accurate account of what could have been observed on the day of battle. A different observer might have reported, for example, that the day was longer than usual.[73] In addition, there is no reason to think that biblical reports of miracles display any philosophical insight into their causes. As Scripture attests, natural reason enables us to understand both God and nature, and with this type of knowledge in hand we can assess the prophets' imagined conceptions of the processes through which the deity operates.

The argument already developed in the *Treatise* therefore gives us ample grounds for questioning the view that miracles are God's providential interruptions of the natural order. However, as Spinoza now points out, his analysis of prophecy is mainly grounded on hermeneutic evidence. Since the Bible is our only source of trustworthy information about divine revelation, he 'was compelled to put together a history of prophecy, and draw from it certain tenets about prophecy's nature and properties, insofar as this can be done'.[74] Among the conclusions he arrived at was the tenet that prophetic signs or miracles do not *have* to be understood as God's interventions in the order of nature, because another explanation is available. But, compelling as this result may be, it does not incontrovertibly establish that miracles as the Bible describes them are impossible. No interpretative method can arrive at such a definitive conclusion, which can only be reached by natural reasoning. It is to bridge this gap that Spinoza now launches an investigation into the purely philosophical question of 'whether we can grant that anything happens in nature that is

---

[72] Spinoza, *Tractatus Theologico-Politicus*, ch. 6, p. 92.
[73] Ibid.   [74] Ibid. ch. 6, p. 95–6.

contrary to its laws, or could not follow from them?'[75] Can there, he wants to know, be miracles in this sense of the term?

Once again, the answer is already clear. If we accept the account of divine law he has laid out, we shall agree that God's decrees are universal and eternal natural laws, and that everything God wills follows necessarily from his perfect nature. If God were to issue a command that ran contrary to natural law he would be acting against his own nature, and this self-contradiction is incompatible with his perfection. 'Nothing, therefore, happens in nature which is contrary to its universal laws.... For whatever happens, happens by God's eternal will and decree, i.e. according to laws and rules that involve eternal necessity and truth'.[76] Furthermore, since God's decrees are infinite, the same must be true of the laws of nature. They must 'be so broad that they extend to everything that is conceived by the divine intellect'.[77] There can, then, be no miracles in the sense of interruptions of the natural order. When people use the term in this way, they are simply putting a gloss on unfamiliar and surprising events for which they are unable to assign any natural causes.[78]

At this point it seems that nothing more need be said. Miracles in the imaginary sense cannot occur, and that is that. However, this is not Spinoza's view, and the additional arguments he goes on to offer are a mark of his determination to completely dismantle the 'ordinary' conception of miracles by pressing home the claim that they cannot tell us anything about God's essence and existence or about his providence. People who look to miracles as a source of knowledge about God are barking up the wrong tree. The demonstrations that follow are dry and rapid. We acquire our philosophical knowledge of the law-bound order of nature by progressively inferring clear and distinct ideas from self-evident common notions. In doing so we extend our knowledge of God and come to understand that he necessarily exists. If miracles were events contrary to the order of nature we would not be able to infer them from common notions, and this would put the common notions in doubt, along with the inferences that follow from them. Rather than confirming our clear and distinct idea of God's necessary existence, the effect would be to undermine it. So miracles would put our idea of God's existence in doubt.[79] Again, if miracles were events that cannot be explained by natural causes it would be impossible for us to understand them clearly and distinctly. But in that case they could tell us nothing clear and distinct about God's existence or essence.[80] Yet again, since miracles would be limited events, we would have no grounds for

---

[75] Ibid. [76] Ibid. ch. 6, p. 83. [77] Ibid.
[78] Ibid. ch. 6, p. 84. [79] Ibid. [80] Ibid. ch. 6, pp. 85–6.

attributing them to an infinitely powerful cause such as God, and could not infer from them anything about his nature.[81]

By enumerating these arguments, Spinoza is aiming to achieve several different goals, the first of which is to further his critique of Calvinist providentialism. The miracles recounted in the Bible appear to confirm the Reformed Church's conception of a God who has a design for humanity; but if, contrary to appearances, they tell us nothing about God's nature or essence, they cannot confirm his providence. Insofar as the Church rests its theological position on this kind of biblical evidence, it has no case. More generally, Spinoza is contending that miracles should have no place in theological doctrine. Since they are merely professions of ignorance, they cannot bear directly on the truths about God that are relevant to salvation, and churches do not need to pontificate about them. They would do better to recognize (and here Spinoza addresses himself to a second goal) that the philosophical position he has laid out provides a far superior knowledge of God's essence. 'When we know that all things are determined and enacted by God, that the operations of nature follow from God's essence, and that the laws of nature are God's eternal decrees and volitions, we must conclude absolutely that we know God and God's will better as we know natural things better, and understand more clearly how they depend on their first cause, and how they operate according to the eternal laws of nature'.[82] As Spinoza must be aware, this broadside could never be acceptable to the Reformed Church. Besides flying in the face of its conception of God, it proposes to dismiss miracles as insignificant, and to give philosophers authority to pronounce on them.

Spinoza is here making a bid for the power of philosophy over theology; but he is also keen to point out that the 'ordinary' view of miracles is liable to be harmful. At one level, his account suggests that narratives about miraculous events can play a role in religion as long as they are not treated as sources of insight into the nature of God but are used only to encourage devotion. Teaching them in this spirit is a legitimate part of the Church's ministry.

---

[81] Ibid. ch. 6, pp. 85–6. It is worth bearing in mind Bacon's comment on this topic: 'Miracles have been wrought to convert idolaters and the superstitious, because no light of nature extendeth to declare the will and true worship of God. For as all works do shew for the power and skill of the workman, and not his image; so it is of the works of God; which do show the omnipotency and wisdom of the maker, but not his image: and therefore therein the heathen opinion differeth from the sacred truth; for they supposed the world to be the image of God, and man to be an exact and compendious image of the world'. Francis Bacon, *The Advancement of Learning*, ed. James Spedding, Robert Ellis, and Douglas Heath, vol. IV, *The Works of Francis Bacon* (London: Longmans, 1858), II.58.

[82] Spinoza, *Tractatus Theologico-Politicus*, ch. 3, p. 54.

However, another strand of his argument is more critical. By dwelling on miracles, religious practices play to the pleasure that ordinary people gain from worshipping a God whose capacity to confound expectation puts him outside nature, and whose extraordinary works inspire the passions associated with wonder—veneration, consternation, devotion, and dread.[83] Natural reasoning undermines these pleasures by making hitherto inexplicable events explicable. Because it deprives people of a familiar and satisfying form of imaginative excitement, they prefer not to give up their beliefs for a firmer understanding of natural causes.[84] Focusing on miracles is therefore one of the tools that churches and their theologians use to block the growth of philosophical understanding and feed hostility to people who cultivate the natural sciences. Like the fear that drives superstition, with which it is intimately connected, wonder binds ordinary people to outlooks and practices that are obstacles to philosophizing and stand in the way of the benefits it can deliver. Teaching them about miracles is not only unnecessary to their salvation. It is also, as Spinoza remarks to Henry Oldenburg, to side with ignorance against wisdom and turn faith into superstition, thus damaging people's capacity to live in a manner that realizes the full potential of human nature.[85]

A theologian who believed in miracles would find it natural to retort that Spinoza's argument was impious, conflicting as it did with the teaching of Scripture. As usual, Spinoza is anxious to head off this objection. It is true, he concedes, that Scripture does not openly teach that we cannot come to know about God or his providence through miracles. But it is nevertheless easy enough to infer these views from the text. For instance, despite the numerous miracles they had observed, the Jews under Moses clearly did not understand the nature of God and were willing to worship a golden calf. ('What shame!' Spinoza interpolates.[86]) Equally, it is clear that the nature of divine providence was not as well understood by the prophets as it is by philosophers, who have always recognized that 'God directs nature as its universal laws require, but not as the particular laws of human nature require, and that God takes account not only of the human race, but of the whole of nature'.[87] Furthermore, while Scripture is not a philosophical or speculative work, and does not explicitly teach that all events have natural causes, careful interpretation of its narratives

---

[83] Spinoza, *Ethics*, 3p52, p. 181.
[84] Spinoza, *Tractatus Theologico-Politicus*, ch. 6, p. 81. See also Spinoza, *Ethics*, 1app.
[85] Spinoza, in Wolf ed. *The Correspondence of Spinoza*, p. 343. Letter 73.
[86] Spinoza, *Tractatus Theologico-Politicus*, ch. 6, p. 87.
[87] Ibid. ch. 6, p. 88.

shows that miracles have various antecedents and are not solely dependent on what is called the absolute command of God.[88] Finally, certain biblical passages endorse the more general view that nature observes a fixed and immutable order.[89]

Spinoza has to allow that none of these conclusions are written on the surface of the text. One needs to apply specialized interpretative skills in order to recognize that Scripture accords with, rather than contradicts, the account of miracles he has provided. This being so, his view cannot be counted as part of the Bible's central doctrine, and has no bearing on salvation. 'So everyone is free to judge of these things for himself, as he thinks best for the purpose of entering wholeheartedly into the worship of God and religion'.[90] However, by suggesting that churches should not place too much weight on the 'ordinary' conception of a miracle, because this can impede the growth of philosophical understanding, Spinoza is demanding that church teaching should do better than take the Bible at face value. Its theology should be carefully honed to encourage forms of devotion that are friendly, or at least not hostile, to philosophy.

---

[88] Ibid. ch. 6, p. 90.   [89] Ibid. ch. 6, p. 95.   [90] Ibid. ch. 6, p. 96.

Demystifying the Bible

Chapter 6

The Meaning of Scripture

The opening chapters of the *Treatise* provide an account of what Scripture does not offer. Properly interpreted, it does not contain philosophical insights into the nature of God or natural things. It does not challenge the authority of human law, whether civil or divine. Nor does it guide worship by requiring us to follow or shun specific ritual practices. In defending these claims, one of Spinoza's principal aims is to undercut the authority of theologians who have in his view corrupted religion by misrepresenting the sense in which Scripture is the word of God. As he had initially emphasized in his *Preface*, and now reiterates, these authorities have promoted superstitious beliefs and practices which 'teach men to scorn reason and nature and to admire and venerate only what is contrary to both'.[1] The Church's insistence that everyone must accept its own, biblically based conceptions of God, nature, and law gets in the way of open investigation and creates an environment where independent reasoning is frowned upon. At worst, this may result in despotism and destroy the hard-won liberty of the United Provinces. But even in the absence of such a dramatic political outcome it can do an impressive amount of damage. 'We see that the theologians have mainly been anxious to twist their own inventions and beliefs out of the Sacred Texts and to fortify them with divine authority. They have no scruple about interpreting the Scriptures. They read the mind of the Holy Spirit with great recklessness. If they fear anything, it is not that they may factitiously ascribe some error to the Holy Spirit and stray from the path of salvation, but that others may convict them of error, thus lessening their authority and exposing them to scorn'.[2] Equally, 'the common people seem to care nothing about living according to Sacred Scripture; we see that almost everyone hawks his own inventions as the word of God, and is concerned only

---

[1] Benedictus de Spinoza, *Tractatus Theologico-Politicus*, ed. Carl Gebhardt, vol. III, *Opera* (Heidelberg: Carl Winter, 1924), ch. 7, p. 97.

[2] Ibid.

to compel others to think as he does under the pretext of true religion'.[3] Superstition therefore fosters and thrives on a coercive environment in which people have fixed and invested in opinions that they are unwilling to change.

Spinoza, too, has arrived at some positive opinions. Alongside his negative judgements, he has simultaneously been developing a preliminary account of what the Bible teaches. When we read the text correctly, he has argued, we find that the divine law requires us to love God. Since philosophical investigation confirms that loving God constitutes our highest good, we can be confident that we are on the right interpretative track. The doctrine of Scripture is not contrary to reason. However, reassuring as this conclusion is, we have still not ascertained on the basis of purely scriptural evidence what the Bible teaches. To be as sure as possible of his conclusions, Spinoza needs to confirm that he has accurately and comprehensively identified the doctrines to be found in the text; and to satisfy himself of this, he needs to examine Scripture using a method that is appropriate to this kind of investigation.

Since the argument of the *Treatise* has been relying on an interpretative method all along and, as Spinoza will shortly point out, has used it to give an account of some of the trickiest speculative claims made in the Bible, this is a puzzling turn in the argument.[4] Why does he need a more refined hermeneutic approach to consolidate conclusions that have already been established? Furthermore, it is not clear why a more elaborate method should be required, given that Scripture's key doctrines are taught 'so clearly and explicitly that no one has ever disputed their meaning'. For example, we do not need a formalized interpretative method, any more than we need a full philosophical deduction, to grasp Scripture's assurance that a unique and omnipotent God exists, who alone is to be worshipped, who cares for all, and who loves above all those who worship him.[5] The same goes for the moral teachings necessary for salvation, which are expressed in simple language and are as easy to understand as Euclid's geometry.[6] Why then, can't we just accept the Bible's teachings at face value?[7]

If the entire text were as clear as the particular doctrines he has been discussing, Spinoza replies, this would be sufficient. But in many places Scripture's meaning is obscure and an explicitly formulated method can help us, first by guiding our attempts to work out what the text actually says, and then by

---

[3] Ibid.   [4] Ibid. ch. 7, p. 104.
[5] Ibid. ch. 7, p. 102.   [6] Ibid. ch. 7, p. 111.
[7] Spinoza argues that we comprehend many things without having to have them demonstrated. This applies to Euclid's geometrical theorems, and to all sorts of other things 'that we are accustomed to embrace without moral certainty and hear without wonder', including stories that 'do not surpass human belief, laws, institutions and customs'. Ibid. ch. 7, p. 111, fn. 12.

indicating how to decode what the prophets intended or meant by their utterances and actions.[8] In some cases this may turn out to be a largely scholarly enterprise—a matter of resolving textual puzzles that have little practical significance. But in other instances much more may be at stake, and until we try the method out we cannot know what it will yield. From a distance, Spinoza's determination to spell out his hermeneutic practice may seem over anxious, but in seventeenth-century Holland the interpretation of Scripture was, as we have seen, a subject of tense theologico-political conflict. If he is to vindicate his conclusions, he needs to show that the method by which they have been reached can withstand a number of predictable criticisms and silence a range of opponents.

Among the most politically powerful challenges that Spinoza now sets out to overcome is the Reformed Church's account of what it takes to interpret Scripture correctly. Taking its official stance from St Paul's assertion that 'all Scripture is given by inspiration of God, and is profitable for doctrine, for reproof, for correction, for instruction, for righteousness',[9] the Church held that one could only fully understand and internalize biblical doctrine with the special intervention of the Holy Spirit. In the early decades of the seventeenth century, however, supporters of the theologian Jacob Arminius (known in the United Provinces as the Remonstrants) had protested against this orthodox position, arguing instead that right reason is sufficient. As their spokesman Episcopius had put it, 'the proper understanding of scripture requires no other external or internal light than simply the aid of natural grace, or at least that grace that is universal and available to all—that is to say, only through the dictates of right reason or the blessings of common grace'.[10] The Arminians' opponents within the Church (known for obvious reasons as the Counter Remonstrants) had immediately rejected this formulation with a determination that Spinoza's contemporaries had not forgotten. Recalling their response in the book he published in 1666, Lodewijk Meijer quotes from the censure they delivered. 'If by right reason [the Arminians] understand here the use of human reason unenlightened by the Holy Spirit, what they say is absurd. . . . But if they speak here of man enlightened by the Holy Spirit, we recognise that right reason is capable of judging the authentic meaning of Scripture, as long as it constantly follows the dictation of the

---

[8] Ibid. p. 102.   [9] 2 Timothy 3:16.
[10] Quoted in W. J. van Asselt, *The Federal Theology of Johannes Cocceius (1603–1669)* (Leiden: Brill, 2001), p. 109.

Holy Spirit, and is guided by it rather than by a merely natural capacity for reasoning'.[11]

This orthodox position was upheld at the Synod of Dort in 1618, after which the Arminians were temporarily expelled from the United Provinces; but as Meijer's book illustrates, the theological issues to which they had drawn attention never disappeared. The Church's official doctrine remained unchanged; but theologians and others continued to consider what kinds of natural reasoning were relevant to interpreting Scripture. Faith, Cocceius writes in defence of the orthodox position, animates our capacity to reason. It 'subdues speculations and captivates every thought for obedience to God. . . . It does not confuse reason but sets it in order. . . . Indeed, faith liberates one from lusts, errors, ignorance, hasty judgments and opinions, and complaints against the truth of God—such snares that Satan employs to hold reason captive to his will'.[12]

The view of biblical interpretation that the *Treatise* now sets out to defend stands on the Arminian side of this debate, and is therefore opposed to the Reformed Church's stance. But it is also more extreme than the positions held by many Arminians. Spinoza does not simply hold with the Remonstrants that natural reason is capable of interpreting Scripture. Rather, he holds that it is the *only* way to interpret Scripture, and that appeals to the Holy Spirit are incomprehensible. Although he occasionally and concessively refers to the Holy Spirit, he repeatedly reiterates his contempt for the very notion of what was generally known as a supernatural light: 'What this light is beyond the natural light I leave it to them to explain'.[13] He casts aspersions on the motives of its defenders: 'But why should I wonder that men who boast that they have a supernatural light are unwilling to grant superiority in knowledge to the philosophers, who have nothing but the natural light?'[14] And he ridicules their lack of interpretative insight: 'Far be it from me to judge that people [who make such blunders] possess a supernatural divine gift'.[15] The attitudes and practices that theologians have been able to build on the assumption that one can only understand Scripture with the help of the Holy Spirit are, he claims, intellectually indefensible; but they also encourage a dangerous form of superstition. By removing the interpretation of the Bible from the realm of natural enquiry and making it depend on a quasi-magical process that lies

---

[11] Lodewijk Meijer, *Philosophia S. Scripturæ Interpres* (Amsterdam, 1666), xvi.4, p. 99; Louis Meyer, *La philosophie interprète de l'écriture sainte*, trans. Jacqueline Lagrée and Pierre-François Moreau (Paris: Intertextes, 1988), xvi.4, pp. 222–3.

[12] Asselt, *Federal Theology*, p. 104.

[13] Spinoza, *Tractatus Theologico-Politicus*, ch. 7, p. 112.

[14] Ibid. ch. 13, p. 167.   [15] Ibid. ch. 7, p. 113.

beyond our comprehension, they turn Scripture into an object of wonder, while at the same time claiming for themselves the authority to determine what it means. Self-deception and self-interest then encourage them to read it in ways that sustain their own complacency, strengthen their ability to control their congregations, and make it easier for them to crush forms of enquiry potentially damaging to their status. All in all, they promote the corrupt forms of religion against which Spinoza inveighs in his Preface.

These superstitious habits are, of course, sustained by a range of passions of which the foremost is fear, and are consequently difficult to dislodge. Spinoza is well aware that revealing the flawed reasoning on which they rest will usually not be enough to topple them and does not expect to have more than a limited success. As he observes in an analogous context, 'things have already nearly reached the point where men do not suffer themselves to be corrected, but stubbornly defend what they have embraced on the pretext of religion. Nor does any place seem to be left for reason, except among a very few'.[16] Nevertheless, unmasking the interpretative errors on which superstitious outlooks rest may at least help the very few, by bolstering their ability to interpret Scripture in a rational fashion, and showing where their opponents go wrong.

On this score, then, Spinoza sets himself uncompromisingly against the Reformed Church. But on another point he is outwardly more conciliatory. Among the arguments that the Church used to defend its position was the claim that Scripture must be interpreted by Scripture: since the Bible itself confirms that it can only be understood with the help of the Holy Spirit, those who reject this view set aside biblical authority and, like Jews and Roman Catholics, rest their conclusions on additional authorities that can make no claim to be the word of God. As Lodewijk Meijer had pointed out, the Reformed Church was not alone in sticking to the rule of *sola scriptura*. It was also accepted by 'Papists . . . Lutherans, Anabaptists, Arminians and Socinians',[17] and as the theological differences between these confessions illustrate, it is not at all clear what counts as conforming to it. Does it, for instance, forbid interpreters from appealing to philosophically grounded conclusions or using independent historical evidence? Does it require them to read the Bible literally, as the Voetians claimed? And if so, what is a literal reading?[18] Disputes about these

---

[16] Ibid. ch. 8, p. 118.

[17] Meijer, *Philosophia S. Scripturæ Interpres*, xi.6, p. 74; Meyer, *La Philosophie interprète de l'écriture sainte*, xi.6, p. 172.

[18] Peter Harrison, *The Bible, Protestantism, and the Rise of Natural Science* (Cambridge: Cambridge University Press, 1998), pp. 107–20, 129–38.

issues had rumbled on throughout the century, but while Spinoza was writing the *Tractatus* they had been reignited by the publication of Meijer's book, in which he had argued that Scripture cannot be interpreted by Scripture and must be interpreted in the light of our philosophical understanding instead. This attack made the Church more alert to contraventions of its own interpretative rule, and it was in this climate that Spinoza wrote the *Treatise*. Perhaps partly as a result, he takes great care to distance himself from Meijer's position, and to remind his readers that he is interpreting Scripture by Scripture.

The hermeneutic method that he now sets out can, of course, be assessed in its own right. But to understand why he presents it as he does, and what it is designed to contribute to his argument, we need to see how he is aligning himself in relation to these and other theologico-political debates. They are in fact his first concern. Only when he has dealt with them does he go on to discuss the various benefits that his interpretative method yields.

Interpreting the Bible

When, in the Preface to the *Tractatus*, Spinoza first raises the question of how we should approach the Bible in order to understand its doctrine, he alludes to the opening of Descartes' *Principles of Philosophy*, the text he had put into geometrical order and to which he had appended his own metaphysical thoughts. The *Principles* begins by outlining the method of doubt that had excited loud protests from the Voetian theologians. Since we have arrived at most of our ideas uncritically, Descartes argues, we cannot be sure that they are true. Natural philosophers who want to build their theories on absolutely secure foundations must therefore divide their ideas into two groups: those they know to be true; and those that may be false.[19] The way to do this is to set aside any ideas about which there is even the slightest uncertainty.[20] When only certain ideas remain, philosophers can confidently go ahead and put them to use. Spinoza's account of his biblical hermeneutics echoes this strategy. To formulate a method of interpreting the Bible, he recounts, he resolved 'to examine Scripture afresh with an unprejudiced and free spirit', and to 'affirm nothing as its teaching which it did not most clearly teach me'.[21] Just as

---

[19] *Descartes, Principles of Philosophy*, in *Oeuvres de Descartes*, ed. Charles Adam and Paul Tannery (Paris: Vrin, 1974), vol. VIII A, pp. 16–17. English Translation: *The Philosophical Works of Descartes*, trans. John Cottingham et al. (Cambridge: Cambridge University Press, 1985), vol. I, p. 203.

[20] *Descartes, Principles of Philosophy* I.1–2, AT VIIIA 5/CSM I.193.

[21] Spinoza, *Tractatus Theologico-Politicus*, Preface, p. 9.

Descartes urges us to shed our prejudices about the natural world and only to accept ideas that we cannot doubt, Spinoza extends this project to theology by setting out to shake off his preconceptions about what Scripture says, and only accept claims that he is absolutely sure it asserts.[22]

For Descartes, the method of doubt is a way of removing prejudices that obscure the clear and distinct metaphysical ideas on which a natural philosophy must be grounded. The goal is to arrive at beliefs that are completely trustworthy. When Spinoza applies a comparable method to Scripture, his goal is to arrive at trustworthy beliefs about what the text asserts. As he now explains, the way to do this is to compile what he calls a history of Scripture modelled on a history of nature. 'Just as the method of interpreting nature consists above all in putting together a history of nature, from which . . . we infer the definitions of things, so . . . it is necessary to prepare a straightforward history of Scripture and to infer from it the mind of the authors of Scripture'.[23] At first glance, this project does not after all seem to be a Cartesian one. Descartes does not describe himself as constructing a history of nature, and it looks as though, having bowed in the direction of his predecessor, Spinoza is now going off on a track of his own. But in fact, as we shall see, he sticks more closely to Cartesian principles than at first appears.

The notion of a history that Spinoza invokes is the ancient one of a 'systematic enquiry that moves from particulars, natural, human or other, rather than first principles',[24] which survived into the early modern era and is employed not only in the titles of ancient works such as Pliny's *Natural History*, but also in modern ones such as Jose d'Acosta's celebrated *Natural and Moral History of the Indies*, published in Seville in 1590. This conception of history is discussed, for example, in Francis Bacon's *Advancement of Learning* (a work owned in its Latin version by Spinoza), where Bacon explains that history

---

[22] See Edwin Curley, 'Spinoza and the Science of Hermeneutics', in *Spinoza: The Enduring Questions*, ed. Graeme Hunter (Toronto: University of Toronto Press, 1994).

[23] Spinoza, *Tractatus Theologico-Politicus*, p. 98.

[24] Anthony Grafton, *What Was History? The Art of History in Early Modern Europe* (Cambridge: Cambridge University Press, 2007), p. 27. For debate about Spinoza's treatment of history, see Étienne Balibar, *Spinoza and Politics*, trans. Peter Snowden (London: Verso, 1998); Alessandro Caccarelli, 'L'orizzonte problematico della ragione Spinozista e il concetto della historia scripturae del *Tractatus Theologico-Politicus*', in *Spinoza: Individuo e moltitudine*, ed. Vittorio Morfino and Stefano Caporali (Cesena: Il Ponte Vecchio, 2007); Pierre Macherey, *Hegel ou Spinoza* (Paris: François Maspero, 1979); Pierre-François Moreau, 'Fortune and the Theory of History', in *The New Spinoza*, ed. Warren Montag and Ted Stolze (Minneapolis: University of Minnesota Press, 1997); Michael Rosenthal, 'Spinoza and the Philosophy of History', in *Interpreting Spinoza: Critical Essays*, ed. Charlie Huenemann (Cambridge: Cambridge University Press, 2008).

(including natural history) derives from our faculty of memory, and 'is properly concerned with individuals which are circumscribed by place and time'.[25] The stipulation that histories only deal with individuals may seem unduly restrictive, but Bacon quickly sets his readers' minds at rest. 'Though natural history may seem to deal with species', he explains, 'this is only because of the general resemblance which in most cases objects of the same species bear to one another; so that when you know one, you know all'. Natural historians start with individuals, and then go on to organize them into types or species, allowing for individuals that are 'unique in their species', like the sun or moon, and 'individuals that are notable deviations from their species, like monsters'. Following this lead, though avoiding Bacon's Aristotelian notion of species and replacing it with talk of definitions, Spinoza agrees that classification forms the basis of histories of nature and enables us to arrive at definitions and general principles. The way to use it is to begin by formulating definitions of the things that are most universal, such as motion and rest, and of the laws by which they are governed. Once these are in place, one can gradually move on to define more specific things.[26]

What Spinoza describes as the process of constructing a history has much in common with the method of presenting data and arguments that early-modern philosophers called analysis. This was the method Descartes had used in his *Principles*; and one of the aims of Spinoza's own published work on this text was to recast its arguments and conclusions in a different form, using the so-called synthetic method. As Meijer's Introduction to Spinoza's book explains, Descartes had presented his ideas in the analytic style, which 'shows the true way by which the thing was discovered'.[27] Starting from ordinary opinions, it works back to first principles.[28] However, arguments can also be explicated in the synthetic manner, 'which uses a long series of definitions, postulates, axioms, theorems, and problems, so that if the reader denies one of its consequences, the presentation shows him that it is contained immediately in the antecedents, and so forces assent from him, no matter how stubborn or contrary

---

[25] Francis Bacon, *The Advancement of Learning*, ed. James Spedding, Robert Ellis, and Douglas Heath, vol. IV, *The Works of Francis Bacon* (London: Longmans, 1858), p. 292. For a discussion of Spinoza's indebtedness to Bacon's theory of history, see Sylvain Zac, *Spinoza et l'interprétation de l'écriture* (Paris: Presses Universitaires de France, 1965), pp. 29–33 and ff.

[26] Spinoza, *Tractatus Theologico-Politicus*, p. 102.

[27] Spinoza, *Parts I and II of Descartes' 'Principles of Philosophy'*, in *The Collected Works of Spinoza*, p. 226.

[28] Descartes, *Principles of Philosophy*, AT VII.156/CSM II.111.

he may be'.[29] By setting out the argument of the first two parts of the *Principles* in the synthetic form normally used by mathematicians, Spinoza had shown, in a manner that forces assent, how Descartes' conclusions follow from his premises. By this means, Meijer goes on, Spinoza offers guidance to people who count themselves as Cartesians, but only know how to chatter and babble about this new system, 'as is the custom among those who are still attached to Aristotle's philosophy'.[30]

Meijer makes the familiar point that one of the advantages of synthesis is epistemological: it sets out to show that conclusions originally reached by means of analysis are mathematically certain. However, as Spinoza now acknowledges, it cannot supplant the type of investigation captured by the analytic method—the process of working our way from our experience of individual things to definitions that form the basis of our explanations of natural phenomena. (As Spinoza's examples of motion and rest indicate, analysis can yield definitions that are absolutely fundamental to natural philosophy, and can also enable us to discover the 'laws and rules' to which they conform.[31]) So when Cartesian natural philosophers, including Descartes himself, employ analysis, what they are doing is constructing histories, with the specific purpose of arriving at definitions and principles that are clear and distinct.

In some cases, as Spinoza's presentation of Descartes' *Principles* illustrates, conclusions reached by analysis can be recast in synthetic form. But this is not always the case. One of the great strengths of histories of nature is that they can teach us about the properties and effects of specific types of things, and deal with them at a level of detail that synthetic demonstration cannot match. Philosophical deduction from first principles may, for example, yield the knowledge that all bodies conform to particular laws of motion, and provide a general characterization of the respects in which types of bodies differ from one another. But it cannot tell us, for instance, that among the many types of body that exist in the world are cloves and blackbirds, any more than it can tell us that blackbirds give a distinctive warning cry or that cloves are good for toothache. Our ordinary knowledge of causes and effects, and our consequent

---

[29] Spinoza, *Parts I and II of Descartes' 'Principles of Philosophy'*, in *The Collected Works of Spinoza*, p. 226.

[30] Ibid.

[31] Compare Hobbes, according to whom, one could begin with a piece of gold and resolve it into the universals that are its causes, in this case solid, visible, heavy, and so on. Thomas Hobbes, *Elements of Philosophy. The First Section Concerning Body* in *The English Works of Thomas Hobbes of Malmesbury*, edited by William Molesworth, 11 vols. (London: J. Bohn, 1839-45), vol. 1, p. 69.

ability to deal with our environment, therefore depend on the historical study of nature, and thus on the analytic method. So, too, does our more formal grasp of natural philosophy. We are not in a position simply to posit a batch of clear and distinct definitions and deduce conclusions from them. Rather, we have to derive them painstakingly from our experience of individual things.

Histories can be constructed for many purposes, and can no doubt be based on all sorts of eccentric classificatory principles. ('Animals belonging to the Emperor' comes to mind.) But when their goal is to provide rationally defensible accounts of natural phenomena, they rely on accredited processes of natural reasoning. Historians of nature, so Spinoza assumes, compare and contrast individual things, cross-check their data, make inferences from one case to another, employ basic logical rules such as *modus ponens*, and so forth. Their conclusions are reached by rational means and, as Meijer points out in his discussion of analysis, can sometimes achieve a certainty that is beyond any significant doubt.[32] Even when there remains a distant theoretical possibility that a definition derived from limited evidence may be misleading, or that a commonplace inductive inference could be falsified, these remote contingencies are not enough to undermine the moral certainty of historical conclusions, and unless we are 'sceptics who doubt for the sake of doubting'[33] they do not undermine our confidence in them.

Like synthesis, then, analysis is capable of arriving at ideas, for instance ideas of motion and rest, which satisfy Descartes' standard of clarity and distinctness; and when Cartesian philosophers bring it to bear on nature, this is what they are aiming for. Of course, they do not always succeed. As Spinoza often reminds us, few of our ideas are perfectly clear and distinct, and many of the definitions we formulate by means of the historical method are more indicative of our own experience than of the totality that he calls God or nature. An ornithologist's definition of a blackbird, for example, is adequate for most ornithological purposes; but it still fails to fully capture the nature or essence of blackbird. The classifications that histories arrive at are, therefore, of varying degrees of clarity and distinctness, and thus of certainty.[34]

The way to understand Scripture, Spinoza now proposes, is to approach it via this same historical method. 'To interpret Scripture it is necessary to prepare a straightforward history of it, and to infer from this the mind of the authors of

---

[32] Spinoza, *Parts I and II of Descartes' 'Principles of Philosophy'*, pp. 226–7.
[33] Ibid. p. 231.
[34] On the role of experience in biblical interpretation, see Warren Montag, *Bodies, Masses, Power* (London: Verso, 1999), ch. 2.

Scripture, by legitimate reasonings, as from certain data and principles'.[35] This abrupt transition from nature to Scripture may seem quite a jump. Since the aim of a history of nature is to define natural entities, while the aim of a history of Scripture is to reveal what the text asserts, one might wonder how a single method can be applicable to both. For Spinoza's Calvinist opponents, the answer lay in their conviction that the goal of studying nature is to appreciate how natural things harmoniously combine to realize God's ends.[36] From their point of view, there is no significant gap between the study of natural truths and the study of their meanings. Equally, the aim of studying Scripture is to find out what God intends. So it is not surprising that a single investigative method should be applicable to both the Bible and the natural world. But this argument is evidently not available to Spinoza who, as we have seen, firmly denies that God acts for ends. While we can legitimately try to uncover the meanings or intentions of human agents such as the prophets, there are no intentions to be found in nature. The question therefore recurs: if natural and biblical history have such different kinds of subject matter, why should a single method be appropriate to both?

To appreciate Spinoza's answer, we need to be clear exactly what he is claiming. He is proposing that a single method can be used to produce an account of what there is in nature, and to produce an account of what there is in the Bible. But he is not claiming that the way in which we then go on to explain the things that a natural history has identified is the same as the way we then go on to explain the crucial things that a scriptural history identifies (by citing the prophets' intentions). On the contrary, and as we know, he is adamant that natural things cannot be explained in the purposive terms appropriate for explicating the meaning of Scripture. The question, then, is why Scripture should be susceptible to the historical process of forming definitions from a batch of data, and this is not so difficult to answer once we take account of the fact that the method of constructing histories had traditionally ranged over phenomena of many kinds. It could be used to arrive at definitions of natural things, of human beings (how do Indians differ from Europeans or cannibals from Christians?), of the societies in which they live (how do democracies differ from oligarchies and what happens when republics become dictatorships?) and of the artifacts that they produce (how did Greek ships differ

---

[35] Spinoza, *Tractatus Theologico-Politicus*, p. 98. On this analogy, see Stanislas Breton, *Spinoza, théologie et politique* (Paris: Desclée, 1977), ch. 2, especially §8.

[36] One example: Martinus Schookius, *Physica Generalis* (Grongingen, 1660), pp. 138–9. On this topic generally, see J. A. van Ruler, *The Crisis of Causality: Voetius and Descartes on God, Nature, and Change* (Leiden: Brill, 1995).

from Phoenician ones and what do Indians wear?). In many of these cases, the information from which definitions are derived included testimonies bequeathed by earlier authors ('according to Pliny', or 'as Aristotle says'). So it is perhaps not such a stretch to propose that this approach can also be used to deal with data contained in a single text to define the phenomena that it describes. This is presumably an aspect of Spinoza's thinking. But there is in addition a sense in which a historical or analytical approach suits his view that Scripture and the events it records are all part of nature. The Bible is a material object; the prophets are human beings much like any others; and their revelations are the fruit of the operation of natural laws. There is therefore no reason why Scripture should not be explained by the same method as any other natural phenomenon.

Although Spinoza is not so rash as to say so, but as we are now in a position to see, constructing a history of the Bible is in effect a matter of borrowing the method of analysis integral to Descartes' natural philosophy and applying it to theology. Scripture, Spinoza proposes, can be subjected to the same form of enquiry that Cartesian philosophers use to investigate nature. Furthermore, since Cartesianism proceeds entirely on the basis of natural reasoning, it follows that interpreting the Bible in this fashion does not require a supernatural light. The interpretative method that Spinoza is about to set out is, therefore, far from politically neutral. On the one hand it directly challenges the Reformed Church. On the other hand it associates Cartesian philosophy with a radical position that was deeply alarming to many Dutch followers of Descartes: the view that natural reason is all that theology requires, and thus that one can reach philosophical and theological conclusions by using a single method. This was just the kind of position that they had agreed not to press for, so that theology should retain a clear domain of its own.

When Spinoza begins to explicate his method, he produces a familiar recipe. The first step in constructing a history of Scripture is to work out what the text asserts,[37] and here the problems are primarily philological. What makes the Bible hard to understand, Spinoza claims, is not the loftiness of its theme but the language in which it is written,[38] and the initial task of an exegete is therefore to acquire a good knowledge of biblical Hebrew. This in itself is not straightforward, partly because there are no ancient Hebrew dictionaries, grammars, or

---

[37] Spinoza, *Tractatus Theologico-Politicus*, ch. 7, p. 100. This style of interpretation departed from the normative commentaries of Scripture favoured by Calvinist theologians. See Peter T. van Rooden, *Theology, Biblical Scholarship and Rabbinical Studies in the Seventeenth Century: Constantijn L'empereur (1591–1648): Professor of Hebrew and Theology at Leiden* (Leiden: Brill, 1989), pp. 132–49.
[38] Spinoza, *Tractatus Theologico-Politicus*, ch. 13, p. 167.

books of rhetoric, and partly because the language has become impoverished in the course of history, to the point where the meanings of some words and idioms cannot be recovered. In addition, there are distinctive features of Hebrew that can easily lead one astray. The exegete needs to remember that conjunctions and adverbs have multiple meanings, that many tenses used in other languages do not exist, and that the original text of the Bible was not pointed—it was written without vowels or punctuation, and the vowels later added by scribes and commentators can be a further source of ambiguity.[39]

Bearing these obstacles in mind, the exegete must next make a list of the main topics the Bible discusses and collect material by subject: for example, as Spinoza has already illustrated, an interpreter needs to gather together all the passages in which the spirit of God is mentioned in order to compare and contrast them.[40] This stage of the project mirrors a procedure used in classical rhetoric—collecting instances or *sententiae* under headings or *loci communes*— that had been taken up in various forms by Renaissance and early-modern historians.[41] Spinoza does not engage with the questions they asked about the best way to sort material, but given the length of the Bible, he is evidently envisaging an enormous and indeterminate project.[42]

Once it is complete, the exegete must attempt to resolve inconsistencies within the text by concentrating on passages that are obscure in the sense that it is difficult to work out their meaning from the context in which they occur. For example, Spinoza explains, when Moses' statement that 'God is fire' is taken by itself it is clear enough what it means, and although it is contrary to reason, the exegete must take it literally. Its obscurity only emerges when we consider it in the context of the prophet's other utterances about God, which include the claim that God does not resemble any of the visible things in the heavens, earth, or sea. How is this contradiction to be resolved? All the exegete can do is to re-examine the text in the hope of finding a solution, and must suspend judgment if none is forthcoming. In this case, however, help is at hand. 'Fire' is metaphorically used in the opening books of the Old Testament to mean 'anger' or 'jealousy'. So there are textual grounds for inferring that when Moses says that God is fire he means that God is jealous; and since he nowhere denies that God has passions or other human properties, there is nothing in Scripture to block this interpretation, despite the fact that it remains contrary to reason.[43]

[39] Ibid. ch. 7, p. 100.   [40] Ibid.
[41] Grafton, *What Was History?*, pp. 208–26.
[42] Spinoza, *Tractatus Theologico-Politicus*, ch. 7, p. 109.
[43] Ibid. ch. 7, pp. 100–1.

Finally, the exegete must search for circumstantial evidence by trying to find out who wrote each individual text, for whom they wrote it, what language they used, and what they were trying to achieve. As Spinoza points out, this last variable bears immediately on our understanding of the genre to which a work belongs. If we only take account of the content of texts, we are liable to misclassify them. For example, one can find superficially similar narratives about winged monsters in Ariosto's epic *Orlando Furioso*, in Ovid's *Metamorphoses*, and in the Old Testament's account of Elijah, and in order to judge these works one needs to be aware that their authors had diverse ends. 'The first wanted to write only trifles, the second, political matters, and the third, sacred matters'. So 'for writings that are obscure or incomprehensible to the intellect, a knowledge of their authors is very necessary'.[44] Equally, as the *Treatise* will later go on to show in more detail, our reading of sacred texts is shaped by our knowledge of their past. We therefore need information about how they were received, how many different versions existed, when they entered the canon, and so forth.

By means of all these familiar techniques one can compile a history of Scripture. But this is only the first of two interpretative steps, and the next is to use the resulting history to 'investigate the intentions of the prophets and the Holy Spirit'.[45] Here again natural history provides a model. Just as historians of nature start by investigating the most universal things, so 'the first thing to be sought from a history of Scripture is what is most universal, what is the basis and foundation of the whole of scripture, and finally, what all the prophets commend in it as an eternal teaching, most useful for all mortals'.[46] Fortunately, Spinoza seems to regard this part of his project as unproblematic; as we have seen, he takes it that the prophets' central teachings about the nature of a virtuous life and the beliefs that it requires are so easy to recover from Scripture that they have never been disputed and are as clear as Euclid.[47] The next step is therefore to proceed to less universal things, which 'flow from this universal teaching like streams', and concern the way in which we conduct our ordinary lives.[48] Here there are further inconsistencies to be resolved, but the task is still not overwhelmingly difficult. For example, when Christ instructs us to turn the other cheek he seems to 'destroy the law of Moses' which commands that an eye should be paid for an eye, leaving us in a quandary about which policy to live by. To overcome it, we need to take account of the contexts in which

---

[44] Ibid. ch. 7, p. 110.   [45] Ibid. ch. 7, p. 102.   [46] Ibid. ch. 7, p. 103.
[47] Ibid. ch. 7, pp. 102–3.   [48] Ibid. ch. 7, p. 103.

Christ and Moses were speaking. Christ, we soon discover, was not a legislator, and when he spoke these words was giving advice to an oppressed people who were living in a corrupt state. Moses, by contrast, was a ruler working to establish a good state. It follows that Christ's teaching—'that we should submit to injuries and yield to the impious'—is only appropriate in times of oppression, and that in good states we should demand and defend justice.[49]

The interpretative strategy that Spinoza uses in this case assumes that all the prophets converge on a single moral doctrine, and that, since Moses and Christ are fundamentally in agreement, we can adjust our reading of one in the light of our reading of another. We do not need to worry that their respective moral teachings may simply have been different. However, as he now reminds his readers, this is not always the case, and the greatest interpretative difficulties arise in relation to speculative matters about which different prophets hold diverse opinions. Here we need to be careful not to mistake the speculative beliefs of a particular prophet for biblical doctrine. The way to avoid this error is to follow the rules Spinoza has set out and start by defining the most universal of the relevant notions, such as prophecy, revelation, and miracles. This is what the *Treatise* has already done. With this stage of the investigation complete, we are in a position to try to determine what particular prophecies mean, and this, too, seems to be a move that Spinoza has already made. For example, he has established to his own satisfaction that when Moses describes the Jews as God's chosen people, what he means is that their state will be long lasting and successful. In some cases, then, we can work out what a prophet intended, but in others cases this information will be irrecoverable. Even if we can be pretty sure what a prophet 'really' saw or heard, we often cannot tell what they meant their signs and revelations to signify, and must be willing to admit interpretative defeat.[50]

This conclusion is not offered in a pessimistic spirit. Where the Bible talks about things that can be grasped with the intellect, Spinoza reassures us, we have no difficulty in comprehending it. Furthermore, as it happens, the moral teachings revealed by the prophets are too clear for us to misunderstand them and 'it is evident that we can grasp with certainty what it intends concerning things that are salutary and necessary for blessedness'. It is only when the Bible discusses imagined ideas that lie beyond our comprehension that the prophet's intentions escape us. But since this failure does not stand in the way of salvation

---

[49] Ibid. ch. 7, p. 104.   [50] Ibid. ch. 7, p. 105.

'there is no need for us to be so anxious about it'.[51] Constructing a history of Scripture enables us to understand all we really need to know.[52]

The view that we cannot always recover the prophets' intentions embodies a further criticism of the Reformed Church. If the correct way to interpret Scripture is to use our capacity for natural reasoning, but natural reasoning sometimes runs out on us, there is nothing more we can do to resolve our perplexities. We simply have to accept that we do not know what certain passages of Scripture mean, and therefore have no authoritative grounds for defending any particular interpretation of them. When reasoning runs out, so does doctrine. However, this conclusion runs counter to the Church's view that there are some doctrines which the faithful are required to believe, despite the fact that they are incomprehensible. In the words of the *Belgic Confession*, although mysteries such as the Trinity 'surpass all human understanding, nevertheless we now believe in it by means of the word of God'.[53] Spinoza is scornful of this feature of Christianity. On close inspection, he argues, what churches call mysteries turn out to be a jumble of old philosophical opinions drawn from the work of figures such as Plato and Aristotle, and consequently have no claim to be regarded as particularly authoritative.

Situating a proper interpretative method

Spinoza's insistence that the best way to interpret the meaning of the prophets' utterances is to employ a historical method that relies on ordinary forms of natural reasoning sets him against a range of critics whose views he now goes on to reject. When he was writing the *Treatise*, philosophers and theologians were still bound by the edict that the States of Holland had passed in 1656, forbidding each group from antagonizing the other.[54] To avoid being accused of breaking this law, authors had to be cautious about the way they expressed themselves, and one obvious device was to pin objections directed against living opponents on historical substitutes or accredited enemies. Spinoza now adopts this strategy. Rather than targeting his contemporaries, he inveighs against a series of other figures and confessions, casting his critical net over a broader area than the polemics of his argument require.

---

[51] Ibid. ch. 7, p. 111.   [52] Ibid. ch. 7, p. 112.
[53] 'The Belgic Confession', in *The Creeds of Christendom: The Evangelical Protestant Creeds*, ed. Philip Schaff (New York: Cosimo Books, 2007), Article 9.
[54] See Chapter 1, fn. 8.

If the meaning of Scripture can be determined by natural reasoning, it is in principle accessible to anyone. While some individuals will no doubt be better than others at interpreting the text, no one has a special *kind* of access to the minds of the prophets or is intrinsically better placed to determine the significance of their revelations. Among the various religious groups which reject this view, Spinoza now identifies two: the Pharisees, who believed that they had passed down a knowledge of the divine word originally vouchsafed to them by Moses; and the Roman Catholic Church, which holds that the Pope cannot be mistaken about the interpretation of Scripture. Both these traditions, he claims, should be viewed with deep suspicion, and neither set of claims will in fact stand up to scrutiny.[55] As we have seen, however, Spinoza is confident that an equally powerful case can be made against the Reformed Church's belief that the Holy Ghost imbues the faithful with a special capacity to know what Scripture teaches. Along with the Pope and the Pharisees, the *Treatise* could have singled out the Elect, together with the theologians who took it upon themselves to represent them.

Spinoza's allusion was hardly likely to go unnoticed, and could presumably have been expected to provoke displeasure among Reformed theologians. In addition, however, his method of interpretation was in danger of exposing him to the grave charge of subordinating theology to philosophy. Since this method is a version of the analytical approach to natural enquiry used by Descartes and favoured by many Dutch Cartesians, applying it to the Bible amounts, as we have seen, to using philosophy to interpret Scripture. From there it was a small step to the charge that not only philosophy, but worse still Cartesian philosophy, can take over the task of theology. For several reasons, this was a dangerous conclusion to reach. At a practical level it overstepped the boundaries of free philosophizing laid down by the States General and broke the rule that philosophers and theologians must keep off each other's territory.[56] Moreover, at an intellectual level it threatened to abolish the division between the two disciplines. Spinoza's next step is therefore to reaffirm their distinctness by showing that philosophy cannot after all do theology's work. To hold that properly philosophical methods of investigation are capable of interpreting the meaning of Scripture is, he now contends, a serious mistake.

---

[55] Spinoza, *Tractatus Theologico-Politicus*, ch. 7, p. 105.

[56] Perhaps this factor contributed to Spinoza's decision to present the *Treatise* as published outside the Netherlands. Although it was published in Amsterdam by Jan Rieuwertsz, the imprint on the title page is 'Hamburg. Henry Kunraht. 1670'. Ibid. p. 3. See Piet Steenbakkers, 'The Text of Spinoza's *Tractatus Theologico-Politicus*', in *Spinoza's 'Theologico-Political Treatise'*, ed. Yitzhak Y. Melamed and Michael A. Rosenthal (Cambridge: Cambridge University Press, 2010), pp. 33–5.

Part of the motivation for the argument that Spinoza now goes on to offer lies in a desire to distance himself from the inflammatory position defended by his friend Lodewijk Meijer, to the effect that only philosophy can judge theology, which has no independent authority of its own. Instead of interpreting Scripture by Scripture, we must test interpretations of the Bible against our philosophical understanding of the truth. As we would by now expect, Spinoza does not name Meijer as an opponent. Instead, he directs his criticisms of Meijer's view against Maimonides, who is accused of arguing that, whenever a passage of Scripture asserts something that is contrary to reason, we must interpret it in a way that accords with reason, even when its meaning is perfectly clear.[57] For example, if Moses says that God is a fire and we know that this is contrary to reason, we must reinterpret his utterance in such a way that it comes out true. This is the very approach that Spinoza has just rejected. As he now explains, Maimonides/Meijer has mistakenly assumed that, despite the apparent diversity of the prophets' opinions, they all propounded a single speculative doctrine that accords with our philosophical understanding.

To appreciate what is at stake in this discussion, it will be helpful to look more closely at some of Meijer's arguments. The conviction that the many ambiguities to be found in the sacred texts can be internally resolved is based, he proposes, on a number of false assumptions. In the first place, it presupposes that we can distinguish clear from obscure passages. But since a passage that is obscure to one reader may be clear to another, there is no single way of making this distinction.[58] Furthermore, it presupposes that the project of resolving inconsistencies has a single solution. But even if we could settle the meanings of a given set of passages and find a way to make them mutually consistent, another inconsistency would soon crop up somewhere else in the text. Finally, since the whole enterprise of interpretation depends on independent linguistic knowledge that cannot be derived from the text itself, Scripture cannot be interpreted by Scripture. Since these problems are utterly intractable, the only way forward is to assess biblical claims in the light of some independent standard. But what better standard could there be than that of philosophy, that is to say, the 'light of reason refined by study, application, experience, and practice'?[59]

---

[57] Spinoza, *Tractatus Theologico-Politicus*, ch. 7, pp. 113–14. See Chapter 5, fn. 58.

[58] Meijer, *Philosophia S. Scripturæ Interpres*, III.3, p. 7; Meyer, *La philosophie interprète de l'écriture sainte*, III.3, p. 46.

[59] Meijer, *Philosophia S. Scripturæ Interpres*, V.2, p. 40; Meyer, *La philosophie interprète de l'écriture sainte*, V.2, p. 106.

Meijer takes pains to show that relying on philosophy to interpret Scripture is not a new idea. Theologians have already employed it to dispel mistaken Catholic and Lutheran interpretations of the Eucharist, by showing that these conflict with our knowledge of physics.[60] (The same approach had been taken, we might add, to Joshua's claim about the sun.) In addition, theologians have employed it to confirm the central biblical doctrines that are, as virtually everyone agrees, both clear and necessary for salvation. (Here Spinoza could not but have recognized some of his own arguments.) The approach has therefore already proved its worth. However, so Meijer enthuses, it has had new life breathed into it by Descartes' innovations. The emergence of a philosophy that guarantees the certainty of its conclusions has provided an indubitable standard against which interpretations of biblical teaching can be assessed. Because we can be absolutely confident of the claims Cartesianism vindicates, we can look forward to an era in which philosophy will reveal the means to eternal life and put an end to the interminable disputes that have torn the Church apart.[61]

Having observed the furore that arose when Meijer's book was published, Spinoza undoubtedly had pragmatic reasons for dissociating himself from its opinions; but he is also intellectually out of sympathy with them. While he acknowledges many of the interpretative problems that Meijer raises, he does not accept his solutions. A first point of disagreement concerns the construction of a history of Scripture. Spinoza willingly concedes that his method cannot clarify all the obscurities to be found in the Bible,[62] but remains convinced that if one's project is to work out what the Scriptures say, one must rely so far as possible on the text itself. It is of course necessary to use external linguistic and historical sources when they are relevant. (For example, the *Treatise* occasionally appeals for support to Josephus's *History of the Jews*.[63]) What we must *not* do, however, is to use our own beliefs about what is true to decode what a passage says, even when we are absolutely certain that these beliefs are correct. Rather, we must try to let the text speak for itself, and confront it in all its strangeness.

Spinoza is equally unimpressed by Meijer's treatment of what the *Treatise* presents as the second stage of interpretation: finding out what the prophets intend or mean. Here again, he rejects the suggestion that we should interpret

---

[60] Meijer, *Philosophia S. Scripturæ Interpres*, VI.3, pp. 47–8; Meyer, *La philosophie interprète de l'écriture sainte*, VI.3, pp. 120–1.

[61] Meijer, *Philosophia S. Scripturæ Interpres*, Epilogus; Meyer, *La philosophie interprète de l'écriture sainte*, Epilogue, p. 249.

[62] Spinoza, *Tractatus Theologico-Politicus*, ch. 7, p. 109.

[63] Ibid. ch. 2, p. 42, ch. 3, p. 49, ch. 6, p. 96, ch. 9, pp. 132, 140, ch. 10, pp. 143, 146.

the prophets' utterances and actions in the light of our own philosophical knowledge. Anyone who takes this path will ride roughshod over the prophets' imaginative grasp of their situations, and ignore their capacity to express their insights in a form accessible to ordinary people. In doing so, they will misread their purposes. Many of the things they say are not, and were not intended to be, literally true, and if we try to make them so we shall end up with a travesty of their meaning and significance. So in order to understand Scripture, we have to try to think in the prophets' imaginative register while being prepared to admit failure.

When Spinoza claims to be interpreting Scripture by Scripture, he means that he is interpreting Scripture by Scripture as opposed to interpreting it against the standard of clarity and distinctness used by Cartesian philosophers. His method does not prevent him from appealing to non-biblical historical and philological sources; on the contrary, it demands that he do so whenever these can help him to work out, for instance, what a word means or when a book was written. What it forbids him to do, however, is to treat the Bible as a work whose purpose is primarily to present a sequence of clear and distinct ideas; and here, he urges, Meijer/Maimonides misses something important. Maimonides, and by implication Meijer, fail to see that the prophets were neither philosophers engaged in demonstration nor theologians aiming to understand the truth about a text.[64] Rather, they were people of great imagination who were trying to convey their insights in a persuasive fashion in order to encourage a certain way of life.[65] To try to interpret and test their claims in the light of clear and distinct ideas is therefore to apply an inappropriate standard. Furthermore, the attempt is bound to fail. Since the Bible mainly consists of narratives about individual things, it contains very few clear and distinct ideas on which philosophical reasoning can get a purchase, and the efforts of philosophers to explain Scripture will consequently come to naught.[66]

Finally, there is an important sense in which advocates of the view that Scripture must be interpreted by philosophy reproduce one of the objectionable features of the Calvinist claim that it can only be interpreted with the help of a supernatural light. It is clear from the Bible that the prophets and Apostles preached not only to the faithful, but addressed the impious as well, expecting to be understood. The Reformed Church's belief that natural reason is not enough to enable us to grasp their teachings therefore implies that the prophets and Apostles largely preached to people who could not understand them, and

---

[64] Ibid. ch. 7, p. 115.   [65] Ibid. ch. 2, p. 43.   [66] Ibid. ch. 7, p. 115.

that Moses prescribed his laws in vain. Most of their audiences, endowed with natural reason but not with faith, would have been incapable of following their meaning.[67] Equally, authors such as Meijer, who insist that one must have an education in Cartesian philosophy in order to grasp the meaning of Scripture, place its meaning beyond ordinary reach. People 'who have no knowledge of demonstrations, or are unable to give their time to them, will be able to admit nothing about scripture, and will depend on the authority and testimony of those who philosophise.... This would obviously introduce a new sort of authority into the Church, and a new kind of minister or priest, whom ordinary people would mock rather than venerate'.[68] The supernatural light returns in a new guise. 'This method of Maimonides', Spinoza bluntly concludes, 'is utterly useless'.[69]

One could hardly look for a more uncompromising rejection. But what exactly does Spinoza offer in place of Maimonides' hermeneutic approach? Does he succeed in avoiding its deficiencies, while meeting the Church's demand that theology must be kept separate from philosophy? Spinoza certainly does defend a distinctive view. While Maimonides and Meijer propose that philosophy should take theology over by subjecting its claims to philosophical standards of assessment, Spinoza aspires to form a coalition between the two forms of enquiry by bringing theology into the Cartesian fold. As he has argued, both philosophy and theology rely on natural reasoning; more specifically, both employ analysis or the historical method to identify and define the entities that they then attempt to understand. Theologians who study the Bible in the way that Spinoza recommends therefore rely on a method that Cartesians also employ in their study of the natural world, and in doing so interpret Scripture by Scripture as the Church requires. So far, then, there is no methodological divide between the two subjects, and nothing for their exponents to fight about.

It is of course true that philosophers can also do something else that theologians cannot. They can recast some of their conclusions in a synthetic or demonstrative form, and where this is possible it enables them to test the mathematical certainty of their results and demonstrate further clear and distinct conclusions. But the Bible, like some of the things that natural philosophers study, is not adapted to this form of inquiry, and that's an end of it. We have to accept with Aristotle that different sorts of things require different methods of investigation. So while some areas of philosophy do not use the historical

---

[67] Ibid. ch. 7, p. 113.   [68] Ibid. ch. 7, p. 114.   [69] Ibid. ch. 7, p. 116.

method that it shares with theology, other areas do. Methodologically, the two forms of inquiry overlap.

For the more orthodox theologians of the Reformed Church, this was not a significant improvement on the position held by Maimonides and Meijer. Although Spinoza allows that theology undertakes a distinctive task that is not itself a philosophical one (namely interpreting the teachings of the prophets and Apostles), he nevertheless brings theology into the ambit of philosophy. Theology, he asserts, relies on norms of natural reasoning that philosophers among others also employ, so that some of the skills cultivated by philosophers also fit them to do theology. Putting the point the other way round, theologians who construct a history of Scripture and draw inferences from it are, from a methodological point of view, philosophizing. Methodologically speaking, there is no sharp boundary between philosophy and theology, and many distinctive features of theology have been lost.

Worse still, the kinds of natural reasoning that are necessary to work out what the Bible's central doctrines consist in are so straightforward that they are not restricted to any professional group, theological or philosophical. 'The standard of interpretation must be nothing but the natural light which is common to all, and not any supernatural light or external authority. Nor must it be so difficult that it can only be applied by the most acute philosophers, but must be accommodated to the natural and common intelligence and capacity of men'.[70] Ordinary people who can read or hear the Scriptures do not need theologians or other religious officials to identify the fundamental doctrines on which their salvation depends, and to some extent they can resolve interpretative problems by using their ordinary capacity for reasoning. In defending the first of these claims Spinoza is, as we have seen, upholding a view shared by more moderate Calvinists within the Reformed Church. But in defending the second, he is implicitly voicing his support for nonconformist religious movements such as the Collegiants, who treated the interpretation of Scripture as a collective project in which everyone could take part, untrammelled by any authority other than the text itself. This is a far cry from the aspirations of the theologians Spinoza is opposing, who are bent on using their purported authority as a means of maintaining their own power. Even had his diagnosis been fair to them, they were hardly likely to have accepted it.

---

[70] Ibid. ch. 7, p. 117.

Chapter 7

Putting the Interpretative Method to Work

The interpretative approach that Spinoza has outlined is designed to capture what he describes as the foundations and principles of our knowledge of the Scriptures.[1] As long as exegetes stick conscientiously to his historical method, they will be able to understand the teaching of the Bible as well as it can be understood. Rather than distorting its meaning and enhancing superstition, their efforts will enable them to decode the prophets' metaphors and affirm its central message. That, at least, is the claim. But while the *Treatise* goes to great lengths to defend this hermeneutic stance against a string of potential criticisms, it remains to show what it can do. What exegetical errors can a history of Scripture put right and what superstitious practices can it unmask? Unless the answers are compelling, readers may be forgiven for wondering what all the fuss has been about.[2]

Spinoza, is more than willing to rise to the challenge, and sets out to show that his method can overcome 'the common prejudices of theology'.[3] Despite the fact that parts of the history of Scripture have fallen into oblivion[4] and that

[1] Benedictus de Spinoza, *Tractatus Theologico-Politicus*, ed. Carl Gebhardt, vol. III, *Opera* (Heidelberg: Carl Winter, 1924), ch. 8, p. 117.

[2] On Spinoza's analysis of the Bible, see Michael Heyd, *Between Orthodoxy and the Enlightenment: Jean-Robert Chouet and the Introduction of Cartesian Science in the Academy of Geneva* (The Hague: Nijhoff, 1982); Jacqueline Lagrée and Pierre-François Moreau, 'La lecture de la Bible dans le cercle de Spinoza', in *Le grand siècle et la Bible*, ed. Jean-Robert Armogathe (Paris: Beauchesne, 1989); Steven B. Smith, *Spinoza, Liberalism, and the Question of Jewish Identity* (New Haven: Yale University Press, 1997), ch. 3; Sylvain Zac, *Essais spinozistes* (Paris: Vrin, 1985); Sylvain Zac, *Philosophie, théologie, politique dans l'œuvre de Spinoza* (Paris: Vrin, 1979); Sylvain Zac, *Spinoza et l'interprétation de l'écriture* (Paris: Presses Universitaires de France, 1965).

[3] Spinoza, *Tractatus Theologico-Politicus*, ch. 8, p. 118.

[4] Ibid. ch. 8, p. 117.

commentators have 'concocted new things out of their own brains',[5] it is still just about possible to circumvent their errors and identify the true teachings of Scripture. In a sequence of chapters he takes on four theological prejudices (the first three closely interlocking), each of which bears in different ways on the development of his argument; and by showing where these prejudices go wrong he puts himself in a stronger position to dismiss them. The conclusions of this section of the *Treatise* are therefore partly negative, although as we shall see they have a number of radical implications. By far the most important of these, from Spinoza's point of view, is that Spinoza's analysis puts him in a position to take up the main thread of his discussion and explain what a religious way of life consists in. By discrediting his Calvinist opponents, he clears the way for his own account of the substance of Scripture's doctrine.

The first stage in this process focuses on the authorship of the various books of the Bible. Continuing his critique of the Reformed Church, Spinoza first employs his method to demolish the view that the Old Testament as a whole is the word of God. In fact, he argues, it is a compilation, written by several hands and only assembled in its present form during the era of the Maccabees.[6] The aim of this lengthy exercise (which begins with an examination of the Pentateuch, Joshua, Judges, Ruth, and Kings, and then moves on to consider the books of the prophets), is partly to vindicate a piecemeal approach to the books of Scripture. 'Proving the divinity of one book', Spinoza urges, 'is not enough to establish the divinity of all'[7]; rather, the authority of each individual book must be considered on its own merits. Next in line to be dismissed is the belief that 'by a certain special providence, God has kept the whole Bible uncorrupted'. Rather than simply assuming that the moral doctrine of the text remains decipherable, we have to use the historical method to find out whether this is so, and whether the meaning of Scripture, 'the only thing in a statement that gives us a reason for calling it divine, has reached us without corruption, even though we may suppose that the words by which it was first signified have very frequently been changed'.[8] Here Spinoza will reach a positive conclusion; but in the course of doing so he will set aside what he regards as a third error, this time concerning the marginal notes in the Masoretic version of the Old Testament. The Masoretic text, he argues, was created during the latter part of the first millennium CE by scholars who inserted vowel points in the earlier Hebrew manuscripts. As they did so, they also added marginal annotations known as the 'Masorah', which subsequently became the subject of fierce

---

[5] Ibid. ch. 8, p. 118.   [6] Ibid. ch. 10, p. 150.   [7] Ibid.
[8] Ibid. ch. 9, p. 135.

scholarly controversy.[9] According to certain commentators, some of these annotations indicate divine mysteries concealed in the main body of the text,[10] and this is one of the views that Spinoza will contest.[11]

In all these cases, Spinoza is determined to show that problems for which commentators have sought supernatural solutions can be resolved by appeal to the natural reasoning on which his method relies. To be sure, he concedes, he is not likely to persuade everyone. 'Those who consider the Bible, as it is, as a letter God has sent men from Heaven will doubtless cry out that I have committed a sin against the Holy Ghost, because I have maintained that the word of God is faulty...that we have only fragments of it, and finally that the original text of the covenant God made with the Jews has been lost'.[12] But Spinoza, on his side, is engaged in a campaign against these opponents, who, 'in their excessive zeal to be holy, may turn religion into superstition, and indeed, may begin to worship likenesses and images, i.e. paper and ink, in place of the word of God'.[13]

Before leaving the theme of interpretation, Spinoza turns his attention to a fourth prejudice specifically about the status of the New Testament. Looking forward to the positive account of religion he will go on to offer, he pauses to show how his historical approach to Scripture can deal with a difficulty that threatens to stand in his way. As with the Old Testament, we need to resist the view that the New Testament as a whole is the word of God by distinguishing its core doctrines from other elements in the text. By sticking to the historical method and paying careful attention to the style of the Apostle's utterances we can separate prophecy from teaching. Thus released from the need to accept everything the Apostles say as authoritative, Spinoza is ready to give an account of the teaching expressed in one form by Moses and in another by Christ.

Diverse as they are, each of these discussions plays a part in building an overall case for a conception of the Bible as a text compiled and transmitted over many generations, in which numerous ordinary human actions and attitudes are recorded. The interpretative method that Spinoza has set out now begins to produce what is from a Calvinist point of view poisonous fruit, as he progressively undercuts all attempt to associate the Scriptures with the supernatural. Failing to treat the biblical books as human artefacts written by human authors is, so Spinoza repeatedly insists, a form of superstition. Even if it does not

---

[9] Noel Malcolm, *Aspects of Hobbes* (Oxford: Clarendon Press, 2002), pp. 398–9.
[10] Spinoza, *Tractatus Theologico-Politicus*, ch. 9, pp. 135–6.
[11] Ibid. ch. 9, p. 136.   [12] Ibid. ch. 12, p. 158.
[13] Ibid. ch. 12, p. 159.

directly arouse hopes and fears that stifle the capacity for independent thought, it is integral to practices that do so.

The authors of the Old Testament

According to the *Belgic Confession*, 'God commanded his servants, the prophets and apostles, to commit his revealed word to writing; and he himself wrote with his own finger the two tables of the law'. Furthermore, 'the Holy Ghost witnesseth in our hearts that [the canonical books] are from God, whereof they carry the evidence in themselves'.[14] Officially, then, Dutch Calvinists were committed to some version of the belief that the Bible is a communication from God, and that the individual prophetic books are the work of the particular prophets to whom he revealed himself. For example, so it was traditionally assumed, the author of the Pentateuch was Moses.[15] This assumption was not of course confined to Calvinism. It was held by other Christian churches and, as Spinoza points out, was an important part of Jewish tradition as well. 'Indeed,' he adds, 'the Pharisees maintained it so stubbornly that they regarded anyone who seemed to think otherwise as a heretic'.[16] Furthermore, in all these confessions, the view that the Pentateuch contained Moses' testimony of revelation is used to sustain the belief that Scripture possesses a special kind of authority.

While the view that Moses is the author of the Pentateuch remained standard, inconsistencies in the text had led a series of biblical commentators to raise doubts about it, and Spinoza now adds his voice to their sceptical chorus. Moses, he claims, was not the author of the Pentateuch. In support of his contention, he cites the work of a twelfth-century Spanish rabbi, Abraham Ibn Ezra (1089–1164), who 'possessed an independent mind and no slight learning and was the first of those I have read to take notice of this prejudice'.[17] Ibn Ezra had obliquely proposed that certain passages of the Pentateuch are later interpolations. For example, Moses is sometimes mentioned in the third person, as in 'Moses wrote the law'; Deuteronomy contains words that Moses is

---

[14] 'The Belgic Confession', in *The Creeds of Christendom: The Evangelical Protestant Creeds*, ed. Philip Schaff (New York: Cosimo Books, 2007), Articles 3 and 6.

[15] i.e. the books of Genesis, Exodus, Leviticus, Numbers, and Deuteronomy.

[16] Spinoza, *Tractatus Theologico-Politicus*, ch. 8, p. 118.

[17] Ibid. On Spinoza and Ibn Ezra, see M. Goshen-Gottstein, 'Bible et Judaïsme', in *Le grand siècle et la Bible*, ed. Jean-Robert Armogathe (Paris: Beauchesne, 1989); Warren Zev Harvey, 'Spinoza on Ibn Ezra's "Secret of the Twelve"', in *Spinoza's 'Theologico-Political Treatise'*, ed. Yitzhak Y. Melamed and Michael A. Rosenthal (Cambridge: Cambridge University Press, 2010).

said to have uttered after he had crossed the Jordan, which he never did; the author makes it clear, when he speaks about Moses' life, that he is describing events that happened long ago; and the author inserts explanations that Moses himself would not have needed to provide.[18] On the basis of scattered pieces of evidence such as these, Ibn Ezra concluded that sections must have been added to the original text. Spinoza, however, goes further. He argues for the much stronger thesis that none of the surviving text of the Pentateuch was written by Moses, which as far as we can tell is the work of the scribe Ezra.[19]

The belief that Ezra had helped to re-establish the Mosaic Law after the Jews' return from Babylonian captivity derives from the book of Nehemiah. According to Jewish tradition, Ezra, acting under divine guidance, not only recovered the content of Moses' original books of the law but produced the surviving Masoretic text. Together with a Grand Synagogue or council of wise men, including some of the prophets, he then fixed the canon. The view that Ezra had miraculously reconstituted the original text of the Bible was also confirmed by the Church fathers on the basis of the apocryphal book of Esdras, and was used by Islamic writers to undermine the Jewish and Christian claim that the Old Testament is the word of God.

Ibn Ezra's critical suggestions about the origin of the Pentateuch were subsequently taken up and developed by a series of Christian scholars, the most influential being a fifteenth-century Spanish Hebraist, Alfonso Tostado Ribera de Madrigal (Tostatus) (1400–55), whose works remained widely known throughout Europe in the sixteenth and seventeenth centuries.[20] Although Tostatus rejected some of Ibn Ezra's specific hypotheses, he agreed that the Pentateuch contains later additions, and shared the traditional view that these were the work of Ezra.[21] In doing so, moreover, he reminded his readers that the authorship of the Pentateuch was debatable, and released a string of increasingly radical critical speculations. During the following century, Andreas Masius (d. 1573), a Flemish Catholic theologian and a distinguished Hebrew scholar, argued that Ezra had compiled the books of Joshua, Judges, and Kings from an assortment of earlier materials, and had at the very least inserted additional phrases into the Pentateuch.[22] Among the writers who

---

[18] Spinoza, *Tractatus Theologico-Politicus*, ch. 8, p. 127.

[19] See Malcolm, *Aspects of Hobbes*, pp. 398–413.

[20] See A. Tostado, *Opera Omnia*, 23 vols. (Venice, 1596), V, fols. 183-4. See also Malcolm, *Aspects of Hobbes*, pp. 404–7.

[21] Tostado, *Opera Omnia*, V, fol.15v. Malcolm, *Aspects of Hobbes*, p. 405.

[22] A. Masius, *Iosuæ imperatoris historia illustrata atque explicata* (Antwerp, 1574), p. 2 (2nd pagination). See Malcolm, *Aspects of Hobbes*, pp. 407–9.

developed this set of claims was another native of Flanders, the Jesuit Cornelius à Lapide (1567–1637), who voiced Masius' implicit suggestion that not only the later books of the Old Testament, but those of the Pentateuch as well, may have been compiled from earlier texts written by Moses.[23]

This line of thought was taken over by two of Spinoza's immediate predecessors, Isaac La Peyrère and Thomas Hobbes. In *Leviathan*, Hobbes is at his most deadpan as he points out that we cannot infer from the title of the Books of Moses that Moses was their author; 'The history of Livy', he writes 'denotes the writer; but the history of Alexander is denominated from the subject'.[24] The Pentateuch, he concludes, was compiled after Moses' death, though the account of the law in Chapter 11 of Deuteronomy is the work of Moses himself.[25] Moreover, the other books of the Old Testament were written long after the events they describe. 'The whole Scripture of the Old Testament, was set forth in the form we have it, after the return of the Jews from their captivity in Babylon, and before the time of Ptolemaus Philadelphus, that caused it to be translated into Greek by seventy men, which were sent him out of Judea for that purpose'.[26] Equally, La Peyrère argues in his *Pre-Adamitae*, that the Scriptures were assembled from a collection of diverse sources. As Noel Malcolm has shown, however, almost all the evidence to which these two writers, and indeed Spinoza, appeal, had already been assembled by Tostatus, Lapide, and others. So, although the only forerunner that Spinoza actually mentions is Ibn Ezra, it is safe to assume that he, like La Peyrère and Hobbes, is drawing on a wider debate in order to defend what the more conservative theologians of the Reformed Church regarded as an unacceptable conclusion: that the text of the Bible as we know it is based on earlier manuscripts that have since been lost, and was assembled over a considerable period of time.

Spinoza's grounds for affirming that Moses is not the author of the Pentateuch can be quickly summarized. He starts out by bolstering Ibn Ezra's claim that the text contains interpolations, citing further examples, all except one of which had been mentioned by Tostatus or Cornelius à Lapide.[27] For example,

---

[23] C. à Lapide, *Commentarius in Esdram, Nehemiam, Tobiam, Judith, Esther, et Machabæos* (Antwerp, 1734); C. à Lapide, *In Pentateuchum Mosis Commentaria* (Paris: 1630). See Malcolm, *Aspects of Hobbes*, pp. 409–10.

[24] Thomas Hobbes, *Leviathan*, ed. Richard Tuck (Cambridge: Cambridge University Press, 1996), p. 261.

[25] Ibid. p. 262. Compare Spinoza, *Tractatus Theologico-Politicus*, ch. 8, p. 119.

[26] Hobbes, *Leviathan*, p. 265.

[27] See Malcolm, *Aspects of Hobbes*, p. 412. See also M. H. Goshen-Gottstein, 'The Textual Criticism of the Old Testament: Rise, Decline, Rebirth', *Journal of Biblical Literature*, 102. 3 (1983).

Deuteronomy includes an account of Moses' death and the events that followed it, which he himself could not have written, and some of the place-names it mentions date from a later period.[28] If we press this line of reasoning to its logical conclusion, Spinoza points out, we are bound to wonder whether Moses is the author of any of the Pentateuch, and the only way to answer the question is of course to consult Scripture. According to Exodus, Moses wrote an account of the war between the Israelites and Amalek, and recorded the laws that God imposed when he first entered into a covenant with the Israelites. After the initial covenant had been broken, he also wrote an account of the laws governing the new agreement with God, which was later expanded by Joshua.[29] But since it is clear that none of these works is contained in the Pentateuch, the balance of evidence indicates that Moses did not write any of the books we now possess.

Engaging with his readers' expectations, Spinoza allows that this conclusion may seem unduly revisionist. Because we know that Moses recorded some laws, it is tempting to infer that he probably also wrote down the laws listed in Deuteronomy. However, this is not an inference that the historical method permits us to make. To do so would be to import our own independent beliefs into the interpretative process, thus departing from the rule of interpreting Scripture by Scripture and 'twisting its words to our liking'. And this would amount to denying Scripture and making up a new version of it to suit ourselves.[30] If we are to stick to a defensible interpretative method, we simply have to admit our ignorance. As far as we can tell, we no longer possess the works originally written by Moses and must assume that they have been lost.[31] We therefore have no grounds for claiming that he is the author of any surviving book of Scripture.[32]

This is a striking argument. The commentators with whom Spinoza is engaging largely worked with the assumption that, except where the evidence explicitly indicated otherwise, it was safe to conclude that Moses wrote the Pentateuch. This approach enabled them to root out later additions, thus disclosing an *ur* text in all its divine purity. Spinoza, however, shifts the burden of proof. Unless the surviving text explicitly indicates that Moses *did* write a particular book, we cannot legitimately conclude that he was its author. 'Even though I might grant that it seems consistent with reason that Moses should have written down the laws at the very time and place in which he happened to communicate them, nevertheless I deny that it is permissible for us to affirm on

---

[28] Spinoza, *Tractatus Theologico-Politicus*, ch. 8, p. 119.   [29] Ibid. ch. 8, p. 122.
[30] Ibid. ch. 8, p. 123.   [31] Ibid.   [32] Ibid. ch. 8, p. 124.

this ground that he did so'.[33] One of the distinctive features of his method is therefore that it vindicates this much stiffer test of authorship.

The critical techniques that have yielded this conclusion about Moses can, of course, be applied to other sections of the Old Testament. Echoing both Lapide and Hobbes, Spinoza offers evidence that the Book of Joshua was not written by Joshua, that the Judges did not write Judges, and that Samuel did not write Samuel.[34] Internal evidence reveals that the Book of Kings is a compilation, and inconsistencies between one biblical book and another show that Chronicles was written long after Ezra; that the Psalms were collected during the era of the Second Temple, five hundred or so years after the rule of David; and that Proverbs was probably written about the same time.[35] As for the books of the prophets, it is clear that these were collected from various sources and are fragments of earlier texts.[36] The origin of the Book of Job, Spinoza allows, is a matter of conjecture, but he is inclined to follow Ibn Ezra's view that it was translated into Hebrew from another language.[37] Finally, Daniel, Ezra, Esther, and Nehemiah were all written after the restoration of the Temple, by a historian who was certainly neither Ezra nor Nehemiah.[38] The aim of this catalogue is progressively to undermine the prevalent assumption that the Bible is a direct and unified record of the divine word, while simultaneously displaying the virtues of Spinoza's method. Much depends, as his conclusions show, on evidence about when a text was written, whether it was copied from another extant work, and whether it contradicts other existing sources. Commentators who fail to consider these issues allow themselves to go astray.

This is a predominantly negative result; but the historical method on which it is grounded also allows Spinoza to arrive at positive hypotheses about the authorship of the Old Testament. Because the first five books tell a connected narrative, it is reasonable to assume that they were the work of a single author who 'wanted to write about the past history of the Jews from their first origin to the first destruction of the city'.[39] Since we also know that they were written long after the events they describe, it is probable, as both Jewish and Christian commentators agree, that the historian in question was Ezra.[40] If so, we can tell from internal evidence that Ezra compiled information from a collection of earlier histories by more than one hand, but he was for some reason unable to complete the project.[41] The precepts and stories he recounts are 'collected and piled up indiscriminately, so that afterwards they might be more easily

---

[33] Ibid.   [34] Ibid. ch. 8, p. 125.   [35] Ibid. ch. 10, pp. 141–2.
[36] Ibid. ch. 10, p. 142.   [37] Ibid. ch. 10, p. 144.   [38] Ibid. ch. 10, p. 145.
[39] Ibid. ch. 8, p. 125.   [40] Ibid. ch. 8, p. 128.   [41] Ibid. ch. 9, p. 129.

examined and put in their place'.[42] As they stand, they are full of repetitions, unaltered transcriptions, and discrepancies.

Many of the most glaring inconsistencies in the Pentateuch are chronological, and although strenuous attempts had been made to reconcile the various lengths of time it mentions, Spinoza is adamant that such efforts are doomed.[43] In a rare autobiographical aside, he assures his readers that he was educated in the rabbinical tradition and has tried for many years to vindicate its commitment to consistency, but has come to the conclusion that in this respect it simply will not work.[44] The chronology of the Old Testament does not add up, and in order to make it do so one has to invent fanciful interpretations that corrupt the language of the text. But this is 'insane'.[45] For example, the fourteenth-century rabbi Levi ben Gerson, also known as Gersonides,[46] attempted to vindicate the transparent claim that Solomon built the Temple four hundred and eighty years after the Jews' expulsion from Egypt by adjusting other equally clear assertions elsewhere in the text, such as that Moses governed his people in the wilderness for forty years. 'It is quite evident', Spinoza comments, 'that this rabbi...and those who follow in his footsteps...are correcting Scripture rather than explaining it',[47] and are more concerned to uphold its divinity than to establish its truth.[48]

There is no reason to suppose that the commentators whom Spinoza describes as following in Gersonides's footsteps are all and only Jews. Here, once again, Spinoza is criticizing not only the rabbinical tradition, but also Christian authors who are prepared to revise clear passages in order to sustain their prejudices about the Bible's overall meaning. 'As for their thinking it pious to accommodate some passages of Scripture to others, it is surely a ridiculous piety, in that they accommodate the clear passages to the obscure, the correct to the faulty, and corrupt sound passages with those which are spoiled'. To avoid these types of error, one must among other things be prepared to face up to the chronological claims made in the text, and refuse, in Spinoza's Cartesian metaphor, to treat Scripture as though it were a piece of wax, capable of taking on an infinity of different forms.[49]

---

[42] Ibid. ch. 9, p. 131.

[43] Used for example by Josephus, *Antiquities*, VI.xiv.9. (See Spinoza, *Tractatus Theologico-Politicus*, ch. 9, p. 133.)

[44] Ibid. ch. 9, p. 135.   [45] Ibid. ch. 9, p. 134.   [46] 1288 – 1344.

[47] Spinoza, *Tractatus Theologico-Politicus*, ch. 9, p. 132fn.

[48] Ibid. ch. 9, p. 130fn.

[49] Ibid. ch. 9, p. 136fn.

To understand the Old Testament, then, we must treat it as a bundle of texts derived from earlier works that have not survived and put together by historians whose powers of imagining and reasoning were nothing above the ordinary. There is consequently no reason to accept the view upheld by some seventeenth-century commentators that Ezra acted under divine guidance.[50] Spinoza owned a copy of a commentary on the Masoretic Bible, published in 1620 by the Hebrew scholar Johannes Buxtorf the elder (1564–1629), who argued that Ezra, together with the other learned men who made up the Grand Synagogue or council at which the text of Scripture was determined, were inspired by God.[51] The *Treatise* may therefore implicitly be referring to Buxtorf when it dismisses what it presents as a rabbinical claim. Ezra, Spinoza asserts, was not even present at the Great Synagogue, let alone divinely inspired, and the hypothesis that he was is an unfounded and ridiculous invention. All the evidence suggests that his efforts were thoroughly human.

While a sceptical attitude to scriptural chronology is undoubtedly what Spinoza's interpretative approach recommends, applying it carried certain risks. La Peyrère, for example, had grounded his claim that Adam was not the first man on chronological evidence,[52] but in doing so had put himself in the heterodox position of questioning the widespread assumption that the Old Testament records the beginnings of terrestrial and human history. The *Pre-Adamitae* had been publicly burned in Paris, and its author imprisoned.[53] Chronological arguments could therefore be dangerous, and in Spinoza's hands they are combined with other techniques to undermine the Reformed Church's view of Scripture. No longer dictated by God, it becomes a compilation of works written by various historians over a period, Spinoza calculates, of at least two thousand years.[54] In what sense, then, can it be said to be divine? In due course Spinoza will reassure his readers that Scripture is more than simply one text among others by explicating a sense in which it can properly be said to teach the divine word. Before that, however, he needs to resolve a set of problems about its authenticity.

[50] Malcolm, *Aspects of Hobbes*, p. 399.

[51] J. Buxtorf, *Tiberias sive commentarius masorethicus* (Basel, 1620). See no.1 of the list in J. Freudenthal, *Die Lebensgeschichte Spinozas in Quellenschriften, Urkunden und Nichtamtlichen Nachrichten*, 2 vols. (Leipzig, 1899), vol. 1, p. 342.

[52] Isaac la Peyrère, *Systema theologicum, ex præadamitarum hypothesi. Pars prima* (n.p., 1655).

[53] Richard H. Popkin, *Isaac La Peyrère (1596–1676): His Life, Work, and Influence* (Leiden: Brill, 1987).

[54] Spinoza, *Tractatus Theologico-Politicus*, ch. 14, p. 173.

The authenticity of the text

Drawing on the biblical scholarship of his time, Spinoza embraces the view that only a few copies of Ezra's original history survived to be copied by later generations of scribes. Furthermore, the canonical books were selected by a council of Pharisees, whose decisions may or may not have been well grounded.[55] With a swipe at the integrity of official deliberations about religious doctrine (and by implication at the Synod of Dort where the Reformed Church's confession had been confirmed), Spinoza paints a dark picture of the motivations and procedures by which they are driven: 'the wise', he comments, 'who know the causes of Councils and Synods, and also the controversies of the Pharisees and Sadducees, will easily be able to conjecture what were the causes of the convocation of that great Synagogue or Council'.[56]

Given the Bible's chequered past and the prejudices of religious councils, it is natural to wonder whether the essential doctrines revealed to the prophets have been transmitted to the surviving text, and thus whether even our best interpretative tools are capable of disclosing them. Perhaps the doctrine of Scripture has been systematically doctored. Perhaps its moral teachings have been utterly corrupted and are beyond our hermeneutic reach. Since Spinoza agrees that tracts of the history of Scripture are irrecoverable, he is vulnerable to this sceptical line of questioning; but he also has strong motives for resisting it. If the texts of the Bible were comprehensively corrupted there would be no point in devising an elaborate interpretative method for recovering their original meaning. In addition, it would be impossible to maintain, as Spinoza has done, that the central teachings of Scripture are clear and transparent. In order to hold on to this assumption, which he shares with his Calvinist contemporaries, he needs to establish that the Bible is sufficiently uncorrupted to bear it. 'The fact that some passages are corrupt', he will argue, 'does not permit us to suspect them all'. On the contrary, we need to identify mutilated passages in order to make sure that they do not contaminate those that are clear.[57]

The debate into which Spinoza now enters had engrossed generations of biblical scholars, and touched on fundamental differences between Protestant and Roman Catholic theology.[58] Protestants had traditionally resisted the Catholic claim that religious authority lies with the Church by arguing that it lies solely with Scripture. However, the more problematic the interpretation of the Bible became, the more Catholics were able to retort that, like

---

[55] Ibid. ch. 10, p. 150, ch. 12, p. 164.   [56] Ibid. ch. 10, p. 150fn.
[57] Ibid. ch. 10, p. 149.   [58] Malcolm, *Aspects of Hobbes*, pp. 414–22.

them, Protestants needed some authority to adjudicate between competing claims about the text. Scripture, they argued, cannot be interpreted by Scripture alone; the judgment of the Church is also required. In the seventeenth century, Catholic writers gathered support for their position from new information about the history of the Masoretic text. According to rabbinical and early Christian tradition, the vowel points had been inserted into this version of the Bible by Ezra and his scribes; but by the seventeenth century the work of Jewish and Christian scholars had shown that the points were added at a considerably later date. (Part of the Jewish side of this debate was summarized in a work by Joseph Salomon Delmedigo, of which Spinoza had a copy.[59]) The Masoretic Bible, it emerged, was not compiled, ordered, and overseen by Ezra. Instead, it was a descendant of Ezra's text, modified by later Jewish scribes who may have corrupted it, either intentionally or out of ignorance.

For the Catholic Church this was welcome news. For example, it allowed Robert Bellarmine (1542–1621) to defend what became the standard Catholic view that, although there was no reason to think that the Jews maliciously mutilated the Bible, the insertion of vowel points and the process of copying had undoubtedly introduced errors. These had in turn generated misunderstandings and variant readings that could only be resolved by an authority such as the Church. However, the same textual discoveries put Calvinist and other Protestant commentators in an awkward spot. To concede that the text of Scripture contained errors was to open the way to Popery. Yet to insist that the Bible is a single, consistent work was to open oneself to scholarly ridicule. Among the commentators willing to take the latter risk was Johannes Buxtorf, who defended the purity of the Masoretic text, vowel points included.[60] Again, it is possible that Buxtorf is at least one of the objects of Spinoza's uncompromising complaint that commentators who adopt this view 'expose the writers of the Bible to contempt'. If other kinds of historians were to adopt the interpretative strategies that these commentators regard as required by piety, they would be laughed out of court. 'And if they think that a person who says that Scripture is faulty is guilty of blasphemy, I want to know what I should call

---

[59] See Benedictus de Spinoza, *Traité Théologico-Politique*, ed. Fokke Akkerman, Jacqueline Lagrée, and Pierre-François Moreau, vol. 3, *Œuvres de Spinoza* (Paris: Presses Universitaires de France, 1999), ch. 9, p. 737, fn. 34.

[60] Johannes Buxtorf, *Tiberias sive commentarius masorethicus* (Basel, 1620), pp. 93–105. See Stephen G. Burnett, *From Christian Hebraism to Jewish Studies: Johannes Buxtorf (1564–1629) and Hebrew Learning in the Seventeenth Century* (Leiden: Brill, 1996), pp. 219–25; Malcolm, *Aspects of Hobbes*, p. 418.

those who ascribe to Scripture whatever invention they please . . . or who deny its clearest and most evident meanings'.[61]

In the circumstances, the only intellectually respectable response was to acknowledge that the text of the Bible contains errors. But such a concession was theologically and politically contentious. Aside from Hobbes, one of the very few Protestant writers who publicly embraced the implications of recent scholarship was Louis Cappel (1585–1658), a Huguenot professor of Hebrew and theology at Saumur.[62] Cappel allowed that the Masoretic text is unreliable, and that the Protestant claim that it does not differ from the versions written by Moses or Ezra is untenable. Nevertheless, he went on, the text is not so corrupted that its meaning is impossible to recover, and by means of careful interpretation we can find out what it teaches.[63] This did not go down well in Holland, where some Reformed theologians viewed it as a betrayal of faith and consequently blocked the publication of Cappel's *Critica Sacra*.[64] When the work appeared in Paris in 1650 it was fiercely attacked by Buxtorf's son, Johannes Buxtorf II, who shared his father's theological outlook.[65] Nevertheless, Cappel's position has much in common with the one Spinoza defended twenty years later.

Like Cappel, Spinoza starts from what his most hard-line Calvinist contemporaries continued to view as a blasphemous position. No one of sound judgement, he claims, can deny that the surviving text of the Old Testament contains errors and mutilations.[66] Moreover, these flaws certainly pose grave exegetical problems. Fortunately, however, they do not prevent us from understanding the Bible, and 'are of little importance, at least for those who read the Scriptures with a comparatively independent judgment'.[67]

Among the difficulties to be overcome are the ambiguities surrounding vowel points and punctuation. In order to defend the antiquity and thus greater authenticity of the biblical text, some commentators continued to insist that the points were added at an early stage. But Spinoza rejects this view. Following more up-to-date scholarship, he takes it that, since they were introduced

---

[61] Spinoza, *Tractatus Theologico-Politicus*, ch. 10, p. 148.

[62] Ludovico Cappel, *Critica sacra, siue de variis quæ in sacris Veteris Testamenti libris occurrunt lectionibus libri sex*. Paris, 1650). See Malcolm, *Aspects of Hobbes*, p. 419.

[63] Spinoza, *Tractatus Theologico-Politicus*, ch. 10, p. 148.

[64] Malcolm, *Aspects of Hobbes*, p. 419.

[65] Burnett, *From Christian Hebraism*, pp. 229–39.

[66] Spinoza, *Tractatus Theologico-Politicus*, ch. 9, pp. 135–6.

[67] Ibid. ch. 9, p. 135.

relatively late, interpreters should not put too much faith in them. Instead, they should take account of variant readings and use them to resolve inconsistencies.[68] A further series of problems is posed by marginal additions. These interpolations, Spinoza claims, are of several kinds. Some are simply variants arising from the fact that it can be hard to distinguish one Hebrew letter from another that closely resembles it.[69] Where a phrase containing the first letter occurs in the text, a scribe has appended the phrase containing the second letter in the margin. Equally, some marginal variants note quiescent or unpronounced letters, which are not included in the main body of the text, in order to show how it should be read. A further class of marginalia records words that have become obsolete; and yet another is designed to show how the text should be read to audiences whose wicked conduct and extravagant way of life has given obscene connotations to certain natural functions. For example, the annotations offer euphemistic substitutes for Scripture's unembarrassed references to sex or excrement.[70]

As Spinoza presents the matter, interpolations of these kinds do not pose an insurmountable obstacle. The exegete must work out what type a particular addition belongs to and be guided by the resulting information. The tension surrounding debates about the status of textual additions arises, he suggests, from the claim that explanations such as the ones he has just offered are not adequate, and that the only satisfactory way to explain the scribes' interpolations is to view them as signs of secret mysteries contained within the main body of the text.[71] 'Most people' he complains, refuse to admit that scribes have introduced errors into the text, and prefer to interpret their divergent readings as signs of some deeper meaning. But this is a ludicrous view. 'Whether they have said these things out of foolishness and credulous devotion, or out of arrogance and malice, so that they alone would be believed to possess God's secrets, I do not know. But I do know this: that in their writings I have read nothing that had the air of a secret, but only childish thoughts. I have also read, and for that matter know personally, certain Kabbalistic triflers, whose insanity always taxed my capacity for amazement'.[72] Elsewhere in the *Treatise*

---

[68] Ibid. ch. 7, pp. 107–8.
[69] Ibid. ch. 9, p. 136.
[70] Ibid. ch. 9, pp. 137–8.
[71] Ibid. ch. 9, pp. 136–7.
[72] Ibid. ch. 9, p. 135. Moreau points out that Spinoza would have known a kabbalistic text published by the Amsterdam Sephardic community: Abraham Cohen de Herrera, *Gate of Heaven*, trans. Kenneth Krabbenhoft (Leiden: Brill, 2002), and also that Spinoza possessed a collection containing kabbalistic writings: *Collecteana decerpta . . . ex magno opere absconditorum*

Spinoza makes it clear that what he regards as a crazy and diversionary preoccupation with mysteries is not confined to Kabbalists, but extends to Christian commentators. Theologians who concentrate on identifying mysteries and attributing them to the Holy Spirit are often motivated by the desire to arouse admiration and veneration for a doctrine that exceeds the reach of natural reasoning.[73] At the same time, they use these mysteries to introduce so many speculative questions into religion that 'the Church seems to be an Academy and religion science, or rather, a disputation'.[74] On inspection, however, mysteries that are supposed to be so profound as to be inexplicable turn out to be 'the inventions of Aristotle or Plato, or someone like that',[75] and do not even have a claim to novelty, let alone divinity.

As these criticisms indicate, Spinoza regards any attempt to find mysteries in the masora as just one example of a more general interpretative trend that encompasses several traditions and is opposed to his own determination to make the Bible rationally accessible. Elsewhere in the *Treatise*, for example, he berates a Jewish medieval commentator, Rabbi Jehuda Alpakhar,[76] for insisting on an excessively literal reading of Scripture that makes it virtually unintelligible. When the Bible asserts that God is a fire, for example, Alpakhar decrees that we must not only accept that this is what it says. We must also renounce any attempt to assess the claim that God is a fire, and accept that it is true. Energetically repudiating this opinion, Spinoza 'marvels that a man endowed with reason should be so eager to destroy it'.[77] Rather than subordinating our capacity for reasoning to Scripture, we must of course bring our judgment to bear on the claims it makes; and since we are incapable of believing assertions that we regard as contrary to reason, Alpakhar in any case demands the impossible.

Like Maimonides, Alpakhar stands in here for some of Spinoza's contemporary opponents, including the theologians of the Reformed Church, whose doctrine committed them to mysteries such as the Incarnation and the Trinity. While a Calvinist theologian might agree with Spinoza that no deep mysteries were concealed in the marginal annotations of the Bible, the fact that he runs

---

sapientiae by Joseph del Medigo. See no. 56 of the index in Freudenthal, *Die Lebensgeschichte Spinozas*.

[73] Spinoza, *Tractatus Theologico-Politicus*, ch. 7, p. 98.

[74] Ibid. ch. 13, p. 167.

[75] Ibid. ch. 13, p. 168.

[76] Harry Wolfson, *The Philosophy of Spinoza* (New York: Meridian Books, 1958), II.258.

[77] Spinoza, *Tractatus Theologico-Politicus*, ch. 15, p. 181.

this specific critique together with a broader attack on biblical mysteries made his position threatening to a confession that imbued them with deep significance. Equally, Spinoza's position would have troubled Dutch Cartesians, who followed Descartes in holding that the Christian mysteries were inexplicable, rather than forthrightly condemning them as empty or ridiculous. Spinoza, however, does not hold back. 'I cannot marvel enough that people should want to make reason, the divine light and [God's] greatest gift, subordinate to dead letters. How can it be thought no crime to speak unworthily against the mind, the true original text of God's word, by maintaining that it is corrupt, blind or lost, yet considered a very great crime to think such things about the letter, the image of God's word?... What are they afraid of? Do they think that religion and faith cannot be defended unless men deliberately know nothing about anything and say farewell to reason completely? Surely, if they believe this, they fear Scripture more than they trust it'.[78]

The fact that, in attacking mysteries, Spinoza is implicitly putting a great deal of pressure on a central Calvinist doctrine may help to explain the fact that he takes care to engage with various interpretations of the masora, despite regarding them as wrong-headed, and examines several arguments in their favour. For example, the proponents of what we might call the mystery view are puzzled by the fact that generations of scribes have retained variant readings, despite the fact that some of them are obviously mistaken. If they are simply errors, why should the scribes have replicated them? Spinoza's pragmatic response points once again to the limits of our knowledge of the history of Scripture. 'I do not know', he comments, 'what superstition persuaded them to do'. But we can conceive of various explanations. Perhaps they were not sure which reading was correct. Perhaps they were indicating how they wanted the text to be read. Either way, we do not need to resort to anything as bizarre as the mystery view.[79]

More interesting is a hypothesis about what appear to be systematic but obvious errors. Since these mistakes could not have occurred by chance, and were not corrected, 'the Pharisees conclude that the first writers made them according to a definite plan, to signify something'.[80] Once again, however, the solution to the puzzle is mundane. For instance, proponents of the mystery view are excited by the fact that the Hebrew word for 'girl' is always written defectively in the Pentateuch, but correctly in the margin. Why, they ask, did the scribes not correct the text? The answer, Spinoza explains, lies in linguistic

---

[78] Ibid. ch. 15, p. 182.   [79] Ibid. ch. 9, p. 137.   [80] Ibid.

change. Because the word in the text had become obsolete, the scribes added the modern variant in the margin. There is nothing to get excited about.

In these and the other arguments he considers, Spinoza contends again and again that the resources of ordinary reasoning on which his interpretative method depends can deal with difficulties that have been held to stand in the way of understanding the text. While the marginal annotations and vowel points have undoubtedly introduced errors and ambiguities, these can usually be resolved, and there is no reason to suppose that they have a superstitious or mysterious explanation. Nevertheless, all these conclusions are grounded on the assumption that we can understand the language in which the text is written; and this in turn presupposes that the meanings of individual words have not been so systematically altered that their original sense is irrecoverable. Is this a defensible presupposition? Reflecting on the possibility that biblical Hebrew might have been wilfully corrupted, Spinoza rules it out. It is extremely difficult for an individual writer to change even the meaning of a single word, because other writers and speakers continue to use it as before. Furthermore, since a language is made up of individual words, it is still more difficult—in fact impossible—deliberately to corrupt an entire language. Contrary to the view held by some commentators, that the scribes had the power to corrupt Scripture but refrained from doing so, Spinoza defends the stronger view that such a course was beyond them.[81] We can therefore rest assured that the Hebrew in which the Masoretic text is written has not been deliberately distorted out of recognition, and that as long as we proceed carefully, we can understand what it says.

However, an obvious problem remains. Even if a whole language cannot be corrupted, it is easy enough for a group of people who exercise control over a text to alter its meaning, for example by modifying the speeches that it contains. If the Bible as we know it is the fruit of a long process of compilation and transmission, how can we be sure that its original doctrines have not been systematically changed? How can we tell that the precepts it now teaches are the ones it originally professed? Once again, Spinoza is optimistic, this time on the grounds that the core teaching of all the biblical books is evident and consistent. To alter this, one would have to change each book in the same way, so that Scripture as a whole would be a different work. But this is so improbable

---

[81] e.g. Petrus Cunaeus, *The Hebrew Republic*, trans. Peter Wyetzner (Jerusalem: Shalem Press, 2006), p. 367. See Aaron L. Katchen, *Christian Hebraists and Dutch Rabbis: Seventeenth Century Apologetics and the Study of Maimonides' Mishneh Torah* (Cambridge, Mass.: Harvard University Press, 1984), p. 52.

that we can confidently put the worry aside. The doctrine of Scripture has not only survived. It is also so clear that almost anyone can grasp it.[82]

The position Spinoza defends is a delicate one. On the one hand, he aligns himself with up-to-date biblical criticism by examining the history of the text and identifying errors and additions. On the other hand, he keenly protests that his approach does not undermine or threaten the divinity of Scripture. His interpretative method protects the Bible by enabling us to separate its true message from the dross of corruption.[83] Moreover, by upholding the rule that Scripture must interpret Scripture, it respects the integrity of the text and isolates it from merely human history. There is, however, something equivocal about the way Spinoza aligns himself with this principle. Once we take seriously the fact that the text of the Bible has changed over time and been translated from one language into another, we are bound to conclude that whatever is important about it cannot be identified with the particular set of words that make up the canon. To deny this is to fall prey to superstition and to worship paper and ink, as many theologians and commentators who squabble over particular phrases are guilty of doing.[84] Perhaps, then, the divinity of Scripture resides in the uncorrupted passages of the text that make up its central doctrine? But here the same objection applies. There is, for example, nothing divine about the words of God's revelations to Moses as they are recorded in the Pentateuch. They are simply sounds, or paper and ink, readily translatable into other sounds or other pieces of paper and ink; and this will apply to any statement of biblical teaching.

Because scriptural interpretation has got so bogged down in tortuous interpretative strategies, many of which Spinoza regards as manifestations of superstition, we need a method of interpretation that will cut through the misreadings to which theologians cling. By revealing the hermeneutic errors on which textually based religions ground their creeds, it is at least possible to show that their claims have no scriptural authority. However, it is important not to erect a new worship for the words of Scripture as the historical method allows us to understand them. In many cases we are incapable of determining what a particular passage means, and while we can detect errors we cannot always put them right. So while biblical hermeneutics is a worthwhile scholarly activity, we should not let the text dominate religion in such a way that it, rather than its teaching, becomes the object of our reverence. The point of developing a sound method of interpretation is thus partly negative: it is a

---

[82] Spinoza, *Tractatus Theologico-Politicus*, ch. 12, p. 165.
[83] Ibid. ch. 10, p. 149.   [84] Ibid. ch. 12, p. 159.

means of overcoming and preventing the growth of superstitious practices that feed on misunderstandings of biblical doctrine. At the same time, however, the method plays a positive role that can counter superstition. Applying it to Scripture enables us to see that the Bible itself is not divine, and that its divinity must reside in something other than the text.

Preaching and prophesying

Considering that Spinoza is writing for a largely Christian audience and is primarily addressing the views of Christian theologians, it may seem curious that he has said so little about the teachings of the New Testament. Although he has distinguished the imaginative form of revelation experienced by the Old Testament prophets from the intuitive form experienced by Christ, he has remained virtually silent about the doctrines taught by the Apostles. 'No one who has read the New Testament', he now asserts, 'can doubt that [the Apostles] were prophets', whose imaginative gifts enabled them to elaborate and communicate the doctrine that they had themselves learned from Christ. But just as it was important in the case of the Old Testament to distinguish the prophets' revelations from their ordinary utterances, so we now need to try to do the same with the teachings of the Apostles.

This is a crucial step in the argument of the *Treatise*. One of the primary aims of Spinoza's initial discussion of prophecy was to discount the prophets' speculative opinions about nature and God on the basis of biblical evidence. Nothing suggests that Moses or Joshua, for example, were philosophically sophisticated people whose speculative views are worthy of respect. Furthermore, their project was not to understand God, nature, or the good in a philosophical fashion, but to persuade their audiences to adopt a particular way of life. The question now is whether the speculative opinions of the Apostles also lack authority; but the problem has taken on a new dimension. Whereas the prophets taught particular nations, the Apostles taught the universal form of the divine law that they had learned from Christ. Although they did, of course, address distinct groups of people in their various Epistles, their doctrine was applicable to everyone, including the philosophically educated. This suggests that their speculative claims may be harder to dismiss. It is possible that these claims were transmitted to the Apostles by Christ (who in turn had them from God), and that they are part of divine doctrine. With this in mind, we need to work out when the Apostles are communicating truths revealed to them by God, and when are they simply offering views of their own.

On the whole Spinoza would prefer to avoid this topic, and it is easy to see why. An excommunicated Jew with a reputation for atheism might have well hesitated to challenge Calvinist biblical scholars in what they regarded as the sanctuary of their religious faith. Excusing himself from investigating the New Testament fully, he remarks that the task has already been undertaken 'by men who are learned in the sciences, and especially in languages'; that he does not know enough Greek (although this does not prevent him from commenting on the correct interpretation of certain Greek passages);[85] and that Hebrew versions of the texts are not available.[86, 87] Nevertheless, there is an issue that he needs to address. His analysis of accommodation has enabled him to open up a large space for free philosophical enquiry by showing that there are many topics on which the prophets' utterances are not intended to be philosophically compelling. But this space will be snatched away from him unless he can establish that the same applies to the Apostles' speculative claims. If they have to be taken *au pied de la lettre* and treated as part of biblical doctrine, the fence between theology and philosophy that Spinoza has been constructing will collapse. Furthermore, since the speculative claims of one Apostle sometimes contradict those of another, the discrepancies between them will make the interpretation of Scripture contentious. Philosophical issues will inevitably become tangled up with endless theological disputes, schisms, and superstitions, so that the question of what one can affirm about philosophy will be theologically tainted.[88] If Spinoza is to sustain his view that philosophical enquiry can proceed independently of Scripture, it is therefore vital to show that the Apostles' speculations are not part of their core doctrine.

How can this conclusion be sustained? Returning to his initial classification of types of accommodation, Spinoza reminds his readers that the capacity to prophesy is only intermittent. Because it is a function of imaginative powers that vary with time and place, it can only occur when conditions are right, and at other times the forms of imagining and reasoning on which prophets rely are

[85]   Ibid. ch. 10, p. 151fn.

[86]   Ibid. ch. 10, p. 150.

[87]   In suggesting that there might be 'copies of the books [of the New Testament] which were written in the Hebrew language', Spinoza seems to be supposing that the original language of the New Testament texts was Hebrew. Though this is doubtful, there is a modern theory of 'Aramaic primacy', which holds that the original language of the New Testament texts was a Semitic one rather than *Koine* Greek. For some discussion of this theory, see Joseph Augustine Fitzmeyer, *The Semitic Background of the New Testament* (Grand Rapids, Mich.: Eerdmans 1997); Frank Zimmermann, *The Aramaic Origin of the Four Gospels* (New York: Ktav, 1979).

[88]   Spinoza, *Tractatus Theologico-Politicus*, ch. 11, p. 157.

not exceptional. Their lives are shaped by the experience of revelation; but only some of the things they say and do are revealed to them by God. Interpreters therefore need to pick and choose, basing their readings of revelation on a critical examination of the biblical record, and subjecting it to the interpretative techniques that Spinoza has outlined.

Among the many features of Scripture that interpreters need to take into account is the style of its speeches and narratives. By attending to style, Spinoza now claims, we can distinguish prophetic from non-prophetic utterances. When prophets are inspired, they speak in a particular fashion. Phrases such as 'thus says God' make it clear that they are issuing divine instructions; and because they are conveying the divine word, they simply issue judgements without giving any reasons for them. (God does not give reasons, nor has the prophet reasoned his way to the view he expresses.) Conversely, the more that prophets argue, 'the more the knowledge they have of the matter revealed approaches natural knowledge'.[89] Guided by these stylistic differences, and applying them to the text of the New Testament, Spinoza concludes that the Apostles rarely prophesy, and in their letters merely offer their own opinions. 'The way the Apostles both spoke and discussed things in their Epistles indicates most clearly that they were not written in accordance with revelation and a divine command, but only in accordance with their natural judgment, and contain nothing but brotherly advice, mixed with a politeness far removed from prophetic authority'.[90]

It may seem troubling, Spinoza allows, that on the basis of their natural reason the Apostles were able to teach things that are beyond reason's grasp. But the puzzle is easily solved. We have seen how, with the help of a proper interpretative method, we can use our ordinary powers of reasoning to create a history of Scripture, which tells us what the Bible says about events such as revelations and miracles whose causes we do not understand. Interpretation enables us to recover the meaning of a text which deals with events that we cannot rationally account for. However, whereas we bring the interpretative method to bear on the Bible, the Apostles applied it to the things they had seen and heard, and created a history of the life of Christ. They brought their interpretative skills to bear, not on a text, but on their immediate experience of Jesus, including the revelations and miracles that he, and to a lesser extent they themselves, performed. Using the same historical method, they assembled information from which they first extracted and then transmitted Christ's

---

[89] Ibid. ch. 11, p. 153.   [90] Ibid.

teaching. Parts of this do indeed exceed the power of natural understanding. But since much of it consists of moral lessons that are accessible to everyone, their teaching is in general easy to understand.

The techniques of textual interpretation that Spinoza has defended therefore indicate that the Apostles were predominantly preachers rather than prophets, and that their teachings were not based on divine revelation. But what, then, is the status of the advice they offer, and are we bound to attend to it? Approaching this question in his usual exegetical manner, Spinoza first points out that the Apostles themselves testify that they have been given authority to teach as well as prophesy. For instance, Timothy describes himself as an 'appointed preacher and Apostle . . . a teacher of the nations with faith and truth'.[91] However, even if we accept that this is the case, we still do not know *what* they had authority to teach, and whether an Apostle could authoritatively teach in any way he wished. A further trawl through the biblical evidence divulges the answer. While all the Apostles taught the same religious precepts, each of them built these on a different foundation adapted to the mentality of his particular audience. Like other teachers, many of whom 'prefer to teach people who are completely uneducated' so that they can put their own stamp on them, each Apostle had their own pedagogical method, and defended religion on a different basis.[92] This basis was in turn accommodated to distinct audiences. For example, the Apostles mainly preached to Jews who, according to Spinoza, disdained philosophy. They consequently 'accommodated themselves to their audience and taught a religion devoid of philosophic speculations'.[93] Paul, by contrast, preached to all the nations and based his teaching on 'the foundations that were best known and accepted at that time'. As a result, he philosophized more than the rest.

As Spinoza implies, this has had disastrous effects. Generations of theologians who have failed to recognize the reason for the divergences in the Apostles' doctrines have read them as authoritative. This in turn has 'given rise to disputes and schisms which have tormented the Church incessantly from the time of the Apostles until the present day, and will surely torment it until religion is separated from philosophical speculations and reduced to the very few and very simple tenets taught by Christ and his followers'.[94] Moreover, since the resulting religious debates are a source of superstitious anxiety, they feed the opposition to natural reason against which Spinoza is pitting himself. 'How

---

[91] Ibid. ch. 11, p. 156. 1 Timothy 2:7.   [92] Ibid. ch. 11, p. 157.
[93] Ibid. ch. 11, p. 158.   [94] Ibid. ch. 11, pp. 157–8.

happy our age would be', he concludes, 'if we saw religion again free of all superstition'.

By applying his account of accommodation to the Apostles, Spinoza is thus able to argue that their diverse philosophical opinions are not authoritative. As the interpretative method confirms, our philosophical convictions about nature, God, interpretation, or the foundations of morality may be as good as, or better than, theirs, and we are free to work out for ourselves what sort of foundation Christ's moral teaching requires.

Interpreting the divine word

Spinoza's chief anxiety is that he will now be accused of claiming that the word of God has been mutilated, distorted, corrupted, and fragmented. By treating Scripture in the same way as any other historical text, so his opponents will claim, he has not only denied its divinity but undermined religion.[95] As he is forced to acknowledge, these charges are not entirely empty. 'I confess that certain profane men, to whom religion is a burden, will be able to take what I have said as a licence to sin' by inferring that Scripture is so thoroughly falsified that it completely lacks authority. But this, he protests, is not a good enough reason to keep quiet.[96] People who are determined to ignore the demands of a religious way of life and indulge in sensual pleasures will always find some justification for doing so, and it would be silly to cling to a mistaken conception of scripture in the hope of making them virtuous.[97] Moreover, setting aside this point, his opponents' charges are unjustified. Their indefensible commitment to the view that Scripture is the unadulterated and sometimes mysterious word of God has given rise to a superstitious form of religion that not only distorts the true doctrine of the Bible but also generates damaging conceptions of piety. It is they who undermine religion, and the goal of Spinoza's critique is to strengthen it by freeing it from superstitious embellishments.[98]

Nevertheless, theologians who are used to viewing the Scriptures as the (mainly) unadulterated word of God are bound to find Spinoza's conclusions threatening. If the books of the Bible were written at different times, and if the canon was assembled by various Councils, the Scriptures may not all be equally authoritative. If the four Gospels of the New Testament were written with different audiences in mind, then the word of God cannot be identical with the surviving biblical text.[99] Furthermore, access to the divine word cannot depend

---

[95] Ibid. ch. 12, p. 158–9.   [96] Ibid. ch. 12, p. 159.   [97] Ibid.
[98] Ibid.   [99] Ibid. ch. 12, p. 164.

on the fact that we now possess a certain number of books, any more than we take ourselves to be deprived of its teaching because certain other books have been lost.[100] Rather than being inextricably embedded in the Bible, the word of God threatens to float free of any particular book, and thus of Scripture itself. To make good his claim that his arguments have unmasked superstition rather than destroyed religion, Spinoza therefore needs to show that the divine word is still legible, and up to now he has simply asserted that the central message of Scripture is easy for everyone to understand. His next task is to explain what this message is, and how it can be known.

[100] Ibid. ch. 12, p. 163.

Meeting the Demands
of a Religious Life

Chapter 8

True Religion

The account of biblical hermeneutics discussed in the two previous chapters has yielded a method for distinguishing dogmatic or superstitious forms of worship from the true religion taught in the Bible. By identifying and setting aside the doubtful, accommodated or merely historical claims that Scripture contains, theologians can raise their eyes from the minutiae of the text and focus on Scripture's central message. But this is not all that Spinoza intends to achieve. He also aims to vindicate a particular interpretation of scriptural teaching that both upholds the separateness of theology and philosophy, and is, he claims, so straightforward, and so consistently expounded throughout the Bible that it cannot be misunderstood and cannot have been corrupted.[1] This step is absolutely crucial to the overall argument of the *Treatise*. Unless Spinoza can provide an uncontroversial account of the biblical doctrines with which theology should concern itself, he will have failed to show that his method can resolve the quarrels by which theology is bedevilled. And unless he can establish that this theological doctrine is independent of the various philosophical contentions advanced in the Bible, the disputes about the extent to which biblical doctrine can limit philosophizing, which he has worked so hard to outlaw, will sneak back in. The meaning and significance of speculative claims will once again become a subject of theological dispute, and biblical interpretation will be back where it started in a viperous pit of schism and superstition. To avoid these failures, so Spinoza reasons, he has to offer an account of the doctrine taught in Scripture that is so transparent, and so evidently free of controversial philosophical commitments, that no one can sensibly contest it. This is clearly not an easy task; but because it is the only way to silence his opponents, 'the settlement of the whole of religion depends on it'.[2]

---

[1] Benedictus de Spinoza, *Tractatus Theologico-Politicus*, ed. Carl Gebhardt, vol. III, *Opera* (Heidelberg: Carl Winter, 1924), ch. 12, p. 165.

[2] Ibid. ch. 13, p. 168.

The fundamental teaching of the Bible, as the *Treatise* now goes on to summarize it, is an exhortation to obey the word of God. However, as we saw in Chapter 4, Scripture uses the phrase 'the word of God' in three complementary senses. In its most overarching sense it signifies the divine law. Obeying the word of God is equivalent to living as the divine law demands. In addition, Scripture metaphorically identifies the word of God with the order of nature, particularly, Spinoza now adds, with the fragments of it foreseen by the prophets. To put the point in the terms he has already spelled out, 'the word of God' sometimes refers to the natural divine law. Finally, when the prophets represented the divine law as a set of commands made by a divine legislator, they referred to it as the word of God.[3]

As we have already discovered, the word of God in the first two of these senses can be understood by natural reasoning as well as learned from Scripture. We can understand the order of nature and the central tenets of the divine law by means of the natural light, because they are 'inscribed by divine agency in the hearts of men, i.e. in the human mind, which is the true original text of God that he himself has stamped with his seal'.[4] At this point, however, Spinoza is concerned only with the word of God as it is taught in the Bible. What he has to show is that it is possible to obey the divine law without having a philosophical understanding of God or nature, and that Scripture shows us how this can be done. One of the things that the Bible allows us to appreciate is that the word of God does not depend on specialized philosophical learning, but is available to ordinary people.

Appealing only to what he presents as the most evident biblical doctrines, Spinoza now embarks on this task. However, at this point his formulation of the divine law, and thus of the word of God, undergoes an abrupt change. Whilst he has so far always summed it up as a requirement to know and love God, where loving God depends upon knowing him, this epistemological emphasis suddenly disappears. Instead, the central precept of the law is characterized in what appears to be a quite different way: Scripture makes it obvious, the *Treatise* claims, that the divine law demands one 'to love God above all else, and to love your neighbour as yourself'.[5] So love rather than knowledge is what we have to aim for, and the objects of our love now include other people.

To modern eyes, this may seem a perplexing transition; but for Spinoza the second formulation seamlessly draws out an implication of the first. In fixing on

---

[3] Ibid. ch. 12, p. 162.   [4] Ibid. ch. 12, p. 158.   [5] Ibid. ch. 12, p. 165.

the interpretation of the law central to the teaching of the New Testament,[6] Spinoza appeals to the expectations of his mainly Christian audience and offers a reformulation that many of them would have taken for granted. (Calvin, for example, explains that love of one's neighbour flows directly from the love of God.)[7] Moreover, Spinoza is not opportunistically pandering to his audience by offering them an interpretation of the law that he knows they will find acceptable, but which diverges from his own understanding of it. Rather, he is articulating in familiar terms a set of philosophical conclusions that he himself holds, and defends at greater length in the *Ethics*. There he argues both that our love of God grows with our knowledge of him, and that the development of this knowledge or love strengthens our capacity to love one another.[8] The more we understand the natural order that is the manifestation of God's power and perfection, the more we appreciate that the best way to empower ourselves is to co-operate with one another, or as the New Testament puts it, to love our neighbour.[9] Spinoza is adjusting his account of the substance of the divine law in a fashion that highlights the features of it that are most relevant to religion, while leaving in shadow those that pertain particularly to philosophy. As we shall see, the formulation that he now begins to use is not a rejection of what went before but a rearticulation of it, suited to the biblically-based analysis of true religion that he is about to explicate.

In presenting the teaching of Scripture as straightforward and uncontentious, Spinoza follows in the footsteps of a series of ecumenically inclined writers who had attempted to bypass the elaborate and contentious requirements of established religions by reducing religious doctrine to a minimum. For example, whereas the Reformed Church's *Belgic Confession* sets out official teachings about the Bible, the Trinity, the creation, providence, original sin, eternal election, the incarnation of Christ, justification through faith in Christ, and

---

[6] Romans 13:8.

[7] 'And surely that is true, the whole law is fulfilled when we love our neighbours; because true love towards men proceedeth not but from the love of God, and is a testimony as well as an effect thereof.' Calvin's Commentary on Romans 13:8. John Calvin, *Commentary Upon the Epistle of Saint Paul to the Romans*, ed. Henry Beveridge, trans. Christopher Rosdell (Edinburgh: The Calvin Translation Society, 1844), p. 371.

[8] Benedictus de Spinoza, *Ethica*, ed. Carl Gebhardt, vol. II, *Opera* (Heidelberg: Carl Winter, 1924), 5p25, p. 33.

[9] To love one's neighbours, as Spinoza represents it in the *Treatise*, is to treat other people justly and charitably (Spinoza, *Tractatus Theologico-Politicus*, ch. 12, p. 165). And as he argues in the *Ethics*, 'the things that beget harmony are those related to justice, fairness and being honourable' (Spinoza, *Ethics*, in Curley ed. *The Collected Works of Spinoza*, vol. I, 4app.15). Reason enjoins a man 'to aid other men and join them to him in friendship' (3p59). Within the state, it is an aspect of uniting oneself to others in friendship that one treats them justly, i.e. in accordance with the law (4p37s2).

many other topics, it became the aspiration of minimalists to reduce this list as far as possible. We have already observed this trend at work among millenarians aiming to settle on theological commitments that would be acceptable to both Christians and Jews; and the same strategy had been used by Arminian opponents of the Reformed Church's *Belgic Confession* in protest against the rigidity of a Church that, as some of them put it, preached Calvin rather than Christ.[10] The jurist Hugo Grotius, for example, had argued that the Church should 'define only the absolute minimum, and leave to each individual his own free judgment on many questions, because many things are very obscure'.[11] The minimum, as he later explained, consisted of four principles that constitute true religion. 'The first is that there is a God, and but one God only. The second, that God is not any of those things we see, but something more sublime than them. The third, that God takes care of human affairs and judges them with the strictest equity. The fourth, that the same God is creator of all things but himself'.[12] Beyond these principles, other doctrinal points should be investigated 'without prejudice, preserving charity and under the guidance of the Holy Scriptures'.[13] Despite its non-Trinitarian leanings, this approach remained influential. In Spinoza's generation it was taken up by Lambert Van Velthuysen, who provided his own list of religious fundamentals.[14] At the same time, it was advocated by various non-conformist sects,

---

[10] 'Our office is to preach Christ, not Calvin. We are Christians, and for that reason we must give ourselves no other names and no one may follow anyone else but God'. Kaspar Coolhaes (1536–1615), quoted in Benjamin J. Kaplan, *Calvinists and Libertines: Confession and Community in Utrecht, 1578–1620* (Oxford: Clarendon Press, 1995), pp. 98–9. See also John Marshall, *John Locke, Toleration and Early Enlightenment Culture: Religious Intolerance and Arguments for Religious Toleration in Early Modern and 'Early Enlightenment' Europe* (Cambridge: Cambridge University Press, 2006), p. 341. Compare Grotius: 'Immense evils must inevitably beset any kingdom where the rulers allow themselves to be led, not by God, but by the spirit of Calvin who is much closer to the spirit of Elias than to that of the Gospel'. Hugo Grotius, *Hugonis Grotii opera omnia theologica, etc.*, ed. Pieter de Groot (Amsterdam, 1679), iii.675, quoted in Marshall, *Early Enlightenment Culture*, p. 349.

[11] Hugo Grotius, *Ordinum Hollandiae ac westfrisiae pietas* (1613), ed. Edwin Rabbie (Leiden: Brill, 1995). Quoted in Marshall, *Early Enlightenment Culture*, p. 343. See also *Hugo Grotius Theologian: Essays in Honour of G. H. M. Posthumus Meyjes*, ed. H. J. M. Nellen and Edwin Rabbie (Leiden: Brill, 1994); Jonathan Israel, *The Dutch Republic: Its Rise, Greatness and Fall, 1477–1806* (Oxford: Clarendon Press, 1995), pp. 428–32; Richard Tuck, *Philosophy and Government, 1572–1651* (Cambridge: Cambridge University Press, 1993), pp. 184–90.

[12] Hugo Grotius, *The Rights of War and Peace*, ed. Richard Tuck (Indianapolis: Liberty Fund, 2005), II.1032.

[13] Quoted in Tuck, *Philosophy and Government*, pp. 184–6.

[14] Lambert van Velthuysen, *Nader bewys, dat noch de leere van de sonne stilstandt en des aertryx beweging, noch de gronden van de philosophie van Renatus Des Cartes strijdig sijn met Godts-woort*

including Socinians,[15] Collegiants, Quakers, Anabaptists, and Mennonites. For all their differences, these confessions were united in their opposition to the restrictive and complex doctrines established, as the Mennonite leader, Menno Simons, had expressed it, by 'the subtlety and philosophy of the learned ones'.[16]

Following this trend, Spinoza aims to provide an analysis of the demands that Scripture imposes on the faithful shorn of all 'lofty speculations',[17] and in due course he will set out a list of the tenets of faith. But this is not where his argument begins. Focusing as narrowly as possible on what is involved in loving God and one's neighbour, the *Treatise* first aims to show that one can obey the law without holding any speculative or philosophical beliefs about God at all. Contrary to the claims of the many churches and confessions which impose excessive intellectual demands on their members, true religion requires us to hold very few beliefs about the deity, and the small number of beliefs that we must hold need not be philosophical ones.[18]

Running over ground he has already covered, Spinoza begins by reminding his readers that this view has ample scriptural support. For example, Moses successfully taught the divine law to his people, but clearly failed to give them a speculative grasp of it. If he had been aiming to make them fully understand the law he would have appealed to reason; but in fact 'God assailed the Jews with the blare of trumpets rather than arguments', and Moses relied on covenants

---

(Utrecht: 1656–7), pp. 1, 37–8. This book is reprinted in Lambert van Velthuysen, *Opera Omnia*, 2 vols. (Rotterdam; 1680), pp. 1037–2000. See Wiep van Bunge, *From Stevin to Spinoza: An Essay on Philosophy in the Seventeenth-Century Dutch Republic* (Leiden: Brill, 2001), p. 82.

[15] The Socinians were Unitarians, many of whom emigrated to Holland after they were banished from Poland. The Reformed Church was extremely hostile to Socinianism, which it often associated with Arminianism. In 1628 the Synod of Holland petitioned the States to have Socinianism banned; in 1653 the Faculty of Theology at Leiden recommended that Socinian works should be diligently suppressed; in mid-century, Voetius campaigned to limit toleration of Socinians still further. See Voetius, *Politica Ecclesiastica*, II, pp. 538–44, 551, cited in Pierre Bayle, *Historical and Critical Dictionary*, trans. Richard H. Popkin (Indianapolis: Bobbs-Merrill, 1965), 'Socinus'; Israel, *The Dutch Republic: Its Rise, Greatness and Fall, 1477–1806*, p. 638; Marshall, *Early Enlightenment Culture*, pp. 367–9; K. H. Mechoulan, 'Morteira et Spinoza au carrefour du Socinianisme', *Revue des études juives* 135, nos. 1–3 (1976).

[16] Menno Simons, *The Complete Writings of Menno Simons*, ed. J. C. Wenger, trans. Leonard Verduin (Scottdale, Pa.: Herald Press, 1956), pp. 210–11. Quoted in Marshall, *Early Enlightenment Culture*, p. 314. Menno Simons (1496–1561) was a leading Anabaptist and the founder of the Mennonite sect.

[17] Spinoza, *Tractatus Theologico-Politicus*, ch. 13, p. 167.

[18] See Étienne Balibar, *Spinoza and Politics*, trans. Peter Snowden (London: Verso, 1998), pp. 88–95.

and threats, which can produce obedience but not knowledge.[19] The manner in which he and other prophets communicate their revelations shows that one can obey the law without understanding the true nature of God. Furthermore, and here Spinoza moves into a philosophical key, it would be fruitless to try to command this kind of understanding. As we saw in Chapter 4, laws are made for human beings and can only impose demands that they are capable of fulfilling. It would, for example, be pointless to command a person to turn herself into a frog; but by the same token it would be ludicrous to command her to be wise. 'No one', Spinoza comments, 'can be wise on command, any more than he can live on command, or exist on command'.[20] The reason for this is that philosophical truths deal with invisible things that are objects of the mind rather than the senses, which can only be understood by means of demonstration. But since one cannot demonstrate a claim unless one already knows an appropriate set of premises, one cannot do it to order, and any attempt to command an understanding of philosophical truths is consequently bound to fail. Unfortunately, this does not stop religious authorities from demanding that the faithful should believe speculative truths without under-standing them. Nor does it prevent people from repeating truths they have been told as if they understood them. But these are empty exercises. When someone asserts a philosophical claim that they are unable to demonstrate, their words 'no more touch or show their minds than do the words of a parrot or an automaton, which speaks without a mind and without meaning'.[21]

This Cartesian description of an automaton parroting wise saws and modern instances sits oddly with the account of body and mind that Spinoza expounds in the *Ethics*. More to the point, however, his insistence that you cannot know a philosophical claim unless you can demonstrate it appeals to a tendentiously narrow conception of philosophical reasoning. Because the objects of philo-sophical insight are invisible, Spinoza is claiming, they 'cannot be seen by any eyes other than those of demonstration, and someone who doesn't have demonstrations doesn't see them at all'.[22] Philosophical understanding, it seems, must either result from demonstration or be non-existent, and there is no possibility of a middle ground. This argument serves Spinoza's immediate purpose by conveniently establishing that, when theologians expect people who lack philosophical training to grasp speculative truths, they are asking the impossible. But it also represents philosophy as isolated from other forms of rational enquiry, and rejects the more open conception of philosophical

---

[19] Spinoza, *Tractatus Theologico-Politicus*, ch. 14, p. 174.
[20] Ibid. ch. 13, p. 170.   [21] Ibid.   [22] Ibid.

reasoning we have found elsewhere in the *Treatise*.[23] Here, then, philosophy seems to be defined as a highly specialized form of knowledge, with its own rarefied and distinctive method, but at other points in Spinoza's argument it encompasses a wider range of synthetic and analytic attempts to understand the truth by means of natural reasoning. Spinoza's project of separating philosophy from theology sometimes pushes him towards the narrower conception, even where doing so obscures the richness of his own overall argument.

Setting this strain aside, if true religion is to be within the grasp of ordinary individuals it cannot incorporate philosophical claims about God, since most people will be unable to understand them. So any ideas of God that it does require must be non-speculative, and in order to support this conclusion, Spinoza again turns to the Bible. 'We see that Jeremiah, Moses and John sum up the knowledge of God that each person is bound to have by locating it only in this: that God is supremely just and supremely merciful, or that he is the unique model of the true life. To this we may add that Scripture does not explicitly give any definition of God, does not prescribe us to embrace any other attributes of God beyond those just mentioned'.[24] Or again, 'through the prophets, God asks no other knowledge of himself from men than the knowledge of his divine justice and his loving-kindness (*charitas*), i.e. such attributes of God as men can imitate in a certain way of life'.[25]

In the light of Spinoza's earlier discussion, it is obvious that justice and loving-kindness or *charitas* are not, philosophically speaking, among God's attributes. The deity does not possess any anthropomorphic properties, and the prophet's depictions of him as an embodied judge consequently belong within the realm of imagination. However, these imaginary representations of the deity can play a vital role in helping us to grasp what is involved in obeying the divine law, regardless of the fact that they do not satisfy a philosophical standard of accuracy. Biblical images of God, as Spinoza now goes on to explain, serve two distinct functions, the first of which is to provide a model of the way of life that the divine law demands. One aspect of the prophets' imaginative genius was their capacity to represent the way of life that is optimal for human beings as exemplified and required by a legislating God. As the prophets portray him, God accordingly possesses virtues from which we ourselves can benefit. However, not all the attributes that they ascribe to the deity are equally well adapted to this purpose.[26] Some, such as God's infinite power, are rendered irrelevant by the fact that we are incapable of imitating

---

[23] See Chapter 6.   [24] Spinoza, *Tractatus Theologico-Politicus*, ch. 13, p. 171.
[25] Ibid. ch. 13, p. 170.   [26] Ibid. ch. 13, p. 171.

them; others, such as God's sight and hearing, have little bearing on the way we treat our neighbours. There are, however, two divine attributes that we are capable of imitating, which also relate directly to our capacity to obey the divine law, namely God's justice and his *charitas*. Unless we attribute these properties to God, Spinoza holds, we shall have no model of the good life to imitate, and will not know how to go about obeying the divine law. Of all the qualities that the prophets ascribe to God, these two are inseparable from the law's requirement to love one's neighbour.

A second, implicit reason for thinking that one cannot obey the law unless one conceives of God as just and charitable stems from the role that these qualities play in motivating us to obey a figure of authority. To follow the divine law consistently, so Spinoza's discussion suggests, one needs to possess a range of steady character traits, such as the dispositions to defend justice, aid the poor, avoid murder, and refrain from coveting other people's goods.[27] This is what it is to love one's neighbour. But acquiring and maintaining these dispositions is not easy, because the affective constitution of human beings ensures that each of us is prone to passions such as anger and envy, which sometimes motivate us to treat our neighbours badly. Among the beliefs that may help to modify this destructive tendency is the scripturally supported conviction that we are subject to a divine judge who will punish our disobedience; but if this judge is conceived, for example, as vengeful or arbitrary, our desire to obey him will be compromised by fear and resentment.[28] We are liable to view the divine law as burdensome or illegitimate, and may decide to rebel against it in the manner of Milton's angels.

In the final section of the *Treatise*, Spinoza will appeal to a human disposition that he regards as utterly fundamental, a disposition to strive to resist situations and things that we experience as actually or potentially disempowering, including those of which we are afraid. This striving or *conatus* manifests itself in each individual's attempts to pursue ends that they believe will be broadly

---

[27] Ibid. ch. 12, p. 165.

[28] As we shall see in Chapter 11, Spinoza acknowledges that fear sometimes has a role to play in political life (see also Spinoza, *Ethics*, 4p54s). But as he states in the *Ethics*, harmony born of fear is without trust and does not pertain to the exercise of reason (4app.16). In arguing against attempts to ground obedience on fear, Spinoza distances himself from both orthodox Calvinists and Arminians, who regarded fear of God as appropriate. According to Episcopius, for example, 'it concerns us that we fear him who is able to cast body and soul into hell; and that we dread his terrible anger, and the evils, indeed, which he threateneth, that we seriously fear them...' Simon Episcopius, *The Confession or Declaration of the Ministers or Pastors Which in the United Provinces Are Called Remonstrants, Concerning the Chief Points of Christian Religion*, trans. Thomas Taylor (London, 1676), p. 91.

empowering, and to avoid those that will have the contrary effect. Although Spinoza does not allude to the workings of the *conatus* in his discussion of true religion, they nevertheless underlie his interpretation of the beliefs that promote obedience to the divine law, and ground his implicit assumption that people will do what they can to resist the dictates of an unjust god.[29] Equally, it explains his assurance that people who think of themselves as subject to a just deity will be motivated to obey the divine law in the confidence that they will not be double-crossed or singled out for mistreatment. There is therefore a psychological and indeed a metaphysical justification for the biblical claim that one needs to imagine God as just and charitable in order to obey him, and when the prophets represent the deity in these terms they convey a profound truth about human motivation.

One may nevertheless wonder what enables Spinoza to assume that human passions are responsive to images of the kind that the prophets evoke, and thus to assume that these images will play an effective part in motivating people to follow the law. Is it enough that Scripture says they do? Or are there other reasons for taking these claims seriously? Without spelling them out, Spinoza is appealing to psychological assumptions that seventeenth-century writers tend to take for granted, and that he himself systematizes in the *Ethics*.[30] At one level, he is drawing on the ancient view that our affects or passions are primarily stimulated both by the objects of our senses (sights and sounds, smells and tastes), and by images of these perceptions such as fantasies or memories.[31] God

---

[29] On the complexities of Spinoza's conception of the *conatus*, see Jonathan Bennett, *A Study of Spinoza's Ethics* (Cambridge: Cambridge University Press, 1984), §10; Jonathan Bennett, 'Teleology and Spinoza's Conatus', *Midwest Studies In Philosophy* 8, no. 1 (1983); Laurent Bove, *La strategie du conatus: Affirmation et résistance chez Spinoza* (Paris: Vrin, 1996); Edwin Curley, 'On Bennett's Spinoza: The Issue of Teleology', in *Spinoza: Issues and Directions* (Leiden: Brill, 1990); Michael Della Rocca, 'Spinoza's Metaphysical Psychology', in *The Cambridge Companion to Spinoza*, ed. Don Garrett (Cambridge: Cambridge University Press, 1996); *Desire and Affect: Spinoza as Psychologist*, ed. Yirmiyahu Yovel (New York: Little Room Press, 1999), §1; Daniel Garber, 'Descartes and Spinoza on Persistence and Conatus', *Studia Spinozana* 10 (1994); Don Garrett, 'Spinoza's *Conatus* Argument', in *Spinoza: Metaphysical Themes*, ed. Olli I. Koistinen and John I. Biro (Oxford: Oxford University Press, 2002); Don Garrett, 'Teleology in Spinoza and Early Modern Rationalism', in *New Essays on the Rationalists*, ed. Rocco J. Gennaro and Charles Huenemann (Oxford: Oxford University Press, 1999); Martin Lin, 'Spinoza's Metaphysics of Desire', *Archiv für Geschichte der Philosophie* 86, no. 1 (2004); Martin Lin, 'Teleology and Human Action in Spinoza', *The Philosophical Review* 115, no. 3 (2006); Wallace Matson, 'Death and Destruction in Spinoza's Ethics', *Inquiry* 20 (1977); Andrew Youpa, 'Spinozistic Self-Preservation', *Southern Journal of Philosophy* 41, no. 3 (2003).

[30] Susan James, *Passion and Action: The Emotions in Seventeenth-Century Philosophy* (Oxford: Clarendon Press, 1997), ch. 6.

[31] Spinoza, *Ethics*, 2p17c, 2p18, 2p40s2.

does not in fact have sensible properties. But when we imagine that he possesses them, by endowing him with a body or a throne, we turn him into an object that can arouse our passions. Furthermore, as the *Ethics* again explains, our feelings are most intensely directed to things that have a lot in common with us, so that the objects of our strongest passions are other people. By imagining God as a human being we make him into the kind of object that affects us, and incorporate him into the community of individual things with which we are most passionately engaged. He becomes, for instance, a being with whom we can compare ourselves, and thus for whom we can feel passions—such as veneration—which rest on comparisons between our own qualities and those of others.[32] However, while we may in principle venerate God for any anthropomorphic attribute such as his power, wisdom, or knowledge, the Bible rightly fixes on his justice and *charitas*. To obey the law with confidence, it implies, we need to conceive of God as a merciful judge who can be trusted to protect us from injustice and neglect.

Spinoza is adamant that the doctrine he has identified sums up the entire teaching of Scripture and is all that the divine law requires of us. 'Who can fail to see', he exclaims, 'that neither Testament is anything other than an education in obedience, and that neither has any aim but that people should obey from a true heart?'[33] Contrary to the Socinian claim that Jesus Christ ushered in a new teaching, and to the Calvinist belief that God has made several successive covenants with man, the *Treatise* cleaves to the view that the divine law is everywhere and always the same. Although it is taught in different forms by the prophets and by Christ, its precepts remain unchanged: one must obey the law by loving God and one's neighbour; and in order to do so, one must conceive of God as charitable and just.

Philosophy and the law

Whereas Spinoza insists that it is impossible to hold philosophical beliefs on command, he seems to take it for granted that there is nothing incoherent about requiring people to imagine God in a particular way. Why, though, should it be any easier to convince oneself that the deity is charitable and just than to conceive of him in a philosophical fashion, for example as the immanent cause of the order of nature? Spinoza's answer takes us back to the kinds of evidence on which these two types of belief are based. Unless one can

---

[32]   Ibid. 3p52s, 4p29–36.
[33]   Spinoza, *Tractatus Theologico-Politicus*, ch. 14, p. 174.

demonstrate a philosophical conclusion, he has claimed, one cannot gain the kind of clear and distinct idea that constitutes philosophical knowledge of it. But using one's imaginative capacities to form a more confused idea of a just deity is not so demanding. As long as one can recognize the difference between justice and injustice, one can go on to form some sort of anthropomorphic idea of a God who deals justly, or not unjustly, with human beings. The exercise draws on ordinary experience, including, perhaps, experience of the Bible; and since there are no other constraints that the idea has to satisfy, it lies within normal reach.[34]

Even if one is willing to accept this view, however, merely forming an image or idea of a just God is not enough. If it is to motivate one to act, one must also be convinced that God possesses the qualities that one imaginatively attributes to him. Spinoza is willing to allow that we sometimes use fantasies to motivate ourselves, and then go on to act as they dictate; but he implicitly assumes that they exert a weaker hold over us than our considered beliefs, and consequently cannot ground a steady determination to live in a particular way. While one might occasionally stir oneself to act lovingly towards one's neighbour by fantasizing about pleasing a just God, only the belief that God really is just will get one to obey the divine law on a regular basis.[35]

For many of the prophets and their peoples, this condition was easily met: their anthropomorphic conceptions of the deity disposed them to be able to accept that he is just and charitable.[36] Moreover, so Spinoza seems to assume, the same applies to many of his contemporaries, who also imagine God anthropomorphically as he is presented in the Bible. Where, though, does this leave individuals such as Spinoza himself, who hold that no such God exists? How are they supposed to think of the deity in anthropomorphic terms, when their best-supported judgments tell them that this conception is false? On the face of things, it looks as though the philosophers whom Spinoza regards as most enlightened are bound to view biblical narratives about God as fictions, roughly on a par with romances and equally devoid of epistemological authority.

Spinoza does not dissent from this conclusion. As he has explained, following the teaching of the Bible is not the only way to live in accordance with the divine law. It is also possible to adhere to it on the basis of a philosophical understanding of its central tenets. By acquiring a rational understanding of the nature of the supreme good, philosophers can emancipate themselves from

---

[34] Ibid. ch. 13, p. 170.   [35] Ibid. ch. 13, p. 172.   [36] Ibid. ch. 13, p. 171.

Scripture, and conform to the divine law without relying on an anthropomorphic conception of a just God.[37] Central as it is, the biblical conception of God therefore does not speak directly to Spinoza or to other philosophers of his bent. It is important, however, not to exaggerate the distance between Spinoza's philosophical outlook and the more ordinary style of obedience with which he is now concerned. Philosophers are human beings whose grasp of what is going on and how to respond to it continues to be shaped by their imaginative experience of the world around them. While some of their ideas are clear and distinct, and are therefore capable of being integrated into the demonstrations that constitute the high ground of mathematical certainty, many will fall short of this standard. Some will straddle the divide between reason and imagination, like the ideas on which Spinoza has built his history of Scripture. Others, including the passions as the *Ethics* defines them, will be firmly planted on the imaginative side of the border.[38] Rather than withdrawing into a purely philosophical realm, philosophers who are trying to live in accordance with the divine law will appreciate the need to work with all their ideas, adequate and inadequate, to refine their models of the true life and motivate themselves to imitate them. Whether they continue to make use of Scripture in order to do so is to some extent an open question, and depends on the direction and distance in which their reasoning has carried them. Spinoza has suggested that Christ's intuitive understanding of the divine law offers a model of the true life that philosophers can imitate; but as he has also shown, such a model can be drawn from resources other than the Bible, so that it is possible to follow the divine law without relying on Scripture.

The fact remains, however, that once philosophers have shed an anthropomorphic conception of the deity, they cannot subscribe to the precept that Spinoza has made a condition of obedience—that God is just and charitable. This brings us back to the question of how they are supposed to understand this requirement, and thus to another key feature of Spinoza's account of biblical doctrine. What makes the belief that God is just a significant one is not its truth, but rather its function—its capacity to motivate us to live together cooperatively or love our neighbours. When a prophet such as Moses describes the divine law as the work of a just God, he finds a persuasive way of imaginatively articulating the instrumental claim that, in order to obey a law willingly, people must be able to trust it. Readers who believe in an anthropomorphic God may find Moses' articulation satisfying and be able to take him at

---

[37] This is implied at ibid. ch. 15, p. 188. See also Spinoza, *Ethics*, 4p22c, 4p24, 5p41s.
[38] Spinoza, *Ethics*, 3.App.'General definition of the affects'.

his literal word. But philosophers will recognize that he and the other prophets are representing a general truth in imaginative terms, and will see beyond the representation to the truth itself. Underlying the Bible's insistence that God is just and charitable is the psychological truth that people are only able steadily to obey the divine law if they can be confident that, in doing so, they will be treated fairly. Moreover, as a philosophical reader will appreciate, this truth applies to philosophers as much as to anyone else. If their philosophical understanding is to motivate them to live co-operatively, as Spinoza believes it will, they too need some reason for believing that such a way of life will not be thwarted by distributions of benefits of the kind that we usually describe as unjust.

Different philosophies attempt to fill out this requirement in different ways, as the history of the problem of theodicy attests. In Spinoza's case, however, the solution is given by his own philosophical system and the conception of God around which it is organized. This God manifests himself, as we have seen, in laws of nature that are simultaneously divine decrees by which all human beings are equally bound and to which everyone must of necessity conform. Furthermore, their unchanging and exceptionless operation ensures that they apply to everyone on exactly the same terms so that, in this metaphorical sense, God can be described as equitable or just. Finally, as Spinoza explains in the *Ethics*, the natural order operates in such a way that groups of people who love their neighbours or live in a co-operative fashion benefit from doing so.[39] Again in a metaphorical sense, a God who makes this way of life available can be described as charitable. These philosophical interpretations of the law do not of course capture the letter of the Bible's conceptions of divine *charitas* and justice. The propositional content of the two sets of formulations is obviously not the same. But there is nevertheless a sense in which they capture its spirit. Like the prophets, philosophers trade on a functional relationship between a certain conception of God and the ability to live co-operatively, though each articulates it in terms of their own beliefs. To put the point another way, each assents to a view about God that can be imaginatively expressed in the claim that he is just and charitable. The prophets, who had an inadequate idea of God, took this claim literally. Spinoza, by contrast, treats it as a gesture in the direction of certain speculative truths about the deity that philosophy can elucidate. So although he and other philosophers cannot straightforwardly assent to the precept that God is just and charitable, they need not straightforwardly reject

---

[39] Ibid. 4p20.

it. By bringing their understanding to bear on it, they can identify and approve the kernel of truth it contains.[40]

In a philosophical discussion, the incompleteness and inaccuracy of the biblical divine law would need to be examined and put right. But in a theological context, Spinoza insists, what matters about our beliefs is not their truth but their efficacy. The only relevant question is whether a belief helps an individual or community to live in the co-operative fashion that the divine law requires. As far as theology is concerned, each individual should therefore be 'permitted to accommodate scripture to his own opinions if he sees that in that way he can obey God more wholeheartedly in matters concerning justice and lovingkindness'.[41] It is simply a fact of life that people vary a great deal, and that beliefs which move one person to behave justly may move another to laughter and contempt.[42] If a community is to live obediently, it will have to countenance a variety of beliefs and outlooks without worrying too much about their truth. The great mistake of theologians is to confuse their calling with that of philosophy, and to concern themselves with the truth of the beliefs that enable and encourage people to obey the law. Gripped by this misconception, they become, as Spinoza puts it, Antichrists, who refuse to tolerate differences of doctrine and persecute those who disagree with them.[43] But this is an egregious error, because the small number of beliefs on which obedience depends are open to individual or collective interpretation. A philosopher will interpret them in speculative terms, which accord with a relatively abstract conception of obedience to the divine law; but this is only one of the multitude of forms that they can legitimately take. They do not have to be philosophical or demonstrable, and generally are not.

As the *Treatise* presents it here, theology gives individuals and communities a great deal of latitude to form beliefs and outlooks that will help them to live in a particular fashion: to obey the divine law or love their neighbours. While the Bible enjoins us to follow this way of life, the primary purpose of its teaching is not to communicate truths about God. Rather, it is a rhetorical or persuasive tool, which seeks to shape our actions by arousing our affects and modifying or reinforcing our motivations. As we have seen, Spinoza has strong reasons for standing by this view. But it nevertheless exposes him to the old and dangerous complaint that rhetoric deals in a tissue of falsehoods designed to pacify an

---

[40] On the epistemological status of such claims, see *Ethics*, 2p33–35.
[41] Spinoza, *Tractatus Theologico-Politicus*, ch. 14, p. 173.
[42] Ibid. ch. 14, p. 177.   [43] Ibid. ch. 14, p. 176.

ignorant multitude.[44] His account of religion, it might be charged, downgrades Scripture to this level by presenting it as a panoply of persuasive fictions, and turns theologians into rhetoricians whose task is in effect to keep their congregations quiet. Rather than offering a way to counter ignorance, theology thus conceived allows it to run riot.

Still more serious, from Spinoza's point of view, is the fact that this kind of theology seems to welcome superstition. If there are very few limits to the beliefs that religious people can legitimately hold or to the practices that they can use to cultivate piety, many superstitious outlooks will surely be beyond reproof. As long as they result in obedience, there will be no theological basis for criticizing or opposing them, and the devious priests against whom Spinoza speaks so bitterly in his Preface will be free to indulge their self-aggrandizing desires. The conception of true religion at which the *Treatise* has now arrived will undermine its initial goal of unmasking and discrediting superstition.

While Spinoza does not directly address this objection in the *Treatise*, it is clear how he would reply to it.[45] Arguing in pragmatic vein, he has conceded that the aim of the doctrine taught in Scripture is to persuade, and that the truly religious way of life it recommends may indeed be sustained by beliefs that are untrue. If one wants to encourage a group of people to live co-operatively in accordance with the law, one has to take them as they are; and when a majority of their ideas and attitudes are imaginary ones, one must draw on imaginative resources to make the divine law compelling. In this type of situation, most of the ideas to which one appeals will of course fall short of a philosophical standard of truth. This, however, does not immediately open the way to either falsehood or superstition. In the first place, as we have seen, the beliefs we derive from imagining are by no means straightforwardly false. Many of them are morally certain, and even those that are deeply misleading when viewed from a philosophical perspective may capture aspects of the truth, albeit in an indirect and metaphorical fashion. It is consequently a drastic and distorting simplification to imply that theology, any more than rhetoric, must trade in falsehoods and is therefore bound to encourage ignorance. Rather, it takes the beliefs and attitudes that a particular community of people find credible, and uses them as best it can to cultivate a certain way of life.

---

[44] Koerbagh, for example, criticizes Machiavelli for arguing that religion is just a set of stories designed to control the *vulgus*. Bunge, *From Stevin to Spinoza*, p. 104.

[45] See Letter 73 to Oldenburg where Spinoza distinguishes superstition, founded on ignorance, from religion, founded on knowledge. *The Correspondence of Spinoza*, ed. and trans. A. Wolf (London: Frank Cass, 1966) p. 343.

In some cases, of course, such beliefs are radically false; but this alone does not pose a theological problem. What makes beliefs and outlooks suspect, from a theological point of view, is the fact that they are embedded in superstitious practices; for although theology is largely tolerant of falsehood, its toleration does not extend to superstitious ways of life. As we saw in Chapter 1, superstition is rooted in a corrosive fear of God, and becomes particularly dangerous when it is used to maintain the influence of religious or political authorities. It usually arises, in Spinoza's view, when priests or rulers trade on fear and the disempowering sequences of passion to which it can give rise, in order to pressurize people into adopting the beliefs and practices on which their power and authority depends. However, the type of religious practice recommended by the *Treatise* is quite the opposite. Instead of trying to impose debilitating beliefs and habits, as superstition does, true religion encourages people to empower themselves by living in the light of convictions that will help them live co-operatively with others; and instead of playing on their fear of God, it attempts to foster a confidence-inspiring conception of a deity who is just and charitable. Such a religion is organized, then, around love and devotion for God rather than fear, and is designed to counteract the poisoned ways of life that arise from superstitious anxiety.

Finally, superstition is habitually used to keep the populace ignorant: for example, Spinoza rails against superstitious theologians who 'love as God's elect those who assent to their own opinions, even when these are the most weak-minded'.[46] But this, as he protests, is outrageous. 'You cannot imagine anything more wicked or more fatal to the state'. True religion of the kind that the *Treatise* is advocating opposes this kind of oppression by allowing people to think for themselves and extend their understanding at their own rate. As the inadequacy of an individual's ideas diminishes and their beliefs about the deity change, they may come to find that different aspects of the Bible strengthen their ability to obey. Equally they may discover non-biblical sources of religious inspiration, and make them sacred by using them to strengthen their commitment to the divine law. But whatever direction this process takes, no one's ideas are to be condemned on theological grounds, as long as they do not obstruct a co-operative way of life. And this last proviso rules out ways of life that are superstitious.

Implicitly answering the criticism that he is ushering in an irresponsible form of persuasion, Spinoza agrees with the traditional opponents of rhetoric that the

---

[46] Spinoza, *Tractatus Theologico-Politicus*, ch. 14, p. 173.

true understanding at which philosophical investigation arrives sustains the highest values of human life. But this does not cause him to share their hostility to the art of persuasion. If a community is significantly to increase the level of its understanding, he proposes, it must create circumstances in which this goal can be pursued; and in order to do this, it needs to persuade its members to develop and sustain a mutually supportive way of life. In Jewish and Christian societies, the divine law taught in the Bible offers a model of co-operation that appeals powerfully to the imagination, and the proper task of theology is to make this model efficacious. But theologians are not always good at their job, and sometimes get sidetracked into policies that inhibit rather than promote conditions in which understanding can grow. This, for example, is what has happened in the United Provinces, where religious factions have tried to limit the freedom to philosophize. However, the way to deal with the problem is not to endorse the old fear of rhetoric by trying to police the imagination—in any case a hopeless enterprise. A more practical way forward is to use such understanding of ourselves as we possess to differentiate between imagination's constructive and destructive uses. Rather than settling for superstition—one of the most damaging fruits of imaginative thinking—we should try to promote a form of true religion that does not enforce, but nevertheless enhances, the pursuit of understanding. We need to create conditions in which people treat one another justly and kindly, and are consequently able to reflect critically on the strengths and limitations of their beliefs and practices.[47]

The religious life that the *Treatise* recommends is consequently designed to resist rather than encourage the corrupt forms of persuasion that worry the enemies of rhetoric. Without denying that theology, like other human practices, can go terribly wrong, Spinoza envisages a form of religion that serves a vital practical function by helping us to live together. In the process, it creates conditions in which we can try to develop the kind of understanding to which philosophy aspires. So, left in the hands of theology, the tools of persuasion need not be given over to deceit and self-aggrandizement. The problem is to see how to exploit their positive potential by using them to create co-operative

---

[47] Moira Gatens, 'Spinoza's Disturbing Thesis: Power, Norms and Fiction in the *Tractatus Theologico-Politicus*', *History of Political Thought*, 30. 3 (2009); Moira Gatens, 'The Politics of Imagination', in *Feminist Interpretations of Benedict Spinoza* (University Park, Pa.: Pennsylvania State University Press, 2009); Susan James, 'Creating Rational Understanding: Spinoza as a Social Epistemologist', *Proceedings of the Aristotelian Society*, supplementary volume, 85, no. 1 (2011); Susan James, 'Narrative as the Means to Freedom: Spinoza on the Uses of Imagination', in *Spinoza's 'Theologico-Political Treatise'*, ed. Yitzhak Y. Melamed and Michael A. Rosenthal (Cambridge: Cambridge University Press, 2010).

ways of life in which communities are not only able to live peacefully, but also to enhance the scope and certainty of their knowledge.

Defining faith

To shore up the analysis of true religion that he has just offered and make it compelling to his readers, Spinoza needs to convince them that it provides a satisfactory account, not only of obedience, but also of faith. Since this virtue was generally regarded as a mark of salvation, it assumed the utmost importance, and the question of what constituted saving faith remained a topic of vehement theological debate. As we would by now expect, Spinoza aims to resist the practice, standard in many religions such as that of the Dutch Reformed Church, of providing lists of highly specific and often speculative tenets of faith. Apart from the fact that he regards it as futile to try to make ordinary people accept speculative claims that they do not understand, he was only too aware that tenets of faith functioned as flashpoints for conflict. As long as these tenets remained numerous and contestable, faith was bound to be a topic of controversy, giving rise to disputes and superstitions of the kind that the *Treatise* is anxious to exclude.

Spinoza's approach to this problem harks back to his view that Scripture teaches a universal doctrine. If this doctrine is to be accessible to everyone, he reasons, it cannot rest on tenets of faith 'about which there can be controversy among honourable men'.[48] As we shall see in Chapter 9, the Latin term translated here as 'honourable', *honestus*, has many connotations, but in this context it is used to distinguish people who make a sincere or well-intentioned attempt to grasp the divine law taught in the Bible from those who are self-deceiving, indolent, or stubborn. Tenets of faith must be sufficiently evident to solicit general assent. In addition, they are defined by their purpose. Returning to his claim that the primary religious virtue is obedience, Spinoza now claims that the point of faith is to enable us live obediently by loving one's neighbour.[49] It therefore consists 'in thinking such things about God that if the person is not familiar with them, obedience to God is destroyed, and such that, if obedience to God is posited, these beliefs are necessarily posited'.[50] To be faithful, according to this careful if slightly contorted formulation, is just to think about God in a way that enables one to live co-operatively, as the divine law requires.

---

[48] Spinoza, *Tractatus Theologico-Politicus*, ch. 14, p. 177.
[49] Ibid. ch. 14, p. 174.   [50] Ibid. ch. 14, p. 175.

Innocuous as it may appear, this definition was, for two reasons, a controversial one. First of all, it directly challenges the conception of faith upheld by the Reformed Church. If faith simply consists in holding beliefs about God that are sufficient for obeying the divine law, it follows, as Spinoza points out, that anyone who obeys the law satisfies this condition, and must therefore count among the faithful. 'He who is obedient necessarily has a true and saving faith.'[51] To put the point another way, obedience is a sufficient sign of faith, so that 'obedience being posited, faith is also necessarily posited'. The mark of one's faith therefore lies entirely in one's way of life and is guaranteed by the fact that one consistently acts justly and charitably, aids the poor, does not murder, does not covet other people's goods, and so on.[52]

By making faith rest entirely on what the English translation of the Bible calls 'works', Spinoza sets himself against the Calvinist claim that works are neither necessary nor sufficient for salvation. As the *Belgic Confession* pronounces, 'We say with Paul that we are justified by faith alone, or by faith without works'. Indeed, works 'are of no account towards our justification. It is by faith in Christ that we are justified, even before we do good works, otherwise they could not be good works any more than the fruit of a tree can be good before the tree itself is good'.[53] Flatly contradicting the Church's official view, Spinoza takes up a position that it associated with Catholicism. 'The person who displays the best faith', he asserts, 'is not necessarily the one who displays the best arguments, but the one who displays the best works of justice and lovingkindness'.[54]

A second controversial feature of Spinoza's definition concerns the content of faith. If we take his claim that being faithful is just a matter of having a view of God that enables one to obey the divine law, and put it together with his analysis of obedience, we arrive at the conclusion that faith only requires us to conceive of God as just and charitable. By the going standards this was already an exceptionally minimal requirement, but it shrinks still further when we remember that it is open to many interpretations. Faith, the *Treatise* explains, does not require us to believe tenets that are true, but only to cleave to tenets that will strengthen our love for our neighbours; and since people vary so much in their patterns of motivation, one should not try to provide a precise

---

[51] Ibid.

[52] Ibid. ch. 12, p. 165.

[53] 'The Belgic Confession', in *The Creeds of Christendom: The Evangelical Protestant Creeds*, ed. Philip Schaff (New York: Cosimo Books, 2007), Articles 22, 24.

[54] Spinoza, *Tractatus Theologico-Politicus*, ch. 14, p. 179.

specification of the beliefs that will enable them to succeed. Better to look at an individual's actions and infer their faith from how they live.[55] 'If their works are good they are faithful, however much they disagree with other faithful people as to their tenets. Conversely, if their works are bad they are unfaithful, even if their words do not differ from those of faithful individuals'.[56]

Perhaps Spinoza would have liked to leave the matter there, but because the position he has so far defended lies right at one end of an existing spectrum of opinion, this is not a practical option. As well as conflicting with the stance of the Reformed Church, his analysis of faith (as he has so far enunciated it) rubs up against an Erasmian tradition according to which salvation flows from a combination of faith and works. According to this view, the faithful must live virtuously in the manner taught by Christ; but they must also affirm certain tenets. Needless to add, the correct balance between beliefs and works could be struck at various points, and different denominations determined their own tipping points, some placing more weight than others on the importance of belief. However, by reducing the convictions on which faith depends so drastically, Spinoza puts himself outside the accepted range of possibilities, and therefore needs to explicate his view with great care.

Elaborating his position, Spinoza now brings it closer to other minimalist interpretations of scriptural doctrine. Adopting a broadly Erasmian stance, he pulls back from the end of the spectrum by spelling out a number of further tenets of faith on which obedience depends. The reason for this strategy, so he himself claims, is that if one leaves the content of faith almost completely unspecified, one creates a space that theologians can fill with their own favourite doctrinal commitments. If there are almost no fixed tenets of faith, anyone can choose whatever tenets they like; but this will replicate the state of affairs that the *Treatise* aims to overcome, by producing a cacophony of conflicting confessions, together with a string of disputes about their relative merits. To block this self-defeating possibility, one needs a more specific definition of faith. 'Unless I show here how to determine the tenets of faith from the foundation we have discovered . . . people will rightly think I have done little to advance the discussion, since everyone will be able to introduce whatever he wishes under the pretext that it is a necessary means to obedience, particularly when it is a question of the divine attributes'.[57]

At first glance this seems an uneasy concession. If faith is merely the capacity to live obediently, and does not depend on holding any particular beliefs, then

---

[55] Ibid. ch. 14, pp. 176–7.   [56] Ibid. ch. 14, p. 175.   [57] Ibid.

surely theologians—and indeed everyone else—*should* generate their own tenets, while also respecting the need for others to do the same. 'Since each person knows himself better [than anyone else does], he must think what he sees will be better for him, for the purpose of confirming himself in his love of justice'.[58] In trying to pin down specific tenets of faith when he has already explained why this is impossible, is Spinoza not simply giving way to the expectations of his readers and adversaries? This is clearly a worry; but Spinoza is not in the habit of making significant concessions, and as we shall see, has reasons of his own for developing his argument as he does. While he wants to keep faith to a minimum, and to exclude from it the philosophical contentions about which theologians quarrel so bitterly, he does not want to allow that absolutely any beliefs are compatible with an obedient way of life. Like his opponents, he holds that some convictions are antithetical to true religion and deserve to be censured. To make this clear, he needs to give a fuller account of the content of true faith.

On reflection, Spinoza seems to suggest, it emerges that his exposition of the core doctrine of Scripture is incomplete. While it captures the fundamental insights that ordinary people need to accept in order to follow the divine law, it fails to spell out all the ideas about God on which obedience depends. Rather than making them explicit, it tacitly assumes that someone who regards God as just and charitable will also have a range of other convictions about the deity, and that these will play a part in determining their way of life. But what might these convictions be? We already know that they must function to support the doctrine 'that there is a supreme being who loves justice and lovingkindness; and that everyone, if he is to be saved, is bound to obey this being and to worship him by practising justice and lovingkindness towards his neighbour'.[59] But at present this is as far as we can go. In order to protect his reading of the divine teaching of Scripture from misunderstanding, Spinoza now needs to spell out the purportedly uncontentious tenets of faith on which obedience depends.

The tenets of the universal faith

The tenets that Spinoza goes on to enumerate—seven in number—look much like the essential doctrines proposed by other theological minimalists. But this appearance is deceptive. Whereas tenets of faith were usually presented as accredited truths to which the faithful must consent, Spinoza's are designed

---

[58] Ibid. ch. 14, p. 177.   [59] Ibid.

not to communicate the truth but to guide our actions. This aim is reflected in the way that he presents them. According to the first, for instance, one must hold that God, 'a supreme being who is supremely just and merciful, or a model of the true life', exists.[60] However, the justification for this tenet is not that it is true. Rather, the point is that it is impossible to obey the divine law without accepting it, because a person who 'does not know or does not believe that God exists cannot obey him or know him as a judge'.[61] As we have seen, it is not enough to ground one's behaviour on a fantasy about such a deity; one must sincerely believe that there is something there to obey. Nevertheless, the tenet says nothing about *how* one is to envisage God, and as Spinoza has gone to such pains to show, one can do this in any number of ways. His tenets therefore appear more conventional than they are. At first glance they replicate some of the doctrines standardly upheld by Christian confessions, with which his readers would have been familiar; but on closer inspection, it emerges that they do not endorse a specifically Christian, let alone a Calvinist viewpoint. For example, they do not rule out Spinoza's own conception of a God who takes no interest in the affairs of human beings and cannot strictly speaking be obeyed. Furthermore, many of the Christians who read Spinoza's tenets would have been struck by a number of deafening silences, which mount up as the list proceeds, progressively bringing home the extent to which they license unorthodox beliefs.[62]

Like the Ten Commandments, the tenets of faith that Spinoza identifies can be divided into two tables, the first concerning the essential attributes of God and the second the relations between God and humankind. In addition to specifying that God exists, the first table requires the faithful to conceive of him as unique, because the devotion, admiration, and love that they need to feel for him 'arise only from the excellence of one by comparison with the others'.[63] There is nothing theologically unusual about the supposition that only a unique deity can command our undivided loyalty, and virtually no one in seventeenth-century Holland would have wanted to make a case for polytheism. Nevertheless, in invoking God's unity, Spinoza pointedly refuses to endorse the

---

[60] Ibid.   [61] Ibid.

[62] 'And so we can see that the author makes no mention in his writings of the use of prayer, just as he makes no mention of life or death, or of any reward or punishment through which men are influenced by the judge of the universe'. Velthuysen, Letter 42. Spinoza, *The Correspondence of Spinoza*, ed. A. Wolf, p. 241. For further discussion, see Jacqueline Lagrée, *La raison ardente: Religion naturelle et raison au xviie siècle* (Paris: Vrin, 1991).

[63] Spinoza, *Tractatus Theologico-Politicus*, ch. 14, p. 177 .

Belgic Confession's pronouncement that 'God is one in essence, yet distinguished into three persons'.[64] Readers would have recognized this as a slightly risky gesture of sympathy towards Socinianism, the Unitarian heresy outlawed in the Netherlands in1653, which the Church continued to use as a convenient stick for beating some of its opponents.[65] And in fact, although there are clear divergences between Spinoza's theological position and that of the Socinians, he does endorse their rejection of the Trinity. Discussing the relation between God and Christ, he allows that there is a sense in which Christ's voice can be called the voice of God, but warns that he is not agreeing with 'the things that certain churches maintain about Christ', because he simply cannot grasp them.[66] Writing to his friend Henry Oldenburg he is more frank. 'As to the doctrine of certain churches. . . . that God assumed a human nature, I expressly warned them that I do not grasp what they say. Indeed, to confess the truth, they seem to me to speak no less absurdly than if someone were to tell me that a circle assumed the nature of a sphere'.[67] Since Spinoza himself conceives of God as the one existing substance, these reservations are not surprising; but they also indicate the latitude with which his tenet of faith can be interpreted. In order to venerate God, one is required to think of him as one; but because the kind of unity that one attributes to him is left open, the tenet does not impose the doctrinal commitments required by the Reformed Church.

Comparable points can be made about Spinoza's next two tenets. The second, that God is present everywhere, is justified on the grounds that, if one were to think that some things are hidden from him, or that there are some things he does not see, one might doubt the equity of his justice. Because this rationale is accommodated to the anthropomorphic God of Scripture rather than a philosophical deity, it answers comfortably to the Church's biblically based insistence that God knows our thoughts and requires us to love him unconditionally. But it is obviously not acceptable to a philosopher, who will therefore have to interpret it non-literally, in the light of his philosophical knowledge. Spinoza's God, for example, has no spatial properties and certainly

---

[64] 'The Belgic Confession', Article 8.
[65] See Bunge, *From Stevin to Spinoza*, pp. 73–4.
[66] Spinoza, *Tractatus Theologico-Politicus*, ch. 1, p. 21.
[67] Letter 72. *The Correspondence of Spinoza*, ed. Wolf, p. 344. Translation adapted. See also 'If [theologians] claim to have any spirit other than [reason] which makes them certain of truth, they are making a false boast. They are either speaking on the prejudiced basis of their affects or fleeing to sacred things for protection, under pressure from a great fear that they may be defeated by the philosophers and exposed to public ridicule' (Spinoza, *Tractatus Theologico-Politicus*, ch. 15, p. 188).

does not check up on us in order to dispense remedial justice. But he (or it) is nevertheless infinite and eternal, and the unchanging natural laws of which he is the immanent cause affect all human beings in the same way. In a remote and impersonal sense, then, he can be described as omnipresent.

Moving to the third tenet, Spinoza claims that one can only be convinced that one is absolutely bound to obey God if one believes that he has supreme right and dominion over all things, and is not himself bound to obey any law or any other power. Again, while this does not explicitly challenge the Reformed Church's voluntarist conception of the deity as a being whose will is entirely unconstrained (the more so because Spinoza describes God as acting 'from his absolute good pleasure and special grace'), there is nothing to prevent Spinoza from subscribing to it, despite the fact that there is a vast gulf between the Church's position and his own.[68] Where Calvinism conceives of God as possessing an unlimited will, Spinoza identifies divine will and intellect. Where Calvinism holds that humans can disobey the divine law, Spinoza denies that this is possible. Where Spinoza claims that God does not act for ends, Calvinists are committed to the view that he does little else. These differences affect the sense in which one can view oneself as absolutely bound to obey God, and thus how this belief bears on one's obedience. But the tenet as Spinoza states it, is from a Calvinist point of view, suspiciously inclusive.

The four divine attributes (existence, uniqueness, omniscience, and omnipotence) on which Spinoza has so far focused make up the first table of his tenets of faith. In the remaining three, he turns to the relationship between God and man, first taking up the issue of worship. 'The worship of God, and obedience to him, consist only in justice and lovingkindness, or in the love of one's neighbour'.[69] As we have already seen, such utter indifference to ritual would have touched the Reformed Church on the raw, as would the absence of any mention of prayer. Given that Spinoza's God neither hears nor answers human supplications, this silence is not surprising; but it once again emphasizes the extent to which he aspires to make religious practices entirely optional. If the Reformed Church were to accept his position, it would not only have to allow that a life without prayer or sacraments can be a faithful one; it would also have to accept that there is nothing irreligious about the ceremonies of its rivals, whether Catholics, Anabaptists, or Jews.

The sixth tenet concerns salvation. It contends that, unless people believe that only those who obey God are saved, while those who live under the

---

[68] Spinoza, *Tractatus Theologico-Politicus*, ch. 14, p. 177.   [69] Ibid.

control of the pleasures are lost, they will lack any firm motivation to live co-operatively, and are liable to give themselves up to selfish goals.[70] Running obedience and salvation together, Spinoza skirts round a host of contentious claims that give his opponents endless trouble: the faithful are not required to believe that salvation is achieved by any particular process such as divine predestination, redemption through Christ, or the intercession of grace; nor are they required to have any particular view of what salvation and loss are like—whether, for example, they involve the flight of the soul to purgatory, heaven, or hell. All such issues are up to individuals or groups to work out for themselves, so that the power of an established religion to enforce or contest any particular view is drastically reduced.

In the *Treatise*, Spinoza advocates a comparatively austere understanding of salvation as the benefit that flows from living co-operatively as the divine law commands. People who love their neighbours are able to create cohesive communities in which their individual and collective powers are greatly increased, and their capacity to protect themselves against harm is strengthened. At the same time, they are able to reflect on the nature of God and enjoy the comfort and illumination that this brings, free from interfering religious authorities. By contrast, people who are not just and charitable, but devote themselves to selfish pleasures, are deprived of these benefits. They dedicate their lives to goals that are ultimately unsustaining, suffer the psychic and social costs of failing to live co-operatively, and never become secure enough to concentrate on the satisfactions that come with the growth of rational understanding. Thus conceived, salvation lies within ordinary reach. It is not, as the most orthodox of Calvinists would have it, an apparently arbitrary gift from God; nor does it depend, as the Arminians within the Church contend, on the intervention of divine grace.

To be motivated to live obediently, Spinoza suggests, we must believe that we shall benefit from doing so; and this in turn requires us to believe that, prone to injustice as we are, the benefits or rewards of obedience are nevertheless a realistic goal for which to strive. According to the seventh and last tenet, this in turn depends on the conviction that 'God pardons the sins of those who repent'. If we fear, for example, that God has predestined us to eternal damnation, we may despair of salvation and decide that we have no reason to obey the divine law. Or if we doubt that salvation lies within our reach, the effort of attaining it may not seem worth the struggle. But as long as we are

---

[70] Ibid. ch. 14, pp. 177–8.

confident that past transgressions do not rule out the benefits of obedience, and that all we have to do is to contribute to the growth of empowering ways of life within which we can avoid conflict, we shall always have a reason to keep trying to adhere to the divine law, and can always expect to benefit from the satisfactions of salvation. To grasp Spinoza's point, it is important to avoid thinking of repentance as a form of sadness at something we have done. (The *Ethics* makes it clear that he does not regard this passion as a virtue.[71]) Instead, we need to conceive the kind of repentance now under discussion as a sustained determination to renew one's efforts to live well when one has failed to live up to the demands of the divine law, however one conceives it. Once again, a familiar feature of Christianity is implicitly being reinterpreted.

To bring home just how little his tenets of faith require in the way of speculative commitments, Spinoza spells out a long list of topics on which they do not pronounce. It does not matter, as far as faith is concerned, what one believes God is like; one can, for example, conceive of him as fire or as spirit as long as these ideas are compatible with the view that he is just and charitable. As long as one believes that God is the exemplar of true life, it does not matter what one's reasons are. As long as one believes that God is omnipresent, one does not have to determine whether he is omnipresent in essence or potency. As long as one believes that he has supreme dominion, one can believe that he directs events either by free will or by necessity. As long as one believes that he lays down rules for men, one can conceive these rules as teachings or as eternal truths. As long as one believes that we are bound to obey divine decrees, it does not matter whether one thinks that we do so freely, or from the necessity of the divine decrees. And as long as one believes that we are rewarded for obedience and punished for disobedience, it does not matter whether one conceives of our rewards and punishments as natural or supernatural.

While these stipulations drive home the point that theologians who turn speculative opinions into dogmas exceed their authority, they also have a range of critical implications. For example, if it is immaterial whether one believes that we obey God freely or of necessity, the Reformed Church's persecution of Arminianism was irreligious, and its continued insistence on the doctrine of salvation established at the Synod of Dort is completely unjustified. As well as loosening the hold of religious power, however, the tenets constitute a plea for Spinoza's own philosophy. He happens to think that God directs everything of necessity, that the rules he lays down for men take the form of eternal truths,

---

[71] Spinoza, *Ethics*, 4p54.

and that rewards and punishments are natural. But while the truth or falsehood of these claims is crucial to his philosophical enquiries, it is not important to religion, since one can obey the divine law whether one accepts them or not. There is therefore no theological objection to these aspects of Spinozism, which do not contradict any of the tenets of faith that are essential to a religious life. Aside from the tenets 'which obedience to God absolutely posits, and which, if they are ignored, make obedience absolutely impossible', true religion leaves it up to each individual to think in a way that confirms his love of justice.[72]

Because individuals can only accept the tenets without mental conflict or hesitation if they are accommodated to their understanding, each one should be viewed as an infinite disjunction.[73] The tenet that God is omnipresent, for example, stands in for an endless sequence of alternative interpretations, united by the fact that each plays a particular role in encouraging people to live in accordance with the divine law. Some of them, such as the philosophically grounded account of God's omnipresence that Spinoza spells out in the *Ethics*, will be clear and distinct, but the great majority will remain vague and unarticulated. As the *Treatise* emphasizes, evidence of one's commitment to the tenets is not supplied by one's ideas but by one's actions, and the fact that one lives obediently is proof that one holds them. In principle, then, there are any number of ways in which one can interpret the tenets of faith on which

---

[72] This interpretation contrasts with the view of some commentators, who have argued that Spinoza is implicitly rejecting religion. See, for example, Jonathan Israel, *Radical Enlightenment: Philosophy and the Making of Modernity, 1650–1750* (Oxford: Oxford University Press, 2001), p. 11; Steven B. Smith, *Spinoza, Liberalism, and the Question of Jewish Identity* (New Haven: Yale University Press, 1997), p. 202; Yirmiyahu Yovel, *Spinoza and Other Heretics*, 2 vols. (Princeton: Princeton University Press, 1989), I.153. It also contrasts with Strauss's claim that the tenets of faith are fictions designed to pacify the common people. See Leo Strauss, 'How to Study Spinoza's "Theologico-Political Treatise"', in *Jewish History and the Crisis of Modernity* (Albany NY: SUNY Press, 1997), reprinted from Leo Strauss, *Persecution and the Art of Writing* (Glencoe Ill.: Free Press, 1952). Opponents of this view include Daniel Garber, 'Should Spinoza have Published His Philosophy?' in *Interpreting Spinoza: Critical Essays*, ed. Charlie Huenemann (Cambridge: Cambridge University Press, 2008); Richard Mason, *The God of Spinoza: A Philosophical Study* (Cambridge: Cambridge University Press, 1997), p. 200; Steven M. Nadler, *Spinoza: A Life* (Cambridge: Cambridge University Press, 1999), p. 247; Richard H. Popkin, 'Spinoza and Bible Scholarship', in *The Cambridge Companion to Spinoza*, ed. Don Garrett (Cambridge: Cambridge University Press, 1996); J. Samuel Preus, *Spinoza and the Irrelevance of Biblical Authority* (Cambridge: Cambridge University Press, 2001); Michael Rosenthal, 'Spinoza's Dogmas of the Universal Faith and the Problem of Religion', *Philosophy and Theology*, 13, no. 1 (2001); Sylvain Zac, *Spinoza et l'interprétation de l'écriture* (Paris: Presses Universitaires de France, 1965).

[73] Spinoza, *Tractatus Theologico-Politicus*, ch. 14, p. 179.

obedience depends, though each formulation will be more intelligible to some people than others. (For example, the formulations that Spinoza himself finds most compelling will only make sense to a small band of philosophers.) In presenting them as he does, Spinoza chooses his audience, favouring readers who are immersed in biblical doctrine and the image of God around which it is organized. Relying on their imagined conceptions of the divine attributes, and of worship, salvation and repentance, he presents his views in a familiar religious guise, so that on the surface of things his tenets are not particularly extreme, and not very different from those specified by other minimalists. What sets his position apart, however, is the fact that each tenet is in effect a variable, to be filled in by each believer as they see fit; and this is what makes them universal.

Chapter 9

Theology and Philosophy

Spinoza's practical conception of religion, stripped bare of ceremonial duties and epistemologically taxing doctrines, amounts to a condemnation of the authority habitually claimed by many religious officials, theologians included. It still gives them a legitimate interest in how people behave, and allows them to use 'brotherly exhortation' to encourage obedience. But it does not license them to police people's beliefs or interrogate them about their religious convictions, as Catholic inquisitors and Calvinist consistories were wont to do. As long as individuals conform to the going standards of justice and charity, thus manifesting their commitment to the tenets of true religion, church authorities cannot censure them for failing to grasp the niceties of established confessions or for holding eccentric beliefs. And since individuals themselves are best placed to judge what will stir them up to obey, theologians have no authority to insist that they sustain their devotion by any particular means. If star-gazing, sung vespers, or silent meditation helps them to imitate the true life, theologians are not in a position to complain. Altogether, then, the scope of theological authority is vastly reduced. While there is nothing to stop members of the Reformed Church from worshipping in their own fashion as long as this helps them to live obediently, they have no grounds for condemning the Anabaptists, Socinians, and Quakers whom they denounce as heretical.

With this analysis in hand, Spinoza is now in a position to conclude his argument for one of the key claims he originally set out to defend: that conflict between theologians and philosophers is unnecessary because theology and philosophy are independent practices, neither of which is subordinate to the other. Competition and antagonism only arises from mistaken conceptions of their relationship. On the one hand, theologians claim that philosophy must be subordinate to theology because they mistakenly believe that Scripture teaches revealed philosophical truths that no philosophical system has the authority to challenge. But as Spinoza has gone to great lengths to show, the premise of this argument is false. The Bible is written in an imaginary register and its doctrines aim to inculcate obedience. It makes no claim to philosophical truth, and therefore does not impose any significant limits on philosophical enquiry. On the other hand, philosophers who try to subordinate theology to philosophy find themselves distorting biblical doctrine in order to make it cohere with their philosophical beliefs. They, too, fail to appreciate the purpose of Scripture when they try to cram it into a philosophical framework for which it was not intended.

Each of these mistakes gives rise to an unnecessary anxiety. Theologians think that they need to exercise control over philosophy because they wrongly suppose that it can challenge their authority to interpret biblical doctrine; and philosophers want to control theology because they wrongly regard it as offering truth claims that they are best placed to judge. However, once we appreciate the character of each practice, it becomes clear that both worries are misplaced. Philosophy and theology have different purposes; they also employ different methods, each of which produces rationally grounded conclusions of an appropriate level of certainty.[1] While '[philosophical] reason is the domain of truth and wisdom, theology is the domain of piety and obedience'.[2] To view them as competitors is nothing less than insane, and also perpetuates damaging conflicts that undermine both obedience and philosophical understanding.[3]

Divide and conquer

Summing up his own achievement, Spinoza will claim to have shown 'how philosophy is to be separated from theology, what each of these principally consists in, that neither is the handmaid of the other, and that each remains in charge of its own domain, without conflicting with the other'.[4] However, the strategy that he employs to reconcile these two antagonistic parties is by no means new, and follows in the tracks of a series of earlier Dutch Cartesian writers. To resist the Voetian claim that philosophical enquiry must be controlled by the Reformed Church, and to carve out a space for Cartesian philosophizing, theologians such as Abraham Heidanus[5] and Christopher

---

[1] Benedictus de Spinoza, *Tractatus Theologico-Politicus*, ed. Carl Gebhardt, vol. III, *Opera* (Heidelberg: Carl Winter, 1924), ch. 15, p. 187.

[2] Ibid. ch. 15, p. 184.

[3] Ibid. ch. 15, p. 180.

[4] Ibid. ch. 15, p. 188.

[5] Abraham Heidanus (1597–1678) was a professor of theology at Leiden University from 1648 to 1676.

Wittich,[6] together with Lambert Van Velthuysen[7] and the natural philosopher Johannes de Raey,[8] had already argued that philosophy and theology deal with different subject matters and serve different ends. While the former concerns itself with clear and distinct ideas about nature, the latter deals with salvation; while the purpose of theology is to persuade, that of philosophy is to enunciate natural truths.[9] Spinoza's general approach is therefore a familiar one; but, characteristically, he takes it to new heights. According to the consensus of opinion among Dutch Cartesians, philosophy can deal authoritatively only with problems about nature. Questions about God, ethics, and salvation remain reserved for theology.[10] The *Treatise*, by contrast, draws the line between philosophy and theology in a different place, substantially enlarging the scope of philosophical enquiry so that it can yield not only truths about nature but truths about God and morality as well.[11] Thus, although Spinoza's position has the same structure as those defended by several of his Cartesian contemporaries, it is far more aggressive, and while it formally ratifies theology's independence, it substantially shrinks the area over which it exercises sole control.

Needless to say, the *Treatise* does not draw attention to this divergence. Doing so would have reignited the very anxieties it is seeking to dampen, and jeopardized its goal of persuading as many readers as possible that free philosophizing does not pose a threat to theological authority. Instead, Spinoza

---

[6] Christopher Wittich or Wittichius (1625–87) was a professor of theology, mathematics, and Hebrew at Herborn, Duisburg, Nijmegen, and eventually Leiden University. He was a harsh critic of Spinoza, and condemned both the *Tractatus Theologico-Politicus* and the *Ethics* in many of his published works.

[7] See Chapter 5, fn. 66.

[8] Johannes de Raey (1662–1702) was a professor of philosophy at Leiden University, and later at the Illustrious School in Amsterdam.

[9] See Wiep van Bunge, 'On the Early Dutch Reception of the *Tractatus Theologico-Politicus*,' *Studia Spinozana* 5 (1989), pp. 52–4; Theo Verbeek, *Descartes and the Dutch: Early Reactions to Cartesian Philosophy, 1637–1650* (Carbondale: Southern Illinois University Press, 1992); Theo Verbeek, 'Spinoza and Cartesianism', in *Judaeo-Christian Intellectual Culture in the Seventeenth Century: A Celebration of the Library of Narcissus Marsh (1638–1713)*, ed. Allison Coudert (Dordrecht: Kluwer, 1999); Theo Verbeek, *Spinoza's Theologico-Political Treatise: Exploring 'the Will of God'* (Aldershot: Ashgate, 2003), pp. 95–7; Theo Verbeek, 'Tradition and Novelty: Descartes and Some Cartesians', in *The Rise of Modern Philosophy: The Tension between the New and Traditional Philosophies from Machiavelli to Leibniz*, ed. Tom Sorell (Oxford: Clarendon Press, 1993).

[10] See Verbeek, *Descartes and the Dutch*; 'Tradition and Novelty'.

[11] Alexander Douglas, 'Spinoza's Vindication of Philosophy: Reshaping Early Modern Debate About the Division between Philosophy and Theology' (Phd thesis) (Birkbeck College, University of London, 2011).

goes to some trouble to distract attention from the novelty of his position by conceding as much as he can to the theologians. He presents his case as though it were simply one more defence of the Cartesian point of view that was already in circulation, but on closer inspection there turn out to be two fundamental respects in which it breaks new ground: by redrawing the boundary between philosophy and theology, and by reconceiving the relationship between them. Compared with his Cartesian contemporaries, Spinoza allots philosophy a broader and more flourishing research programme, and correspondingly reduces the theoretical challenges of theology. Still more important, he does not accept that theology and philosophy are entirely independent enterprises. While theology as he interprets it retains a degree of autonomy, it remains in some ways subservient to the greater intellectual power of philosophical thought.

As other Cartesians had pointed out, and as Spinoza also claims, theology and philosophy not only serve different purposes, but focus on different kinds of evidence.[12] Philosophers try to demonstrate general truths and can use them constructively, to generate new conclusions, or critically, to rule out existing opinions. Working in the latter spirit, they can prove, for example, that God does not act for ends or that he is not a legislator, tasks that lie beyond theology's reach. Theologians, by contrast, focus on the particular events and stories narrated in the Bible, and employ what Spinoza has described as a historical method to interpret them. But since none of the claims they deal with are demonstrable, philosophy has nothing to say about them.[13] As long as this distinction between particular and general truths is respected, there is in principle no reason why philosophers and theologians should come into conflict; but in practice it is difficult to keep the two apart, both because theologians tend to rely on general truths in order to interpret their material, and because philosophers tend to rely on their knowledge of individuals in order to formulate general truths. Although the two groups of investigators use their materials for distinct purposes, the materials themselves do not divide neatly down the middle.

This overlap is evident in Spinoza's account of the core doctrine of Scripture. On the one hand, theologians can derive this general teaching from the various specific narratives recounted in the Old and New Testaments, which make the

---

[12] See, for example, Joannes de Raei, *Cogitata de interpretatione, quibus natura humani sermonis et illius rectus usus, ab hujus seculi errore et confusione vindicantur* (Amsterdam, 1692), p. 665.

[13] Spinoza, *Tractatus Theologico-Politicus*, ch. 15, p. 185.

divine law and the various tenets of faith that it presupposes accessible in an accommodated form to people who have no philosophical training or inclination. On the other hand, the same doctrines and tenets are available in a philosophical guise to anyone who is capable of deducing them from other clear and distinct ideas. Philosophers can consequently access the teaching of Scripture in their own terms, and can use their philosophical knowledge to live in a truly religious manner.[14] Spinoza does not find this surprising. Since the imaginative gifts of the prophets enabled them darkly to perceive truths that philosophy fully illuminates, 'it is not without reason that the word of God in the prophets agrees completely with the word of God speaking in us'.[15] But it nevertheless implies that theology and philosophy are not symmetrical as to their scope. While philosophers can use their own investigative method to confirm the key findings of theology, theologians are not in a position to assess any philosophical truths. And while philosophers can use their own resources to achieve the way of life that theology strives to inculcate, theologians cannot use the Bible to extend the mathematically certain understanding at which philosophy aims.

In these respects, then, theology seems to be in a weaker position than philosophy, and Spinoza's attempt to present them as symmetrically placed begins to look a trifle suspect. He himself can hardly fail to be aware of this problem, and may be trying to ameliorate it when he unexpectedly makes what looks like a last-minute concession to theology. So far, we have been led to believe that the entire doctrine of Scripture can be philosophically confirmed. Now, however, Spinoza draws back, claiming that there is one aspect of this teaching that lies beyond philosophical reach. 'We cannot rationally demonstrate', he tells us, 'that the foundation of theology—that men are saved by obedience—is either true or false';[16] and if philosophy cannot offer any judgement on this point, we have no alternative but to trust the doctrine revealed in Scripture.

By awarding theology sole authority over such a crucial issue, the *Treatise* slightly redresses the uneven balance we have just identified. Although it remains the case that there are infinitely many philosophical truths on which theologians cannot pronounce, there is now one theological tenet that philosophers can neither confirm nor deny. Only theologians are officially in a position to reassure people that, according to the Bible, living obediently is sufficient for salvation, and as Spinoza points out, this gives them an important

---

[14] Ibid. ch. 13, p. 168.   [15] Ibid. ch. 15, p. 186.   [16] Ibid. ch. 15, p. 185.

form of power. 'Since we cannot perceive by the [philosophical] natural light that simple obedience is the way to salvation...it follows that Scripture has brought a very great source of comfort to mortals....If we did not have its testimony, we would doubt the salvation of almost everyone'.[17]

It is not immediately obvious why Spinoza claims that this particular piece of biblical doctrine is unlike the rest, and cannot be philosophically confirmed or refuted. Nor is it clear how resistant to demonstration he takes it to be. For the most part, he implies that it is impossible to prove or disprove that obedience is sufficient for salvation. ('I maintain unconditionally that this fundamental tenet of theology cannot be tracked down by the natural light'.) Elsewhere, however, he entertains the much weaker view that the claim has not so far been demonstrated.[18] Given his conviction that revelation shadows reason, this weaker view is what one would expect Spinoza to hold; but if this is all he is claiming he will be back where he started, with the asymmetry between philosophy and theology that he seems to be trying to offset. The fact that a doctrine has not yet been proved or disproved does not show that it is unprovable, and does not rule out the possibility that philosophy will in time arrive at a view about each of the claims taught in Scripture.

Spinoza therefore needs to stand by the stronger view. But why does he think it is impossible to demonstrate that obedience alone either does or does not save? His point seems to revolve around the difference between people who live obediently (and thus achieve salvation) on the basis of tenets of faith that are accommodated to their imaginations, and people who live in the same manner on the basis of their philosophical understanding. For the latter group, the benefits that constitute salvation derive from their understanding, and depend on their ability to provide a philosophical vindication of the tenets of faith. These philosophical achievements are what enable philosophers to live together harmoniously and love God, and are also the source of the intense pleasures that purportedly come with such a way of life.[19] In short, they are what constitute salvation.[20] But this is exactly what biblical doctrine denies when it affirms that salvation can be constituted by ways of life that are not organized around philosophical understanding. By definition, these ways of life do not depend on the kind of thinking that characterizes philosophy, and

---

[17] Ibid. ch. 15, p. 188.
[18] Ibid. ch. 15, p. 185.
[19] See Benedictus de Spinoza, *Ethics*, in Curley ed., *The Collected Works of Spinoza*, vol. I, 4p24, 4p26, 4p28, 5p3.
[20] Ibid.

yet, according to Scripture, they can attain its benefits. Within their own framework, however, philosophers cannot show that benefits which, as far as they are concerned depend on demonstration, can be achieved without it. So although the Bible reliably assures us that obedience is sufficient for salvation, this is not a conclusion that philosophy can reach.

If this interpretation is correct and the argument convincing, Spinoza has indeed gone some way towards rebalancing the relation between theology and philosophy by establishing that each can vindicate claims inaccessible to the other. More specifically, he has put theology in charge of a key teaching about salvation, itself the culmination of a religious life. But even so, he has not put the two practices on an equal footing, nor shown that neither is the handmaid of the other. As we shall see, and as any handmaid knows, there are many ways of subordinating one subject to another.

An unequal relationship

Two further inequalities mark Spinoza's analysis of the relationship between philosophy and theology, one of which derives from the epistemological character of philosophical argument. Suppose, to take a hypothetical case, that a tenet of faith were to be disproved by means of a philosophical demonstration. Officially, this is meant to have no impact on theology, and would not prevent people from using the discredited tenet to sustain their obedience. But the situation is not so simple. A person who knew that the tenet was false could not sincerely appeal to it; and anyone who appreciated the superior level of certainty that philosophy guarantees, and cared about the highest standards of truth, would surely be constrained to accept the philosophical conclusion. Although theology is not primarily directed to the truth, it is not indifferent to it. It works with the beliefs that a particular individual or community hold to be true, and assumes that, as people acquire new evidence, their beliefs are liable to change. Since one of the kinds of evidence that can produce this result is demonstration, people who have been taught to philosophize can be expected to appreciate its epistemological power and accept it conclusions.

Spinoza is confident that biblical doctrine and philosophical reasoning will nevertheless not conflict because, with one unthreatening exception, philosophy confirms the teachings of Scripture. But in arriving at this view, it is arguable that he has already given priority to philosophical reasoning. In assembling his list of tenets of faith, and rejecting many of the other tenets approved by the Reformed Church, he seems to have tacitly required that genuine tenets must not only be taught by Scripture but also be demonstrable.

(Unless this were so, he would not be able to claim that the moral insights taught by the prophets coincide with those of natural reason, and would reopen the way to possible conflicts between theology and philosophy. Nor would he be able to claim that biblical doctrine is uncontroversial, since anything that philosophers and theologians can disagree about is surely a matter of controversy.) However, if philosophers have their own route to the tenets on which obedience and thus salvation depend, the epistemological superiority of their insights once again threatens to undercut the independence of theology. When philosophers and theologians disagree, it is the philosophers who will have the final say about what is true. And since it would be obstinate and irreligious to ground one's obedience to the divine law on beliefs that one knew to be false, or to set one's face against the arguments that philosophers supply, philosophical findings can in principle put pressure on the opinions of theologians, and indeed of anyone else who comes across them.

This asymmetry presents a challenge to any religion, Calvinism included, which regards its own epistemological standards as the highest available. One may respond that, because the morally certain knowledge provided by Scripture is good enough for most purposes, including salvation, the asymmetry is too remote to worry about; and this seems to be what Spinoza wants at least some of his readers to think. But it remains the case that, while philosophy is in principle capable of assessing and confirming all, or almost all, the central claims of theology, theology does not exert the same authority over its philosophical rival. In this respect, philosophy is the more powerful of the two and, like a handmaiden, theology must submit to it.

Alongside this epistemological asymmetry, Spinoza allows philosophy a further and arguably still more consequential kind of power, this time relating to salvation. So far, he has bent over backwards to give theologians authority over the means to salvation, awkwardly insisting that only Scripture can assure us that obedience saves. However, alongside this concession, he continues to maintain that there is a philosophical route to salvation, and that one can attain this cherished state by means of philosophical understanding. Here his view diverges sharply from that of Calvinism. According to the Reformed Church, philosophy can contribute nothing of significance to our grasp of the one true form of salvation, which can only be learned from Scripture. Spinoza, by contrast, turns this view on its head. As he presents the matter, the benefits of the co-operative way of life that theology helps to sustain are enormously valuable, and constitute a form of salvation for which everyone has reason to strive. But as we have seen, philosophical understanding provides the clearest and most compelling form of moral liberation which, as the *Ethics* expresses it, constitutes our *true* salvation.[21] So where the Church gives clear priority to theology, Spinoza gives philosophy a matching power. Instead of accepting the Cartesian view that, while philosophical expertise allows one to study the natural world, it stops short at moral or theological matters, the *Treatise* advocates a more all-encompassing form of philosophy capable of arriving at conclusions about God, morality, and even salvation. As well as yielding mathematically certain conclusions that ultimately trump those of theology, philosophy can outstrip the blessedness to which theology had traditionally laid claim. In its moral as well as its epistemological power, it dominates its theological partner.

Unsurprisingly, Spinoza does not explicitly acknowledge these asymmetries. Nevertheless, the greater power of philosophy hangs over his argument, destabilizing the equality between theology and philosophy that he purports to have established and undermining their supposed independence. Since neither he nor his readers could have failed to notice this problem, and since it is potentially serious enough to vitiate his project, it is not enough to accuse him of an elementary failure of reasoning. We need to read his position in a way that takes the tension into account, seeing how he is able to allow that philosophy is in some respects more powerful than theology whilst also maintaining that neither is the handmaid of the other.

By using the Dutch Cartesians' strategy of divide and conquer, Spinoza successfully identifies two significant differences between philosophy and theology—that each uses a distinct method to pursue a distinct end. This level of independence ensures that they can peacefully co-exist, and is enough to support the central theologico-political claim that Spinoza is aiming to establish. Philosophers and theologians who understand the nature of their own inquiries will not interfere with one another, and theologians can therefore safely grant the freedom to philosophize. As far as it goes, this analysis is all well and good. However, as we have seen, it only captures some dimensions of the complex relationship between theology and philosophy, and Spinoza does not manage, or indeed wish, entirely to exclude the rest. There is something more that he wants his readers to grasp, and this half-submerged set of insights sends ripples across the surface of his text. To salvage it, and thereby gain a fuller picture of the relationship between theology and philosophy, we need to move away from the Dutch Cartesian approach and turn, as Spinoza does, to another powerful strand of seventeenth-century Dutch intellectual culture, which

---

[21] Ibid. 4App.4, 5p42.

provides him with a further source of inspiration. To fill out his explication of philosophy and its relation to theology, he draws on the tradition of northern humanism, and in doing so extends his critique of Calvinism.

The Reformed Church's theology was deeply indebted to Saint Augustine whose influential view of sin and redemption pervaded its entire outlook, and the Church's theologians continued to defend many of his commitments against attack. Setting out the nature of salvation in *The City of God*, Augustine contrasts his own view with a position that he attributes to a group of classical philosophers, among whom Cicero is singled out. These authors, he claims, have failed to appreciate the depths of human depravity, and have made the grave mistake of thinking that salvation or blessedness lies within human power. 'With wondrous vanity', he grumbles, '[they] have wished to be happy here and now, and to achieve blessedness by their own efforts'.[22] What they have failed to realize is that, fallen as human beings are, even individuals who struggle for virtue can never free themselves from vice, and consequently cannot achieve salvation in this life. It has to be given to them by God, who elects some people to eternal life.[23]

In seventeenth-century Holland, this debate remained very much alive. While the Reformed Church continued to reiterate Augustine's opinion, a number of Dutch thinkers indebted to the tradition of Erasmian humanism revived the classical view that Augustine had repudiated. Over time, their position became entrenched in the educational curricula of schools and universities, where one of the most influential sources used to teach it was Cicero's study of public and private duty, *De Officiis*.[24] Educated Dutchmen who had not forgotten what they had learned in their youth would have been familiar with this work, as would Spinoza, who had put himself through a classical humanist education at the Amsterdam school run by Francis Van Enden.[25]

---

[22] Saint Augustine, *The City of God against the Pagans*, ed. and trans. R. W. Dyson, (Cambridge: Cambridge University Press, 1998), xix, ch. 4, p. 919.

[23] Ibid. xix, ch. 4, pp. 918–24.

[24] Marcus Tullius Cicero, *On Duties*, trans. Walter Miller, *Loeb Classical Library* (Cambridge Mass.: Harvard University Press, 1913).

[25] Franciscus Van den Enden (1602–74) ran a small school in Amsterdam that taught Latin, liberal arts, and philosophy. 'Van den Enden would have had his students read the ancient classics of poetry, drama, and philosophy—the literary legacy of Greece and Rome—as well as neoclassical works of the Renaissance. They were introduced, at least in a broad manner, to Platonic, Aristotelian, and Stoic philosophy; to Seneca, Cicero, and Ovid; and perhaps even to the principles of ancient skepticism'. Wim Klever, 'A New Source of Spinozism: Franciscus Van Den Enden', *Journal of the History of Philosophy*, 29, no. 4 (1991); Steven M. Nadler, *Spinoza: A Life* (Cambridge: Cambridge University Press, 1999), p. 109.

One of the main aims of *De Officiis* is to defend the very claim that Augustine subsequently attacked—that a virtuous way of life lies within human reach. Because Cicero's position was widely known, it could be used as a means of contesting the Reformed Church's interpretation of salvation. Revived and rewritten, it could function as a recognizable philosophical counterweight to Calvinism by offering an alternative to the Church's forbidding doctrine of predestination. And this is exactly how the *Treatise* tacitly employs it. Since Cicero was by no means the only classical exponent of this view (though in early-modern Europe he was undoubtedly the most influential), and since this type of position was widely taken up and explored, Spinoza could in principle have encountered it in a range of authors and texts. How far he drew specifically on Cicero's works is therefore impossible to say. But it is striking that, as we shall see, he replicates the precise structure of the account of virtue laid out in *De Officiis*. Rebuilding it in his own materials, he uses a Ciceronian model first to characterize theology and philosophy, and then to explicate the ways in which they are unequal.

Cicero distinguishes two levels of virtue—an everyday one fitted for ordinary people leading ordinary lives, and a more elevated one achievable only by philosophical sages—and characterizes the first as a similitude of the second.[26] At the higher level, perfectly virtuous people are able to blend the various duties to which individual virtues give rise, so that for these comparatively rare individuals, living wisely, justly, temperately, and courageously are not distinct skills directed at distinct ends. Rather, they are embedded in a comprehensive capacity to respond virtuously to all situations, however complex and multifaceted, without sacrificing virtue for utility. In exercising this ability, individuals manifest an overarching quality that Cicero calls *honestas*,[27] which also draws them together in friendship. Each loves the other as himself, so that they become as one.[28]

Contrasted with such unqualified *honestas* is its second-level or second-grade counterpart, *honestas secunda*. People who possess this quality, Cicero explains, are familiar with the duties that each virtue imposes, and are in general able to fulfil them. So they often behave as they would if their *honestas* were perfect. While their grasp of how to live virtuously does not obliterate trade-offs between one virtue and another, or invariably resolve apparent conflicts between virtue and utility,[29] there are nevertheless many circumstances in

---

[26] Cicero, *On Duties*, I.v.15.   [27] Ibid.   [28] Ibid. I.xvii.55–6.
[29] Ibid. III.iii–iv, I.iv.12–13, I.xlii.52.

which they are able to act well. Moreover, second-level *honestas* is relatively easy to achieve, and lies within the reach of ordinary people who, as Cicero puts it, 'are not perfectly wise, and do very well if they achieve a semblance of virtue (*simulacrum virtutis*)'.[30]

However, even second-level *honestas* can be quite demanding, and in order to attain it the members of a community must be motivated to live up to its various requirements, including those of justice, the key value of political society.[31] There are of course various ways of encouraging people to live justly; but Cicero seems to assume that one of the most effective is to supply a range of narratives, illustrating the advantages of a just way of life and offering models of just action for people to imitate. He himself employs this technique in his works, which are stuffed with anecdotes about heroes and virtuous actions, designed to arouse his readers' desire to emulate them.

In his *Ethics*, and less overtly in the *Treatise*, Spinoza replicates this two-tier structure. For him, the flawless virtue that Cicero associates with perfect *honestas* continues to derive from philosophical understanding, which alone enables communities to steer an unswervingly virtuous course through the exigencies of everyday existence. Situated below it are communities bound together by the forms of thought and action belonging to imagination, and in some of them people live very much as they would if they were perfectly virtuous. These communities rely on, and do their best to sustain, second-level *honestas*, and this is where theology comes into play. By using the resources of the Bible to inculcate obedience to the divine law, theologians and other religious officials can help to generate a form of second-level *honestas* that enables individuals to sustain a co-operative way of life which, while it is less perfect than one grounded on philosophical understanding, nevertheless emulates it as far as possible. For Spinoza, as for Cicero, one of the primary virtues of this way of life is justice, and the capacity to live justly is upheld by narratives that provide models for people to imitate. In the *Treatise*, we could say, theology becomes an aspect of what Cicero regards as the fundamentally political project of maintaining just co-operation under the law.

It remains to see how Spinoza's acceptance of this two-tier conception of virtue can help us to understand his account of the relationship between theology and philosophy, and resolve the inconsistencies that seem to plague his analysis. Following Cicero's lead, Spinoza holds that virtue can be viewed from two different angles. From the philosophical vantage point corresponding

---

[30] Ibid. I.xv.46.   [31] Ibid. I.vii.20.

to perfect *honestas* it is unified, while from the everyday vantage point afforded by second-level *honestas* we can distinguish distinct virtues, each aiming at a different goal. When Spinoza sketches a way of life in which theology and philosophy are viewed as separate, we need to ask which vantage point he is speaking from.[32]

Since the main thrust of *the Treatise's* argument contends that the virtue of truth pursued by philosophy is independent of the virtue of obedience at which theology aims, the answer seems clear enough: its author is talking in everyday terms, mainly addressing himself to an audience that only aspires to what Cicero calls second-level *honestas*. Inhabiting this outlook, Spinoza confirms that the practice of theology does not depend upon philosophical skills or knowledge, so that one does not need to be a philosopher in order to live in an obedient or co-operative fashion. Equally, the capacity to arrive at philosophically grounded truths does not depend on imaginative skills or insights, and therefore has no use for Scripture. At this level one can be obedient without being wise, and wise without being obedient, and there is consequently a clear sense in which the two virtues are distinct.

While this is the conclusion that Spinoza wants to stress in the *Treatise*, he also wants to indicate that there is no more to say, and his unwillingness to oversimplify gives rise to instabilities that complicate his account of the relationship between theology and philosophy. As he illustrates more fully in the *Ethics*, it is also possible to appreciate the unity of the virtues by inhabiting a more strictly philosophical vantage point, and when truth and obedience are viewed from this angle it becomes clear that they are mutually dependent. To be convinced of this, one has to have made enough philosophical progress to realize that co-operating with other people and extending one's understanding are so inextricably intertwined that any failure of co-operation compromises understanding, and any limitation of understanding threatens co-operation. But anyone who has achieved this level of insight will acknowledge that the two virtues are not independent, thus graduating to the equivalent of Cicero's perfect *honestas*.[33]

Once a community begins to philosophize, then, the second-level *honestas* sustained by its imaginative practices ceases to constitute its entire outlook, and gradually makes space for a form of life in which the virtues no longer appear to be distinct. Moreover, only this perspective fully reveals what virtue is and enables people to lead a fully virtuous life. Looking back on the second-level

---

[32] Ibid. II.x.35.   [33] Spinoza, *Ethics*, 4App.12.

honestas they formerly possessed, the wise can appreciate the incompleteness of the understanding on which it was based, and the weakness of the bonds that sustained their obedience or co-operation. Although they can still see why they used to regard the virtues as distinct and liable to conflict, they now appreciate what their earlier view lacked, and can correct its practical limitations. From their present perspective, obedience, the goal of theology, has become absorbed into the goal of philosophy, and the pursuit of co-operation has become integral to the pursuit of truth. The viewpoint of second-level *honestas* has been replaced by one in which it is impossible to be fully co-operative without being wise, or fully wise without being co-operative.

When, in the *Treatise*, Spinoza seems to contradict his claim that philosophy and theology are independent by allowing that theology is epistemologically and morally subordinate to philosophy, he is speaking from this philosophical vantage point. Anyone who occupies it, and appreciates that understanding and co-operation form a single virtue, will not be satisfied by practices that ground obedience on falsehood, or by a conception of salvation that only delivers a simulacrum of the delight that they derive from a way of life organized around the pursuit of understanding. From their perspective, such positions can be no more than tarnished compromises, so although we have compelling practical reasons for being satisfied with second-level *honestas*, we should not refuse to acknowledge the limitations of this outlook, and need to remain aware that philosophy holds out the possibility of still more satisfying ways of life.

The tensions that we set out to explain therefore arise from the fact that Spinoza portrays the relationship between theology and philosophy from two different points of view. For the most part, he speaks at the level of everyday virtue, and represents theology and philosophy as separate practices sustaining separate virtues. This account serves the practical purpose that he is trying to achieve in the *Treatise*, and enables him to establish a sense in which theology is not the handmaid of philosophy, or vice versa. At the same time, however, he intimates that there is a further level of perfect virtue, where philosophy takes over theology's role, and the inequality between the two practices is revealed.

Shedding theology

Since the transition from an everyday to a philosophical way of life obliterates the distinction between theology and philosophy by incorporating the first into the second, this aspect of Spinoza's analysis of their relationship is hardly calculated to reassure his theological opponents. While the surface argument of the *Treatise* promises to liberate theologians from philosophical interference, and guarantees them an independent, though limited, domain of enquiry, its underlying implications threaten their existence. Theology and philosophy are not after all independent, and philosophy has the potential to engulf its weaker partner. Spinoza must have recognized that his position was liable to be interpreted in this way, and presumably hoped to limit the damage by focusing on the dimensions of theology and philosophy that hold them apart. But he would also have expected his more sympathetic readers to reject this interpretation of his position on the grounds that it misunderstands his analysis of religion.

It is true, in Spinoza's view, that a philosopher who grasps the rational basis of co-operation ceases to regard the goals of truth and obedience as distinct, and tries to develop practices that will foster both at once, rather than just one or the other. Such a person will not have a deep commitment either to theology, viewed as a practice aiming at obedience, or to philosophy, viewed simply as a practice that aims to extend our knowledge of the truth. However, while they will lose their commitment to these practices, they will not lose their commitment to their goals. Instead, they will aspire to build a philosophical way of life that incorporates the goal of theology by encouraging a particularly strong form of co-operation. At least as they are ideally represented, philosophers will not rely on Scripture or other loci of imaginative thinking to strengthen their commitment to loving their neighbours. But they will love their neighbours nonetheless on the basis of their desire to extend collective philosophical knowledge. This process can be described in various ways. One can say, with Spinoza's opponents, that philosophy progressively engulfs theology. But one can also say, with Spinoza himself, that philosophy becomes a form of religion, sharing its capacity to bind, and transforming devotion to the divine law into rational piety. Rather than focusing on a goal external to true religion, this kind of philosophy offers theology its wholehearted support by cultivating the same end.

This reply might nevertheless trouble even a sympathetic reader of the *Treatise*, afraid that philosophy as Spinoza conceives it will be liable to swamp religious practices and undermine their credibility. And once again, the worry is not altogether misplaced. Spinoza does hold that our beliefs and affects change with our understanding, and that, as this happens, we outgrow the ways of life in which our old commitments were embedded. However, this process is not meant to be coercive. One of the truths that philosophy makes clear is that people cannot be forced to understand, or to act consistently on the basis of an understanding they do not possess. The religious way of life that Spinoza envisages condemns 'opinions which encourage obstinacy, hatred, quarrels and anger', but 'considers faithful all those who, in proportion to the powers of their reason and faculties, encourage justice and lovingkindness'.[34] Philosophy can only proceed at a community's pace, and is bound to respect the genuinely religious practices to which its members are sincerely committed.

To some of Spinoza's contemporaries, the prospect of a multi-faith society might have seemed to be a recipe for the kind of political conflict that the *Treatise* was designed to exclude, and might have been taken to reinforce the criticism that Descartes and Elisabeth had raised against republics—that conflict is the price they pay for freedom. Spinoza's next task is to explain the political implications of his position and show that this doubt is misplaced.

---

[34] Spinoza, *Tractatus Theologico-Politicus*, ch. 14, p. 180.

The Politics of True Religion

Chapter 10

Life in a Republic: The Lessons of Philosophy

The final paragraphs of Spinoza's analysis of the relationship between theology and philosophy have the feel of an ending. Summarizing the conclusions he has reached, and reminding his readers of the 'absurdities, disadvantages and harms' they will resolve, he arrives at the climax of his long argument about the nature and status of religion. As a number of commentators have suggested, it seems likely that this may have been the point at which he originally intended to stop. If, as the title page of the *Treatise* explains, it contains several *dissertationes*, we seem to have reached a break between one and the next.[1] So far, the aim has been to show that theologians have no good grounds for trying to limit the freedom to philosophize. It is now time, as Spinoza explains, 'to ask how far freedom of thinking, and of each saying what each person thinks, extends in an ideal republic (*optima respublica*)'.[2]

At one level, then, the discussion now shifts from theology to politics, but at another level it continues to explore the theologico-political issues with which it has been concerned all along. The religious life, as Spinoza has presented it, is a communal project of devising and maintaining a collaborative form of existence, and sustaining it by as many kinds of beliefs and practices as necessary. These will in turn be embedded in social institutions, some highly structured and others more informal, which must somehow serve the overall function of enhancing co-operation. Viewed from this perspective, however, there are two connected ways in which religion is already political. The end at which it

---

[1] The title page describes the *Treatise* as 'containing several discussion in which it is shown that the Freedom of Philosophising can not only be granted without harm to Piety and the Peace of the Republic, but also cannot be abolished unless Piety and the Peace of the republic are destroyed'. See Verbeek, *Spinoza's Theologico-Political Treatise*, p. 6, fn. 28.

[2] Benedictus de Spinoza, *Tractatus Theologico-Politicus*, ed. Carl Gebhardt, vol. III, *Opera* (Heidelberg: Carl Winter, 1924), ch. 16, p. 189.

aims—a harmonious way of life in which people love their neighbours—
overlaps with the ends of the political realm, which aspires to provide peace
and security. In this respect, then, politics and religion are continuous. Furthermore, the kind of co-operation that religious people aim to achieve can
only be realized with the help of political co-ordination. If many different sub-
groups are to pursue the common goal of loving their neighbours, they will
need some political structure within which they can reach agreement as to what
neighbourly love requires, and adjudicate between competing interpretations
of the divine law. Living a religious life is always a theologico-political enterprise. The problem is to see how political institutions, and above all the state,
can uphold peace and security in conditions where individuals are able to live
openly in the light of their conflicting religious and philosophical convictions.[3]

As we shall find, this is a highly contentious topic among Spinoza's contemporaries, and rather than immediately staking out his own position in a field
of fierce disputes, he first steps back. 'To conduct this examination in an orderly
way, we must discuss the foundations of the state . . . without yet attending to
the state or to religion'. But in spite of this declaration, Spinoza is not really
starting from scratch. The *Treatise* has already defined a state as a society (*societas*)
where one is subject to a supreme power (*summa potestas*) which holds sovereignty (*imperium*) and is capable of enforcing the law (*lex*).[4] Furthermore, we
already know that the aims of the state are to guarantee peace and security by
keeping our more destructive desires in check, and to organize a division of
labour that will allow us to live comfortably.[5] The desire to live in a state is
therefore both rational and honourable (*honestus*), but a range of familiar
obstacles undermine our ability to exist within the limits of the law: individuals
or groups may be convinced that obeying particular laws will put them at a
disadvantage; they may resent the fact that they are bound to obey people
whom they regard as their equals; and, as Machiavelli had emphasized, they are
liable to resist any attempt on the part of a sovereign to remove freedoms they
have previously possessed.[6] In Spinoza's view, two forms of political authority

---

[3] Étienne Balibar, 'Spinoza the Anti-Orwell: The Fear of the Masses', in *Masses, Classes, Ideas: Studies on Politics and Philosophy before and after Marx* (London: Routledge, 1994).

[4] Spinoza, *Tractatus Theologico-Politicus*, ch. 3, p. 48.

[5] Ibid. ch. 3, p. 47, ch. 5, p. 73.

[6] Ibid. ch. 5, p. 74. Niccolò Machiavelli, *The Prince*, ed. Russell Price and Quentin Skinner (Cambridge: Cambridge University Press, 1988). For broader discussion of the relation between Spinoza and Machiavelli, see Étienne Balibar, 'Spinoza: From Individuality to Transindividuality', in *Medelingen Vanwege het Spinozahuis* (Delft: Eburon, 1997); Filippo Del Lucchese, *Conflict, Power, and Multitude in Machiavelli and Spinoza* (London: Continuum, 2009); Douglas den Uyl, *Power, State and Freedom: An Interpretation of Spinoza's Political Philosophy* (Assen: Van Gorcum, 1983).

are best placed to minimize these difficulties. First, as Aristotle had argued, rulers who possess exceptional qualities of leadership, and are able persuade their subjects to trust them, are in a particularly strong position to enforce the law.[7] Because their charisma sets them apart, the people are unlikely to envy them or resent their authority, and this in turn enables them to govern effectively. Second, the rule of law is exceptionally strong where sovereignty is held collectively by a society as a whole. When laws are enacted by common consent, and each citizen plays a part in making them, no one is forced to conform to the command of a sovereign over whom they have no influence. Instead, each person obeys laws that they themselves have helped to make.[8]

Although Spinoza thinks that both kinds of constitutional arrangement can work satisfactorily, he favours the second as the surest means of sustaining a secure and peaceful way of life. So much so that, when he turns to consider how far an optimal state can accommodate the freedom to philosophize, this republican form of constitution is the only kind he considers.[9] Some of his reasons for this choice are undoubtedly theoretical, but it is also important to remember that he is addressing people who live in a republic and see themselves as able (at least to some extent) to influence the course of legislation through town, provincial, and national assemblies. The question he will put to them is whether free philosophizing damages or benefits a republic in which sovereignty is, as he expresses it, democratically held.[10] But rather than simply taking this starting-point for granted, he first sets out to place it on a firmer footing by explicating the main notions on which it is based: the foundations of the state; the natural and civil right of individual persons; and the right of the sovereign.[11]

The state of nature

In their efforts to capture the essential features of political life, early-modern theorists repeatedly contrast life within the state with life in the pre-political

---

[7] Aristotle, *Politics*, trans. Ernest Barker, revised by Richard Stalley (Oxford: Oxford University Press, 1995), 1260a17.

[8] Spinoza, *Tractatus Theologico-Politicus*, ch. 5, p. 74.

[9] Ibid. ch. 16, p. 195.

[10] Only some Dutch republicans describe a free state as a democracy. Among them is Franciscus van den Enden, who ran the school at which Spinoza learned Latin, and who wrote a brief defence of democracy as the form of state in which people could live most freely. Franciscus van den Enden, *Free Political Proposition and Considerations of State*, trans. Wim Klever (Amsterdam: Wim Klever, 2007), p. 151, Franciscus van den Enden, *Vrye politijke stellingen en consideratien van staat, met een inleiding van Wim Klever* (Amsterdam: Wereldbibliotheek, 1992).

[11] Spinoza, *Tractatus Theologico-Politicus*, ch. 16, p. 189.

condition that they call the state of nature. Spinoza is no exception. But while his analysis draws on a long tradition of imagining this kind of life, it is particularly indebted to the revolutionary account of the state of nature that—when he was writing—had recently been offered by Hobbes. The *Treatise* departs from Hobbes's view in a number of significant ways, but its structure of argument is undeniably Hobbesian, and it is difficult not to read it as an attempt to digest and improve upon the positions developed first in *De Cive* and then in *Leviathan*.[12] Hobbes's comprehensive and revolutionary theory of politics sent shock-waves through seventeenth-century Europe and excited many responses, positive and negative. It was widely taken up in the United Provinces where, ironically in the light of Hobbes' own political preferences, it provided defenders of the republic with a series of timely arguments against mixed constitutions.[13] Following this lead, Spinoza uses some of Hobbes's claims for his own ends; but he also adopts many features of Hobbes's 'condition of mere nature', portraying it as a state of affairs devoid not only of law, but of the many concepts and practices that depend on it.[14]

At the same time, Spinoza situates himself within a tradition of anti-monarchical theorizing (on which Hobbes had also managed to draw for his pro-monarchical purposes)[15] by assuming that the fundamental goal of government is the safety of the people. Cicero had described this principle as one of the tenets of the Twelve Tables of the Roman Law,[16] and in the sixteenth and seventeenth centuries it served as the basis of arguments to the effect that the people has a right to preserve itself. It plays an important role, for example, in the argument of the *Vindiciae contra tyrannos*, which had spelled out the case

[12] Edwin Curley, '"I Durst Not Write So Boldly" or How to Read Hobbes' Theologico-Political Treatise', in *Studi su Hobbes e Spinoza*, ed. Emilia Giancotti (Naples: Bibliopolis, 1996); Edwin Curley, 'The State of Nature and Its Law in Hobbes and Spinoza', *Philosophical Topics*, 19, no. 1 (1991); Thomas Heerich, *Transformation des Politikkonzepts von Hobbes zu Spinoza: Das problem der Souveränität* (Würzburg: Königshausen & Neumann, 2000); Christian Lazzeri, *Droit, pouvoir et liberté: Spinoza critique de Hobbes* (Paris: Presses Universitaires de France, 1998); Noel Malcolm, 'Hobbes and Spinoza', in *Aspects of Hobbes* (Oxford: Clarendon Press, 2002); Theo Verbeek, *Spinoza's Theologico-Political Treatise*, pp. 43–6.

[13] Malcolm, 'Hobbes and Spinoza', Catherine Sécretan, 'La réception de Hobbes aux Pays Bas', *Studia Spinozana*, no. 3 (1987).

[14] Thomas Hobbes, *Leviathan*, ed. Richard Tuck (Cambridge: Cambridge University Press, 1996) ch. 13. The phrase 'condition of meer Nature' comes from ch. 14, p. 97.

[15] Ibid. ch. 30, p. 231. 'The Office of the Sovereign, (be it a Monarch or an Assembly), consisteth in the end, for which he was trusted with the Sovereign Power, namely the procuration of *the safety of the people*'.

[16] Marcus Tullius Cicero, *De Re Publica, De Legibus*, trans. C. W. Keyes, *Loeb Classical Library* (Cambridge, Mass.: Harvard University Press, 1977), iii.8–9.

for popular resistance to monarchy in the French religious wars, and had met with considerable success when it was published in Amsterdam in 1586.[17] The principle is likewise fundamental to Althusius's defence of the Dutch Revolt in his *Politica Methodica Digesta* of 1604.[18] *Salus populi suprema lex* became a catch phrase, summing up a republican stance, and by repeating it, as he does, Spinoza aligns himself with the republican cause. The assumption that the point of the state is to guarantee the security of the people frames his analysis, and shapes the account of its foundations that he now sets out to provide.

The state of nature, as the *Treatise* explicitly points out, is prior to both politics and religion. 'No one knows by nature that he is bound by any obedience to God.'[19] Lacking any institutions, it has no means to lay down laws or ways of life that people prescribe in order to achieve particular ends. Because no agent possesses enough sustained power to devise and impose legislation, there can be no civil laws designed to provide peace and security. Equally, there can be no divine laws calculated to generate obedient and collective ways of life. But without these civil and religious constraints, there is nothing to oblige people to act in the name of any common goal, and the only kind of law that remains in operation is the universal and eternal order of nature that Spinoza figuratively describes as the natural divine law. As we have seen, it is possible to interpret the regularities that nature displays as divine decrees, and in this minimal sense the state of nature can be said to be subject to a kind of law. However, since this type of law governs us whether we like it or not, and we cannot coherently be said to obey it, the state of nature remains a condition in which the notion of obedience has no place. By contrast with many of his predecessors and contemporaries, who took the state of nature to be a condition in which everyone is subject to commands imposed by God, Spinoza provides an analysis so stripped of juridical content that the notion of a legal bond can get no purchase.[20] The state of nature is literally nature's state, a

---

[17] Frans Coornhert, *Cort onderwijs eens Liefhebbers des welstandts deser Nederlanden* (Amsterdam, 1586).

[18] Johannes Althusius, *Politica methodica digesta*, trans. Frederick Smith Carney (Indianapolis: Liberty Fund, 1995). See L. Campos Boralevi, 'Classical Foundational Myths of European Republicanism: The Jewish Commonwealth', in *Republicanism: A Shared European Heritage*, ed. Martin van Gelderen and Quentin Skinner, 2 vols. (Cambridge: Cambridge University Press, 2002), vol. 1, pp. 247–61.

[19] Spinoza, *Tractatus Theologico-Politicus*, ch. 16, p. 198.

[20] See ibid. ch. 16, p. 198, fn. 'As for the natural divine law, whose chief precept, as we have said, is to love God, I have called it a law in the same sense the philosophers call laws the common rules of nature, according to which things happen. For the love of God is not obedience, but a virtue which is necessarily in the man who rightly knows God. Obedience is concerned with the

domain where nature alone operates and only the regularities that determine the course of natural events hold sway.

In this context, human beings are just one kind of natural thing among many others, subject to laws that determine them to exist and act in certain ways. How, then, will they behave? Introducing a view that he shares with Hobbes and also develops in the *Ethics*, Spinoza claims that natural laws determine all individual things to strive to persevere in their state (*suo statu*), by preserving and where possible increasing their power to exist.[21] The purposive-sounding notion of striving or *conatus* that Spinoza uses here is liable to be misleading. If each individual thing strives to preserve and increase its power to exist, this must be true, for example, of a stone; but Spinoza does not mean to imply that a stone possesses a consciousness comparable to that of a human being, and can work out how to preserve itself. Rather, the stone's ability to persevere in its state is constituted by the qualities that enable it to endure over time, such as its ability not to break when it is dropped by an eagle or washed down a mountain by a flood. In exercising these qualities, the stone manifests its conatus or 'striving'. Equally, when Spinoza says of a more complex thing such as a woman that she strives to preserve herself, he is not only pointing to her intentional efforts to remain alive or make herself more powerful. Her striving or *conatus* encompasses a multitude of physical and psychological dispositions, only some of them intentional. They include, for example, her regular heart-beat, her sometimes unconscious tendency to keep out of the way of people who make her feel worthless, her recognition that she needs to sleep, and her efforts to help her friends. In Spinoza's view, individual things only continue to exist because they 'strive' to preserve themselves by exercising certain powers that enable them to do so. Moreover, while these powers are comparatively stable in simple items such as stones, they are subject to change in more complex ones. Individuals such as human beings can develop capacities that make them better able to maintain themselves than they were before, as when a

---

will of the one commanding, not with the necessity and truth of the matter'. Spinoza then reaffirms that it is only through revelation that we can come to know whether God wills us to worship him as we might honour a prince. So without revelation, no one can be bound to *obey* God. Since there is no revelation in the state of nature, 'we must not confuse the state of nature with the state of religion, but must conceive it as being without religion or law, and hence without sin or violation of right'.

[21] Ibid. ch. 16, p. 189. See Spinoza, *Ethics* in Curley ed. *The Collected Works of Spinoza*, vol. I, 3p6, 3p9. Here Spinoza describes things as striving to persevere in their being (*in suo esse*). On this doctrine of striving (*conatus*), see Chapter 8, fn. 29.

child learns to feed herself or cross the road. Equally, they can lose some of their power and become more vulnerable than they were.

As the *Ethics* explains more fully, individual persons and things cannot fail to exercise their *conatus*.[22] To be a stone, for instance, is to be determined by the order of nature to exercise the particular range of powers that constitute the kind of *conatus* possessed by stones, and the same applies to other species. To take one of the examples that Spinoza uses in the *Treatise*, the order of nature determines fish to swim, and as a Dutch proverb illustrated by Pieter Breughel has it, also determines big fish to eat little fish.[23] The strivings of human beings are not all that different, and accord with a law that is 'so firmly inscribed in human nature that it ought to be numbered among the eternal truths which no one can fail to know: that no one fails to pursue a thing they judge to be good unless they hope for a greater good or fear a greater harm; nor does anyone submit to an evil unless he hopes to avoid a greater evil or gain a greater good'.[24] Reiterating Hobbes's assertion that this law is 'a real necessity of nature as powerful as that by which a stone falls downwards', Spinoza enunciates what he and Hobbes both regard as the most fundamental principle governing human action.[25]

Elaborating this account, the *Treatise* now claims that, when an individual thing acts in accordance with its *conatus* and strives to persevere in its state, it does so 'by supreme right' or *ius summum*.[26] For example, it is 'by the supreme right of nature that fish are masters of the water, and that the large ones eat the smaller'. Equally, each human being is licensed by supreme natural right to strive to preserve themselves by doing anything in their power that they regard as conducive to their good. Just as a wise man has the supreme right to strive to live as his understanding dictates, 'the ignorant and weak-minded have the supreme right to do everything appetite urges'. The right of nature does not bind one 'to live according to the laws of a sound mind, any more than a cat is bound to live according to the laws of a lion's nature'.[27] It not only determines

---

[22] Spinoza, *Ethics*, 3p7. 'The striving by which each thing strives to persevere in its being is nothing but the actual essence of a thing'.

[23] Spinoza, *Tractatus Theologico-Politicus*, ch. 16, p. 189. Pieter Breughel the Elder. Signed preliminary drawing 1557.

[24] Ibid. ch. 16, pp. 192, 196.

[25] Hobbes, *On the Citizen*, ed. Richard Tuck and Michael Silverthorne (Cambridge: Cambridge University Press, 1998), ch. 1, p. 96.

[26] Spinoza, *Tractatus Theologico-Politicus*, ch. 16, p. 189.

[27] Ibid. ch. 16, p. 190.

us to do whatever we believe will be most beneficial to us, but as it were allows us to act in this way by right.

This analysis sits strangely with Spinoza's efforts to give an account of the order of nature shorn as far as possible of juridical terms. Since natural laws (or God's decrees) operate necessarily and determine everything that occurs, the claim that a person who acts in accordance with the supreme right of nature does so by right seems to mean no more than that the laws of nature determine them to act in that particular way. This is indeed what Spinoza implies. As he explains the matter, God possesses supreme right to exercise his power; and since the power of God is the power of nature, nature, too, exercises its power by supreme right. Furthermore, since the power of God (or nature) as a whole is nothing beyond the power of the individuals of which it is made up, each individual possesses a portion of God's supreme right to do anything it can. To put the conclusion another way, the right of each thing extends as far as its power.[28]

Discussing this argument, critics such as Van Velthuysen would object that it trades on the heterodox claim that the power of natural things to operate as they do is identical with the power of God, and implies, for example, that God exercises his power by eating little fish.[29] Spinoza will respond to the criticism in other works,[30] but at this point he is not interested in justifying the metaphysical basis of his position, and simply takes the conclusion he needs: that according to the law or operation of nature, the right of a human being, like that of any other natural individual, is identical with its power.

To present-day readers, this conception of right is liable to seem profoundly alien.[31] In the first place, it suppresses any distinction between an agent's right and power, and implies, for example, that insofar as a man lives by the right of nature he can rightfully use his power to rape or kill. It also abandons the usual supposition that one's right or rights are relatively stable, and instead allows that they fluctuate from minute to minute. For instance, my right over the food I have just bought is only as strong as my power to hold on to it, and evaporates when someone snatches it and runs off too fast for me to catch them. Finally, and perhaps most alien of all, this conception does not recognize any link

---

[28] Ibid. ch. 16, pp. 189–90.

[29] Letter 42 from Velthuysen to Ostens, *The Correspondence of Spinoza*, ed. and trans. Abraham Wolf, pp. 239–54.

[30] Spinoza, *Ethics* 1p29–30.

[31] On Spinoza's conception of right see Étienne Balibar, *Spinoza and Politics*, trans. Peter Snowden (London: Verso, 1998), pp. 59–63, 101–5; Warren Montag, *Bodies, Masses, Power* (London: Verso, 1999), ch. 3.

between right and obligation. The fact that I have a right to the food I have bought does not imply that you have an obligation to let me exercise my right over it; on the contrary, you have the right to stop me doing so if you can. As Hobbes had put it, under the law of nature 'every man has a Right to every thing; even to one anothers body'.[32]

To make sense of this conception, it is fruitless to try to assimilate it to the suggestion that a right is a kind of claim that others are obliged to respect. A more constructive way forward is to conceive the right in question as a liberty.[33] We find this view, for example, in *Leviathan*, where Hobbes defines the right of nature or *ius naturale* as 'the Liberty that each man hath, to use his own power, as he will himselfe, for the preservation of his own Nature'.[34] Applying it to Spinoza's examples, a pike has the liberty to devour a minnow, and in this sense can be said to act of right. Equally, a woman exercises a liberty when nothing in nature prevents her from snatching the food I am carrying. For all its strangeness, then, Spinoza's amoral conception of right captures what can be described as the kind of liberty that obtains in the state of nature, where the only constraints on action are those that flow from the order of nature, and nothing is prohibited 'except what no one desires and no one can do'.[35]

Without dwelling on its horrors, Spinoza shares Hobbes's view that the state of nature is an insecure and inconvenient condition, and is anxious to remind his readers how far the forms of order on which we routinely rely are artefacts of life in the state.[36] Without civil or divine laws, he emphasizes, our moral landmarks vanish, and normative standards that we usually take for granted are unable to get any purchase. The state of nature contains no legal standard of private civil right. There can be no injuries in the sense of illegal harms, since all harms are done rightfully. There can be no effective distinctions between justice and injustice, or equity and inequity, since these contrasts get their purchase from law. There can no legal norms of duty or authority; and the only available conception of right simply marks what a person can do.[37] Equally, there can be no shared or obligatory moral standards, or as Spinoza

---

[32] Hobbes, *Leviathan*, ch. 14, p. 91.

[33] See Hobbes, *On the Citizen*, ch. 1, p. 27.

[34] Hobbes, *Leviathan*, ch. 14, p. 91. The distinction between a subjective notion of a right as a permission, and an objective conception of a right as the ground of corresponding obligations had been made by Grotius. Hugo Grotius, *The Rights of War and Peace*, ed. Richard Tuck (Indianapolis: Liberty Fund, 2005), ch. 1, iv–x. See Alexandre Matheron, 'Spinoza et la problématique juridique de Grotius', *Philosophie*, 4 (1984), pp. 82–3.

[35] Spinoza, *Tractatus Theologico-Politicus*, ch. 16, p. 190.

[36] Ibid. ch. 16, p. 191.

[37] Ibid. ch. 16, p. 196.

puts it, quoting Saint Paul, there can be no sin before the law. In the absence of a prescribed and common way of life, an individual's judgements of good and evil, or right and wrong, simply mirror their individual assessments of what is and is not desirable. Individuals are not subject to any constraints that can systematically prevent them from satisfying their antisocial appetites, so that they live in what Hobbes designates a state of war, and Locke later disapprovingly describes as a state of licence.[38]

Pursuing this line of thought even further than Hobbes had done, Spinoza defends a view that is crucial both to his analysis of the state of nature and to his overall argument—that in the state of nature there can be no effective convention of promising. Since people always try to maximize their good, we can infer that no one will knowingly make a promise unless they hope to avoid an evil or gain a good by doing so, and that no one can be counted on to keep it for any longer than these conditions obtain. Suppose, Spinoza hypothesizes, that a robber forces me to promise him my goods. Since I can by right do anything in my power, there is nothing to prevent me from making the promise with every intention of breaking it as soon as I can. Equally, if I promise not to eat for twenty days, but realize at the end of the first that starving will damage my health, I can rightfully start eating again.[39] Promises are worthless in the state of nature, where they cannot be systematically enforced. More than that, the notion of a promise makes no sense in conditions where the only norm is the one embodied in the right of nature—that each individual may pursue whatever they judge to be best.

This position diverges significantly from the analysis of the state of nature given by Hobbes. According to *Leviathan*, covenants (including promises) are agreements 'wherein neither of the parties performe presently, but trust one another'.[40] They are binding, even in the state of nature, and are only void 'upon any reasonable suspicion' that the other party is going to break their side of the deal.[41] Thus, for example, 'if I Covenant to pay a ransome . . . for my life, to an enemy; I am bound by it. For it is a Contract, wherein one receiveth the benefit of life; the other is to receive money . . . ; and consequently . . . the Covenant is valid'.[42] Both sides stand to benefit, and as long as neither shows any signs of reneging, each is bound to fulfil their side of the bargain. For

[38] Hobbes, *Leviathan*, ch. 13, p. 88; John Locke, *Two Treatises of Government*, ed. Peter Laslett (Cambridge: Cambridge University Press, 1960), chs. 2, 6.
[39] Spinoza, *Tractatus Theologico-Politicus*, ch. 16, p. 192.
[40] Hobbes, *Leviathan*, ch. 14, p. 96.   [41] Ibid.
[42] Ibid. ch. 14, pp. 97–8.

Spinoza, however, nothing in the state of nature can put one under an obligation to keep promises that no longer strike one as beneficial. To argue otherwise is to import a further normative standard of obligation into this pre-political and pre-religious condition, where no such standards obtain. Unlike Hobbes, he therefore excludes promising from the state of nature and concludes that, just as it contains no norms of justice and injustice, it contains no norms governing the keeping or breaking of agreements.

The *Treatise* therefore sets out a uniquely stark construction of the state of nature, in which there are no divine commands to function as a prototype for civil law or provide a model for a civil legislator to imitate, and no civil laws to contain the untrammelled efforts of individuals to realize whatever they happen to regard as their greatest good. However, while the state of nature puts no legal or moral constraints on what individuals can do, it imposes enormous practical limitations. We would be liable to find ourselves hedged about by the powers of people more persuasive, co-operative, strong, cunning, devious, threatening, or alluring than we are, so that the extent of any individual's power and right would in practice be limited and variable. Still following in Hobbes's footsteps, Spinoza appeals to these psychological and social factors to highlight the disadvantages of the state of nature. Everyone prefers to live securely and without fear, and since no one enjoys anxiety, deception, anger, and hostility, each individual is to some extent prompted by their own affects to exchange the state of nature for a less combative way of life. In addition, there are obvious social and material benefits to be gained by escaping it, which will weigh with anyone who is sufficiently rational to appreciate them. Both reasoning and imagination therefore motivate us to abandon the state of nature for a more peaceful and comfortable way of life; and the fact that states exist is evidence that communities usually manage to do so. The question now is what sort of transformation such communities undergo.

The state

At this stage of his argument Spinoza is not interested in examining the historical processes by which states emerge from states of nature. Instead, he aims to show in general terms how a state of nature differs from an *optima respublica*, and to provide an abstract account of the reasons for making the transition from one to the other. In a state, individuals are subject to a sovereign with the power to make and enforce laws; and in the particular type of state with which the *Treatise* is concerned, sovereignty is collectively shared. The right that individuals exercise for themselves in the state of nature is held by 'everyone together'.[43] Somehow, a domain of individuals has been united into a sovereign, and a new power has arisen, capable of defeating or modifying the natural right of individuals.

Since it starts from a state of nature, this transition can only be governed by the right of nature and is in this respect on a par with the way that big fish eat little fish. Early modern political writers commonly appeal to the animal world to characterize political relationships, comparing the relations between rulers or nations with those between cats, lions, foxes, or even fish.[44] But when Spinoza relies on this device he is not merely employing metaphors to move the imagination; he is also underlining his conviction that the creation of a state is the creation of a natural thing, which possesses the same right of nature as animals and individual human beings, and strives to preserve itself.[45] Here again his view is distinctive. For many natural law theorists who modelled the civil law imposed by a sovereign on laws made by God, the state was situated somewhere between God and nature. It was not entirely a divine creation, because it also depended on rational human activity; but it was not entirely natural either, because in creating it, humans 'read off' and attempted to replicate commands issued by God. Even for Hobbes, the state is a person by fiction or an artificial man, and thus a work of artifice as opposed to nature. However, Spinoza explicitly distances himself from this aspect of Hobbes's position in a letter to Jarig Jelles. Whereas Hobbes grounds the state on a transfer of power that brings nature's right to an end, Spinoza preserves 'the natural right intact, so that the sovereign in a state has no more right over its subjects than is proportionate to the power by which it is superior to its subjects'.[46] The right of nature does not merely determine what happens outside the state; it continues to operate within political society, and sets the terms in which problems can be solved.

The question of how a state can emerge out of a state of nature is therefore a question about how one distribution of nature's right or power can give rise to another. What can induce individuals who are not subject to any legal constraints, and are in a position to pursue whatever they currently regard as most conducive to their own good, to create a sovereign capable of forcing them to obey its laws, even though this will sometimes require them to act in ways that

---

[43] Spinoza, *Tractatus Theologico-Politicus*, ch. 16, p. 191.

[44] See, for example, Pieter de la Court, *The True Interest and Political Maxims of the Republic of Holland* (London, 1746), pp. 168–71.

[45] Cf. Aristotle, *Politics*, Book I, 1252b and ff.

[46] Letter 50. *The Correspondence of Spinoza*, ed. and trans. Abraham Wolf, p. 269.

are contrary to their perceived advantage? How can such individuals unite to form an agent with enough power to impose its will on all of them?

One key to these questions lies in the fact that, while the right of nature does not require people to live in accordance with shared rules, it does not prevent them from doing so. As Spinoza has pointed out, a wise man who does his best to empower himself by entering into agreements with others and sticking to them is still obeying the law of nature by doing what he regards as best.[47] So we can imagine a community of rational or wise individuals who understand that the best way to live securely is to unite to form a collective sovereign and obey its laws. These people continue to pursue what they regard as their greatest good; but their interpretation of this goal is shaped by their understanding of what is truly good for human beings, and by their determination to try to live accordingly. While living under the right of nature, they simultaneously live in accordance with the norms of reason, and this latter fact puts them in a position to ground a state entirely on promises or agreements. Such people would understand that their greatest good lies in imposing laws on themselves, and would therefore agree that the best way to exercise their natural right is to give up their power to try to do whatever they want. They would mutually agree that it is in their best interests to unite into a sovereign, and having done so, the *Treatise* insists, they would invariably follow the law. They would detest deceitfulness, never break their promises, and recognize the overwhelming importance of trustworthiness, 'the supreme protection of the republic'.[48]

This is an enticing image of state formation, but Spinoza is not seduced by it. Humans, he comments, 'are born ignorant, and even when they are well brought up, much of their life passes away before they can come to know the true principle of living and acquire a virtuous disposition'.[49] Many of them are so preoccupied by passions such as greed, envy, and the desire for esteem that they are incapable of appreciating the benefits of mutual co-operation, and even if they were to enter into an agreement to live co-operatively they would break it as soon as it suited them. So on the uncontroversial assumption that people are not entirely rational, it follows that the transition from the state of nature to the state cannot be founded solely on a mutual promise or agreement. As Hobbes had already remarked, and as Spinoza agrees, 'something needs to be added', which will enable a sovereign to impose its will on wayward or intransigent subjects.[50] Moreover, while a variety of threats and incentives can serve this purpose, the most effective is the threat of death. If they are to be

[47] Spinoza, *Tractatus Theologico-Politicus*, ch. 16, p. 195.   [48] Ibid. ch. 16, p. 192.
[49] Ibid. ch. 16, p. 190.   [50] Ibid. ch. 16, p. 193.

sufficiently powerful to do their job, sovereigns must possess the *ius gladii* or power to impose the death sentence, 'which all people, without exception, fear'.[51] To form what Spinoza calls a democratic state, individuals in a state of nature therefore need collectively to endow themselves with the power not only to make law, but to impose capital punishment on those who disobey it.

Once again, rational individuals who appreciate the nature of human passion will understand that this course of action is in their own best interests and will willingly agree to it. They will voluntarily place themselves under a sovereign with enough power to prevent them from doing what they, as individuals, regard as best, on the grounds that this is the only way to make the state effective and realize the benefits they are trying to achieve. But less rational individuals—of whom there are many—will not see this so clearly, and may exercise their right of nature by refusing to give up their own individual power. Alternatively, even if they judge that the best thing to do is to submit, their submission may be less than wholehearted. In their case, transferring their power to the sovereign does not amount to promising to obey, because it does not involve a commitment to obey the law in future. It is simply a concession that—in the circumstances—obeying is the optimal thing to do. Nothing in this attitude prevents such people from continuing to try to break the law whenever it seems to stand in their way, and this helps to explain why sovereignty must be underwritten by force. There is a significant gap between subjects who are capable of promising to obey the law and can be trusted to keep their word, and subjects who submit because they think it is in their best current interests to do so, but have no commitment to obeying when this condition is not met. To concentrate their minds and subdue their willingness to resist, sovereigns need to be able to threaten to use force against them.

At this stage, Spinoza does not enter into the question of how, in practice, the transition from the state of nature to a democratic state might occur. Nor does he need to, since his conception of the state of nature implies that, regardless of how a group of people unites to form a collective sovereign, they do it in accordance with their right. The state of nature contains no basis for condemning sovereigns whose power was gained through force or fraud, or commending those whose rule emerged out of a process of peaceful negotiation.[52] On the contrary, any method of acquiring the power that constitutes sovereignty is rightful. Furthermore, since the right of nature continues to operate within the state, sovereigns as well as subjects retain their right to do

---

[51] Ibid.   [52] Ibid. ch. 16, p. 195.

anything within their power; but while subjects are now constrained by the law, the sovereign is not similarly restricted. As the collective agent responsible for making and rescinding law, the sovereign is not bound by it, and is in principle free to use its power in any way it can.[53]

The creation of a state therefore does not extinguish the right of nature, but it does transform the ways in which it can be exercised. Laws not only impose common and enforceable standards of behaviour; they also bring with them a range of shared norms, so that particular actions can be described, for example, as just or unjust. In place of a state of nature in which the only standards of right and wrong are those that individuals prescribe for themselves, a sovereign determines standards on behalf of the community as a whole. When, for example, a sovereign lays down an edict that no one is to commit murder, it does not merely give notice of its power to punish. It also uses its power or right to create circumstances in which murder can be generally condemned. This common standard can then be used to assess subjects' decisions and actions; but it can also be brought to bear on the status and actions of the sovereign. It provides a way to characterize the sovereign's right and legitimate its power, so that a sovereign can now describe its own actions as right or just.

It may seem that this yields only an impoverished morality in which there is no distinction, for example, between the sovereign's decision to use its power to prevent murder and its claim that murder is unjust. If anything that the sovereign commands counts as just and anything it forbids as unjust, there will be no room for the possibility that it might issue an unjust command or forbid a just course of action. But this underestimates the force of the normative standards that sovereignty makes possible. Once in circulation, they acquire a life of their own and enable subjects, as well as sovereigns, to justify their beliefs and actions in moral terms. Instead of simply asserting their power, sovereigns can, for example, represent their decisions as just; and once they do so, the standards of justice to which they appeal become open to scrutiny and contestation. Moral discourse enters into the balance of power between sovereigns and subjects, so that one of the forms of power that sovereigns now need to hold is the moral high ground. To avoid the disempowerment that comes with moral contempt, they must be able to justify their actions to their subjects in moral terms. Equally, the ability to provide compelling moral arguments becomes a form of power or right. So although the *ius gladii* remains an essential element of sovereignty, sovereign power now takes a wider range of forms.

---

[53] Ibid. ch. 16, p. 199.

The state does not simply redistribute power that already existed in the state of nature. It also creates new powers, including those of morality and religion.

Contract

It is significant that Spinoza first introduces the notion of a contract or *pactum* while discussing an idealized scenario of how a group of philosophically informed or fully rational people would elect to live. In a state of nature, he argues, such a group would enter into a contract or *pactum*—a mutual agreement to obey a collective sovereign.[54] Each would grasp the reasons for making this commitment, and would promise the others to stick by it. Moreover, knowing that such a promise may be difficult to keep, each would agree to make the arrangement generally binding by contracting to give the sovereign enough power to enforce it. Binding themselves by both force and reason, they would commit themselves to obey the law. As Spinoza portrays them, these individuals are so clear about the nature of their own collective good, and so confident of their ability to realize it, that they are able to operate in accordance with the norms of reason and, by contracting, prescribe for themselves a new way of life. Although they inhabit a state of nature in which there are no generally recognized standards of right and wrong, and no generally respected conventions of contracting, they are nevertheless able to converge on a single interpretation of the good, and use the device of contract to put it into practice. Contracting, as it first enters Spinoza's argument, is therefore part of an abstract, philosophical conception of the basis of the state.

As we have seen, however, the practices of promising and contracting only become available within the state, where a sovereign's power to impose laws makes way for a notion of objective right and wrong. So when Spinoza imagines a group of people in the state of nature whose converging desires enable them to generate a shared and rational way of life, he suppresses the fact that, according to his own account, they would be unable to appeal to generally articulated moral or legal norms. He asks us to imagine a community external to the state, which is nevertheless equipped with robust moral standards, and can therefore ground a common way of life on contract or agreement. Here, however, he is surely speaking from a point of view only made possible by the state. Taking the existence of moral and legal norms for granted, he is projecting them onto the state of nature and making the hypothetical claim that rational people in the state of nature would contract with one another to

---

[54] Ibid. ch. 16, p. 191.

form a collective sovereign and obey its laws. Speaking from the rational perspective made available by the state, and addressing readers who share it, he uses its resources to provide a rational justification of obedience. Contract is now an established aspect of everyday life, which can be used to articulate and examine reasons for obeying the law, and in Spinoza's view, rational, philosophical argument should in principle convince each one of us that contracting to obey it is the optimal and maximally empowering course of action. Understanding why this is so will shape our motivations and bring about a state of affairs where, whether or not we have actually made such an agreement, we shall think of ourselves as having done so. Rather than envisaging the requirement to obey as something that has happened to us or been imposed by an external authority, we shall conceive of it as an obligation that we have ourselves brought about because it is conducive to our good, and for which we bear responsibility. It would always be rational to agree to it, and we therefore have agreed to it. This outlook in turn opens up new justificatory possibilities. For example, an individual may reproach themselves for feeling tempted to flout the law, be regarded as untrustworthy and unjust when they break it, and feel ashamed when they are punished. Equally, a person who does the legal thing in difficult circumstances may arouse admiration or take pride in their own achievement. Abiding by a contract to conform to the sovereign's commands becomes a moral matter, and can be justified in moral terms.[55]

Viewed like this, the moral force embodied in the presumption that we have contracted to obey the law is ultimately grounded on a rational judgement about the best way to realize the human good. However, since this judgement is not accessible to everyone, it remains unclear whether the notion of contract can do much justificatory work in real states inhabited by people who are less than fully rational. Here Spinoza begins to explore several ways in which the view that our obligation to obey the law rests on a contract can become detached from its rational foundation and set up on its own. A first cause of

---

[55] For broader discussion of Spinoza's conception of contract, see Don Garrett, '"Promising Ideas": Hobbes and Contract in Spinoza's Political Philosophy', in *Spinoza's 'Theologico-Political Treatise'*, ed. Yitzhak Y. Melamed and Michael A. Rosenthal (Cambridge: Cambridge University Press, 2010); Moira Gatens and Genevieve Lloyd, *Collective Imaginings: Spinoza, Past and Present* (London: Routledge, 1999), chs. 4–5; Alexandre Matheron, *Individu et communauté chez Spinoza* (Paris: Les Éditions de Minuit, 1969); Alexandre Matheron, 'Le "droit du plus fort": Hobbes contra Spinoza', *Revue philosophique de la France et de l'étranger* 110 (1985); Michael Rosenthal, 'Two Collective Action Problems in Spinoza's Social Contract Theory', *History of Philosophy Quarterly*, 15, no. 4 (1998); Uyl, *Power, State and Freedom*, Douglas den Uyl, 'Sociality and Social Contract: A Spinozistic Perspective', *Studia Spinozana*, 1 (1985); Sylvain Zac, 'État et nature chez Spinoza', *Revue de méthaphysique et de morale*, 49 (1964).

this split is the conviction that contracting to obey the sovereign is widely taken to be rational. Even when people do not fully understand the reasons for contracting, the fact that it is presented as a rational course of action can be enough to persuade them to adopt the stance of contractors, and view themselves as having voluntarily bound themselves to obey the law. The reason for this, Spinoza points out, is that no one 'dares openly to reject the dictates of reason, for fear of seeming mindless'.[56] Aside from its internal power to convince, the capacity to live on the basis of rational judgments is imbued with a superiority that makes it an object of desire, and therefore shapes both thought and action.

Another factor that detaches contractualism from its rational ground and gives it a broader persuasive power can be traced to the character of ordinary practices of contracting. Some of these generate binding obligations whether or not the contract in question can be rationally justified, and if one thinks of one's contractual obligation to the state in these terms, one does not need to understand why it is rational in order to be bound by it. All one needs to understand is the substance of the agreement one has made. Spinoza sometimes speaks about contracting in these terms, for example when he claims that people who contract to transfer their right of defending themselves to the sovereign are bound by their agreement, even if they later come to regret it. 'If they wished to keep anything for themselves, they ought to have taken precautions so that they could defend it safely'.[57] The fact that one has entered into an agreement can be enough to make it valid, whether or not it was rational to have done so.

By these various means, Spinoza shifts away from the claim that our contractual obligation to obey the law is ultimately grounded on philosophical argument, and acknowledges that it can also be justified in imaginative terms. Much as the narratives revealed in Scripture provide people with grounds for action that motivate them to act more or less as Spinoza's conception of rationality dictates, so political narratives can encourage them to live in ways that enhance peace and security. And one of the most powerful of these narratives represents individuals as having contracted to obey the law. In some cases, an imagined contract may be modelled on a real-life social practice; but in others it may be grounded on fantasy. When, for example, the Jews contracted to obey God, they regarded themselves as bound to obey a super-powerful legislator, although, as the *Treatise* has repeatedly argued, no such being exists. However,

---

[56] Spinoza, *Tractatus Theologico-Politicus*, ch. 16, p. 191.
[57] Ibid. ch. 16, p. 193.

this difficulty did not prevent them from regarding themselves as parties to a contract who would be punished for breaking it; and their self-perception in turn played a part in motivating them to obey the law promulgated by Moses.

When Spinoza speaks about a foundational contract in which individuals transfer their right or power to the sovereign, he is not implying that such an event must actually have taken place. Rather, he is acknowledging that the rational grounds for contracting, which provide the strongest justification for obeying the law, are mirrored in the ways that we imagine ourselves as contractually bound, and that these in turn exercise justificatory force. The various kinds of contract we encounter in everyday life provide us with examples, precedents, and arguments in terms of which we can characterize (and question) our obligation to obey the state; and although these resources are local, they are often more persuasive than philosophical reasoning, and consequently form much of the substance of contractarian theorizing and debate. Once they have been put into play, they shape the way that sovereigns and subjects understand their relationship, form part of a society's ongoing attempts to figure and reconfigure its own past and future, and justify its political order. Like images of God, images of the contract and the state of nature in which it occurs are continually accommodated to particular circumstances, as communities project their conceptions of the risks and benefits of political life.[58]

Sovereign and subject

Spinoza does not doubt that the key to a secure and prosperous way of life is an enforceable system of law. However, since the individual members of a state will only obey the law if they think they will gain more good than harm by doing so, a sovereign must convince them that obedience is in their interests. To put the point in contractual terms, 'no contract can have any force except by reason of its utility.... It is consequently foolish to demand that someone should keep faith with you to eternity, unless you at the same time strive to bring it about that breaking the contract you are entering into brings more

---

[58] See Louis Althusser, 'The Only Materialist Tradition, Part 1: Spinoza', in *The New Spinoza*, ed. Warren Montag and Ted Stolze (Minneapolis, Minn.: University of Minnesota Press, 1997); Étienne Balibar, '*Jus-Pactum-Lex*: On the Constitution of the Subject in the *Theologico-Political Treatise*', in *The New Spinoza*, ed. Warren Montag and Ted Stolze (Minneapolis, Minn.: University of Minnesota Press, 1997); Gatens and Lloyd, *Collective Imaginings: Spinoza, Past and Present*.

harm than advantage to the one who breaks it'.[59] This consideration, which 'must be especially applicable to the institution of the state', indicates that sovereigns will need a great deal of power—both the coercive power that makes subjects prefer to obey than be punished, and the power to persuade them by rational or imaginative means that obedience is preferable to its opposite.

Like Hobbes, Spinoza dramatizes what it takes to endow a sovereign with these resources. Each individual, he initially claims, must transfer all their natural right to the sovereign, so that they no longer possess the power to flout the law, and are bound to obey it either freely or out of fear.[60] Moreover, in giving up their right, they create and submit themselves to a sovereign who remains in a state of nature and can rightfully exercise its power in any way that it sees fit. They thus put themselves in a position where it will always be advantageous to 'carry out absolutely all the commands of the sovereign, even though it commands the greatest absurdities',[61] where any failure to recognize the right of the sovereign makes one an enemy of the state, and where anyone who tries to seize or transfer sovereignty is a traitor, regardless of their motives.[62]

This account is hardly calculated to increase confidence in the state.[63] The conditions for producing a secure way of life seem to be identical with those for undermining it, and the sovereign's untrammelled power appears to endanger subjects as much as to guarantee their protection. If Spinoza is to provide a persuasive analysis of the benefits of living in the state, he will somehow have to dispel these negative impressions and show that the position of subjects is not as bad as it looks. To meet this demand, he offers a sequence of ameliorative arguments.

The first thing to remember is that the *Treatise* is only talking about democratically governed republics, and is not trying to justify obedience to any other type of sovereign. Spinoza's aim, as he explains, is to provide an account of the foundations of a democratic state (*imperium democrati...*) while 'passing over the foundations of other forms of political power (*potestas*)'.[64] By contrast with Hobbes, who had offered a general account of the obligation to obey the law,

---

[59] Spinoza, *Tractatus Theologico-Politicus*, ch. 16, p. 194.
[60] Ibid. ch. 16, p. 193.   [61] Ibid. ch. 16, p. 194.   [62] Ibid. ch. 16, p. 197.
[63] Edwin Curley, 'Kissinger, Spinoza and Genghis Khan', in *The Cambridge Companion to Spinoza* (Cambridge: Cambridge University Press, 1996); Moira Gatens, 'Spinoza's Disturbing Thesis: Power, Norms and Fiction in the *Tractatus Theologico-Politicus*', *History of Political Thought*, 30, no. 3 (2009).
[64] Spinoza, *Tractatus Theologico-Politicus*, ch. 16, p. 195.

he is only concerned with the situation of subjects who transfer their natural right to a *societas*, 'which alone will retain the supreme right of nature over all things', and submit to rule by a general assembly of which they are members.[65] Such citizens play a part in making the law, and are not forced to obey a sovereign over whom they have no control. The cost of giving up one's individual natural right and the burdens of obedience are consequently minimal.

Nevertheless, there remains the worry that even an individual with a voice in the sovereign assembly of a state may become part of an entrenched minority that is persistently subject to the will of a majority. If that majority becomes tyrannical, members of the minority will be forced to obey laws that significantly diminish their quality of life by thwarting some of the goals that they most care about. Instead of strengthening their ability to live in the light of their own desires and aspirations by providing a secure environment, such a state will have the opposite effect, and may effectively enslave them to the will of the majority. With this possibility in view, would individuals in a state of nature be wise to transfer all their natural right to the sovereign?

Spinoza works hard to allay this anxiety by elaborating his account of sovereign power. Although his formal model requires subjects to transfer the entirety of their natural right to the sovereign, it now emerges that this is an oversimplification, which neglects the fact that some forms of natural right are not transferable.[66] A sovereign cannot take over its subjects' right to make their own judgements.[67] Nor can it altogether shape their responses to its rule. Some patterns of affect, such as our desire to be free from fear, our dispositions to hate people who have harmed us, and our tendency to be offended by insults, are so deeply etched in human psychology as to be ineradicable. When, for example, a sovereign makes a law that its subjects find insulting, it must expect them to take offence.[68] So while sovereigns may alter judgements and feelings in a great many ways, some aspects of natural right are inalienable.[69]

Sovereigns are therefore not quite as invincible as Spinoza's formal model suggests, and what appeared to be an entirely one-sided relationship is in fact an ever-shifting balance between two sets of powers. To fulfil its role, a sovereign needs to ensure that it can enforce the law; but to achieve this, it needs to take account of its subjects' powers and the uses to which they may put them. It

[65] Ibid. ch. 16, p. 193.   [66] Ibid. ch. 17, p. 201.
[67] Ibid. ch. 20, p. 240.   [68] Ibid. ch. 16, p. 193.
[69] Ibid. ch. 17, p. 201. Compare Hobbes, *Leviathan* ch. 21, pp. 150–3; Hobbes, *On the Citizen* ch. 6, pp. 80–4, §§10–13.

needs to be aware that people will always exercise their *conatus* by doing what they perceive to be for their greatest good, and that disaffected subjects are liable to resist. Emphasizing this risk, Spinoza echoes the classical view that the greatest threat to sovereignty is posed by the people, and that a ruling body which fails to control them is unlikely to survive. The question, then, is how control can best be achieved. While force may seem to offer the answer, sovereigns who resort to tyrannical methods are in practice unlikely to last. When a sovereign makes its people afraid, it strengthens their desire to be free from fear and thus their desire to resist the sovereign who is the source of their alarm. In an attempt to weaken its people, the sovereign encourages them to resist and puts its own survival in doubt. Thus, a sovereign has the greatest authority when it 'reigns in the hearts of its subjects' and they obey its commands willingly, so that the ruling body has every reason to court their loyalty, both by 'consulting the common good and directing everything in accordance with the dictates of reason', and by using the resources of imagination to justify its laws.[70] As we have seen, the language of contract has an important role to play here. The assumption that the obligation to obey the law is grounded on contract enables both sovereigns and subjects to represent obeying the law as a matter of honouring one's agreements, and thus as a matter of moral obligation rather than mere submission.

These arguments may go some way towards reassuring anxious subjects. However, the fact remains that, while a sovereign's power is not limitless, it is still sufficient, even in a democracy, to force an entrenched minority of subjects to submit to its will. Such a strategy may be short sighted and ill judged, but what can stop an unwise sovereign from pursuing it? Spinoza is deeply sensitive to this criticism. As he puts it, the objection charges that subjects who have no legitimate means of protecting themselves against their sovereign's power are in effect enslaved, and thus that the state licenses servitude.[71] Drawing on a traditional republican line of argument, he resists this view, responding that the democratic form of state with which he is concerned is in fact optimally designed to exclude slavery and produce a community of free men.[72]

---

[70] Spinoza, *Tractatus Theologico-Politicus*, ch. 17, p. 202, ch. 16, p. 194.

[71] Ibid. ch. 16, p. 194.

[72] On this republican ideal, see Quentin Skinner, *Liberty before Liberalism* (Cambridge: Cambridge University Press, 1998). On its place in Dutch political thought and Spinoza's use of it, see Susan James, 'Freedom, Slavery and the Passions', in *The Cambridge Companion to Spinoza's Ethics*, ed. Olli Koistinen (Cambridge: Cambridge University Press, 2009); Jonathan Scott, 'Classical Republicanism in Seventeenth-Century England and the Netherlands', in *Republicanism: A Shared European Heritage*, ed. Martin van Gelderen and Quentin Skinner, vol. 1, pp. 61–81. Justin

One might argue, so the *Treatise* allows, that the state turns subjects into slaves simply by virtue of the fact that it prevents them from doing anything they want, and forces them to act in accordance with the sovereign's commands. But this, Spinoza claims, is a seriously misguided objection. Being able to do what you want does not in itself make you free, any more than obeying commands in itself makes you a slave. On the contrary, 'the one who is drawn by his own pleasure ... is most a slave' and 'only he who lives wholeheartedly according to the guidance of reason alone is free'. People who live under laws that constrain them to live rationally are therefore more free than those who follow their own irrational desires, and insofar as the state brings such a condition about, it enhances freedom.

However, since sovereigns do not always act rationally, it remains to ask whether subjects are enslaved when, as is often the case, a sovereign's commands fail to promote security or, as Spinoza also puts it, do not protect the common good. To answer this question we need to know more about what it is to be a slave, and Spinoza accordingly provides a definition. Subjects becomes slaves when they are forced to follow commands that further the sovereign's advantage as opposed to their own.[73] Judged by this criterion, sovereigns can sometimes enslave their subjects, as for example when a king orders a noble to hand over his goods so that the king can build himself a bigger palace. However, as long as laws enhance the interests, not just of the sovereign, but of its subjects as well, they do not enslave. When, for instance, a republican assembly requires a subject to pay his share of taxes in order to fund public services, the subject is not reduced to slavery, because the services for which he is helping to pay benefit him as well as everyone else. The law takes his advantage into account, so that by obeying it he serves his own *utilitas*, and at the same time furthers the common good.

Underlying this argument is a deeply entrenched republican doctrine derived from Roman Law, according to which one is enslaved when one is dependent on the arbitrary will of another agent, and free when one is bound only by one's own will. A sovereign enslaves its subjects when it subjects them to its arbitrary will; and its will is said to be arbitrary precisely when it is not constrained to take their interests into account. But subjects are also turned into slaves in circumstances where, although their sovereign has not in fact enacted any laws of this kind, it is nevertheless in a position to do so. For

Steinberg, 'On Being *Sui Iuris*: Spinoza and the Republican Ideal of Liberty', *History of European Ideas*, 34, no. 3 (2008).

[73] Spinoza, *Tractatus Theologico-Politicus*, ch. 16, p. 194.

example, a king may have the power to confiscate his subjects' goods for his own purposes even if he has not yet used it; and the very fact that he possesses and is known to possess this power is enough to enslave his subjects. To be a slave, and to forfeit the status of a free man, is thus to be exposed to the risks that are implicit in a political order where the sovereign is not constrained to track its subjects' interests, as well as to the psychological and social pressures that such a system creates.

This conception of slavery helps to define a corresponding notion of political freedom, and yields an account of the conditions that a free state must meet. It is clearly not enough that the sovereign is, as it happens, benign, and has not so far imposed laws that sacrifice its subjects' interests to its own advantage. There must also be some guarantee that it will not go down this path, and that the law can be relied on to uphold the common good. A free state must therefore contain some constitutional protection against slavery—some means of preventing an overweening sovereign from turning its back on the common good. Taking up a long-established view supported in his own day by a number of Dutch republicans, Spinoza argues that the best way to ensure that a sovereign lacks the power to enslave its subjects is for the subjects themselves to hold sovereignty collectively.[74] Of all types of state, he claims, a democracy seems 'the most natural, and the one that approaches most nearly to the freedom that nature concedes to everyone. For in it, no one so transfers his natural right to another that thereafter there is no consultation with him; instead he transfers it to the greater part of the *societas* of which he is a part. In this way everyone remains equal, as they were before in the state of nature', and *salus populi suprema lex*—the wellbeing of the whole people as opposed to that of the ruler is the supreme law.[75]

Spinoza is advocating a state where all individuals are able to identify with the law because they have played, or are eligible to play, some part in making it. To

[74] For this widespread view, see also P. de la Court, *True Interest*, pp. 35, 37. For further discussion of Spinoza's conception of democracy, see Alexandre Matheron, 'The Theoretical Function of Democracy in Spinoza and Hobbes', in *The New Spinoza*, ed. Warren Montag and Ted Stolze (Minneapolis, Minn.: University of Minnesota Press, 1997); Antonio Negri, '*Reliqua Desiderantur*: A Conjecture for a Definition of the Concept of Democracy in the Final Spinoza', in *The New Spinoza*; Antonio Negri, *The Savage Anomaly: The Power of Spinoza's Metaphysics and Politics*, trans. Michael Hardt (Minneapolis, Minn.: University of Minnesota Press, 1991).

[75] Spinoza, *Tractatus Theologico-Politicus*, ch. 16, p. 195. See Jonathan Israel, *Radical Enlightenment: Philosophy and the Making of Modernity, 1650–1750* (Oxford: Oxford University Press, 2001), ch. 15.

put the point in traditional republican terms, when subjects obey the law, they are not subjecting themselves to the will of another by conforming to commands imposed on them by someone else; rather, they are acting in conformity with their own wills by obeying laws that they themselves have made. By itself, this does not of course rule out the possibility that a minority of subjects may become enslaved, and Spinoza concedes that can be no absolute guarantee that an over-enthusiastic majority will not back a destructive legislative programme and make the law an ass. Nevertheless, appealing once again to the distinctive features of democratic sovereignty, and heading off the deep fear that democracy amounts to rule by the unruly masses, he reassures his readers that things can be arranged in such a way that this is extremely unlikely to happen. 'If the assembly is large, it is almost impossible that the majority of its members should agree on one absurd action. . . . As we have shown, the foundation and end [of such a state] is precisely to avoid the absurdities of appetite, and to confine men as far as possible within the limits of reason so that they may live harmoniously and peacefully'.[76] A constitution where sovereignty is exercised by a large assembly of subjects is more likely than any other to produce laws that uphold the common good, and this is the most that we can hope for.

The appeal and power of this argument largely rides on the assumption that everyone in a democratic state can contribute to making the law. The capacity of subjects to play a part in this process is meant to ensure that the law reflects the common good, and to reduce the risk that the state will become dominated by factional or sectarian interests. But while Spinoza accedes to this view, he only supports it in a qualified form. Drawing again on Roman law, he argues that democracies are not only made up of sovereign and subjects. They also contain individuals who occupy a third political status, one exemplified by children, who 'do what is to their own advantage in accordance with the command of their parents'.[77] As long as parents only command courses of action that are not simply for their own benefit but for that of their children as well, their children are not slaves. But neither are they subjects, because they are primarily bound to obey their parents rather than the sovereign. The sovereign gives parents discretion to determine what is best for their children, so that the family functions as a sort of sub-state under the sovereign's overall control, and a child will only be enslaved if its parents abuse their power. But whether they do or not, the child lives outside the primary political bond

---

[76] Spinoza, *Tractatus Theologico-Politicus*, ch. 16, p. 194.
[77] Ibid. ch. 16, p. 195.

between sovereign and subject, and is only indirectly under the sovereign's command.[78]

The territory over which a sovereign rules therefore contains children, and as Spinoza later explains in the *Tractatus Politicus*, many other categories of person, including wives and servants, who are not in a position to ensure that the law takes account of their interests by playing a part in making it. Their interests can only be indirectly represented by people who have a voice in the legislative assembly. Spinoza has frequently been represented as a democrat, particularly in some recent strands of scholarship, but it is important to recognize that the democracy he envisages is one in which only a proportion of individuals are in a position to will the law in the fullest sense. Many others are subject not only to the will of the sovereign, but also to the wills of subsidiary authorities, and while a virtuous subject will defend his dependants, a vicious one may use them for his own ends. The many individuals who are not subjects therefore remain relatively unprotected. Even if, as Spinoza contends, they are not slaves, they are excluded from the fullest form of political right, and do not possess the status that republicans describe as that of a freeman.

Resistance

Spinoza's extended defence of republican sovereignty clarifies the grounds of his claim that it is rational to obey the law. Republics are far from perfect, but they are the strongest available means of preventing tyranny and protecting subjects, so that it is better to obey their laws than to resist, even in those rare cases where the law is absurd. 'For reason commands that we carry out even those orders, in order to choose the lesser of two evils'.[79] However, for all its apparent confidence, this judgement must be a fine one. One of Spinoza's principal reasons for writing the *Treatise* is to decry the damaging effects of superstition and religious division on the Dutch Republic, and draw attention to the threat they pose to liberty. Presumably these political deficiencies are ultimately the responsibility of the sovereign, so that even republics can go wrong. But is it then so obvious that, even in a republic, it is always right to knuckle under and follow the law? Would it necessarily be irrational, for example, to refuse to obey a particularly unjust piece of legislation in the hope of getting it repealed?

---

[78] Susan James, 'Democracy and the Good Life in Spinoza's Philosophy', in *Interpreting Spinoza: Critical Essays*, ed. Charlie Huenemann (Cambridge: Cambridge University Press, 2008); Alexandre Matheron, 'Femmes et serviteurs dans le democratie Spinoziste', in *Speculum Spinozanum* (London: Routledge, 1977).

[79] Spinoza, *Tractatus Theologico-Politicus*, ch. 16, p. 194.

Spinoza's attitude to this issue, like that of Hobbes, is informed by an underlying conviction that the threat of anarchy is greater than that of tyranny. Invasive as the power of a state may be (and Spinoza is well aware that there are all sorts of ways in which sovereigns can oppress their subjects)[80] it is always safer, and thus more rational, to try to reform it from within, rather than directly challenging sovereignty by disobeying the law. This claim is surely questionable. While a group of people who break the law will be punished, their action may in the long run lead to reform. Moreover, it is highly unlikely that a few strategic infractions of the law will destroy the sovereign and usher in the anarchic state of war that both Spinoza and Hobbes are justifiably afraid of. Both of them acknowledge this objection, but neither finds it persuasive. The danger it overlooks is in their view that disobedience contributes to a climate where subjects feel able to make their own judgements about whether or not to obey the law, and it is consequently harder for the sovereign to enforce its decrees. Disobedience need not immediately destroy the sovereign, but it increases its vulnerability. Furthermore, when subjects break the law they alter their own horizon of possibilities, and may begin to inculcate a habit of disobedience. ('Everyone knows what the wicked man's aversion to the present, and his desire to make changes in the status quo, will lead him to, and what impetuous anger and disdain for poverty will result in'.[81]) In the case of a single individual this will hardly matter, but once a disposition to treat the law as optional becomes widespread, the sovereign again faces a steeper challenge. The fact that some people regularly take the law into their own hands gives others a reason to do so, and the sovereign's evident inability or unwillingness to prevent them provides further grounds for discounting its commands. Despite the fact that it has far more power than its subjects they can always undermine it, and because the stakes are high it is rational not to start.

The image of the sovereign that best fits this line of reasoning is not the supremely powerful one of Spinoza's model, but a vulnerable authority, exposed to the whims and preferences of an unruly population. It is not a modern nation state equipped with vast security forces and a military complex, but a relatively fragile assembly whose subjects have not fully internalized the risks of undermining the law, and still need to be encouraged to cultivate mores that will fully secure the benefits of living in the state. Spinoza's claim that it is always rational to obey the law is an unconditional one, and he is not suggesting that it only obtains in the kind of state in which he himself lived. Nevertheless,

---

[80] Ibid. ch. 20, pp. 244–6.   [81] Ibid. ch. 17, p. 203.

it is reasonable to assume that his experience of the Dutch Republic helped to shape the general conclusions he arrived at, including his belief that incursions into the sovereign's power should not be tolerated.

Setting these historical considerations aside, what enables individuals to commit themselves to obeying the law is the extent to which the sovereign relies on their obedience. As Spinoza puts it, 'if men could be so deprived of their natural right that subsequently they could do nothing except by the will of those who held the supreme right, then the latter would be permitted to rule over their subjects most violently and with absolute impunity'.[82] But this is fortunately impossible. Although the model 'agrees in no small measure with practice, and a practice could be established which approached more and more nearly to the condition contemplated', the model 'will nevertheless always remain in many respects merely theoretical'. The power of a sovereign can never completely eclipse that of its subjects or vice versa, and their respective rights always have to be balanced against one another.[83] The law is thus a *modus vivendi*—a way of life that can in practice be sustained, and the art of politics lies in finding ways to sustain it.

The question, then, is how to create ways of life in which the powers of sovereign and subjects are balanced in a manner that enables individuals to enjoy the benefits of life within the state as fully as possible. But what approach will best enable us to answer it? The philosophical mode of enquiry that Spinoza has so far been pursuing shows that the preservation of the state 'depends chiefly on the loyalty of its subjects, on their virtue, and on their constancy of heart in carrying out its commands'.[84] Because people who obey only out of fear and other negative passions are not loyal, both sovereign and subjects are much more secure when they are moved to co-operate by positive passions such as love, or clearly understand the advantages of doing so. Sovereigns therefore need to find ways of cultivating these motivations, and establishing states 'where everyone, no matter what his mentality, prefers public right to private advantage'.[85] As we have seen, Spinoza is convinced that a broadly democratic constitution provides the optimal framework within which to pursue this project; but the precise character of the constitution is less important than the specific arrangements through which sovereign power is exercised and freedom upheld. Here we have to turn to experience, and specifically to the lessons taught by theology.

---

[82] Ibid. ch. 17, p. 201.   [83] Ibid. ch. 17, p. 203.
[84] Ibid. ch. 17, p. 201.   [85] Ibid. ch. 17, p. 203.

Chapter 11

Life in a Republic: The Lessons of Theology

The burden of devising a balance of power that will maintain liberty and security falls primarily on the sovereign, who must take the initiative by determining 'what it ought to grant its subjects for the greater security and advantage of the state', what will make them loyal and virtuous, and how it can best prevent them from becoming subversive.[1] It is above all rulers who face the tasks of getting people to limit their private pursuits in order to contribute to the processes of government, and of finding ways to direct their conflicting desires to productive political ends. Spinoza places this project at the heart of politics and, emphasizing its difficulty, portrays the common run of people in a deeply unflattering light. The *multitudo*, he complains, rushes headlong into decisions and is easily corrupted. Each individual among them is convinced that his own view is correct, wants everything to be ruled in accordance with his outlook, and grounds his judgements of policies on his beliefs about the extent to which they will benefit himself. Driven by a craving for esteem, citizens ordinarily disdain their equals and cannot bear to be directed by them. Gnawed by envy of other people's good fortune, they wish them ill and are delighted when they come to harm. 'Everyone knows what the wicked man's aversion to the present, together with his desire to make changes in the *status quo*, will lead him to; what his impetuous anger and disdain for poverty often result in; and how far these passions fill and disturb the hearts of men'.[2]

As a range of classical authorities had pointed out, the gravest threat to the security of the state consequently lies within, and the most immediate task of sovereigns is to protect themselves against it by learning to deal effectively with

---

[1] Benedictus de Spinoza, *Tractatus Theologico-Politicus*, ed. Carl Gebhardt, vol. III, *Opera* (Heidelberg: Carl Winter, 1924), ch. 17, p. 203.

[2] Ibid.

the multitude.[3] While a philosophical understanding of the principles of politics can undoubtedly contribute to this skill, rulers can also learn the art of government by studying the successes and failures of past states. History indicates what strategies one should follow; but it can also teach one what to avoid. For example, it indicates that hard-pressed sovereigns such as Alexander the Great or the Emperor Augustus made a mistake when they tried to subdue the multitude into unquestioning obedience by representing themselves as divine.[4] This ruse is liable to fail; for instance, Alexander's claims to divinity were so crude that, although they deceived the barbarian Persians whom he was trying to conquer, they did not fool his more prudent countrymen.[5] But even when the device succeeds it is harmful, not because it immediately produces political instability or conflict, but because it diminishes the freedom at which good government aims. By knowingly inculcating a distorted conception of sovereignty, rulers undermine their subjects' understanding of the nature of political power and degrade their ability to play the co-operative role on which a flourishing state depends. The resources on which the sovereign can draw to sustain its subjects' loyalty and virtue are accordingly diminished, and whether or not this results in tyranny or insurrection, the proper purposes of the state are thwarted.

As a modern instance of these dangers, Spinoza cites the theory of the divine right of kings. While the Macedonians were not duped into believing that Alexander was a god, some recent rulers 'have been more successful in persuading men that Majesty is sacred and is God's agent on earth, that it has been established not by men's vote and consent but by God, and that it is preserved and defended by God's particular providence and aid. In this way monarchs have devised other means to secure their rule'.[6] The strong implication here is that early-modern conceptions of sovereignty as divinely ordained are no less deceptive and delusory than their classical counterparts, and that people who encourage them do equally great damage to freedom. Flawed as it may be, the strategy of equating sovereignty with divinity is alive and well in seventeenth-century political culture, and both sovereigns and subjects need to be on their guard against it. Spinoza does not directly link this phenomenon to

---

[3] Spinoza gives the following examples. Alexander of Macedon is reported to have remarked that he was safer in battle than at home; Quintus Curtius Rufus claims that more kings have been killed by their own people than by their enemies; and the same moral can be drawn from Tacitus's account of the civil wars between Vespasian and Vitellius (ibid. ch. 17, p. 204).

[4] Ibid.

[5] Ibid. ch. 17, p. 205.

[6] Ibid.

superstition, but as he has already explained, the greatest secret of monarchical government is to mislead subjects, 'by cloaking the fear by which they must be checked in the specious name of religion, so that they will fight for slavery as for freedom'.[7] The divine right accorded to a sovereign (and more specifically to a king) is designed to convert the fear that makes people obey a human being into a range of feelings for God, of which fear remains one; and the immense power attributed to God is meant to diminish the tendency of superstitious people to flit from one allegiance to another by generating a constant desire to obey a ruler invested with divine authority.[8] Seen in this light, conceptions of sovereignty such as divine right absolutism are superstitious in the standard sense of exploiting an orchestrated and debilitating fear. As well as propagating false ideas about the nature of political rule, they trade on their ability to excite anxieties which, once they gain a hold, tend to make people's patterns of thought and action inflexible and reduce their capacity for critical and constructive thinking. As fear dulls their confidence and creativity, both sovereign and subjects become less able to create a free way of life.

The fundamental reason for sovereigns to refrain from representing themselves as invested with divine power is, therefore, that this mode of legitimation, being superstitious, opens up a Pandora's box of dangers. However, a ruler who takes this conclusion to heart may be tempted by the different strategy of encouraging subjects to obey by handing out honours that answer to their desire for glory and self-esteem. Again, however, the *Treatise* suggests that this approach tends to inflame the multitude by stimulating invidious and competitive passions that make it harder to rule. Those whom the sovereign honours disdain their equals, while the rest become envious of rewards they have not been given.

With these arguments, Spinoza implicitly rejects the political psychology on which Hobbes had grounded his political theory. According to *Leviathan*, the most effective way to direct a person's passions is to appeal above all to their fear, and then to their desire for honour.[9] The *Treatise* disagrees. Our knowledge of history confirms the psychologically grounded truth that, although each of these strategies may secure short-term advantages, neither is suited to achieving a free way of life, because fear generates hatred, and the desire for

---

[7] Ibid. p. 7, Preface.
[8] Ibid. p. 6, Preface.
[9] Thomas Hobbes, *Leviathan*, ed. Richard Tuck (Cambridge: Cambridge University Press, 1996), chs. 10 and 27.

honour brings with it the destructive passions of envy and disdain.[10] If the sovereigns of republics are to survive and flourish, they must search for more effective ways of creating the peace and security on which freedom depends. But to which histories should they look for inspiration? On which past republics should a state such as the United Provinces try to model itself?[11]

An obvious and much-studied candidate was Rome; but Dutch seventeenth-century writers tended to break with the long humanist tradition of treating Roman history as a fount of political instruction, and Spinoza is no exception. Rather than focusing on the merits of the ancient republic, he tends to dwell on the obtuseness of its leaders and the turbulence of its history. One reason for this lies, perhaps, in the fact that the United Provinces had its own historical reasons for disparaging the Romans. Reviving their own past, early-modern Dutch writers represented the expulsion of the Spanish as a reiteration of an earlier struggle against Rome by their ancestors, the Batavians. The story of the Batavian Revolt (recounted in Tacitus's *Annals* and other classical sources)[12] was rapidly transformed into a heroic precedent designed to show that the Dutch had always been an independent nation and that, far from being a constitutional innovation, the modern Dutch state had simply restored the ancient freedoms of the people. Versions of this narrative were defended by a series of influential political, historical, and jurisprudential writers, who explored the similarities between ancient and modern government in the Netherlands.[13] Grotius, in particular, offered a detailed account of the Batavian constitution, representing it as an uncanny anticipation of the federal system of the Dutch republic, and painting the Batavians as paragons of republican virtue

[10] Spinoza, *Tractatus Theologico-Politicus*, ch. 17.

[11] On Venice as a model republic, see E. O. G. Haitsma Mulier, *The Myth of Venice and Dutch Republican Thought in the Seventeenth Century* (Assen: Gorcum, 1980).

[12] Cornelius Tacitus, *Histories 4–5. Annals 1–3*, trans. C. H. Moore, *Loeb Classical Library* (Cambridge, Mass.: Harvard University Press, 1931) *Histories*, Book 4.IV. Dutch histories of the Batavian revolt contained 'lavish marginal references to Tacitus, Pliny, Strabo—any classical source making mention of the Batavians'. Simon Schama, *The Embarrassment of Riches: An Interpretation of Dutch Culture in the Golden Age* (London: Collins, 1987), p. 77.

[13] Schama cites Emmanuel Van Meteren, *Belgische ofte Nederlantsche Historian van Onser Tidjen* (1605); Wouter Van Goudhoeven, *D'oude chronijke ende historien von Holland* (s'Gravenhage, 1636); P. C. Hooft, *Nederlande Historien* (Amsterdam, 1642); Joh Gijsius, *Oorsprong en Voortgang der Neder-Lantsche Beroeten ende Ellendicheden* (Leiden?, 1616). Schama, *Embarrassment*, pp. 76–80. Black notes that the historical map of the Low Countries made by Ortelius in the 1590s purported to depict the area in the Roman period, but 'consists of the seventeen provinces belonging to the Hapsburgs, creating a sense of territorial coherence that was misplaced for the earlier age'. Jeremy Black, *Maps and History: Constructing Images of the Past* (New Haven: Yale University Press, 1997), p. 10. Quoted in Raia Prokhovnik, *Spinoza and Republicanism* (Basingstoke: Palgrave Macmillan, 2004), p. 38.

who had ruled themselves by periodic popular assemblies, had been led by *primores* rather than kings, and had fiercely defended their independence.[14]

This anti-Roman myth, extolled in plays and prints as well as treatises, portrayed the valiant struggle of an independent republic against a conquering empire.[15] But it was told alongside an arguably even more powerful narrative, in which the United Provinces figured as the New Israel, and its constitution was represented as a revival of the divine law given to Moses. Although Spinoza mentions the Batavians in passing, it is principally to the so-called Hebrew Republic that he looks for examples of good and bad government.

During the early years of its history, the image of the United Provinces as the New Zion had played a potent legitimating role. Just as the Jews had liberated themselves from Pharaoh, so the Dutch had thrown off their Spanish oppressors and, by setting up a republic, had established a society modelled on one ordained by God himself. These analogies were enthusiastically propagated by Protestants of various kinds, by scholarly Hebraists, and by statesmen from all political parties. The paintings on the walls of Amsterdam's town hall showed scenes from the Old Testament alongside heroic episodes from the Dutch past; plays and epics compared the United Provinces' sufferings and achievements with those of the Jews; and the comparison was pressed home in hymns, sermons, pamphlets, and political speeches. Addressing the Assembly of Provincial States in 1650, the Grand Pensionary Jacob Cats declared that the Hebrew Republic 'corresponded wholly to this state'.[16] In a similar vein, Constantijn L'Empereur compared the Calvinist church to the tabernacle of the Jews. Much as the former had been carried through several nations before coming to rest in Jerusalem, he claimed, the Church had finally arrived in the United Provinces, where it had been 'transmuted, as it were, into an utterly immovable edifice'.[17]

---

[14] Hugo Grotius, *Liber de antiquitate republicae batavicorum* (1610). See Schama, *Embarrassment*, p. 76.

[15] Ibid. pp. 78–83; Arthur Weststeijn, 'The Power of "Pliant Stuff"': Fables and Frankness in Seventeenth-Century Dutch Republicanism', *Journal of the History of Ideas*, 72, no. 1 (2011).

[16] L. V(an) A(itzema), *Herstelde Leeuw of Discours Over't Gepasseerde in De Vereenigde Nedelanden in 'Tjaer Ende 1651* (Amsterdam, 1652), p. 187. Quoted in Haitsma Mulier, *Myth of Venice*, p. 121.

[17] Aaron L. Katchen, *Christian Hebraists and Dutch Rabbis: Seventeenth Century Apologetics and the Study of Maimonides' Mishneh Torah* (Cambridge, Mass.: Harvard University Press, 1984), p. 81. L'Empereur was a professor of Hebrew at the University of Leiden from 1627–46, and wrote a guide to the Talmud. Amongst his many works was a translation of the chapters on idolatry from Maimonides' *Mishneh Torah* (1641). See Eric Nelson, *The Hebrew Republic: Jewish Sources and the Transformation of European Political Thought* (Cambridge, Mass.: Harvard University Press, 2010), p. 15.

Popular representations of Amsterdam as Jerusalem and of the River Scheldt as the Red Sea were complemented by more scholarly explorations of the Hebrew state. Drawing on the works of Josephus and a variety of Talmudic texts, Dutch authors described the historical phases of the Hebrew constitution and explained how it was and should be mirrored in the contemporary United Provinces. According to Althusius, for example, 'no state has been established since the beginning of the world which was more wisely and more perfectly organized than the Jewish state'; moreover, the best replication of its arrangements was to be found in 'the cities, constitutions and customs... of the confederated provinces of the Netherlands'.[18] His view was echoed by Grotius, who argued in an early work (unpublished in his lifetime) that the constitution of the United Provinces should be made to resemble that of the Hebrews even more closely than it did;[19] and the same theme was elaborated at length in 1617, when Grotius's friend and contemporary, Petrus Cunaeus, published his *De Republica Hebraeorum*.[20] Cunaeus was a Hebraist and professor of Latin at the University of Leiden, where he also taught politics and law. In the *Preface* of his book, addressed to the Estates of Holland and West Frisia, he reminds the Estates that the Hebrew republic is 'very like your own', and praises it as the most exemplary and holy in the world. Repeating an opinion held by Josephus, he remarks that, although people think of the Greeks as the great law makers, Greek legislators lacked the stature of Moses, 'the first writer and publisher of laws' who taught the Hebrew people 'what was right or wrong, just or unjust, and by what decrees the commonwealth was to be established'.[21] The state that Moses established therefore provides a constitutional model; but its history also contains important lessons. As long as the Hebrews maintained concord, as though their whole state were a single city,[22] they went from strength to strength; but when Jeroboam 'changed the old religion into a vain and senseless

---

[18] Johannes Althusius, *Politica methodica digesta*, trans. Frederick Smith Carney (Indianapolis: Liberty Fund, 1995). Quoted in Lea Campos Boralevi, 'Classical Foundational Myths of European Republicanism: The Jewish Commonwealth', in *Republicanism: A Shared European Heritage*, ed. Martin van Gelderen and Quentin Skinner (Cambridge: Cambridge University Press, 2002), vol. 1., p. 257.

[19] Hugo Grotius, 'De Republica Emendanda (1601)' (The Hague: 1984).

[20] Petrus Cunaeus, *De Republica Hebraeorum*, ed. and intro. Lea Campos Boralevi (Florence: Centro Editoriale Toscano, 1996). Cunaeus was a pupil of Scaliger and had studied Hebrew with Drusius. He was a careful reader of Maimonides' *Mishneh Torah* and uses it as an authoritative source of evidence about the Hebrew Republic.

[21] Cunaeus, De Republica Hebraeorum, p. 37.

[22] Ibid. p. 9.

superstition', war broke out between the tribes and the commonwealth collapsed. This should be a warning to the leaders of Holland and West Frisia, many of whose subjects are already embroiled in religious conflict. They should 'apply seasonable remedies to this distemper, lest your flourishing affairs receive some detriment . . . more pernicious than foreign war, famine or pestilence'.[23]

De Republica Hebraeorum traces the history of the Jews from the founding of the Hebrew state by Moses to the time of Jesus Christ, and ends with a sequence of commonly-expressed anti-Jewish sentiments. Because the Jews refused to recognize the Messiah, God rejected them, 'and to this day they eat pottage and deplore their birthright'.[24] However, since the Bible promises that they will one day return to God, 'we cannot be altogether averse from them, as if they were given up to public hatred, when as yet so great hopes are remaining for them'.[25] While 'all the Jews at this day are of a very base and illiberal disposition',[26] this is simply the result of their history. 'Verily, the same day that deprived them of that fair light of liberty, and struck the sceptre out of their hands, did also abase the edge of their ingenious spirits . . . Servitude dwarfs the mind and enchains the spirit, and chokes all the seeds of generosity. What high thought can they possibly have, who for so many years throughout the whole world, have been wearied out with so great scorn and contumely? Whom children in contempt have pulled by the sleeve and men by the beard? Lastly upon whom all the fury of the Caesars has spent itself?'[27] Thus, 'whithersoever they turn themselves, their night goes along too, and overshadows them; nor shall it be dispelled before they have thoroughly smarted for their ingratitude and their obstinacy, and the hardness of their hearts'.[28]

Because Jewish history, as Cunaeus portrays it, culminates in such desolation, his warning to the Estates is a grave one: if you sacrifice constitutional arrangements resembling those that God himself ordained, you too may lose your

---

[23] Ibid. p. 23.

[24] Ibid. p. 357. For example, in 1637 Voetius had accepted the blood-libel, and had argued that ritual infanticide accorded well with a people who denied the doctrine of justification by faith. Gisbertus Voetius, *Disputationes Theologicae Selectae*, 5 vols. (Utrecht, 1648–69), ii, pp. 77–102. See John Marshall, *John Locke, Toleration and Early Enlightenment Culture: Religious Intolerance and Arguments for Religious Toleration in Early Modern and 'Early Enlightenment' Europe* (Cambridge: Cambridge University Press, 2006), p. 348; Peter T. van Rooden, 'Conceptions of Judaism in the Seventeenth Century Dutch Republic', in *Christianity and Judaism*, ed. D. Wood (Oxford: Oxford University Press, 1992).

[25] Cunaeus, *Republica Hebraeorum*, p. 361.

[26] Ibid.

[27] Ibid. pp. 363–5.

[28] Ibid. p. 381.

freedom and be enslaved. But what are these arrangements and what part did they play in the success of the Hebrew state? As we shall see, Cunaeus emphasizes three features, all of which reappear in Spinoza's own analysis. First, as Josephus had argued, the state set up by Moses was a theocracy, 'that is, a commonwealth whose ruler and president is God alone',[29] in which the magistrates were not lords and masters, but keepers of the laws and ministers (*custodes* et *ministri*),[30] and in which the laws themselves did not change.[31] At the same time, however, sovereignty or *maiestas* belonged to the people,[32] 'and this majesty of the sceptre ... continued theirs, although the state of the commonwealth was sometimes altered, and the power was in the hand, one while of the best men and the priests, another while of the kings and princes ... For what people so ever enjoys a commonwealth of their own and a law of their own, may justly glory in their empire and their sceptre'.[33] The Jewish people were therefore sovereign under God, and retained this status until they ceased to be bound by the Mosaic Law.[34] Secondly, the Hebrew constitution as it evolved after Moses' death had a federal structure; and a final, defining feature of the Hebrew constitution was its Agrarian Law, which guaranteed a level of economic equality. Each of the twelve tribes was given an equal amount of land, and 'in order that the wealth of some might not tend to the opposition of the rest', it was decreed that people who had been forced to sell were able to redeem their land every fifty years, at the Jubilee.[35] By contrast with Rome, this arrangement ensured that agriculture was maintained and the corruption of urban life avoided.[36]

---

[29] Ibid. p. 41.   [30] Ibid. p. 43.

[31] '[S]ome peoples have entrusted the supreme political power to monarchies, others to oligarchies, yet others to the masses. Our lawgiver, however, was attracted by none of these forms of polity, but gave to his constitution the form of what—if a forced expression be permitted—may be termed a "theocracy", placing all sovereignty and authority in the hands of God. To him he persuaded all to look, as the author of all blessings, both those which are common to all mankind, and those which they had won for themselves by prayer, in the crises of their history'. Flavius Josephus, *The Life. Against Apion*, trans. H. St J. Thackeray, *Loeb Classical Library* (London: Heinemann, 1926), p. 359. Quoted in Nelson, *Hebrew Republic*, p. 89.

[32] Cunaeus, *Republica Hebraeorum*, pp. 189ff.

[33] Ibid. pp. 191–3.

[34] The view that the people do not lose their sovereignty by changing their ruler was widely accepted, and was also defended by Grotius in *De Iure Praedae* (1604). Martin van Gelderen, 'Aristotelians, Monarchomachs and Republicans: Sovereignty and *Respublica Mixta* in Dutch and German Political Thought 1580–1650', in *Republicanism: A Shared European Heritage*, ed. Martin van Gelderen and Quentin Skinner (Cambridge: Cambridge University Press, 2002), vol. II, pp. 201–4.

[35] Cunaeus, *Republica Hebraeorum*, p. 53.

[36] Ibid. pp. 63, 73.

Cunaeus uses his case study to praise the virtues of a federal republic in which sovereignty rests ultimately with the people. However, while this was a common line of argument, it was not the only way to read the history of the Jewish state, and modern authors characteristically organized their interpretations of it around their own political preferences. We find this phenomenon across Europe. To take only two examples, Calvin cites the case of the Hebrews as confirmation of his view that aristocracy, or a system compounded of aristocracy and democracy, far excels all others. God 'ordained among the Israelites an aristocracy bordering on democracy, since he willed to keep them in the best condition'.[37] Hobbes, by contrast, contended that Moses alone held sovereignty, and that after the prophet's death the Hebrew state became a sacerdotal kingdom.[38] The same diversity of interpretation existed within the United Provinces, where writers of different political persuasions stressed the aspects of the ancient Hebrew republic that best supported their own points of view, and the *Treatise* follows this pattern. Its narrative echoes many of the political morals drawn by Cunaeus and other supporters of a republican system of government. At the same time, it is designed to support Spinoza's philosophical account of the state by illustrating his conception of an original contract, defending his commitment to popular sovereignty and vindicating his conception of law.

Founding a theocracy

The *Treatise* divides the history of the Hebrew state into two phases, the first of which runs from its foundation to the death of Moses. When the Israelites fled from Egypt, they ceased to be bound by any contract or *pactum* and re-entered a state of nature where there were no legal limits to individual natural right. 'Each could decide anew whether he wanted to keep it, or surrender it and transfer it to someone else'.[39] Acting on Moses' advice, the Israelites decided to transfer their right to God and, as the book of Exodus records, promised with one voice to obey God's commands. 'By an explicit covenant and an oath they freely surrendered and transferred their right to God, without being compelled by force or terrified by threats'.[40] They thus created a state of which God was

---

[37] Jean Calvin, *Institutes of the Christian Religion*, ed. and trans. John Thomas McNeill and Ford Lewis Battles, *The Library of Christian Classics* (Philadelphia: Westminster Press, 1960–1), IV.xx.8.

[38] Hobbes, *Leviathan*, ch. 40.

[39] Spinoza, *Tractatus Theologico-Politicus*, ch. 5, p. 75, ch. 17, p. 205.

[40] Ibid. ch. 17, p. 205.

the sovereign, and in which 'civil law and religion were one and the same thing'.[41] However, as Spinoza goes on to explain, they found themselves in a curious condition. Since they 'were not bound by any law except that revealed by God', their state was formally a theocracy. But because its theocratic status was upheld only by the Israelites' beliefs, it 'consisted more in opinion than fact'. The Israelites' idea of their deity as a theocratic sovereign was a fiction, and only their commitment to it made it efficacious. So although they believed that they had transferred their right to God, they had not in fact succeeded in doing so. Instead, they had entered into a covenant whereby, 'as in a democracy', everyone remained equal. Each person retained an equal right to consult God and to receive and interpret his laws, and 'all equally held the whole administration of the state'.[42]

The state therefore answered simultaneously to two descriptions. As in a democracy, 'the people retained absolutely the right of sovereignty'. But as in a theocracy, the people were bound to obey laws imposed by God. Because the founding agreement to obey God was simultaneously a covenant to obey themselves, obedience to God *was* obedience to the people, and obedience to the people *was* obedience to God.[43] This dual-aspect conception of the covenant is critical to Spinoza's account of the Hebrew state, because it enables him to argue that, as long as one version of the founding contract was upheld, so too was its counterpart. As long as God continued to be the sole legislator, sovereignty continued to reside with the people. Moreover, on the strength of this interpretation, Spinoza can agree with Cunaeus that the Israelites retained their sovereignty throughout much of their history, despite the fact that their government underwent a series of changes, most notably when Moses' powers were divided after his death. At first glance, these modifications look like fundamental constitutional transformations that abolish whatever sovereignty the people originally held. But in Spinoza's view they are not. As long as the state's human rulers were not its legislators, but continued to receive the law from God, popular sovereignty endured, only ceasing when the people became subject to kings who took the task of law-making into their own hands.[44]

This is an elusive position. It allows that a people can be sovereign without recognizing its own sovereignty, can remain sovereign in a constitution where

[41] Ibid. ch. 17, p. 206.

[42] Ibid.

[43] Ibid. ch. 19, pp. 230–1.

[44] See Étienne Balibar, 'Jus-Pactum-Lex: On the Constitution of the Subject in the *Theologico-Political Treatise*', in *The New Spinoza*, ed. Warren Montag and Ted Stolze (Minneapolis, Minn.: University of Minnesota Press, 1997).

its power is exercised on its behalf, and can symbolically vest its sovereignty in an imaginary or fictive idea of a legislating God. However, while Spinoza's interpretation of Hebrew sovereignty has novel elements, it is by no means entirely original. The claims that God was the sovereign of the Hebrew Republic, that its rulers were consequently God's representatives rather than sovereigns, and that its religious and civil law were one, went back to Josephus and had been taken up by Grotius and Cunaeus.[45] Thus, when Spinoza sets out to integrate his version of the story into his philosophical account of the state, he is covering familiar territory.

A first continuity between the *Treatise's* abstract analysis of sovereignty and its history of the Hebrews lies in the assumption that sovereignty fundamentally consists in the right to make law. This was accordingly God's only role within the Hebrew constitution, and other political responsibilities, such as interpreting or implementing his edicts, could consequently be distributed among human actors without undermining divine (and hence popular) supremacy. In addition, the Hebrew Republic was founded on an explicit, voluntary *pactum*, made by people who already possessed the normative concepts that are essential preconditions of contracting. While their escape from Egypt put the Israelites back into a state of nature, their experience of political life had given them the idea of a binding *pactum*, which they were able to put to use. However, their covenant derived its forcefulness, in a manner for which Spinoza has already allowed, from elements of fantasy. The Israelites elevated an imaginary conception of a legislating God into a symbolic representation of themselves as a sovereign people, and in doing so provided an external and vastly enhanced image of their own sovereign power. Rather than conceiving their sovereignty as that of a group of displaced tribes wandering in a desert, they projected it onto the figure of an omnipotent deity whose capacity to legislate on their behalf was backed by an infinite power to punish and protect.

Addressing this last point, Spinoza traces the process that enabled the newly exiled Israelites to create the simultaneously democratic and theocratic state for which their founding contract laid the ground. Echoing a standard analysis of the effects of servitude to which Cunaeus also appeals, the *Treatise* describes them as 'crude in their understanding and weakened by wretched slavery', and thus as incapable 'of ordaining legislation wisely'. Sovereign as they were, they were not equipped to live democratically in the manner that Spinoza regards as optimal, and therefore followed what he has already characterized as another

---

[45] Nelson, *Hebrew Republic*, pp. 89–91.

effective strategy for creating a free state—that of delegating power to a charismatic leader. In the circumstances, 'sovereignty had to remain in the hands of one person only, who would command the others and compel them by force, and who would prescribe laws and afterwards interpret them'.[46] This further transition occurred when the experience of hearing God's voice filled the Jews with such terror that they asked Moses to communicate with the deity on their behalf, and agreed to obey any commands that God might give him. In doing so, 'they clearly abolished the first covenant and unconditionally transferred to Moses the right to consult God and interpret his edicts'.[47] Moses consequently became the 'supreme authority'—the sole interpreter of the law, and the supreme judge 'whom no one could judge, and who was the sole agent of God among the Hebrews'. As the *Treatise* points out, his position closely resembled that of a monarch[48]; but there remained a crucial difference. Unlike a monarch, Moses did not make the law. Because he was a prophet, he was able to rule in accordance with decrees revealed to him by God, and thus to uphold the sovereignty of the Hebrew people. By giving him the power to interpret God's commands, the Israelites moved from a situation in which, despite their symbolic allegiance to God, they were not effectively bound by any edicts, to one where a human agent acquired the right to represent God and prescribe an obligatory way of life. With this transition, law in Spinoza's ordinary sense of the term came into existence. So, too, did a viable state, in which laws could be interpreted, promulgated, and enforced, and an orderly way of life sustained.

While this analysis has a number of Dutch antecedents, there is also a pervasive sense throughout Spinoza's account that he is simultaneously drawing and playing on the analysis of sovereignty outlined by Hobbes in *Leviathan*. According to Hobbes, a multitude of people in a state of nature turns itself into a unity when all its individual members covenant with one another to transfer their right to a single agent, who represents their collective will.[49] Moreover, in binding themselves to obey this agent, who 'bears their person' and is their sovereign, the multitude creates a *civitas* or state.[50] As Hobbes puts it, they generate 'that great Leviathan' or 'mortal God', represented on the frontispiece of his book as a gigantic king whose body is made up of, and unifies, the many

---

[46] Spinoza, *Tractatus Theologico-Politicus*, ch. 5, p. 75.

[47] Ibid. ch. 17, p. 207.

[48] Ibid. ch. 19, p. 230.

[49] Hobbes, *Leviathan*, ch. 17, p. 120.

[50] 'The Multitude so united in one Person, is called a COMMON-WEALTH, in latine CIVITAS', ibid. ch. 17, p. 120.

bodies of the members of the multitude.[51] In this celebrated portrait, the mortal God or state is clearly human; but Spinoza's discussion of the first Hebrew covenant introduces the further possibility that the same figure might also be divine. The Israelites agree to transfer their right to God, and to obey only the laws that he commands; and it is their agreement to let God represent their collective will that first unites them. Their mortal God is consequently none other than the immortal God.[52] However, as we have seen, this is a fictional state of affairs, because God does not issue commands. To give themselves an effective government, the Israelites therefore needed to appoint someone capable of representing God's will, and in Spinoza's narrative this is exactly what they did. They appointed a prophet, that is to say, an interpreter (*interpres*) and spokesperson (*orator*) of God and, rather than making Moses a sovereign, made him God's representative.[53] Thus, according to their second covenant, the Israelites remained bound by the terms of their first covenant to obey God as the source of law, but each of them now transferred to Moses their individual right to interpret divine decrees.

By reading Spinoza's account alongside both *Leviathan* and Hobbes's earlier political treatise, *De Cive*, we can clarify this analysis of the Hebrews' two covenants. On one level, Spinoza agrees with Hobbes' pronouncement in *Leviathan* that 'there is no covenant with God, but by mediation of some body that represents God's person'.[54] The Hebrew commonwealth only became an effective state when Moses became God's representative. However, Spinoza seems to combine this view with a different position that Hobbes had advocated nine years earlier. According to *De Cive*, the individual members of a multitude can only subject themselves to a representative once they have entered into a mutual contract, to the effect that each will have an equal voice in choosing a form of representation. This initial contract generates a democracy, and until such an association has been formed, a people cannot enter into a further contract to transfer its collective right to a representative. In Hobbes's view, the second contract annuls the first and turns a democracy into some other kind of state, for example an oligarchy or monarchy. But according to Spinoza the two contracts can complement one another, as they did in the case of the Israelites. The Israelites' first *pactum* constituted a democracy in

[51] Horst Bredekamp, *Thomas Hobbes Visuelle Strategien* (Berlin: Akademie Verlag, 1999); Quentin Skinner, *Hobbes and Republican Liberty* (Cambridge: Cambridge University Press, 2008).
[52] Compare Hobbes, *Leviathan*, ch. 40, where Hobbes discusses the basis of Moses' authority.
[53] *Tractatus Theologico-Politicus*, ch. 1, p. 15.
[54] Ibid. ch. 18, p. 122.

which the collective sovereignty of the people was symbolized by the sovereignty of God. The second *pactum* then duly made Moses God's representative and gave him the right to interpret and impose the law. However, because it did not challenge divine sovereignty, the second *pactum* also did not challenge the ultimate sovereignty of the people.[55] Popular sovereignty therefore continued to exist alongside Moses' power to represent this sovereignty by representing God.

In the first section of the *Treatise*, Spinoza showed how prophetic imagination can posit images of God that exert tremendous power over prophets and people, shaping the courses of action available to them. In his account of the Hebrew Republic he now returns to this theme and explores the part played by collective fictions in creating political entities such as states and sovereigns. Although the Israelites were not in a position to set up and run an explicitly democratic state, they were able to endow themselves with sovereignty by imagining their power as that of God. Moreover, as long as the Israelites' allegiance to God as sole legislator endured, so too did their popular sovereignty.

Once Moses acquired the power to rule, one of the many problems with which he had to contend arose from the fact that his right to interpret the law had been born of fear. When the Israelites had assembled as a body to consult God and had heard him speaking, 'they were so terrified, so stunned by thunder and lightning, that they thought their end was near'.[56] This in turn prompted them to ask Moses to communicate with God on their behalf. But it also meant that he faced the task of ruling a people whose political life was highly imaginative, whose obedience was primarily motivated by anxiety, and who were therefore primed to become superstitious. To transform them into a stable community he needed both to counteract the leanings to inconstancy and conflict that are integral to superstitious ways of life, and to inculcate a habit of voluntary obedience, grounded on a recognition of the benefits of life within the state. At one point, the *Treatise* claims that Moses relied on fear to achieve these ends, teaching the Israelites 'in the way that parents customarily teach children who are lacking in reason', and 'terrifying them with threats'

---

[55] As Spinoza will later explain, 'We have shown that in a democratic state (which comes closest to the natural condition) everyone contracts to act according to the common decision, but not to judge and reason according to the common decision, i.e. because it cannot be that all men think alike, they agreed that the measure that has the most votes has the force of a decree, all the while retaining the authority to repeal such decrees if they saw better ones. The less this freedom of judgment is granted to men, the more we depart from the most natural condition, and hence the more violent is the rule' (Spinoza, *Tractatus Theologico-Politicus*, ch. 20, p. 245).

[56] Ibid. ch. 17, p. 206.

about what would happen if they transgressed the law.[57] For the most part, however, Spinoza takes a different line, contrasting superstitious governments such as those of Alexander or the Ottomans with the wiser and more comforting policies of the Hebrew Republic. Rather than fanning superstition by exploiting the Israelites' anxieties, Moses did his best to ensure 'that the people should do their duty not so much from fear as from devotion', promising that they would be rewarded rather than punished. Moreover, because the laws that he enacted were not severe and did not impose demands that would themselves be a source of anxiety, the memory of old fears gradually gave way to devotion to the law, and superstition became correspondingly less liable to take hold.

As we have already seen, however, the requirements imposed by the Mosaic Law were extremely numerous. The law determined every aspect of life, including, for example, how men shaved, dressed and cut their hair, what signs they put on their doorposts or wore on their foreheads, how they ploughed, sowed, and reaped, and what ceremonies they performed. Such a system, ensuring as it did that 'men should do nothing by their own decision . . . but should confess in all their actions and meditations that they were not their own master in anything, but were completely subject to someone else'[58] may seem to have been calculated to prevent people from developing the kind of critical outlook that, in Spinoza's view, provides the strongest protection against superstition. But he insists that it was well judged. Because the Israelites were incapable of ruling themselves, the only way to create a stable state was to ensure that they 'hung on the words of their ruler'.[59] Without demanding a greater level of self-control than his people could achieve, Moses inculcated and enforced the habit of obedience, gradually transforming them into a united body whose commitment to their law-governed way of life was exceptionally strong. In its first phase, the Hebrew Republic therefore offers a model of an unusually peaceful state, in which popular sovereignty was sustained and civil war was exceedingly rare. Under a regime where there was no distinction between civil and religious law the Israelites lived securely and freely, despite the fact that relatively few of their actions were not subject to legal control.

Maintaining the integrity of the law

Towards the end of his life, Moses bequeathed a new system of government to the Israelites and the state entered on what Spinoza represents as a second constitutional phase. Anticipating a time when the republic would no longer be

---

[57] Ibid. ch. 2, p. 41.   [58] Ibid. ch. 5, p. 76.   [59] Ibid. ch. 5, p. 75.

ruled by a prophet who could communicate directly with God, Moses reinforced God's supreme authority in a variety of ways, thus ensuring that the
state would remain 'neither popular, nor aristocratic, nor monarchical, but
theocratic'.[60] The entire people contributed to the cost of building a temple,
which represented the supreme authority of the state; all citizens swore allegiance to God as their supreme judge and promised to obey him unconditionally; the army swore loyalty to God when it went to war and took the Ark of
the Covenant into battle; and when a military leader was needed to command a
force made up of soldiers drawn from all the tribes, he was 'chosen by God'.[61]
At the same time, Moses instituted what was to prove a fateful change in the
administration of the law. Rather than bequeathing his powers to a successor,
he divided them between different officials or *administratores*, who 'seemed to
be his deputies (*vicarii*), administering the state as if a king were absent rather
than dead'.[62] While the prophet had possessed both the right to consult God
whenever he wanted and the power to interpret and impose the divine law,
these functions were now separated. The leaders of eleven of the twelve tribes
of Israel were made jointly responsible for the security of the state, initially
under the overall military and administrative command of a single *imperator*,
who could impose the law but was not allowed to interpret it. The latter task
fell to the leader of the twelfth and priestly tribe, the Levites. So whereas Moses
had been able to consult God whenever he saw fit, only the *imperator* could
now initiate this process by asking the high priest to petition God on behalf of
the people. Moreover, whereas God's words had, as Spinoza puts it, been
decrees in the mouth of Moses, the high priest could not issue commands but
only answer questions. 'Not until his answers had been accepted by [the
imperator] and his councils did they at last acquire the force of a command
and decree', so that each party held the other in check.[63] Accompanying these
changes was a further shift of power. As a mark of their priestly status, the
Levites were made responsible for the Temple and deprived of the right to own
land. They became the guardians of religion, but also became dependent on the
other tribes for material support.

In the first generation after Moses, the role of *imperator* was held by Joshua,
and that of high priest by Moses' brother Aaron. However, after Joshua's death,

---

[60] Ibid. ch. 17, p. 208.
[61] Ibid. ch. 17, pp. 209, 211.
[62] Ibid. ch. 17, p. 209, ch. 19, p. 234. Cunaeus also says that Moses made his magistrates not
masters of the law but their guardians and servants. Cunaeus, *Republica Hebraeorum*, Book I, ch. 1.
This may well be taken from Josephus.
[63] Spinoza, *Tractatus Theologico-Politicus*, ch. 17, p. 209.

his powers passed to the eleven leaders or *principes* of the tribes, each of whom became responsible for consulting the high priest about the affairs for which he was responsible, 'and administering all matters of war and peace without exception'. The tribes continued to be united by the fact that they were bound to obey God's decrees, and to this extent were fellow citizens (*concives*). But once a tribe had its own territory, and a *princeps* who possessed the right to found and fortify cities, appoint judges, ensure that the divine law interpreted by the high priest was enforced, and decide on war and peace, it increasingly ran its own affairs. In relation to one another, the tribes were related not as citizens, but as allies (*confoederatae*)—independent states who had agreed to co-operate, but whose agreement was only binding for as long as it remained advantageous.[64]

Reflecting on this state of affairs, Spinoza first relates it to the ancient Batavian Republic, explicitly comparing the history of the Jews with that of the Dutch. The situation of the tribes was, he claims, 'almost like that of the *Confoederati Belgarum Ordines* (as long as you discount the common temple)'.[65] What had been a single state had become a confederation of smaller states under a single sovereign legislator, each largely responsible for ruling itself. In stressing the federal character of the Batavian Republic, Spinoza broadly follows Grotius' celebrated interpretation of its constitution. But on another key point the *Treatise* parts company with Grotius and with Cunaeus too. As we have seen, Spinoza is adamant that only Moses, and later the high priests, possessed authority to interpret the law. However, according to Josephus and a series of Talmudic writers, this power also lay with the Sanhedrin. Taking his lead from these authorities, Grotius had argued that the Sanhedrin possessed juris-diction over religious matters, including the right to interpret the law and to elect the high priest.[66] Cunaeus had agreed that Joshua and the Judges who followed him were supported by three councils, the most powerful of which was the Sanhedrin, made up of seventy senators selected for their wisdom from noble families and the Levites.[67] This body was responsible for appointing town magistrates, and also functioned as a supreme court. It made statutes in sacred matters, interpreted the law, and decided after consulting the people whether the state should go to war.[68] Spinoza, however, is unconvinced. The rabbis have made a mistake, he claims, 'and many Christians are as foolish as they are'.[69] Defending his earlier contention that there is no textual basis for these

---

[64] Ibid. ch. 17, p. 210.   [65] Ibid.
[66] Nelson, *Hebrew Republic*, pp. 100–3.   [67] Cunaeus, *Republica Hebraeorum*, p. 241.
[68] Ibid. pp. 342–5.   [69] Spinoza, *Tractatus Theologico-Politicus*, ch. 17, p. 210fn.

accounts of the Sanhedrin's role in government, Spinoza allows that Moses appointed seventy *coadjutores* to help him rule, but insists that they never had any independent power to interpret or judge the law. Throughout the history of the Hebrew Republic, the high priest remained the supreme interpreter of the law, and was never subject to any higher human authority. Instead, sovereign powers continued to be divided between the high priest and the leaders of the tribes, in such a way that religious and civil authority were inextricably intertwined and the ultimate sovereignty of the people remained intact.

What is at stake in this dispute? Authors such as Grotius and Cunaeus are anxious to present the Sanhedrin as a civil rather than a religious power. In claiming that it had authority to interpret the law they are claiming that this right lay with a civil body, thus holding up a model of the state in which civil officials have at least some control over legislation. In doing so, they are, as we shall see, trying to establish a precedent for their own view that, in a modern republic, the right to make and impose law should belong to the civil sovereign. While Spinoza entirely agrees with their conclusion, he does not attempt to derive it from the Hebrew case. To do so he would have to allow that, within the Hebrew Republic, authority to interpret the law was divided between the high priest and the Sanhedrin; and it will be vital to his own conception of a free state that no such division occurs. Rather than giving way on this point, he prefers to go out on a limb by dismissing the textual evidence on which Cunaeus and other rely, a bold strategy that leaves his interpretation of Jewish history highly exposed, and sets him apart from a generally accepted position.

Turning to the benefits of the Hebrews' theocratic division of right, the *Treatise* claims that it was it able to 'contain both rulers and ruled so that the latter did not become rebels and the former did not become tyrants'.[70] In a detailed analysis, Spinoza first identifies a series of checks on the powers of tribal leaders. A sovereign acquires a potentially dangerous amount of power, he asserts, when it both interprets and administers the law, because it can then use legal mechanisms to justify actions contrary to the good of the state. Since those who administer sovereignty are always eager to cover their crimes with a pretext of right, and to persuade the people that they have acted honestly, a state must be designed to prevent them from misusing the law for these nefarious ends. One way to achieve this outcome is to divide the right to

---

[70] Ibid. ch. 17, p. 212.

interpret and administer the law, as happened in the Hebrew state after Moses. A further method is to ensure that the law is widely known and understood, and here again the Jewish state serves as a model. Its people were obliged to study the law, and were instructed in it every seven years by the high priest. They were consequently in a position to keep a watch on their leaders and protest if they began to use existing legislation improperly. At the same time—and particularly in a state where the normative significance of civil law was shaped by the fact that it was simultaneously the law of God and the basis of popular sovereignty—the knowledge that the people were well informed served to restrain their rulers. In Spinoza's view, leaders who abused their power 'could not escape their subjects' extreme hatred, since there is usually no greater hate than theological hate'.[71]

Four further provisions also limited the tribal leaders' misuse of sovereign power. They were chosen on the basis of age and virtue rather than nobility or hereditary right, and were probably drawn, Spinoza speculates, from a select group of families.[72] Because leaders could only alter the law after consulting the high priest, but usually hesitated to compromise their own authority by seeking advice, they tended to interpret the law conservatively rather than introducing innovations. Furthermore, they were constrained by the need to be able to face down new prophets. A leader who diminished his power, for example by implementing novel and unpopular laws, made himself vulnerable to prophets who claimed that their revelations gave them privileged insight into who should rule. Finally, Hebrew armies were made up of citizens rather than mercenaries. Reiterating a traditional republican claim, Spinoza appeals to Quintus Curtius Rufus to illustrate his conviction that, because citizen armies pay for the freedom and glory of the state with their own blood, they cannot be used to suppress the people. Their loyalty to the populace limits what a ruler can achieve.

Although Spinoza claims that the constraints he has so far listed were made particularly effective by the Jews' allegiance to God, the constraints themselves are not special to theocracies. However, when the *Treatise* turns to examine the checks that the Hebrew constitution imposed on the Levites and the people, the distinctively theocratic character of the state, and the crucial position of its law, begin to plays a larger role. Since the authority of the Levites lay entirely in their right to interpret the law, they had an overwhelming interest in upholding it. 'Their whole fortune and honour depended on interpreting the laws

---

[71] Ibid.   [72] Ibid. ch. 17, p. 211.

truly'.[73] Furthermore, both the nature of the law and the way it was taught made it central to the life of the people. The equation of obedience with piety, the imposition of an intensive training in reverence for the law and the Temple, and the requirement to follow legal decrees governing all aspects of everyday life, gave the law a unique significance and inculcated the habit of submission. At the same time, the Israelites' belief that, as the children of God, they were the enemies of other nations and were required by piety to hate them, bound the people to the state. They were convinced that it would be disgraceful to leave a sacred land where daily life constituted worship, where exile was too abhorrent to be used even as a punishment, and where the idea of betraying one's country was unthinkable.[74]

This exceptional patriotism, not to say xenophobia, was reinforced by the benefits that the law guaranteed. One source of gratification lay in its compulsory periods of varied and joyful leisure. 'I do not think', Spinoza comments, 'that anything more effective can be devised for steering people's hearts in a certain direction. For hearts are won by nothing more than by the joy that arises from devotion'.[75] A second and equally substantial advantage was the Agrarian Law, which rescued people from poverty and maintained a level of material equality. 'Things could only go well with Hebrew citizens inside their own country, whereas outside it were the utmost harm and dishonour'.[76] In this account, as in his discussion of the contractual basis of the Hebrew state, Spinoza again makes it clear that the tools and resources through which obedience and security are created are extremely diverse. Individuals are motivated to obey by many factors, which shape their affects, material desires, convictions, habits, and expectations, and to sustain their loyalty a state needs to be sensitive to all these variables. In the case of the Israelites, circumstances combined to create a people whose commitment to upholding their laws, and thus maintaining the peace and security in which they lived, was exceptionally deep. Supported by the constitutional checks that Spinoza has itemized, their outlook put unusual pressure on their leaders to respect the law, and encouraged an exceptionally cohesive culture of obedience, patriotism, and piety.

Why, then, did the state eventually disintegrate? As we have seen, what united the Hebrews after the death of Moses was a commitment to obey the law of God as the High Priest interpreted it, and in doing so to abide by a covenant that symbolized the collective sovereignty of the people. Over the course of the state's history, this sovereignty was exercised on the people's

---

[73] Ibid. ch. 17, p. 212.   [74] Ibid. ch. 17, p. 214.
[75] Ibid. ch. 17, p. 216.   [76] Ibid.

behalf by rulers of various kinds, but in the state's last constitutional phase it was gradually undermined. While it was not completely cancelled until the people of Israel became subject to the King of Babylon and could no longer obey God as their supreme legislator, this defeat was only possible because the state was by that stage already weak and divided.[77] The crucial question is therefore what caused it to decline.[78]

A long tradition of Dutch Christian writers, including Althusius, Grotius, and Cunaeus, had represented the Hebrew constitution as a perfect set of arrangements, fit to be imitated by contemporary states. The fact that the ancient republic had deteriorated and collapsed was not in their view a comment on its original constitution, but an indictment of its people, whose stiff-necked obstinacy provoked God to punish them by allowing their constitution to develop as it did. One of the notable features of the *Treatise* is its forthright rejection of this explanation. Since human beings are much the same the whole world over, Spinoza objects, the stubbornness of a particular people could only be explained by its laws and customs; but if we look at the laws and customs of the later phases of the Hebrew state, we do not find that they are framed to encourage obstinacy. Rather, the stabilizing features of the law came to be offset after Moses' death by a constitutional aberration, namely the Levites' dependence on the other tribes. If Moses had given each tribe a stake in supporting the law by decreeing that all first-born sons were to be priests, he would have effectively guaranteed the security of the state.[79] However, because the Levites were the only group who had not defiled themselves by worshipping the golden calf, he gave the role to them alone.[80] Unfortunately, this arrangement set up an insurmountable structural tension, which first manifested itself during Moses' lifetime and was never satisfactorily resolved.[81] The other tribes resented the Levites' religious authority and chafed against their duty to support them. The Levites, meanwhile, exacerbated this resentment by continually reproaching their compatriots for failing to live up to the law. 'So there was continual murmuring, and then weariness with feeding men who were

---

[77]   Ibid. ch. 19, p. 230.

[78]   Josephus claims that when the Israelites chose to be ruled by a human king they ceased to be ruled by 'the best of rulers' namely God. Flavius Josephus, *Jewish Antiquities*, ed. and trans. H. St J. Thackeray and Louis H. Feldman, 8 vols. (Cambridge, Mass.: Harvard University Press, 1930–65), vi.357. Quoted in Nelson, *Hebrew Republic*, p. 90.

[79]   Spinoza, *Tractatus Theologico-Politicus*, ch. 17, pp. 218–19.

[80]   Ibid. ch. 17, p. 217.

[81]   Ibid. ch. 17, p. 219.

idle, envied, and not related to them by blood, especially when food was expensive'.[82]

In these circumstances, Spinoza concludes, it is hardly surprising that loyalty to the religious law should have tailed off. But this process gradually brought down the Republic. To circumvent the Levites' power, the leaders of the tribes turned to false prophets for religious inspiration, thus degrading true religion and creating theological dissent within the polity. By way of response, the priests struggled for power to make decrees and handle affairs of state.[83] Worse still, the disaffected people eventually demanded to be led by ordinary kings, thus prompting the priests to unite all sovereign powers in their own persons and turn themselves into monarchs. In doing so, the Levites ushered in a monarchical form of government that eclipsed the theocratic form of the state, and destroyed the sovereignty of the people by making it impossible for them to honour their obligation to obey the divine law. The tribes became fellow citizens, 'not in virtue of the divine law and the priesthood, but in virtue of the kings'.[84]

As Spinoza reads it, this turn to monarchy was not merely a temporary low point in Hebrew history, but marked an irrevocable transition to an inherently less secure and peaceful form of government, in which the opportunity to live freely was structurally restricted. Because the power of a monarch is always vulnerable to that of the people, the kings needed to secure their status, and consequently tended to become tyrannical. 'What can a king tolerate less than ruling precariously?' However, this in turn generated rebellion, often provoked in the Hebrew case by prophets, and led to endless 'dissension and civil war'.[85] Once theocracy had given way to monarchy, the chance of restoring a republic was exceedingly slim, and did not in fact occur.

Learning from history

Spinoza's explanation of the downfall of the Hebrew state appeals, as one would expect, to general political and psychological factors that he takes to apply to all human communities. (For example, people normally resent being hectored by authorities for whose upkeep they are having to pay, and making one group subject to the arbitrary will of another is liable to generate discord and insecurity.) However, he also touches on a theological debate surrounding a highly specific question about the Hebrew Republic: why did a divinely-

---

[82] Ibid. ch. 17, p. 218.   [83] Ibid. ch. 18, p. 222.
[84] Ibid. ch. 17, p. 219.   [85] Ibid. ch. 17, p. 220.

inspired leader such as Moses allow his sovereign powers to be so clumsily divided, in a way that sowed the seeds for the collapse of a theocratic state? A popular explanation—offered in the Bible, repeated in Tacitus' *Annals*, and echoed by various Dutch authors including the De la Court brothers, contended that God promulgated a law that would ultimately have disastrous consequences because he wanted to punish the Israelites for their disobedience.[86] This view runs directly against the grain of the *Treatise's* philosophical outlook, but Spinoza nevertheless appears to accept it, albeit unwillingly. 'I cannot sufficiently marvel', he comments, 'that there was so much anger in the heavenly heart that [God] established the laws themselves, which always aim only at the honour, well-being and security of the whole people, with the intention of taking vengeance and punishing the people'.[87] It is difficult to know what to make of this remark. Since Spinoza denies that the deity possesses anthropomorphic properties, he cannot intend his philosophical readers to take it literally. (They will surely rather conclude that the system of necessary causes that constitutes God or nature determined a Hebrew constitution that lasted for a certain period of time but no longer.) He must therefore be talking in imaginative or theological terms, but it remains hard to see why he should do so, since the idea of a vengeful and angry God resurrects a stance he has consistently opposed, and conflicts with several of the conclusions he has defended. However, while Spinoza cannot wholeheartedly accept the claim that the downfall of the Hebrew state was the fruit of divine vengeance, the image that it evokes draws attention to what he regards as a significant truth: that the Jews paid an enduringly high price for abandoning their form of popular sovereignty and replacing it by a monarchical regime. In place of a secure way of life governed by a law that upheld the common good, they found themselves engulfed by civil war, conquest, and slavery. As we have seen, Cunaeus and others had used their interpretations of the history of the Hebrew Republic to warn the United Provinces of its own vulnerabilities. Spinoza now follows their example, and goes on to draw his own morals from the story he has told.

Perhaps the most striking of these lessons is his warning that the constitution of the Hebrew Republic cannot be replicated. Although it was indeed beauti-

---

[86] Johan and Pieter de la Court, *Consideratien van staat, ofte polityke weeg-schaal* (Amsterdam, 1662), *La balance politique de J. et P. de la Court. Livre premier*, trans. Madeleine Francès (Paris: F. Alcan, 1937), 1.10, p. 51; Tacitus, *Histories 4–5. Annals 1–3, Histories*, I.3.

[87] Spinoza, *Tractatus Theologico-Politicus*, ch. 17, p. 217.

fully adapted to the Israelites' circumstances and allowed them to live in peace for many generations, 'no one can now imitate it, nor would this be advisable'.[88] It would not be advisable because the constitution was designed to generate a xenophobic loyalty to the state which, while it sustained cohesion among the isolated Israelites, would be ill suited to a community dependent on foreign trade. (In alluding to the United Provinces' maritime prosperity, Spinoza acknowledges a central theme of Dutch republican thought, championed by the merchant-philosopher Pieter de la Court. The welfare of Holland, de la Court had insisted, is founded on 'manufactures, fisheries, trade and navigation', and such a populous country cannot feed itself, let alone maintain its independence, without them.[89]) In addition, the Hebrew constitution can no longer be replicated because it was founded on a contract with God. Such a contract, Spinoza goes on, depended not only on the will of the individuals who transferred their right, but also on the will of God to whom their right was transferred. 'God, however, has revealed through his Apostles that his covenant is no longer written with ink, or on stone tablets, but in the heart, with the spirit of God'.

This argument needs to be handled with care. As we have seen, Spinoza's philosophical account of the contract on which a state is founded follows that of Hobbes, and characterizes the contract as a mutual agreement between the individual members of the multitude. The people agree with one another to transfer their power to a sovereign, but the sovereign is not a party to their agreement.[90] If the Israelite contract to obey God had conformed to this model, it would not have needed to depend on the will of God, since the people would only have had to agree among themselves to obey divine decrees. Moreover, Spinoza's earlier description of their decision seems to accord with his abstract model. The Hebrews agreed with one another to obey the law of God, imagining him as a legislating sovereign; but since God is not in fact the kind of being who can contract with human beings, he could not, and therefore did not, agree to anything. When Spinoza now implies that the founding contract was made between the Israelites and God, and that this is why the contract cannot be imitated, he stands back from his philosophical account of sovereignty and adopts the imaginative viewpoint of Scripture. However, he does so as a prelude to pointing out that the viewpoint of the

---

[88] Ibid. ch. 18, p. 221.

[89] Pieter de la Court, *The True Interest and Political Maxims of the Republic of Holland* (London, 1746), pp. 7, 50.

[90] Spinoza, *Tractatus Theologico-Politicus*, ch. 16, p. 199.

Israelites is no longer available. While they imagined God as a legislator who wrote his side of the contract on tablets of stone, people now recognize that this is not how God communicates his decrees. For seventeenth-century European communities, obeying the divine law is no longer a matter of contracting with a sovereign deity, but rather one of internalizing the law's recommendations and living accordingly. Those of Spinoza's contemporaries who call for a New Jerusalem modelled on the old have failed to appreciate the scale of the historical and theological break that divides the era of the Old Testament from the early modern world. A form of political legitimation that was once available is available no longer, and it is important to realize that the clock cannot be turned back. The will of God, in the sense of the order of nature, has bequeathed a new situation, and the Dutch must confront their constitutional problems in contemporary terms, without nostalgia for the contracts of the biblical past.

Nevertheless, there are lessons to be learned from the history of the Hebrew Republic, which 'still has many features well worth noting, that might be highly advisable to imitate'.[91] Many of these have to do with the legal powers of religious authorities, but as we should by now expect, others concern the nature of popular sovereignty. A first and vital point to note is that, in the Hebrew case, popular sovereignty was uniquely conducive to peace. 'As long as the people maintained their rule, they had only one civil war, and even it was completely stamped out'.[92] Furthermore, what brought peace to an end was the transition to monarchy. 'After the people, who were not at all accustomed to kings, changed their first form of state into a monarchical one, there was hardly an end to civil wars, and their battles were so fierce that they surpassed all others in reputation'. The moral, Spinoza concludes, is that states whose people are not used to monarchy should not try to institute it, because they will find themselves swept up in a pernicious and destructive dynamic. A newly installed monarch who continues to defend laws and rights instituted by the people under a republic will be regarded as their slave rather than their master, and will lose authority. To avoid this outcome, he will do all he can to secure his position by diminishing the power of the people and making new laws that serve his own interests. However, this in turn will excite the resentment of a people unaccustomed to kingly authority. The balance of power will consequently be unstable, and the state will be exposed to tyranny on one side and rebellion on the other.

---

[91] Ibid. ch. 18, p. 221.   [92] Ibid. ch. 18, p. 224.

In appealing to the history of the Hebrew state to illustrate the dangers of monarchy, Spinoza joins a chorus of Dutch republicans who were anxious to uphold the claim that sovereignty belonged to their Estates.[93] After the Dutch Revolt, the United Provinces had instituted what was represented as an ancient form of government, dividing power between regional and central States or assemblies, and a hereditary Stadtholderate traditionally occupied by the leader of the House of Orange. The Stadtholder, who commanded the Provinces' military forces and exercised considerable influence within the States, was initially the popular William the Silent; but his successors proved less adept at winning respect and loyalty, and in 1650 the then Stadtholder tried to usurp the right of the Estates General by staging an unsuccessful coup. In response, the States of Holland led by De Witt deposed him from office, and until 1672 the province was ruled by its States alone. Needless to say, this development was opposed by the Stadtholderate's traditional supporters, who remained loyal to the old regime.[94] But the States and its sympathizers energetically defended their action. Drawing on Grotius' analysis of the Batavian Republic, they argued that, because ultimate sovereignty lay with the States rather than the Stadtholder, their action was legitimate and had restored true freedom.[95] To discredit the Stadtholder still further, republicans tended to represent him as aspiring not only to usurp the Estates' powers but also to become a monarch. We see this, for example, in the work of Pieter de la Court who, while he protests that he is not writing in order to criticize the House of Orange,[96] is nevertheless adamant that the prosperity of the United Provinces depends upon wealthy and fortified cities, 'all which, to a monarch or one supreme head, is

---

[93] The superiority of republics to monarchies was a favourite theme within Dutch Republican discourse. See, for example, de la Court, *True Interest*, pp. 7–8, 37–41. See also Hans Blom, 'Spinoza on *Res Publica*: Republics and Monarchies' in *Monarchisms in an Age of Enlightenment: Liberty, Patriotism and the Public Good*, ed. John Christian Larsen, Lisa Simonutti, and Hans Blom (Toronto: University of Toronto Press, 2007); Raia Prokhovnik, *Spinoza and Republicanism*; Jonathan Scott, 'Classical Republicanism in Seventeenth-Century England and the Netherlands', in *Republicanism: A Shared European Heritage*, ed. Martin van Gelderen and Quentin Skinner, 2 vols. (Cambridge: Cambridge University Press, 2002), vol. 1, pp. 61–81; Wyger R. E. Velema, 'That a Republic Is Better Than a Monarchy: Anti-Monarchism in Early Modern Dutch Political Thought', in *Republicanism: A Shared European Heritage*, ed. van Gelderen and Skinner, 2 vols. (Cambridge: Cambridge University Press, 2002), vol. 1, pp. 9–25.

[94] Maarten Roy Prak, *The Dutch Republic in the Seventeenth Century: The Golden Age*, trans. Diane Webb (Cambridge: Cambridge University Press, 2005), ch. 3; Prokhovnik, *Spinoza and Republicanism*, ch. 3.

[95] Herbert H. Rowen, *John De Witt, Grand Pensionary of Holland, 1625–1672* (Princeton: Princeton University Press, 1978), p. 381.

[96] de la Court, *True Interest*, Preface, pp. 6, 7.

altogether intolerable'.[97] If a Stadtholder were to be restored, de La Court implies, he would again try to take away the ancient liberties of the Dutch and subject them to a form of kingly rule that might well become tyrannical. By the time Spinoza was writing the *Treatise* in the second half of the 1660s, the United Provinces was at war on several fronts, and the call for a Stadtholder to command its forces had become increasingly strident. In a desperate attempt to silence it, the States of Holland abolished the Stadtholder's office in 1667, specifying in addition that no one who held the post could act as supreme commander.[98] Not surprisingly, however, this strategy failed to resolve the problem, and as the decade drew to a close the republican leader of the States, Johan De Witt, was steadily losing his political power.[99]

Spinoza's emphasis on the damaging effects of monarchy is therefore among other things a warning to his fellow citizens: be careful not to reinstate a Stadtholder with monarchical pretensions. Commenting briefly on the local situation, he reiterates the Grotian view that the Dutch were never ruled by kings, but only by counts (*comites*) who owed their authority to the Estates. The Estates alone were therefore sovereign, and possessed the right to defend their own authority, advise the counts of their duties, defend the freedom of the people, avenge themselves against counts who degenerated into tyrants, and generally ensure that the counts did not act without the States' endorsement.[100] Moreover, since the Estates represent popular sovereignty, Stadtholders who try to usurp the Estates' powers threaten the freedom of the people.

To press his conclusion home and underline the risks involved in ignoring it, Spinoza dwells on the futility of attempting to overthrow a monarchy once it has been instated. 'But here I cannot pass over the fact that it is also no less dangerous to remove a monarch from your midst, even if it is established in every way that he is a tyrant'.[101] Because people who have become used to being ruled by kings will regard any lesser authority with contempt, there is no route from a monarchy back to a republic. Nor is there any comfort to be had from the thought that it is possible to replace a tyrannical king with a more moderate one. Suppose, for example, that a people assassinates a tyrant and installs an apparently more benign monarch. To avoid popular derision, the

---

[97] Ibid. p. 37.

[98] Prak, *Dutch Republic*, p. 50.

[99] Jonathan Israel, *The Dutch Republic: Its Rise, Greatness and Fall, 1477–1806* (Oxford: Clarendon Press, 1995), pp. 780–5; Prak, *Dutch Republic*, pp. 47–55; Rowen, *John De Witt*, pp. 793–7.

[100] Spinoza, *Tractatus Theologico-Politicus*, ch. 18, pp. 227–8.

[101] Ibid. ch. 18, p. 226.

new king will have to show that he rules by his own authority and is not subject to the people; but he also knows that his people have just assassinated a king. To warn them not to do the same thing again and establish himself as a ruler to be reckoned with, he will have to avenge his predecessor's death. But in order to represent this action as legitimate, he will have to 'defend the cause of the former tyrant and endorse his deeds'. In effect, he will uphold a tyrannical regime and turn himself into a tyrant. 'This is how it happens', Spinoza concludes, 'that the people can, indeed, often change one tyrant for another, but can never destroy him, or change a monarchic state into a different form'.[102]

Responding to the implied objection that the Romans successfully over- threw a tyrant, the *Treatise* reiterates a view already advocated by de la Court and sweeps the claim aside.[103] All that the Romans achieved by removing one tyrant was to elect several more, and to subject themselves to a series of external and internal wars.[104] Their history is thus a tale of servitude. And if this example is not sufficient to establish the point, one need only look to the current condition of England.[105] Having executed Charles I, the English installed a new monarch under the different name of Lord Protector, 'as if the whole issue had been about the name'. However, the new monarch could only survive by destroying Charles's supporters and distracting the people from his own brutal- ity by waging war. After much loss of life, the English realized that the only way to ameliorate their situation was to reconstitute the monarchy and restore the son of Charles I to the throne. So after a brief and bloody attempt to transform a monarchy into a republic they found themselves back where they started.[106] Spinoza does not pick this example at random. The restored English king, Charles II, was the uncle of the deposed Dutch Stadtholder, and had been pressing De Witt to reinstate his nephew, with some success. What exactly was he trying to achieve? As a king who had suffered under a republic, it seemed

---

[102] Ibid. ch. 18, p. 227.

[103] P. and J. de la Court, *Consideratien van staat*.

[104] Spinoza, *Tractatus Theologico-Politicus*, ch. 18, p. 227.

[105] Spinoza owned a history of the lives of Charles I and Charles II, translated into Dutch by L. van Bos. See no. 158 of J. Freudenthal, *Die Lebensgeschichte Spinoza's in Quellenschriften, Urkunden und Nichtamtlichen Nachrichten*, 2 vols. (Leipzig, 1899), vol. 1, p. 358.

[106] Compare Machiavelli, 'A corrupted people, having acquired liberty, can maintain it only with the greatest difficulty', Niccolò Machiavelli, *The Discourses*, ed. Bernard Crick (Harmonsworth: Penguin Books, 1970), I.17, pp. 157–60.

likely to the Dutch that Charles viewed the restoration of the Stadtholder as a first step towards establishing a Dutch monarchy to complement his own power. So by pointing to England's failure to cast off its king, Spinoza is reminding his fellow Dutch citizens that there would be no easy escape from monarchy, and that, as a people accustomed to republican rule, they should do their utmost to hold on to it.

The *Treatise's* bleak assessment of the consequences of regicide and tyranni-cide suits its overall argument. As the Hebrew Republic illustrates, the form of sovereignty that is optimal for a particular community depends on its history. Because states do best when they stick with what they know, monarchies should remain monarchies and republics remain republics. In addition, repub-lics tend to be more stable than polities ruled by kings. So a community with a republican tradition, such as the Israelites or the Dutch, has both a local and a general reason for doing everything it can to sustain the sovereignty of the people: it is already a republic; and republics are the most secure kind of state. A republic can of course make constitutional innovations, since there are a number of ways in which the people can be represented. However, reformers must beware of the ever-present threat that republics may decline into monarchies.

Chapter 12

Sovereignty and Freedom

For Spinoza and his contemporaries, debate about the optimal constitutional form of the United Provinces was inextricable intertwined with another issue, this time concerned with the division of civil and religious jurisdiction within the state. Should a civil sovereign or magistrate exercise control over religious as well as civil matters? Or should spiritual affairs be directed by religious authorities such as the officials of the Reformed Church? To put the point in broader terms, should the capacity to make and impose legislation be distributed among different representatives of the people, some civil and some ecclesiastical, or should the people be represented by a single sovereign, which 'alone retains the supreme right of nature over all things'.[1]

Almost from its inception, the Republic had been embroiled in struggles about this balance of power, in turn inherited from earlier controversies of the European Reformation.[2] Confronting the Catholic claim that the Pope exercised religious jurisdiction over the rulers of Christian states and could, for example, excommunicate them, Luther had argued that the true church is simply a congregation of the faithful, without worldly authority. Only civil sovereigns have coercive power to enforce religion, and no one is entitled to resist their laws.[3] Advocating a more politicized conception of ecclesiastical

---

[1] Benedictus de Spinoza, *Tractatus Theologico-Politicus*, ed. Carl Gebhardt, vol. III, *Opera* (Heidelberg: Carl Winter, 1924), ch. 16, p. 193.

[2] On these debates and their consequences in the United Provinces, see Jonathan Israel, *The Dutch Republic: Its Rise, Greatness and Fall, 1477–1806* (Oxford: Clarendon Press, 1995), chs. 18, 19; Douglas Nobbs, *Theocracy and Toleration: A Study of the Disputes in Dutch Calvinism from 1600 to 1650* (Cambridge: Cambridge University Press, 1938), esp. ch. 19.

[3] Quentin Skinner, *The Foundations of Modern Political Thought*, 2 vols. (Cambridge: Cambridge University Press, 1978), II, p. 14. The political implications of Luther's position were made fully explicit by the Swiss Zwinglian theologian, Erastus (Thomas Lüber (1524–83)), who argued that a religious practice or observance could only become law if it was promulgated by a civil sovereign. This view is often referred to as Erastian, and some commentators use this term to describe Arminian authors such as Grotius, and indeed Spinoza. See, for example, Eric Nelson,

might, Calvin had responded that, since God alone can determine the divine law revealed in Scripture and interpreted by the Church, no human agent has any authority over it, and the coercive power of civil rulers only extends to *adiaphora* or matters on which divine law does not pronounce. The power of civil sovereigns is consequently limited; but Christian rulers nevertheless have a religious duty to further the work of the Church by upholding the moral law taught in Scripture.[4]

During the early years of the seventeenth century, the scope of ecclesiastical authority became one of several issues contributing to the split between Remonstrants and Counter-Remonstrants within the Dutch Reformed Church. Laying out the Remonstrant side of the case, the preacher Johannes Uytenbogaert (portrayed by Rembrandt with his ruffled, thumb-marked Bible)[5] had argued that divine law gives a Christian ruler power over church and state, and that, since any division of authority is an invitation to conflict, all juridical power must lie with the civil magistrate.[6] Uytenbogaert's stance precipitated replies from a series of Counter-Remonstrant theologians, notably the Leiden professor Franciscus Gomarus who gave his name to the Counter-Remonstrant or Gomarist cause. According to Gomarus, neither church nor state has any discretion in relation to the divine decrees providentially ordained for us by God,[7] which determine that civil sovereigns are responsible for civil matters while the church is responsible for religion. Although church ministers can be punished by civil sovereigns for breaking the law or failing in their duties as ministers, the ministry as a whole is not subject to the sovereign. On the contrary, rulers are subject to the church in spiritual affairs and the church can

The Hebrew Republic: Jewish Sources and the Transformation of European Political Thought (Cambridge, Mass.: Harvard University Press, 2010), pp. 92–105.

[4] Jean Calvin, *Institutes of the Christian Religion*, ed. and trans. John Thomas McNeill and Ford Lewis Battles, *The Library of Christian Classics* (Philadelphia: Westminster Press, 1960–1), IV.xx.9.

[5] Rembrandt van Rijn, 'Jan Uytenbogaert, Preacher of the Remonstrants' (Cambridge: Fitzwilliam Museum, 1635).

[6] Jan Utenbogaert, *Remonstrantie van J. Utenbogaert aen de Staten Generael* (Leiden, 1618). See Israel, *The Dutch Republic: Its Rise, Greatness and Fall, 1477–1806*, p. 425.

[7] Franciscus Gomarus, *Waerschouwinghe over de Vermaninghe aen R. Donteclock* (Leiden, 1609). A response to Uytenbogaert, who replied in Jan Uytenbogaert, *Tractaet Van T'ampt Ende Authoriteyt Eener Hoggher Christelicker Overheydt, in Kerckelicke Saecken* (The Hague, 1610).

rightfully excommunicate them from the spiritual community if they fail to uphold the divine law.[8]

The Remonstrant or Arminian side of this dispute was immediately taken up by a number of consequential thinkers including Episcopius,[9] Vossius,[10] and Grotius,[11] each of whom argued that sovereignty lies with the civil magistrate, and contended that, although the Church can teach or persuade rulers, it has no authority to control them by means of law.[12] Their stance suffered a temporary setback in 1618, when the Arminian wing of the Reformed Church was censured at the Synod of Dort, but it nevertheless remained central to the conception of Dutch freedom subsequently developed in the 1640s and 1650s by De Witt and his supporters. It was vehemently defended by the De la Court brothers;[13] it drew fresh inspiration from Hobbes's *Leviathan* after the book appeared in Dutch translation; and as late as 1670, it remained sufficiently contentious for Spinoza to feel the need to defend it in the *Treatise*.[14] Its continuing topicality sprang from the fact that the Counter-Remonstrants were equally persistent in advocating their position, and in the 1640s developed a new strand of argument against civil authority. Returning to a broadly

---

[8] Israel, *The Dutch Republic: Its Rise, Greatness and Fall, 1477–1806*, p. 426.

[9] Simon Bischop (1583–1643), student of Arminius and Professor of Theology at Leiden from 1612. A leading Remonstrant, he was exiled in 1619 after the Synod of Dort, and wrote a systematic account of Arminianism.

[10] Gerrit Janszoon Vos (1577–1649), director of the Theological College of Leiden University from 1614 to 1619 and subsequently Professor of Rhetoric, Chronology, and Greek. Gerardus Vossius, *Historia Pelagiana sive historiae de controversiis quas Pelagius ejusque reliquiae moverunt* (Leiden, 1608) aimed to vindicate Arminianism by showing that it was not Pelagian. See Israel, *The Dutch Republic: Its Rise, Greatness and Fall, 1477–1806*, p. 440.

[11] Hugo Grotius, *De imperio summarum potestatem circa sacra* (1648), trans. C. Barksdale as *Of the Authority of the Highest Powers About Sacred Things* (London, 1651).

[12] Simon Episcopius, *The Confession or Declaration of the Ministers or Pastors which in the United Provinces are Called Remonstrants, Concerning the Chief Points of Christian Religion*, trans. Thomas Taylor (London, 1676); Hugo Grotius, *Ordinum Hollandiae ac Westfrisiae pietas (1613)*, ed. Edwin Rabbie (Leiden: Brill, 1995); Vossius, *Historia pelagiana sive historiae de controversiis quas Pelagius ejusque reliquiae moverunt.*

[13] See, for example, Pieter de la Court, *The True Interest and Political Maxims of the Republic of Holland* (London, 1746), pp. 38, 70–1.

[14] The need to keep the clergy out of politics was clearly discussed in Spinoza's circle during the 1660s. For example, Adriaen Koerbagh fiercely defended it in a pamphlet published under the pseudonym Vrederyck Waarmond: Vrederyck Waarmond, *'T Nieuw woordenboek der regten, ofte een vertaalinge en uytlegginge van meest alle de Latijnsche Woorden en wijse van spreeken, in alle regten en regtsgeleerders boeken en schriften gebruykelijk* (Amsterdam, 1664). See Jonathan Israel, *Radical Enlightenment: Philosophy and the Making of Modernity, 1650–1750* (Oxford: Oxford University Press, 2001), pp. 185–90. See also P. de la Court, *True Interest*, pp. 70–1.

Lutheran distinction between legislative and spiritual power, Voetius and other ecclesiastical leaders conceded that the church has no authority to make laws.[15] Nevertheless, they claimed, it possesses a form of spiritual power over the faithful that binds the conscience.[16] Because the church's spiritual authority derives from Christ and works at a quite different level from the coercive right of the civil magistrate, there is a sense in which it is self-sufficient and entirely independent of the state. Moreover, while ministers are citizens, and should submit to rulers, rulers are members of the church, and in this role should submit to its authority.[17]

Even-handed as it aimed to appear, this conception of church–state relations was an object of suspicion among de Witt's supporters, not least because the Voetian wing of the Reformed Church seemed bent on extending ecclesiastical power at the expense of the Estates. In theory, membership of the Dutch Reformed Church was entirely voluntary and its rule only applied to the faithful; but in practice the Church's more rigorous defenders did their best to censure religious outlooks that diverged from their own and impose their theological convictions on the populace.[18] De Witt's struggle against this militant strand of Calvinism continued throughout the 1650s and 1660s, focusing now on one issue, now on another. For example, setting the legitimate boundaries of Christianity became a divisive problem in 1653, when the States of Holland gave way to pressure from the Reformed Church and declared Socinianism illegal.[19] A further symbolically significant contest concerned the extent to which the Church should support the government in its sermons, and in prayers for government officials and institutions. In 1654, for instance, De Witt sent judges to two synods to enjoin the Church to preach respect and obedience for legitimate sovereigns; in 1657 he proposed that references to the Stadtholder should be removed from the public prayers

---

[15] Gisbertus Voetius, *Politica Ecclesiastica* (Amsterdam, 1663–76), I.196, III.796. See Nobbs, *Theocracy and Toleration*, p. 139.

[16] Gulielmus Apollonius, *Jus Majestatis circa sacra, sive Tractatus Theologicus, de jure magistratus circa res ecclesiasticas* (Middleburg, 1642–3); Jacob Triglandius, *Dissertatio theologica de civili et ecclesiastica potestate* (Amsterdam, 1642). See Nobbs, *Theocracy and Toleration*, ch. 4.

[17] Nobbs, *Theocracy and Toleration*, pp. 185–7.

[18] On the organization of the Dutch Reformed Church, see Israel, *The Dutch Republic: Its Rise, Greatness and Fall, 1477–1806*, pp. 367–71.

[19] Socinianism was also banned in other provinces, and was outlawed by the States General in 1656. Willem Frijhoff, Marijke Spies, and Myra Heerspink Scholz, *Dutch Culture in a European Perspective. 1, 1650, Hard-Won Unity* (Basingstoke: Palgrave Macmillan, 2004), p. 266.

used in church services, but was forced by a number of town councils to back down; and during the 1660s preachers who refused to follow the law concerning official prayers were regularly reprimanded for sedition. The Church also challenged the States' right to appoint ministers, by gathering local supporters behind its own candidates, and sometimes fanning violent resistance to the States' decisions.[20] As the *Treatise* indicates, disputes about the extent of the Reformed Church's authority ranged over its right to 'choose ministers, determine and stabilise the foundations of the Church and its doctrine, judge what customs and actions are pious, excommunicate or receive members of the Church, and finally, provide for the poor'.[21]

For Spinoza and others like him, these apparently peripheral but nevertheless pernicious struggles reinforced their conviction that religious officials should be entirely subject to a civil sovereign. The only way to maintain peace and freedom, and thus achieve the proper ends of political life, was to give the sovereign sole power over religion.[22] However, as the *Treatise* points out, 'a great many people flatly deny that this right belongs to sovereigns, and do not wish to recognise them as the interpreters of divine law. They consequently assume for themselves a licence to censure them, expose them to scorn, and even excommunicate them from the church'.[23] While the specific arguments that they employ to show that sovereigns do not possess sacred right are, according to Spinoza, too frivolous to merit refutation, the flaws in their overall position nevertheless need to be exposed.[24]

Civil and religious right

Taking up the historical dimension of the problem, Spinoza turns once again to the Hebrew Republic. According to Gomarus and a string of other anti-Arminian theologians, the ancient Jewish state sets a precedent for independent religious authority because priests rather than kings were responsible for

---

[20] See, Israel, *The Dutch Republic: Its Rise, Greatness and Fall, 1477–1806*, p. 697; Herbert H. Rowen, *John De Witt, Grand Pensionary of Holland, 1625–1672* (Princeton: Princeton University Press, 1978), pp. 427–30.

[21] Spinoza, *Tractatus Theologico-Politicus*, ch. 19, p. 235.

[22] See, for example, Lucius Antistius Constans, *De jure ecclesiasticorum, liber singularis* (Amsterdam, 1665). This view was also defended by de la Court and Koerbagh. See Israel, *The Dutch Republic: Its Rise, Greatness and Fall, 1477–1806*, p. 760; Israel, *Radical Enlightenment*, pp. 185–96; Theo Verbeek, *Spinoza's Theologico-Political Treatise: Exploring 'the Will of God'* (Aldershot: Ashgate, 2003), p. 9.

[23] Spinoza, *Tractatus Theologico-Politicus*, ch. 19, p. 228.

[24] Ibid. ch. 19, p. 234.

directing spiritual life.[25] However, Remonstrant writers such as Grotius and Cunaeus had repudiated this interpretation. Appealing to Josephus' claim that in the original Hebrew commonwealth there was no distinction between civil and religious law, and to the purported fact that, after Moses' death, supreme power to make and enforce law lay with a civil sovereign,[26] they had contended that sovereignty was never exercised by priests, but only by magistrates with power over sacred as well as secular affairs.

Although Spinoza's interpretation of Hebrew history does not entirely coincide with that of his Arminian predecessors, he fervently concurs with this conclusion. People who hold the seditious opinion that sovereignty lay with the priests are, he claims, 'wretchedly deceived'.[27] They fail to recognize that, in the first phase of the Hebrew state, Moses possessed the right to command 'absolutely all things to all people' and 'taught the people religion, ordained sacred ministries and chose ministers'.[28] After his death, priests became interpreters of the law; but 'it was still not their function to judge the citizens or excommunicate anyone'. This power lay with the leaders of the tribes and the judges they appointed, in short with civil authorities.[29]

The Hebrew constitution therefore offers no precedent for dividing priestly from civil sovereignty. Furthermore, as Spinoza now reminds his readers, it did not even acknowledge such a division. Because its civil and religious law were one and the same, obedience to the law was simultaneously a matter of religious and civil duty, and any decree articulated a civil as well as a religious demand.[30] The distinction between the two realms of law results, Spinoza claims, from the history of Christianity, a religion originally practised by groups of private citizens who ruled themselves 'without any consideration of the sovereign'. When the Christian faith was eventually introduced into the state, it was taught to civil sovereigns or *imperatores* by ecclesiastics, who consequently came to be seen as the interpreters of religion and the deputies or *vicarii* of God.[31]

---

[25] Gomarus, *Waerschouwinghe*. Also Antonius Walaeus (1579–1639), another professor at Leiden and one of the Counter-Remonstrant delegates at the Synod of Dort. Nobbs attributes this view to him: Nobbs, *Theocracy and Toleration*, p. 12.

[26] On the development of Grotius's argument, see Nelson, *Hebrew Republic* pp. 98–100. For argument to the effect that this is an Erastian trend, see Nelson, *Hebrew Republic*, pp. 92ff.

[27] Spinoza, *Tractatus Theologico-Politicus*, ch. 19, p. 234.

[28] Ibid. ch. 18, p. 222, ch. 19, p. 237.

[29] Ibid. ch. 18, p. 222.

[30] Ibid. ch. 19, p. 236.

[31] Ibid. ch. 18, p. 223, ch. 19, p. 237.

This apparently incidental historical digression introduces a crucial claim. Many of the political theorists to whose work Spinoza is responding took it for granted that religious and civil affairs can be distinguished, and went on to ask who should have legal power over each realm. Should sovereignty be divided, and if so, how? As we shall shortly see, Spinoza has a strong view; but it is shaped by a deeper concern about the nature of the problem to be solved. If there really are two spheres of law, the problem that his contemporaries grapple with is rightly framed; but if the distinction between civil and religious law is merely an artefact of the history of Christianity, there may be another way to approach it. The Hebrew Republic offers a model of a state in which there is not only no division between religious and civil sovereignty, but also no division between religious and civil legislation. Following this example, might one not resolve the tension between church and state that is such a marked feature of Christian communities by rejecting their fissured conception of law? Perhaps, by providing a general and unified conception of the law, one can close the gap between religious and civil obligation, and eradicate the juridical compartmentalization that has generated such bitter strife.

The suggestion that this might be one of the main lessons to be learned from the Hebrew Republic is not made explicit in the *Treatise*, but it nevertheless guides the remainder of Spinoza's discussion of sovereignty and sustains his culminating analysis of religious and philosophical freedom. Developing his argument in stages, he begins in a straightforward fashion by assembling historical evidence in favour of the view that states do better when sovereignty is undivided. As soon as the Israelites' priests and tribal leaders began to struggle for control of the law their state began to deteriorate, and its ability to maintain a peaceful way of life was compromised. Each side issued decrees to suit its own interests, with the result that legal contradictions arose between one law and another. Legislation became a tool of superstition so that people obeyed it out of fear rather than confidence, and the law as a whole ceased to command respect. Worse still (and here Spinoza echoes a claim already made by Cunaeus), religious controversies within the law gave rise to fierce theological disagreements, which the civil magistrates could only resolve by licensing the creation of sects.[32] Again, however, this was a pernicious compromise. Once competing sects try to impose their doctrines on society as a whole, Spinoza comments, 'what rules most is the anger of the mob', whose 'impudent licence cannot easily be restrained, because it is obscured by the deceptive appearance

---

[32] Ibid. ch. 18, pp. 222–3.

of religion'. The history of the Hebrews therefore indicates, and that of Christianity confirms, that it is 'fatal for both religion and the state to grant the right to make decrees or handle the business of the state to the ministers of sacred affairs; and everything is much more stable if these people are held in check'.[33]

Why exactly is this so dangerous? On the assumption that the vast majority of agents are less than rational, it is safe to assume that they will tend to pursue their individual or factional goals. Where power is divided between two authorities, each is consequently liable to promote its own interests to the detriment of the other; and this pattern will in turn produce tensions that risk destabilizing the state. Such frictions tend to be particularly acute when one of the authorities concerned wields religious power, because people respond exceptionally strongly to the imaginative conceptions of the deity that religious leaders promote. Prophets, preachers, and churchmen can exercise enormous influence over the *populus*, so much so that ecclesiastics have won greater loyalty and devotion 'merely with the might of their pens', than monarchs have gained 'by the use of iron or fire'.[34] Once a religious leader gains the ear of the people, the right of the civil magistrate is inevitably diminished and sovereignty is in effect divided. Civil sovereigns can therefore easily find themselves in an unhappy situation like that of the Catholic princes of Europe, and above all the Holy Roman emperors, who became so dependent on the papacy that they were unable to act without its approval.[35] Where power is split between civil and religious authorities, the two parties will struggle for power, and peace will be destroyed.

Psychological and social dispositions therefore militate in favour of a single sovereign in whom all power is vested, and Spinoza is clear that this type of constitutional arrangement is the best way to maintain harmony and security. However, it remains to ask how a sovereign who is responsible for upholding

---

[33] Ibid. ch. 18, pp. 223–4, 225. 'This argument yields a problem about the right of Christ's disciples to preach religion to the people. Spinoza discusses this in ch. 19, pp. 233–4, and offers an account of the disciples' activities that makes them legitimate. Cf. de la Court's attack on pro-monarchical church ministers: 'Wherefore all the rabble ... being void of knowledge and judgment, and therefore inclining to the weather or safer side, and mightily valuing the vain and empty pomp of kings and princes, say amen to [attacks on republics]; especially when kept in ignorance, and irritated against the lawful government by preachers, who aim at dominion, or would introduce an independent and arbitrary power of church government'. de la Court, *True Interest*, p. 38.

[34] Spinoza, *Tractatus Theologico-Politicus*, ch. 19, p. 235.

[35] Ibid.

both civil and religious values can be constrained to allow each its proper weight. If it has sole control over the law, what can prevent it favouring security over piety, or piety over security? And how is it to reconcile them when they conflict? These problems carry Spinoza to the next stage of his discussion. His strategy for dealing with them is to revive the Mosaic conception of a law that is simultaneously civil and religious, by showing that our obligation to obey the divine law by loving our neighbours always accords with our duty to obey the civil law, and vice versa.

The sovereign's chief responsibility, so the *Treatise* claims, is to maintain the safety of the people by making and imposing laws that foster peace and security; but in achieving this end, it simultaneously creates the necessary conditions for living religiously in accordance with the divine law. As we have seen, a co-operative way of life governed by the divine law cannot be realized in a state of nature, and can only arise within a political society where a sovereign prescribes and imposes legislation. In order to live religiously one must therefore maintain the state by maintaining the law, and anyone who wants to achieve the former end must also commit to the latter. Furthermore, since disobeying the law is in Spinoza's view always harmful to the state and incompatible with promoting its ends, it follows that disobedience must also be incompatible with a religious way of life. As the *Treatise* puts it, 'no one can practise piety nor obey God unless he obeys all the sovereign's decrees'.[36]

A weakness of this piece of reasoning appears to be that it reduces piety to obeying the law and deprives it of any independent content, so that whatever the sovereign decrees, piety demands. Spinoza does not disagree, but he weakens the force of the objection by arguing in the other direction. Just as creating a secure way of life is part of what it is to create a religious existence, so creating a religious or co-operative way of life is part of what it is to make the state secure. To live religiously is, as the *Treatise* has already explained, to love one's neighbours by practising the virtues of justice and *charitas*. However, as Spinoza now urges his readers to see, living religiously is also a condition of living securely. Unless people co-operate with one another by conforming to common norms of justice, unjust actions will undermine the law, diminish peace and security and damage the state. Subjects who want to live securely must therefore commit themselves to living religiously; or to put the point another way, there is no security without piety. Our grasp of what a pious way

---

[36] Ibid. ch. 19, p. 236.

of life involves informs our understanding of security and shapes our conception of the ends of the state.

Binding religious and civil values together still more tightly, the *Treatise* contends that a community can in practice only live religiously if someone determines what it means to love one's neighbour and thus what patterns of action a religious life requires. If private individuals try to work this out for themselves, disagreements will arise and spiral into conflict, making co-operation or piety impossible; and the only effective way to avoid this problem is to give the sovereign the right to specify what obedience to the divine law involves.[37] Alongside its power to make the civil law, the sovereign must possess the power to interpret and enforce the divine law, by determining what counts as loving one's neighbour. 'Since it is the duty of the sovereign alone to determine what is necessary for the well-being of the whole people and the security of the state, and to command what it judges to be necessary, it follows that it is the duty of the supreme power alone to determine in what way each person must cherish his neighbour in accordance with piety, i.e. in what way each person is bound to obey God'.[38] Or again, because 'God has no special kingdom over men except through those who have sovereignty', the only way to live piously is to obey the laws made by a sovereign who exercises power over both civil and religious life.[39]

It is important to Spinoza's position that the sovereign's power over religion is a power to interpret rather than to make the divine law. Reason and revelation both confirm that the law enjoins us to love our neighbour, and this is not a fact that any sovereign can change. Rulers can only flesh out this injunction by specifying *how* subjects are to love their neighbours or live securely, and enshrining these judgements in law. For example, when the civil law decrees that people can dispose of their property, endows them with rights of self-defence, or makes them liable for rescuing drowning children from puddles, it determines what a co-operative or religious way of life consists in; and when it refrains from binding people to worship in any particular fashion, to profess a particular philosophical opinion, or to provide for the poor of other provinces, the same applies. Through its legislative powers, the

---

[37] Ibid. ch. 19, p. 236.

[38] Ibid. ch. 19, p. 232, ch. 18, p. 228. See also, P. de la Court, *True Interest*, pp. 70–1. Although ecclesiastical authorities have the right to teach and advise, 'the coercive power is given only to the civil magistrate; all power and right which the ecclesiastics have, if they have any, must be derived from [the powers of the civil magistrate], as the same is excellently and unanswerably shown by Lucius, Antistius Constans in his book, *De Jure Ecclesiasticorum*, lately printed'.

[39] Spinoza, *Tractatus Theologico-Politicus*, ch. 19, p. 231.

sovereign makes it possible for its subjects to live religiously, by giving them a shared and enforceable account of what—for them—co-operation consists in. As in the Mosaic Law, then, piety and security are so closely connected that any law promoting one also promotes the other, and a sovereign who undermines the first also damages the second. The fear that subjects face is not that their rulers will favour piety over security or vice versa, but rather that they will jeopardize both by failing to appreciate their interdependence.

By reviving a central feature of the law of the Hebrew Republic, Spinoza offers an elegant solution to a seventeenth-century problem. However, as he acknowledges, an anxiety remains. If we are under both a political and a religious obligation to obey the sovereign, what are we to do when in our opinion a ruler governs badly, and requires us to act in ways that we regard as impious? To take a familiar example, the New Testament claims that, when a man tries to take my shirt, piety requires me to give him my cloak.[40] However, if the civil law classifies the man's attempt to take my shirt as theft, and requires me to report his crime to the authorities, I find myself in a dilemma. Piety requires one thing, civil justice another. What am I to do? Spinoza responds that such problems are easily resolved. Political life familiarizes us with the need to subordinate our private opinions (including our private opinions about what is pious) to the law. Particularly in democratic societies where sovereignty is exercised by the body of the people, subjects are used to accepting decisions with which they do not themselves agree. 'In councils, whether of supreme or lesser powers, it is rare for anything to be agreed by universal consent; but everything is nevertheless done by common decision, both of those who voted for a measure and of those who voted against it'.[41] A comparable rule applies in the case of the shirt. 'When it is judged that [allowing the man to take it] is fatal to the preservation of the state, it is pious to call the man to judgment, even if he will be condemned to death'.[42] Our individual disposition to act on our own conception of what constitutes piety must give way to the collective view enshrined in law, and we should not reproach ourselves for doing what the law decrees.

This is not to deny that it may sometimes be extremely difficult to obey the law, or that individuals may sometimes be incapable of doing so. To illustrate the first of these points, Spinoza takes the celebrated example of the Roman consul, Manlius Torquatus, who condemned his own son to death for disobeying military orders. Torquatus' case had been discussed by Livy, taken up by

---

[40] Matthew 5:40.
[41] Spinoza, *Tractatus Theologico-Politicus*, ch. 20, p. 242.
[42] Ibid. ch. 19, p. 232.

many authors including Machiavelli, and was well known in Holland.[43] In 1661, for instance, the Dutch artist Ferdinand Bol had dramatically depicted the enthroned father overseeing his son's execution, surrounded by a shocked assembly of soldiers and counsellors.[44] We honour Torquatus, Spinoza comments, 'because he valued the safety of the people more than piety towards his son', and as this description implies, we view him as a man who faced a terrible choice. Formally speaking, both piety (upholding a co-operative way of life) and his military responsibilities (upholding the safety of the people) required him to punish anyone who defied his orders, regardless of family loyalties. Spinoza's theoretical account of our obligations therefore vindicates the consul's action and explains why he should be an object of honour. But reason and imagination can still conflict. Because our affects cannot be entirely subordinated to our rational judgements about what is ultimately for our good, doing the right thing is compatible with feeling guilt or anguish. Furthermore, since our affects determine how we act, they shape the extent to which we are capable of obeying the law.[45] Manlius Torquatus was, we must suppose, a person of extraordinary fortitude, who managed to put his patriotism ahead of his love for his son; but because this was an exceptional achievement, sovereigns cannot count on such unswerving loyalty. Many people—including those who understand and accept Spinoza's claim that there is no genuine conflict between the demands of piety and civil law—may be unable to obey laws that contradict their individual apprehension of what is pious, for example by asking them to sacrifice their children. Moreover, as Spinoza has already pointed out, a wise sovereign will bear this fact in mind and will try not to ask more of its subjects than they can deliver. A ruler who tests his or her subjects by requiring them to act in ways that they regard as violating their deepest commitments to a co-operative form of life will find that they do not obey, and put its own power at risk.

In modern states, the unity of the Mosaic Law that gave the Hebrew Commonwealth such exceptional stability can therefore be replicated in a

---

[43] Marcus Tullius Cicero, *De Finibus bonorum et malorum*, trans. Harris Rackham, *Loeb Classical Library* (Cambridge, Mass: Harvard University Press, 1921), I.vii.23, Livy, *Ab urbe condita*, trans. B. O. Foster et al., 14 vols. *Loeb Classical Library* (Cambridge, Mass: Harvard University Press, 1919–59); Niccolò Machiavelli, *The Discourses*, ed. Bernard Crick and trans. Leslie J. Walker (Harmondsworth: Penguin Books, 1970), III.2.

[44] Ferdinand Bol, 'Consul Titus Manlius Torquatus Beheading His Son' (Amsterdam: Rijksmuseum, 1661–3).

[45] For further discussion of these issues see Spinoza, *Ethics*, in Curley ed. *The Collected Works of Spinoza*, vol. I, 4p5–4p17.

new guise, no longer so strongly dependent on the particular imaginary outlook that made it compelling to the Israelites. Their method of creating a climate of obedience by attributing their political authority to a legislating God still has considerable force. (As Spinoza has explained, this ancient conception of the deity continues to move seventeenth-century communities to love their neighbours.) But the inhabitants of the Dutch Republic are also in a position to begin to comprehend and embrace their own sovereignty without projecting it onto an external deity. Rather than representing themselves as subject to a law over which they have no control, they are able to think of themselves in a different fashion, as members of a collective body that can only survive if its various components act in concert to sustain the integrated set of processes on which its life depends. Conceiving of themselves in this way is of course a complex and partly imaginative enterprise. The grounds for doing so can be philosophically understood; but in practice they must also be expressed and sustained by pictorial images, such as the frontispiece of Hobbes's *Leviathan*, literary descriptions of the state as a body of legislators, anecdotes such as the story of Manlius Torquatus, and a host of other political and cultural artefacts. Through these resources, a successful republic represents itself to itself and, by appealing to the imaginations of its subjects and legislators, arouses affects that enable them to live under the law.[46]

Spinoza's contribution to this enterprise has been to trace certain continuities between the Hebrew and Dutch Republics, casting the latter as a community where the stabilizing features of a divinely ordained law are maintained, but the dark glass through which they were murkily descried by the Israelites has been taken away. The law is no longer written on tablets of stone, but in the hearts of Dutchmen who can empower themselves by making and obeying decrees. This image of modern transparency is itself an aspect of the imaginary conception of the republic that Spinoza has been helping to build; but as he has also been arguing, it is supported and fortified by historical and philosophical knowledge.[47] Whether or not we represent the state as a body of a particular

---

[46] This emphasis on the imaginative dimension of social and political institutions is far from unusual in early modern political discourse. See Susan James, 'The Role of *Amicitia* in Political Life', in *The Concept of Love in Seventeenth and Eighteenth Century Philosophy*, ed. Gabor Boros, Herman De Dijn and Martin Moors (Leuven: Leuven University Press, 2007); Arthur Weststeijn, 'The Power of "Pliant Stuff": Fables and Frankness in Seventeenth-Century Dutch Republicanism', *Journal of the History of Ideas*, 72, no. 1 (2011).

[47] Moira Gatens, 'Spinoza's Disturbing Thesis: Power, Norms and Fiction in the *Tractatus Theologico-Politicus*', *History of Political Thought* 30, no. 3 (2009); Moira Gatens, 'The Politics of Imagination,' in *Feminist Interpretations of Benedict Spinoza* (University Park, Pa.: Pennsylvania State University Press, 2009); Susan James, 'Narrative as the Means to Freedom: Spinoza on the

kind, there are independent rational grounds for believing that the best way to secure its ends is to unify the power to make law under a single sovereign, and to ensure that sovereignty is exercised by the people as a whole. By appealing to purportedly universal psycho-social traits, the *Treatise* has provided a reasoned case for these conclusions, which in turn slots into, and gains persuasive force from, the grander philosophical system defended in the *Ethics*. Nowadays, then, a republic can draw on two overlapping resources, imagination and reason, to integrate the demands of piety and security in a manner that both sovereign and subjects can live with, alive to the fact that each party is in a position to destroy the equilibrium.[48] Subjects who refuse to allow the sovereign to interpret the divine or civil law can quickly breed conflicts that destroy peace and usher in servitude. A sovereign who is insensitive to a community's religious or civic sensibilities can easily issue decrees that its subjects cannot and will not follow, thus rendering both itself and its subjects more vulnerable. In practice, a form of government that encourages both piety and stability is neither a *fait accompli* nor a state of affairs that a ruler can simply impose upon its subjects, but rather a *modus vivendi* that sovereign and subjects must collectively envisage and realize. Part of a ruler's skill lies in knowing how to allow subjects to assist in this process, by giving them the freedom to use their energies for legitimate political ends.[49] Instead of suppressing their insights and thwarting their talents, it must try to make its subjects useful, and school itself to learn from their determination to live as their experience and understanding dictate. With this line of thought, Spinoza arrives at his final goal of showing that the freedom to philosophize does not damage the state.

Free thought, speech, and action

Taking stock of the circumstances with which both sovereigns and subjects have to deal, the *Treatise* firmly refuses to idealize. The multitude over which a sovereign rules is passionate, stubborn, and divisive. To some extent, its members will disagree with one another, and each faction within it will struggle to persuade the sovereign to do whatever it regards as best. A competent sovereign who grasps the principles of good government is therefore bound to be drawn into a politics of consensus and compromise, and its more rational

Uses of Imagination', in *Spinoza's 'Theologico-Political Treatise'*, ed. Yitzhak Y. Melamed and Michael A. Rosenthal (Cambridge: Cambridge University Press, 2010).

[48] Spinoza, *Tractatus Theologico-Politicus*, ch. 20, p. 240.
[49] Ibid. ch. 20, p. 245.

subjects will recognize that this is unavoidable. No faction, however wise and well informed, can expect to be ruled entirely as it would wish. No religious confession can expect its beliefs to be shared by the community as a whole. No philosophical movement can expect the world at large to agree with its conclusions. But how are the overlapping values of piety and peace to be maintained in the midst of such diversity?

Since the closing decades of the sixteenth century, a long line of Dutch theorists had discussed the religious aspect of this question. Looking back over the many sectarian wars that had engulfed Europe, and contemplating the theologically motivated disputes that continued to flare up in the United Provinces, they regarded it as clear that religious disagreement cannot be resolved by force. Although some writers held out against religious pluralism (Lipsius, for example, was convinced that it leads to strife and fanaticism, and should only be allowed as a last resort), many argued that religious persecution was not only dangerous to the state, but flew in the face of the traditional freedoms of which the Dutch were so proud.[50] This position could be defended on pragmatic grounds. Persecution only encourages sedition, and leads to civil war; equally, as the De la Court brothers repeatedly insisted, freedom of conscience was a condition of prosperity, and a trading nation such as Holland could not sustain its wealth unless it allowed people of many faiths to congregate in its ports and cities.[51] A further popular defence of religious freedom appealed to the Bible: Scripture, it was claimed, enjoins Christian communities to admonish rather than punish heretics, and urges us to resolve theological conflicts through negotiation and persuasion.[52] Yet a third argument, which formed a mainstay of the Arminian case for freedom of conscience, drew on the originally Lutheran claim that faith cannot be forced. Rulers and churches may manage to control forms of worship, but have no dominion over the relationship between God and man on which faith essentially depends.[53] According to Grotius, for instance, a sovereign can exert

---

[50] Martin van Gelderen, *The Political Thought of the Dutch Revolt, 1555–1590* (Cambridge: Cambridge University Press, 1992), pp. 254–5.

[51] e.g. P. de la Court, *True Interest*, I, chs. 14–15, III, ch. 1.

[52] Dirck Volckertsz Coornhert, 'Proces van't ketterdooden ende dwangh der coscientien. Tusschen Justum Lipsium ... ende Dirck Coornhert. het eerste deel politijck (1589)', in *Wercken* (Amsterdam, 1630), fols. 54, 58, 69; Dirck Volckertsz Coornhert, 'Synodus van der conscientien vryheydt (1582)', in *Wercken* (Amsterdam, 1630), fol. 30; Episcopius, *Confession* ch. 24, §5, 9. See van Gelderen, *The Political Thought of the Dutch Revolt, 1555–1590*, pp. 247–52.

[53] Coornhert, 'Dwangh Der Coscientien', fol. 64. See van Gelderen, *The Political Thought of the Dutch Revolt, 1555–1590*, pp. 252–3.

indirect control over our thoughts or internal actions by governing the external aspects of religion, but the mind itself remains beyond legislation or command.[54]

Nevertheless, the line between external worship and internal conscience proved hard to draw. Both Arminians and some of their Counter-Remonstrant opponents agreed that freedom of conscience is incompatible with the use of violence to alter belief. As Episcopius had put the point, the essence or substance of religion is a matter of individual conviction, over which magistrates have no authority, so that people who try to rule by means of bodily or capital punishment 'do arrogate and assume to themselves too great a power . . . and oppress the liberty of men's consciences'. They turn the saving and wholesome remedy of free religious belief 'into a most deadly poison; and that which was designed for health and safety, these men turn to subversion and ruin; wherefore also those who any ways patronise and defend the killing of heretics or any the like tyranny or persecution for conscience sake, we hold and judge that they are altogether estranged from and contrary to that most meek and mild spirit of Christ'.[55] But was conscience violated when people were subjected to non-violent forms of discipline?[56] For example, did one's conscience remain free if one was allowed to worship as one chose in private?[57] Or was this liberty inseparable from freedom of expression, so that people who were prevented from worshipping in public or propagating their religious views could claim a genuine grievance? Debates about this issue had begun as far back as the 1580s, when Dirk Volckertsz Coornhert, a prominent supporter of the Dutch Revolt, had argued that freedom of conscience encompassed not only freedom of expression and worship, but also the right to publish one's religious opinions.[58] And although almost no one favoured a polity in which

[54] Grotius, *De Imperio*, p. 65. Quoted in Nobbs, *Theocracy and Toleration*.

[55] Episcopius, *Confession*, ch. 24, pp. 253–4.

[56] A view taken by the Calvinist preacher Jan Schuurmann in 1572. Pieter Pekelharing, 'Reflections on Tolerance and Republicanism: The Case of the Dutch Republic (unpublished)', (1999); Andrew Pettegree, 'The Politics of Toleration in the Free Netherlands 1572–1620', in *Tolerance and Intolerance in the European Reformation*, ed. Ole Peter Grell and Bob Scribner (Cambridge: Cambridge University Press, 1996). Also see Mark Goldie, 'The Theory of Religious Intolerance in Restoration England', in *From Persecution to Toleration: The Glorious Revolution and Religion in England*, ed. Jonathan Israel, Nicholas Tyacke and Ole Peter Grell (Oxford: Clarendon Press, 1991).

[57] One upholder of this view was the Counter-Remonstrant preacher, Henricus Arnoldi. See Henricus van der Linde Arnoldi, *Vande Conscientie-Dwangh, dat is: Klaer ende grondich vertoogh, Dat De Staten Generaal in Haer Placcaet Den 3. Julij 1619.* (Delft, 1629), p. 20.

[58] Coornhert, 'Dwangh Der Coscientien', fols. 30–7. See van Gelderen, *The Political Thought of the Dutch Revolt, 1555–1590*, pp. 247–8.

religion was entirely devoid of official control, the extent to which it should be overseen remained fiercely disputed. As Heinricus Arnoldi van der Linde described the problem in 1629, the government of the United Provinces had to steer a middle course between forcing the conscience and permitting an 'unlimited freedom to believe, profess, preach and fool people into the figments of one's own imagination'.[59]

During the 1650s, political debate about what one should be free to say on theological topics became mixed with debates about the freedom to philosophize. Some of the pragmatic and psychological arguments used to justify religious freedom could also be applied to philosophical beliefs. Moreover, when philosophical convictions came into conflict with Church doctrine, disputes about the proper extent of liberty of conscience merged seamlessly into disagreements about the acceptable limits of philosophical speech. Hence the various efforts of Dutch Cartesians to remove philosophy from the arena over which theologians exercised authority. Spinoza's own solution to this problem rests, as we have seen, on the claim that revealed religion requires very few theological commitments. Truly religious people must accept that the divine law requires us to love our neighbours by treating them justly and charitably, and must subscribe in some form to the tenets of faith on which a religious way of life depends, But no further beliefs or practices are essential, and religious institutions consequently have no authority over them. Furthermore, since the most effective way to encourage people to live religiously is to allow them to imagine and worship God in whatever way suits them best, religious officials who try to harass people into professing a particular doctrine merely succeed in undermining neighbourly love.

This extensive freedom of religious belief and worship in turn vindicates the freedom to philosophize. Like anyone else, philosophers must follow the divine law by living justly and charitably, as Spinoza is convinced that they will. (Their philosophical understanding will confirm that a co-operative way of life is a component of our highest good, and motivate them to cultivate it.) Beyond this, however, no demands of piety prevent philosophers from pursuing their distinctive interests and attempting to extend their philosophical knowledge. In sum, nothing in true religion prevents the members of a community either from developing diverse religious outlooks, or from extending their philosophical understanding within the context of a co-operative way of life.

---

[59] Arnoldi, *Vande Conscientie-Dwangh*. Quoted in Pekelharing, 'Reflections on Tolerance and Republicanism: The Case of the Dutch Republic' (unpublished).

Taking up the account of sovereignty that he has now defended, Spinoza draws out the political implications of this view. As the rightful interpreter of divine law, a sovereign will determine what form piety or co-operation is to take, and will use the law to impose its decision on its subjects, philosophers included. The precise scope of religious and philosophical freedom will therefore be fixed by law; but a ruler who accepts the argument of the *Treatise* will be inclined to give his subjects as much freedom as the argument allows. However, as Spinoza acknowledges, a doubt remains. Even if the levels of freedom of religious self-expression and freedom to philosophize that the *Treatise* endorses are consonant with the true religion revealed in Scripture, it remains possible that they may damage the state, for example by fomenting disagreement about the nature of co-operation, or generating arguments for political resistance that may function as an incitement to civil war. Spinoza's account of the relation of philosophy and religion is designed to vindicate both religious and philosophical liberty; but he has not yet said enough to quell the political doubts it is liable to raise, and now goes on to address them.

One of the greatest mistakes that rulers can make is to enact laws that their subjects are unable to obey; so in determining how much religious and philosophical freedom to permit, sovereigns need to consider what the people they are dealing with are capable of. Within any ordinary community there will be disagreement about what is right and wrong, and thus about whether particular laws are good or bad; and because people's beliefs alter with circumstances, areas of consensus and conflict will be in a continual process of formation and dissolution. Explicating the causes of this state of affairs in the *Ethics*, Spinoza focuses on our imaginative grasp of morality. Insofar as we are passionate, we call a thing good when we think it will sustain us and make us joyful, and call a thing bad when we regard it as a source of sadness. But because each of us has a body and a history of our own, conceptions of what is good and bad will vary from one individual or group to another. 'Each person is plentifully supplied with his own faculty of judgment, and there are as many differences between people's heads as between their palates'.[60] This unavoidable diversity is enough to create the potential for conflict; but disagreement is also fuelled by the fact that our ideas about what is good and bad are not merely theoretical observations. Rather, each of us strives on the basis of these ideas to make ourselves joyful; and because our joy increases when other people share our judgments, we are disposed to try to make other people adopt them. 'Each

---

[60] Spinoza, *Tractatus Theologico-Politicus*, ch. 20, p. 239.

of us, by his nature, wants the others to live according to his temperament'.[61]
This struggle may lead us in various directions, but the principle on which it
operates cannot be quenched. The differences of opinion that arise from our
individual constitutions and experience, combined with a passionate tendency
to try to get others to share our views, are a permanent feature of social life and
stand in the way of efforts to create a stable consensus.

The strategies available to sovereigns for dealing with this state of affairs are
limited by the fact that no amount of subjugation can altogether prevent people
from forming their own beliefs. As Spinoza has pointed out, rulers cannot
exercise complete control over their subjects' affects. 'The sovereign would act
in vain if he commanded a subject to hate someone who had benefited him or
love someone who had harmed him, not be offended by insults, or not to desire
to be freed from fear'.[62] Moreover, as the *Treatise* now goes on to reiterate, 'no
one can transfer to another person his natural right or faculty of reasoning
freely'.[63] Once again, the *Ethics* provides a more elaborate justification for this
view. Since the essence of human beings is their striving to maintain themselves, an individual's thinking cannot but be oriented to this end, and as long as
that individual continues to exist, their striving will endure. One manifestation
of this *conatus* is the disposition of human beings to assess and judge their
situations—to work out how things stand and what to do about it. The
judgements they arrive at may be ignorant or well informed, deluded or
insightful, servile or independent, steady or vacillating, but no pressure that a
sovereign can bring to bear can eliminate the disposition to form them. Nor,
for the most part, are we able to prevent ourselves from acting on our judgements. Although subjects and sovereigns may believe that humans are able to
control their actions at will, and consequently have the power to obey or
disobey any decree, Spinoza regards this as an illusion. The complex antecedents of our actions cause us to act as we do, and if we want to change a course
of action we must find ways of modifying them. On the whole, so the *Ethics*
argues, we vastly overestimate our ability to interrupt the passage from thought
to action, failing to recognize that, because we generally do not understand the
causal antecedents on which our actions depend, we do not know how to
redirect them.[64] In more cases than we care to acknowledge, it is not in our
power to do otherwise than act on the basis of our current affects, and this in
turn puts limits on a sovereign's power. When its subjects are not inclined to

---

[61] Spinoza, *Ethics*, 3p31.
[62] Spinoza, *Tractatus Theologico-Politicus*, ch. 17, p. 201.
[63] Ibid. ch. 20, p. 239.   [64] Spinoza, *Ethics*, 3p2s3.

obey the law, it will only be able to make them do so if it can find ways to alter the causes that currently prompt them to disobey.

To be sure, sovereigns sometimes possess this power. By arousing fear or devotion, for example, they can acquire a certain degree of control over the multitude. But in order to make a community completely submissive, rulers would need to understand, and be capable of modifying, the many causes of their subjects' inherently diverse affective dispositions, and no ruler is capable of such a feat. A sovereign's ability to control its subjects' judgements is too limited to force them to abide by its decrees; and their power over their own imaginations is too limited to enable them to agree with a sovereign on demand.

While Spinoza's philosophical arguments for these conclusions are distinctive, the conclusions themselves had already been advocated by other political writers, alive both to the view that belief cannot entirely be forced, and also to the limited power of the will. Sovereigns cannot completely control what people think and feel; but nor, as the *Treatise* now goes on to point out, can they entirely control what people say. Although individuals often pride themselves on being able to conceal their thoughts, 'not even the wisest know how to be silent', and 'it is a common vice of men to entrust their plans to others, even if there is no need for secrecy'.[65] Here, then, is a further limit to sovereign power.

Once again, the limit is not an absolute one. As is all too obvious, sovereigns can cajole or threaten their subjects into taciturnity. But rulers who try to implement this policy will not only come up against a general human incapacity to refrain from saying what one thinks; they will also encounter particularly strong resistance from the philosophically educated. Unlike the vacillating and inconstant beliefs of the ignorant multitude which are open to persuasion and manipulation, rationally grounded conclusions are in Spinoza's view exceptionally hard to shift. So, although a person who fully understands the benefits of obedience will in some respects be tractable and easy to rule, they will nevertheless be incapable of altering an opinion simply because a ruler tells them to do so or offers them an external incentive for changing their mind.[66] To unseat their belief, a sovereign would have to appeal to reason to show them that it was mistaken, and when a belief rests on strong philosophical grounds or compelling imaginative evidence, this may well be impossible. There is consequently something steely about philosophically minded indivi-

---

[65] Spinoza, *Tractatus Theologico-Politicus*, ch. 20, p. 240.   [66] Ibid. ch. 20, p. 244.

duals who are committed to living in the light of their best understanding of the truth, and they will habitually be unable to compromise their integrity by suppressing their genuine opinions. This, too, puts limits on a ruler's power. Sovereigns can no more comprehensively govern the speech of their most rational subjects than they can completely control the passionate tendency of the mob to talk, and thus cannot censor thought or expression 'with absolute right'.[67] As a wise sovereign will acknowledge, thought and its expression partly lie beyond the reach of law.

With these considerations, Spinoza traces the boundaries of political power and maps out the space within which it can operate effectively. There are some forms of oppression that sovereigns cannot impose, but they nevertheless remain relatively powerful, and sometimes have the option of forbidding their subjects to voice religious or philosophical opinions. Should they take advantage of it? Drawing on an established analysis of the dangers of censorship, Spinoza runs through a familiar catalogue of the damaging consequences to which it leads. When people are constrained to think one thing and say another, the loyalty on which a state depends becomes corrupted, flattery and treachery are encouraged, and 'all good arts (artes) are undermined'.[68] Those whom the law penalizes are liable to resent it, and among the subjects who are likely to resist most adamantly are the very individuals whom the state most needs. If they do not opt for exile, these virtuous and independent-minded citizens, who 'do not know how to pretend to be what they are not', will come into confrontation with the law. Unlike criminals who fear death or plead for mercy, 'their mind is not anguished by repentance for a shameful deed; on the contrary . . . they think it honourable to die for freedom'.[69] Faced by their principled disobedience, the sovereign will have no alternative but to punish them; but their courage and integrity are bound to make the sovereign look bad: 'the gallows . . . becomes the noblest stage for displaying the utmost endurance and a model of virtue, to the conspicuous shame of the authorities'.[70] When other subjects view such a spectacle of martyrdom, they may well become vengeful or be filled with compassion for its victims, and this in turn will make them more likely to resist.[71] So if a sovereign is to retain the loyalty and support of subjects who are valuable precisely because they cherish the

---

[67] Ibid. ch. 20, p. 240.
[68] Ibid. ch. 20, p. 243. Similar arguments can be found in P. de la Court, *True Interest*, I, pp. 53–4, ch. 14, pp. 323ff., III, ch. 1.
[69] Spinoza, *Tractatus Theologico-Politicus*, ch. 20, p. 245.
[70] Ibid.
[71] Ibid. ch. 20, p. 246.

honour and freedom that the state should be trying to cultivate, it must acknowledge these dangers. Rather than attempting to eradicate differences of opinion or silence their expression, it should instead put its energy into creating a community where the right to free thought and expression does not undermine the state.

So far, Spinoza's argument is straightforward: freedom of thought cannot be effectively separated from freedom of expression, and since a sovereign cannot prevent the first it should not try to stifle the second. But when he shifts his attention to the delicate relation between freedom of expression and freedom of action, this clearly etched conclusion begins to blur. As we have seen, a sovereign's aim is to get people consistently to obey the law, without paying more attention than necessary to the judgements and affects that motivate them.[72] In some cases, rulers can control what people do without limiting their freedom of expression. (For example, the law may permit a religious sect to express its belief that the ceremonies practised by a rival group are irreligious, while imposing penalties that successfully prevent it from acting on its beliefs by disrupting its rival's acts of worship.) However, as Spinoza has emphasized all along, it is not always possible to hold this line, because there is no sharp distinction between speech and action. We do things with words, and some of the things we do with them are dangerous. Alluding, perhaps, to the Dutch Edict of 1656 by which university professors had been forbidden to philosophize in a fashion that would offend the theological sensibilities of their colleagues,[73] and returning to his earlier observation that the meaning of words and objects is determined by their use, Spinoza acknowledges that our speech acts can be damaging to the state. 'We cannot deny', he claims, 'that treason can be committed by words as well as deeds'. Although it is perilous for a sovereign to attempt to control what people are allowed to say, it will be 'quite as fatal' to grant its subjects unlimited freedom of expression.[74] The difficulty, then, is to determine how far subjects should be permitted to express their opinions, and how far speech and publication should be censored in the name of co-operation and security.

Spinoza's solution to this problem is framed by his theoretical analysis of the transfer of power that constitutes the state. Individuals transfer their right to act as they wish to a sovereign, so that it can secure and enhance their freedom. However, since they cannot transfer their right to form their own judgements, they find themselves in a position where, although they are bound to *act* as the

---

[72] Ibid. ch. 20, p. 240.   [73] Rowen, *John De Witt*, pp. 403–6.
[74] Spinoza, *Tractatus Theologico-Politicus*, ch. 20, p. 240.

sovereign commands, they can rightfully think as they wish. How free does this leave them in respect of speech? Since the state can survive and flourish only if its subjects do not disobey the law, individuals must be prevented from speaking in ways that amount to contravening the sovereign's decrees. But as long as their discourse does not challenge the sovereign's right by violating the law, they should be free to express their opinions. For example, 'if someone shows that a law is contrary to sound reason and argues that it ought to be repealed, and if at the same time he submits his opinion to the judgment of the sovereign, and in the meantime does nothing illegal, he of course deserves well of the state, as one of its best citizens'. Such a course of action is the opposite of treasonous. 'On the other hand, if he acts in order to accuse the magistrates of unfairness and make them hateful to the people, or has seditious reasons for wanting to disregard the law in question . . . he is nothing but a troublemaker (*perturbator*) and a rebel'.[75]

Determining whether an utterance is legitimate is therefore a complex process. As well as taking account of what has been said, one must consider the speaker's intention, the extended context in which the utterance occurred, and how the audience was likely to interpret it. Did the speaker intend to stir up animosity or were they merely trying to draw attention to an injustice? Did they make it clear that they had no intention of breaking the law, or was their manner calculated to excite disobedience? Such questions are often difficult to resolve. As Spinoza observes, there are, for instance, cases where a speaker who appears to be solely concerned to establish the truth about an issue is really motivated by resentment,[76] so that in order to gauge whether their action is harmful one needs to peer beneath its surface. While subjects and sovereigns exercise this skill all the time, the judgements they arrive at will sometimes be contested. In any community, there will be disagreement about what speech acts certain agents are performing and whether their acts pose a threat to the state; and this very debate will in turn make space for further distortion, as agents deliberately misinterpret and polemically redescribe what is going on. Rulers can consequently expect their subjects to hold diverse views, both about the extent to which speech should remain uncensored, and about the types of utterances that people should be free to voice.

To prevent the kind of free for-all-that undermines political authority, someone will have to be given power to judge these difficult issues, and in Spinoza's view that someone is of course the sovereign. As usual, the sovereign

---

[75] Ibid. ch. 20, p. 241.   [76] Ibid. ch. 20, p. 243.

can rightfully use its power in any way it sees fit; but as before, rational sovereigns and subjects will follow certain guidelines. On the assumption that a sovereign has the right to determine how its subjects act, it follows that an act of sedition must consist in challenging or undermining this right. As the *Treatise* puts it, seditious opinions are ones that, 'as soon as they are assumed, destroy the agreement by which each person surrendered his right of acting according to his own decision'.[77] For instance, a person who publicly announces—in appropriate circumstances and with appropriate intentions—'that the supreme power is not its master, or that no one is under an obligation to stand by promises, or that each person ought to live according to his own decision', voices a point of view that challenges the founding principles of the state and therefore counts as seditious.[78]

The argument Spinoza employs here builds on his earlier analysis of the proper limits of religious freedom. As he has already claimed, one lives in a religious fashion by following the divine law; and in order to manage this one must accept a small number of theological beliefs. (For example, so the *Treatise* claims, it is impossible to obey the divine law without believing that God exists.) Since the religious quality of one's life is entirely measured by one's actions, only they can condemn one as irreligious, and as long as one acts in accordance with the divine law one's opinions should not be subject to religious criticism. Nevertheless, some beliefs are incompatible with true religion, and although it may be impossible to prevent people from holding them, their expression can and should be censured. Because a person who publicly denies that God exists, or for that matter challenges any other tenet of faith, undermines the basis of a religious way of life, their act can properly be described as sacrilegious. However—and here Spinoza takes a further step—Scripture's injunction to love one's neighbour only becomes a law when it is interpreted and imposed on a community by the sovereign of a state, who decrees what particular mode of co-operation constitutes a religious way of life. Once such a law is in place, a subject who challenges it by publicly denying the principles on which it depends no longer merely does something that is sacrilegious. Their action also contests the sovereign's right to determine how its subjects should co-operate or act, and is consequently seditious as well. Sacrilege and sedition therefore extend to speech acts that either directly or by implication undermine divine and civil law. One can act seditiously by propounding theological opinions that are incompatible with the co-operative

---

[77] Ibid. ch. 20, p. 242.   [78] Ibid.

form of life laid down by the sovereign, or by voicing political views that threaten the basis of the state.

To twenty-first century ears, this conclusion is liable to sound ominous. The sovereign envisaged in the *Treatise* possesses the sole right to determine which religious and political opinions are seditious, and can legitimately do anything in its power to prevent them from being expressed. However, although this gloss of Spinoza's argument is not wrong, it fails to capture what he presents as its main thrust—that his view gives sovereigns very little power to censor speech, and vindicates wide-ranging freedoms of thought and expression. To see the position in this perspective we need to remember that, in order to act seditiously, one must publicly express an opinion in a manner that is held to be damaging to the state. If one voices the opinion respectfully and shows that one's intentions are constructive, one's act will not be seditious. Furthermore, sovereign power is not as great as it at first appears. Rulers can try to use law to govern what people think; but as we have seen, this is a fruitless enterprise. They can try to make laws that prevent people from expressing their views, but as we have seen, their efforts are liable to backfire. Human psychology being what it is, many people are incapable of obeying such decrees, and their inability to abide by them both brings the law into disrepute and undermines the authority of government. Finally, rulers who try to control opinion often fall into the hands of dangerous factions who want the law to reflect their own particular opinions. 'Laws which command everyone to adopt a particular belief, and prohibit speaking or writing against it, have often been instituted by way of making a concession, or rather surrendering, to the anger of those who cannot endure free minds, but who can, by a certain grim authority, transform the devotion of the seditious mob into frenzy and rouse them against anyone they choose'.[79] To take a case close to home, the struggle between Remonstrants and Counter-Remonstrants is just one example of a religious schism that arose out of an attempt to use law to suppress a religious point of view and resulted in an attempt to usurp the sovereign's right.[80]

A wise sovereign who recognizes these many dangers will therefore try to create an environment where the expression of diverse religious and philo-sophical opinion does not undermine the state and consequently does not need to be limited by law.[81] Nor, Spinoza adds, is this so very difficult. 'In this most

[79] Ibid. ch. 20, p. 244.
[80] Ibid. ch. 20, p. 246.
[81] Justin Steinberg, 'Spinoza on Civil Liberation', *Journal of the History of Philosophy*, 47, no. 1 (2009).

flourishing Republic, this most outstanding city [of Amsterdam], all men of whatever nation or sect live in the greatest harmony. In deciding whether to entrust their goods to someone, they are concerned to know only whether the person is rich or poor, and whether he customarily acts in good faith or deceptively. They don't care at all what religion or sect he belongs to, for that would no nothing to justify or discredit their case before a judge. There is, without exception, no sect so hated that its followers are not protected by the public authority of the magistrates and their forces, provided that they harm no one, give each person his due and live honourably'.[82]

Freedom in the state

If attempts to suppress religious and philosophical liberty are as ineffectual and dangerous as Spinoza claims, sovereigns will obviously be well advised to avoid them. Abolishing freedom of judgement is indeed likely to damage the republic, and it is fair to say, as the title page of the *Treatise* puts it, that 'one cannot destroy the freedom to philosophise without destroying piety and peace'.[83] Although religious and philosophical freedom generate certain inconveniences, these are comparatively insignificant, and need not interfere with a flourishing civic life.[84] If we want piety and peace, and acknowledge a range of psychological constraints that are bound to shape the balance of power between sovereign and subjects, we shall find that there is no realistic alternative to allowing people the freedom to arrive at their own judgements within the limits the *Treatise* has set out, and putting up with any inconveniences that may arise. However, returning again to Spinoza's title page, it looks as though he has more to say on behalf of a freedom of judgement that can be granted 'without damaging piety or peace'.[85] His point is not only that it is excessively risky to suppress this liberty, but also that doing so is not compatible with, or even conducive to, the ends of the state. In the final pages of the *Treatise*, Spinoza indicates how freedom of judgement, and particularly the freedom to philoso-

---

[82] Spinoza, *Tractatus Theologico-Politicus*, ch. 20, p. 246.

[83] Ibid. Preface, p. 3.

[84] Ibid. ch. 20, pp. 245–6. On the implications of Spinoza's defence of freedom of expression for his political philosophy, see Daniel Garber, 'Should Spinoza Have Published His Philosophy?', in *Interpreting Spinoza: Critical Essays*, ed. Charlie Huenemann (Cambridge: Cambridge University Press, 2008); Antonio Negri, '*Reliqua Desiderantur*: A Conjecture for a Definition of the Concept of Democracy in the Final Spinoza', in *The New Spinoza*, ed. Warren Montag and Ted Stolze (Minneapolis, Minn.: University of Minnesota Press, 1997).

[85] Spinoza, *Tractatus Theologico-Politicus*, Preface, p. 7.

phize, can enhance the life of the republic, and strengthen the liberty that is its defining political virtue.

When sovereignty is held by the people, the relationship between sovereign and subjects takes a particular form.[86] Instead of a situation where one agent (such as a monarch) rules over another (a group of individual subjects), the sovereign people rules itself. It exercises its collective power through a legislative assembly whose members are themselves subjects; and all subjects who act as legislators share responsibility for arriving at decrees that benefit the state as a whole. To play a fruitful part in this process, individuals must on the one hand learn to consider themselves as members of a political community on whose collective flourishing their own well-being depends. In their role as legislators, they must do their best to work out how co-operation and security can best be enhanced, and cast their votes accordingly. A minimal requirement of successful republican government is that legislators should achieve the kind of harmony that Spinoza attributes to Amsterdam, by ensuring that everyone is protected under law. But a more ambitious programme requires the sovereign body to create new ways of life in which people are increasingly free to live as they wish, whether because they are subject to fewer constraints than before, or because they find the constraints that bind them less onerous and no longer chafe against them. For a state to progress in this direction, sovereign and subjects must be able to communicate without putting one another at risk. To find out how best to govern, legislators (who are also subjects) need to know what people believe and care about, and in order to acquire this knowledge, they must allow subjects the freedom to express their opinions without fear. However, if these channels of communication are to be kept open, subjects (who may also be legislators) must express their opinions in ways that do not threaten their sovereign. Both overlapping parties play a part in maintaining conversation, by avoiding forms of sedition or exercises of power that will undermine it.

The kind of democratic republic discussed in the *Treatise* does not precisely correspond to this idealized model.[87] As we have seen, Spinoza seems to envisage a polity in which many individuals, including children, women, and

---

[86] Justin Steinberg, 'Benedict Spinoza: Epistemic Democrat', *History of Philosophy Quarterly*, 27, no. 2.

[87] For some discussion of Spinoza's theory of democracy, see Moira Gatens and Genevieve Lloyd, *Collective Imaginings: Spinoza, Past and Present* (London: Routledge, 1999), ch. 3; Israel, *Radical Enlightenment*, ch. 15; Nancy Levene, *Spinoza's Revelation: Religion, Democracy, and Reason* (Cambridge: Cambridge University Press, 2004); Alexandre Matheron, 'The Theoretical Function of Democracy in Spinoza and Hobbes', in *The New Spinoza*, ed. Warren Montag and Ted

servants, are dependent on more powerful parents, employers, fathers, or husbands, and are therefore disadvantaged when it comes to freely voicing their own opinions. Equally, it is unclear how many individuals are eligible to play any part in the business of legislation, and can actually realize the double status that unites the subjects and sovereign of a republic. Nevertheless, there is a democratic tendency in Spinoza's model of the state. To increase a community's security and co-operation, its legislators need to take account of the beliefs and attitudes of its subjects, and the wider the circle of subjects with whom they can communicate, the better they will understand what these beliefs and attitudes are. On the assumption that the most reliable way to find out what people think and care about is to allow them to speak for themselves, they have a reason to extend the right to political inclusion and enable as many people as possible to exercise it. In principle, then, the way to strengthen the state is to devise a way of life that approximates as closely as possible to the republican ideal of liberty, and gives everyone the freedom to speak truth (as they see it) to a power of which they are themselves a part. But this in turn depends upon the freedom to arrive at and express one's opinions about what is and is not true, or to put it differently, on the freedom to philosophize. One benefit of such a liberty is therefore that it contributes to an ethos in which political freedom can grow.

Building a community where this outlook is accepted relies, as Spinoza has pointed out, on more than the blunt instrument of the law. Legislation can certainly help, for example by guaranteeing free speech under certain conditions. But the arts of constructive communication and negotiation on which the strength of a free state rests cannot be created by decree, and here again, the freedom to philosophize plays a crucial role. To allow people this freedom is, among other things, to allow them to express their 'zeal for truth' by publicly rehearsing and debating the arguments and points of view that they take to be most rational. However, the zeal for truth is also, as Spinoza remarks, 'a source of gentleness (*comitas*) and consideration for others (*mansuetudo*)'.[88] People who are genuinely committed to the philosophical project of understanding are open to new ideas and eager to learn. Like all human beings, they want others to accept their point of view; but because they recognize the fruitlessness of trying to force others to reason, they will restrict themselves to encouraging and leading by example. (Somewhat like the ministers of the true church, they will

---

Stolze (Minneapolis, Minn.: University of Minnesota Press, 1997); Negri, '*Reliqua Desiderantur: A Conjecture for a Definition of the Concept of Democracy in the Final Spinoza*'.

[88] Spinoza, *Tractatus Theologico-Politicus*, ch. 20, p. 246.

not resort to verbal or physical aggression, but will rely on encouragement and brotherly admonition. But unlike religious officials, they will aim to ground their views on philosophical understanding rather than imaginative insight.) In a political context, groups who appreciate the value of philosophical reasoning can bring their *mores* to bear on public life and engage in rational discussion and negotiation. The more their habits take hold, the easier it will become for sovereign and subjects to present their points of view and accept criticism, and the more the ability to offer compelling arguments will become a significant form of power or right. Increasingly, a sovereign will be required to justify its policies in rational terms that its subjects can accept, and subjects will be expected to defend their opinions in rational terms that the sovereign can appreciate. By granting the freedom to philosophize, so Spinoza implies, a state extends its ability to develop and become habituated to a respectful, truth-seeking discourse that in turn strengthens the bonds of co-operation on which its security and liberty depend.

How far such a discourse will be able to tame the destructive force of superstition will depend on many circumstances. As the *Treatise* presents the matter, superstition is most dangerous in the hands of monarchical rulers, who may manage to convince their subjects that they possess divine power. This error is less likely to take hold in a republic, where the all-too-human frailties of legislators are harder to conceal, but such states are still vulnerable to the possibility that their religious leaders may try to foment superstition. Spinoza's model of the state is carefully designed to minimize this risk. By drastically diminishing the scope of theological authority and defining true religion as he does, he limits the capacity of preachers or false prophets to make people afraid; and by giving the sovereign the right to interpret the divine law, he awards it a power that traditionally belonged to prophets, the spokesmen or inter-preters of God.[89] What the sovereign cannot be given, however, is the capacity to capture the imagination of the populace, so that even the best governed republics need to be on their guard against charismatic leaders bent on undermining sovereign power. The more the state cultivates a gentle and encouraging ethos in which the people have little to fear, the less will they be susceptible to superstition; but since hope and fear are ineradicable passions, this susceptibility can never be entirely extirpated. Because the darker side of imagination is always present, a democratic sovereign must carefully monitor

---

[89] Ibid. ch. 1, p. 15.

the affects both of its own legislators and of the people, to prevent or halt the growth of superstitious terror.

Spinoza knows that people who call themselves philosophers can be quarrelsome and sophistical, and that many of them have espoused doctrines that are in his view seditious. In defending the freedom to philosophize he is, therefore, not defending everything that has gone by the name of philosophy. Philosophizing, as he presents it in the *Treatise*, is a disciplined form of thinking that aims to improve our understanding of the principles that will best guide us to live peacefully and freely, and which secretes its own norms of truth and considerate discussion. As Spinoza's remarks about his opponents reveal, however, even the most dedicated philosophers can find these norms impossible to maintain, and may, in moments of extreme indignation, express themselves aggressively. To limit the antagonism that such outbursts can cause, philosophizing must be a public activity carried on within the state and subject to certain restrictions. Moreover, while a bad philosopher may resent these limits and find them irksome, a wise one will embrace them gladly. Although philosophical enquiry yields a rational understanding of the need to live harmoniously with others, and generates a deep commitment to this end, philosophers are no more in a position than other subjects to determine precisely how this goal is to be achieved. The conciliatory task of a democratic sovereign is therefore to place philosophy in a political context and, by appealing to both reason and imagination, to cobble together a free way of life.

Bibliography

A[itzema], L. V[an]. *Herstelde Leeuw of Discours Over't Gepasseerde in De Vereenigde Nedelanden in 'Tjaer Ende 1651*. Amsterdam, 1652.

Althusius, Johannes. *Politica methodica digesta*. Translated by Frederick Smith Carney. Indianapolis: Liberty Fund, 1995.

Althusser, Louis. 'On Spinoza'. In *Essays in Self-Criticism*. London: New Left Books, 1976, 132–41.

—— 'The Only Materialist Tradition, Part 1: Spinoza'. In *The New Spinoza*, edited by Warren Montag and Ted Stolze. Minneapolis, Minn.: University of Minnesota Press, 1997, 1–9.

Apollonius, Gulielmus. *Jus Majestatis circa sacra, sive Tractatus Theologicus, de jure magistratus circa res ecclesiasticas*. Middleburg, 1642–3.

Aquinas, Thomas. *Summa Theologica*. Rome: Forzani, 1894.

Aristotle. *Politics*. Translated by Ernest Barker, revised by Richard Stalley. Oxford: Oxford University Press, 1995.

Arminius, Jacobus. *The Works of James Arminius*. Translated by James Nichols and William Nichols. Grand Rapids, Mich.: Baker, 1986.

Arnoldi, Henricus van der Linde. *Vande Conscientie-Dwangh, dat is: klaer ende grondich vertoogh, dat de Staten Generaal in haer placcaet den 3. Julij 1619*. Delft, 1629.

Asselt, W. J. van. *The Federal Theology of Johannes Cocceius (1603–1669)*. Leiden: Brill, 2001.

Augustine. *Confessions*. Translated by R. S. Pine-Coffin. Harmondsworth: Penguin Books, 1961.

—— *The City of God against the Pagans*. Translated and edited by R. W. Dyson. Cambridge: Cambridge University Press, 1998.

Bacon, Francis. *The Advancement of Learning*. Edited by James Spedding, Robert Ellis, and Douglas Denon Heath. Vol. IV, *The Works of Francis Bacon*. London: Longmans, 1858.

—— 'Of Superstition'. In *Francis Bacon*, edited by Brian Vickers. Oxford: Oxford University Press, 1996.

Balibar, Étienne. 'Spinoza: From Individuality to Transindividuality'. In *Medelingen Vanwege Het Spinozahuis*. Delft: Eburon, 1997.

—— 'Spinoza the Anti-Orwell: The Fear of the Masses'. In *Masses, Classes, Ideas: Studies on Politics and Philosophy before and after Marx*. London: Routledge, 1994, 3–37.

—— '*Jus-Pactum-Lex*: On the Constitution of the Subject in the *Theologico-Political Treatise*'. In *The New Spinoza*, edited by Warren Montag and Ted Stolze. Minneapolis, Minn.: University of Minnesota Press, 1997.

—— *Spinoza and Politics*. Translated by Peter Snowden. London: Verso, 1998, 171–208.

Bangs, Karl. *Arminius: A Study in the Dutch Reformation*. Nashville: Abingdon Press, 1971.

Bayle, Pierre. *Dictionnaire historique et critique*. Rotterdam, 1697.

—— *Historical and Critical Dictionary*. Translated by Richard H. Popkin. Indianapolis, Ind. Bobbs-Merrill, 1965.

—— *Écrits sur Spinoza*. Edited by Pierre-François Moreau and Françoise Charles-Daubert. Paris: Berg International, 1983.

Beardslee, John Walter. *Reformed Dogmatics. J. Wollebius, G. Voetius, F. Turretin*. Edited and translated by John W. Beardslee *[Library of Protestant Thought]*. Oxford: Oxford University Press, 1965.

Beck, Andreas J. 'Gisbertus Voetius (1589–1676): Basic Features of His Doctrine of God'. In *Reformation and Scholasticism: Texts and Studies in Reformation and Post-Reformation Thought*, edited by W. J. van Asselt and E. Dekker. Grand Rapids, Mich.: Baker Academic, 2001, 205–26.

Belaief, Gail. *Spinoza's Philosophy of Law*. The Hague: Mouton, 1971.

Belgic Confession, The. In *The Creeds of Christendom: The Evangelical Protestant Creeds*, edited by Philip Schaff. New York: Cosimo Books, 2007, 383–436.

Bennett, Jonathan. 'Teleology and Spinoza's Conatus'. *Midwest Studies in Philosophy* 8, no. 1 (1983), 143–60.

—— *A Study of Spinoza's Ethics*. Cambridge: Cambridge University Press, 1984.

—— *Learning from Six Philosophers: Descartes, Spinoza, Leibniz, Locke, Berkeley, Hume*. Oxford: Clarendon Press, 2001.

Bizer, Ernest. 'Reformed Orthodoxy and Cartesianism'. *Journal for Theology and the Church* 2 (1965), 20–82.

Black, Jeremy. *Maps and History: Constructing Images of the Past*. New Haven: Yale University Press, 1997.

Blom, Hans. 'Spinoza on *Res Publica*: Republics and Monarchies'. In *Monarchisms in an Age of Enlightenment: Liberty, Patriotism and the Public Good*, edited by John Christian Larsen, Lisa Simonutti, and Hans Blom. Toronto: University of Toronto Press, 2007, 19–44.

—— and J. M Kerkohven. 'A Letter Concerning an Early Draft of Spinoza's Treatise on Religion and Politics?' *Studia Spinozana* 1 (1985): 371–7.

Bol, Ferdinand. 'Consul Titus Manlius Torquatus Beheading His Son'. Oil on canvas. Amsterdam: Rijksmuseum, 1661–3.

Boralevi, L. Campos. 'Classical Foundational Myths of European Republicanism: The Jewish Commonwealth'. In *Republicanism: A Shared Europen Heritage*, edited by Martin van Gelderen and Quentin Skinner. 2 vols., Cambridge: Cambridge University Press, 2002, vol. 1, 247–61.

Bove, Laurent. *La stratégie du Conatus: Affirmation et résistance chez Spinoza*. Paris: Vrin, 1996.

Brasz, Chaya, and Yosef Kaplan, eds. *Dutch Jews as Perceived by Themselves and by Others: Proceedings of the Eighth International Symposium on the History of the Jews in the Netherlands.* Leiden: Brill, 2001.

Bredekamp, Horst. *Thomas Hobbes: Visuelle Strategien.* Berlin: Akademie Verlag, 1999.

Breton, Stanislas. *Spinoza, théologie et politique.* Paris: Desclée, 1977.

Brutus, Stephanus Junius. *Vindiciæ contra tyrannos: siue, de principis in populum, populique in principem, legitima potestate.* Edinburgh [Basel], 1579.

Brykman, Geneviève. *La Judéité de Spinoza.* Paris: Vrin, 1972.

Bunge, Wiep van. 'On the Early Dutch Reception of the *Tractatus Theologico-Politicus*'. *Studia Spinozana* 5 (1989), 225–51.

—— *From Stevin to Spinoza: An Essay on Philosophy in the Seventeenth-Century Dutch Republic.* Leiden: Brill, 2001.

Burnett, Stephen G. *From Christian Hebraism to Jewish Studies: Johannes Buxtorf (1564–1629) and Hebrew Learning in the Seventeenth Century.* Leiden: Brill, 1996.

Buxtorf, Johannes. *Tiberias sive commentarius masorethicus.* Basel, 1620.

Caccarelli, Alessandro. 'L'orizzonte problematico della ragione Spinozista e il concetto della historia scripturae del *Tractatus Theologico-Politicus*'. In *Spinoza: Individuo e moltitudine*, edited by Vittorio Morfino et Stefano Caporali. Cesena: Il Ponte Vecchio, 2007, 117–28.

Calvin, John. *Commentary upon the Epistle of Saint Paul to the Romans.* Translated by Christopher Rosdell. Edited by Henry Beveridge. Edinburgh: The Calvin Translation Society, 1844.

—— *Commentaries on the Epistles to Timothy, Titus, and Philemon.* Translated by Rev. William Pringle. Edinburgh: Calvin Translation Society, 1856.

Calvin, Jean. *Institutes of the Christian Religion.* Translated and edited by John Thomas McNeill and Ford Lewis Battles, *The Library of Christian Classics.* Philadelphia, Pa.: Westminster Press, 1960–1.

Cameron, Evan. *Enchanted Europe: Superstition, Reason and Religion, 1250–1750.* Oxford: Oxford University Press, 2010.

Canons of the Synod of Dort. In *The Creeds of Christendom: The Evangelical Protestant Creeds*, edited by Philip Schaff. New York: Cosimo Books, 2007, 550–97.

Cappel, Ludovico. *Critica sacra, siue de variis quæ in sacris Veteris Testamenti libris occurrunt lectionibus libri sex.* Paris, 1650.

Carriero, John. 'Spinoza's Views on Necessity in Historical Perspective'. *Philosophical Topics* 19 (1991), 47–96.

Chalier, Catherine. *Spinoza lecteur de Maïmonide: La question théologico-politique.* Paris: Cerf, 2006.

Cicero, Marcus Tullius. *De natura deorum.* Edited by Joseph B. Mayor. Oxford: Oxford University Press, 1880.

—— *On Duties.* Translated by Walter Miller, *Loeb Classical Library.* Cambridge, Mass.: Harvard University Press, 1913.

—— *De divinatione*. Edited by Arthur Stanley Pease. Urbana: University of Illinois, 1920–1923.

—— *De finibus bonorum et malorum*. Translated by Harris Rackham, *Loeb Classical Library*. London: Heinemann, 1921.

—— *De re publica, de legibus*. Translated by C.W. Keyes. *Loeb Classical Library*. Cambridge, Mass.: Harvard University Press, 1977.

—— *De officiis*. Translated by Walter Miller, *Loeb Classical Library*. Cambridge, Mass.: Harvard University Press, 1913.

Clark, Stuart. *Thinking with Demons: The Idea of Witchcraft in Early Modern Europe*. Oxford: Clarendon Press, 1997.

Cocceius, Johannes. 'Prophetia Ezechielis: commentario illustrata (1668)'. In *Opera omnia theologica exegetica didactica polemica philologica*. Amsterdam, 1673–5.

—— *Summa theologiae ex scripturis repetita*. Amsterdam, 1669.

Cohen de Herrera, Abraham. *Gate of Heaven*. Translated by Kenneth Krabbenhoft. Leiden: Brill, 2002.

Cohen, Hermann. 'Spinoza über Staat und religion, Judentum Und Chistendum'. In *Jüdische Schriften*, edited by Bruno Strauss, Berlin: Schwetschke, 1924, 290–372.

Colie, Rosalie. *Light and Enlightenment: A Study of the Cambridge Platonists and the Dutch Arminians*. Cambridge: Cambridge University Press, 1957.

Constans, Lucius Antistius. *De jure ecclesiasticorum, liber singularis*. Amsterdam, 1665.

Coornhert, Dirck Volckertsz. 'Proces van't ketterdooden ende dwangh der conscientien. Tusschen Justum Lipsium . . . ende Dirck Coornhert. het eerste deel politijck (1589)'. In *Wercken*, Vol. 2, fols. 42–109. Amsterdam, 1630.

—— 'Synodus van der conscientien vryheydt (1582)'. In *Wercken*, Vol. 2, fols. 1–42. Amsterdam, 1630.

Coornhert, Frans. *Cort onderwijs eens Liefhebbers des welstandts deser Nederlanden* (Amsterdam, 1586).

Cunaeus, Petrus. *De republica hebraeorum*. Edited by Lea Campos Boralevi. Florence: Centro Editoriale Toscano, 1996.

—— *The Hebrew Republic*. Translated by Peter Wyetzner. Jerusalem: Shalem Press, 2006.

Curley, Edwin. *Spinoza's Metaphysics: An Essay in Interpretation*. Cambridge, Mass.: Harvard University Press, 1969.

—— 'Spinoza's Moral Philosophy'. In *Spinoza: A Collection of Critical Essays*, edited by Marjorie Grene. Notre Dame, Ind.: University of Notre Dame Press, 1973, 354–76.

—— 'Notes on a Neglected Masterpiece: The *Tractatus Theologico Politicus* as Prolegomenon to the *Ethics*'. In *Central Themes in Modern Philosophy*, edited by M. Kulstad and J. Cover. Indianapolis, Ind.: Hackett, 1990.

—— 'On Bennett's Spinoza: The Issue of Teleology'. In *Spinoza: Issues and Directions*. Leiden: Brill, 1990, 39–52.

Curley, Edwin. 'The State of Nature and Its Law in Hobbes and Spinoza'. *Philosophical Topics* 19, no. 1 (1991), 97–117.

—— 'Spinoza and the Science of Hermeneutics'. In *Spinoza: The Enduring Questions*, edited by Graeme Hunter. Toronto: University of Toronto Press, 1994.

—— '"I Durst Not Write So Boldly" or How to Read Hobbes' Theologico-Political Treatise'. In *Studi su Hobbes e Spinoza*, edited by Emilia Giancotti. Naples: Bibliopolis, 1996.

—— 'Kissinger, Spinoza and Genghis Khan'. In *The Cambridge Companion to Spinoza*. Cambridge: Cambridge University Press, 1996, 315–42.

Curley, Edwin, and Gregory Walski. 'Spinoza's Necessitarianism Reconsidered'. In *New Essays on the Rationalists*, edited by Rocco J. Gennaro and Charles Huenemann. Oxford: Oxford University Press, 1999, 241–62.

Curtius Rufus, Quintus. *History of Alexander*. Translated by John C. Rolfe. 2 vols, *Loeb Classical Library*. Cambridge, Mass.: Harvard University Press, 1946.

Daston, Lorraine, and Michael Stolleis, eds. *Natural Laws and Laws of Nature in Early Modern Europe: Jurisprudence, Theology, Moral and Natural Philosophy*. Aldershot: Ashgate, 2008.

De la Court, Pieter and/or Johan. *Consideratien van staat, ofte polityke weeg-school beschreven door*. Amsterdam, 1661.

—— *La balance politique de J. et P. de la Court. Livre premier*. Translated by Madeleine Francès. Paris, 1937.

De la Court, Pieter. *The True Interest and Political Maxims of the Republic of Holland*. London, 1746.

Del Lucchese, Filippo. *Conflict, Power, and Multitude in Machiavelli and Spinoza*. London: Continuum, 2009.

Della Rocca, Michael. 'Spinoza's Metaphysical Psychology'. In *The Cambridge Companion to Spinoza*, edited by Don Garrett. Cambridge: Cambridge University Press, 1996, 192–266.

Delumeau, Jean. *Catholicism between Luther and Voltaire: A New View of the Counter-Reformation*. Translated by Jeremy Moiser. London: Burns and Oates, 1977.

Descartes, René. *Oeuvres de Descartes*. Edited by Charles Adam and Paul Tannery. Paris: Vrin, 1974.

—— *The Philosophical Writings of Descartes* (3 Vols). Translated by John Cottingham, Robert Stoothoff, and Dugald Murdoch. Cambridge: Cambridge University Press, 1985.

Douglas, Alexander. 'Spinoza's Vindication of Philosophy: Reshaping Early Modern Debate About the Division between Philosophy and Theology'. Phd Thesis. Birkbeck College, University of London, 2011.

Elisabeth, Countess Palatine, and René Descartes. *The Correspondence between Princess Elisabeth of Bohemia and René Descartes*. Translated and edited by Lisa Shapiro. Chicago: University of Chicago Press, 2007.

Enden, Franciscus van den. *Vrye politijke stellingen en consideratien van staat, met een inleiding van Wim Klever*. Amsterdam: Wereldbibliotheek, 1992.

—— *Free Political Proposition and Considerations of State*. Translated by Wim Klever. Amsterdam: Wim Klever, 2007.

Episcopius, Simon. *The Confession or Declaration of the Ministers or Pastors which in the United Provinces are called Remonstrants, Concerning the Chief Points of Christian Religion*. Translated by Thomas Taylor. London, 1676.

Feuer, Lewis. *Spinoza and the Rise of Liberalism*. Brunswick: Transaction, Inc., 1987.

Finocchiaro, Maurice A. *The Galileo Affair: A Documentary History, California Studies in the History of Science*. Berkeley: University of California Press, 1989.

Fisch, Harold. 'The Messianic Politics of Menasseh Ben Israel'. In *Menasseh Ben Israel and His World*, edited by Yosef Kaplan, Henry Méchoulan, and Richard H. Popkin. Leiden: Brill, 1989, 228–39.

Fitzmeyer, Joseph Augustine. *The Semitic Background of the New Testament*. Grand Rapids, Mich.: Eerdmans, 1997.

Fix, Andrew C. *Prophecy and Reason: The Dutch Collegiants in the Early Enlightenment*. Princeton: Princeton University Press, 1991.

Freudenthal, J. *Die Lebensgeschichte Spinozas in Quellenschriften, urkunden und Nichtamtlichen Nachrichten*. 2 vols. Leipzig: von Veit, 1899.

Frijhoff, Willem, Marijke Spies, and Myra Heerspink Scholz. *Dutch Culture in a European Perspective. 1, 1650, Hard-Won Unity*. Basingstoke: Palgrave Macmillan, 2004.

Funkenstein, Amos. *Theology and the Scientific Imagination: From the Middle Ages to the Seventeenth Century*. Princeton: Princeton University Press, 1986.

Garber, Daniel. 'Descartes and Spinoza on Persistence and Conatus', *Studia Spinozana* 10 (1994), 43–67.

—— 'Should Spinoza Have Published His Philosophy?' In *Interpreting Spinoza: Critical Essays*, edited by Charlie Huenemann. Cambridge: Cambridge University Press, 2008, 166–87.

Garrett, Don. 'Spinoza's Necessitarianism'. In *God and Nature: Spinoza's Metaphysics: Papers Presented at the First Jerusalem Conference (Ethica I)*, edited by Yirmiyahu Yovel. Leiden: Brill, 1991.

—— 'Teleology in Spinoza and Early Modern Rationalism'. In *New Essays on the Rationalists*, edited by Rocco J. Gennaro and Charles Huenemann. Oxford: Oxford University Press, 1999, 310–335.

—— 'Spinoza's *Conatus* Argument'. In *Spinoza: Metaphysical Themes*, edited by Olli I. Koistinen and John I. Biro. Oxford: Oxford University Press, 2002, 127–58.

—— '"Promising Ideas": Hobbes and Contract in Spinoza's Political Philosophy'. In *Spinoza's 'Theologico-Political Treatise'*, edited by Yitzhak Y. Melamed and Michael A. Rosenthal. Cambridge: Cambridge University Press, 2010, 192–209.

Gatens, Moira. 'Spinoza's Disturbing Thesis: Power, Norms and Fiction in the *Tractatus Theologico-Politicus*', *History of Political Thought* 30, no. 3 (2009), 455–68.

Gatens, Moira. 'The Politics of Imagination'. In *Feminist Interpretations of Benedict Spinoza*, University Park, Pa.: Pennsylvania State University Press, 2009, 189–209.

—— and Genevieve Lloyd. *Collective Imaginings: Spinoza, Past and Present*. London: Routledge, 1999.

Gebhardt, Carl. *Kommentar zum Tractatus Theologico-Politicus*. Edited by Carl Gebhardt. Vol. V, *Opera*. Heidelberg: Carl Winter, 1987.

Gelderen, Martin van. *The Political Thought of the Dutch Revolt, 1555–1590*. Cambridge: Cambridge University Press, 1992.

—— *The Dutch Revolt*. Cambridge: Cambridge University Press, 1993.

—— 'Aristotelians, Monarchomachs and Republicans: Sovereignty and *Respublica Mixta* in Dutch and German Political Thought 1580–1650'. In *Republicanism: A Shared European Heritage*, edited by Martin van Gelderen and Quentin Skinner. 2 vols. Cambridge: Cambridge University Press, 2002, vol. 1, 195–217.

Geyl, Pieter. *A History of the Dutch Speaking Peoples 1555–1648*. London: Phoenix Press, 2001.

Giancotti, Emilia. *Studi su Hobbes e Spinoza*. Naples: Bibliopolis, 1996.

Goldie, Mark. 'The Theory of Religious Intolerance in Restoration England'. In *From Persecution to Toleration: The Glorious Revolution and Religion in England*, edited by Jonathan Israel, Nicholas Tyacke, and Ole Peter Grell. Oxford: Clarendon Press, 1991, 331–68.

Gomarus, Franciscus. *Waerschouwinghe over de Vermaninghe aen R. Donteclock*. Leiden, 1609.

Goshen-Gottstein, M. 'Bible Et Judaïsme'. In *Le grand siècle et la Bible*, edited by Jean-Robert Armogathe. Paris: Beauchesne, 1989, 33–8.

Goshen-Gottstein, M. H. 'The Textual Criticism of the Old Testament: Rise, Decline, Rebirth', *Journal of Biblical Literature* 102, no. 3 (1983), 365–99.

Gottlieb, Michah. 'Spinoza's Method(s) of Biblical Interpretation Reconsidered', *Jewish Studies Quarterly* 14, no. 3 (2007), 286–317.

Grafton, Anthony. *Joseph Scaliger: A Study in the History of Classical Scholarship*. Oxford: Clarendon Press, 1983–93.

—— *What Was History? The Art of History in Early Modern Europe*. Cambridge: Cambridge University Press, 2007.

Grassi, Paolo. *L'interpretazione del'imaginario: Uno studio di Spinoza*. Pisa: Edizioni ETS, 2002.

—— 'Adam and the Serpent'. In *Feminist Interpretations of Benedict Spinoza*, edited by Moira Gatens. University Park, Pa.: Pennsylvania State University Press, 2009, 145–53.

Grotius, Hugo. *De imperio summarum potestatem circa sacra* (1648). Translated C. Barksdale as *Of the Authority of the Highest Powers About Sacred Things*. London, 1651.

—— *Hugonis Grotii opera omnia theologica, etc.* Edited by Pieter de Groot. Amsterdam, 1679.

—— *De Republica Emendanda (1601)*. The Hague, 1984.

—— *Ordinum Hollandiae ac Westfrisiae pietas (1613)*. Edited by Edwin Rabbie. Leiden: Brill, 1995.

—— *The Rights of War and Peace*. Edited by Richard Tuck. Indianapolis, Ind.: Liberty Fund, 2005.

Haakonssen, Knud. *Natural Law and Moral Philosophy from Grotius to the Scottish Enlightenment*. Cambridge: Cambridge University Press, 1996.

Haitsma Mulier, E. O. G. *The Myth of Venice and Dutch Republican Thought in the Seventeenth Century*. Assen: Gorcum, 1980.

Harrison, Peter. *The Bible, Protestantism, and the Rise of Natural Science*. Cambridge: Cambridge University Press, 1998.

Harvey, Warren Zev. 'Spinoza on Ibn Ezra's "Secret of the Twelve"'. In *Spinoza's 'Theologico-Political Treatise'*, edited by Yitzhak Y. Melamed and Michael A. Rosenthal. Cambridge: Cambridge University Press, 2010, 41–55.

Heerich, Thomas. *Transformation des Politikkonzepts von Hobbes zu Spinoza: Das problem der Souveränität*. Würzburg: Königshausen & Neumann, 2000.

Heidanus, Abraham. *Eenige Stellingen Aengaende den Rust-Dagh en den Dagh des Heeren . . . uyt het Latijn Vertaelt*. Utrecht, 1658.

Heidelberg Catechism, The. In *The Creeds of Christendom: The Evangelical Protestant Creeds*, edited by Philip Schaff. New York: Cosimo Books, 2007, 307–55.

Heyd, Michael. *Between Orthodoxy and the Enlightenment: Jean-Robert Chouet and the Introduction of Cartesian Science in the Academy of Geneva*. The Hague: Nijhoff, 1982.

—— 'Menasseh Ben Israel as a Meeting Point of Jewish and European History: Some Summary Comments'. In *Menasseh Ben Israel and His World*, edited by Yosef Kaplan, Henry Méchoulan, and Richard H. Popkin. Leiden: Brill, 1989, 262–7.

—— *'Be Sober and Reasonable': The Critique of Enthusiasm in the Seventeenth and Early Eighteenth Centuries*. Leiden: Brill, 1995.

—— 'The "Jewish Quaker": Christian Perceptions of Sabbatai Zevi as an Enthusiast'. In *Hebraica Veritas? Christian Hebraists and the Study of Judaism in Early Modern Europe*, edited by Alison P. Coudert and Jeffrey S. Shoulson. Philadelphia, Pa.: University of Pennsylvania Press, 2004, 234–65.

Hobbes, Thomas. *Thomæ Hobbes Malmesburiensis opera philosophica quæ Latine scripsit, omnia . . .* Amsterdam, 1668.

—— 'De Corpore'. In *The English Works of Thomas Hobbes of Malmesbury*, edited by William Molesworth, 11 vols. London: J. Bohn, 1839, vol. 1.

—— *Leviathan*. Edited by Richard Tuck. Cambridge: Cambridge University Press, 1996.

—— *On the Citizen*. Edited by Richard Tuck and Michael Silverthorne. Cambridge: Cambridge University Press, 1998.

Hodder, R. Ward. *John Calvin and the Grounding of Interpretation*. Leiden: Brill, 2006.

Israel, Jonathan. *The Dutch Republic: Its Rise, Greatness and Fall, 1477–1806*. Oxford: Clarendon Press, 1995.

Israel, Jonathan. *Radical Enlightenment: Philosophy and the Making of Modernity, 1650–1750*. Oxford: Oxford University Press, 2001.

Israel, Manasseh Ben. *The Hope of Israel*. Translated by Moses Wall. Edited by Henry Méchoulan and Gérard Nahon. Oxford: Oxford University Press, 1987.

James, Susan. *Passion and Action: The Emotions in Seventeenth-Century Philosophy*. Oxford: Clarendon Press, 1997.

—— 'The Role of *Amicitia* in Political Life'. In *The Concept of Love in Seventeenth and Eighteenth Century Philosophy*, edited by Gabor Boros, Herman de Dijn and Martin Moors. Leuven: Leuven University Press, 2007, 43–54.

—— 'Democracy and the Good Life in Spinoza's Philosophy'. In *Interpreting Spinoza: Critical Essays*, edited by Charlie Huenemann. Cambridge: Cambridge University Press, 2008, 128–46.

—— 'Shakespeare and the Politics of Superstition'. In *Shakespeare and Early Modern Political Thought*, edited by David Armitage, Conal Condren, and Andrew Fitzmaurice. Cambridge: Cambridge University Press, 2009, 80–98.

—— 'Freedom, Slavery and the Passions'. In *The Cambridge Companion to Spinoza's Ethics*, edited by Olli Koistinen. Cambridge: Cambridge University Press, 2009, 223–41.

—— 'Narrative as the Means to Freedom: Spinoza on the Uses of Imagination'. In *Spinoza's 'Theologico-Political Treatise'*, edited by Yitzhak Y. Melamed and Michael A. Rosenthal. Cambridge: Cambridge University Press, 2010, 250–67.

—— 'Creating Rational Understanding: Spinoza as a Social Epistemologist', *Proceedings of the Aristotelian Society*, Supplementary volume 85, no. 1 (2011).

Jarrett, Charles. 'Spinoza on the Relativity of Good and Evil'. In *Spinoza: Metaphysical Themes*, edited by Olli I. Koistinen and John I. Biro. Oxford: Oxford University Press, 2002, 159–81.

Jonge, H. J. de. 'The Study of the New Testament'. In *Leiden University in the Seventeenth Century: An Exchange of Learning*, edited by Th H. Lunsingh Scheurleer and G. H. M. Posthumus Meyjes. Leiden: Brill, 1975, 65–110.

Josephus, Flavius. *The Life. Against Apion*. Translated by H. St J. Thackeray, *Loeb Classical Library*. London: Heinemann, 1926.

—— *Jewish Antiquities*. Translated and edited by H. St J. Thackeray and Louis H. Feldman. 8 vols. Cambridge, Mass.: Harvard University Press, 1930–65.

Kaplan, Benjamin J. *Calvinists and Libertines: Confession and Community in Utrecht, 1578–1620*. Oxford: Clarendon Press, 1995.

—— *Divided by Faith: Religious Conflict and the Practice of Toleration in Early Modern Europe*. Cambridge, Mass.: Belknap Press of Harvard University Press, 2007.

Kaplan, Yosef. *From Christianity to Judaism: The Story of Isaac Orobio De Castro*. Oxford: Oxford University Press, 1989.

—— *An Alternative Path to Modernity: The Sephardi Diaspora in Western Europe*. Leiden: Brill, 2000.

—— Henry Méchoulan, and Richard H. Popkin. *Menasseh Ben Israel and His World*. Leiden: Brill, 1989.

Kasher, Asa, and Shlomo Biderman. 'Why Was Baruch de Spinoza Excommunicated?' In *Skeptics, Millenarians and Jews*, edited by David S. Katz and Jonathan Israel. Leiden: Brill, 1990.

Katchen, Aaron L. *Christian Hebraists and Dutch Rabbis: Seventeenth Century Apologetics and the Study of Maimonides' Mishneh Torah*. Cambridge, Mass.: Harvard University Press, 1984.

Kelin-Braslavy, Sara. 'Bible Commentary'. In *The Cambridge Companion to Maimonides*, edited by Kenneth Seeskin. Cambridge: Cambridge University Press, 2005, 245–54.

Klever, Wim. 'A New Source of Spinozism: Franciscus Van Den Enden', *Journal of the History of Philosophy* 29, no. 4 (1991), 613–31.

—— 'L'erreur de Lambertus Van Velthuysen (1622–85) et des Velthuysiens'. In *The Spinozistic Heresy/L'hérésie Spinoziste: The Debate on the Tractatus Theologico-Politicus, 1670–1677*, edited by Paolo Cristofolini. Amsterdam: APA–Holland University Press, 1995, 138–46.

Koerbagh, Adriaan. *Een Bloemhof von allerley lieflykheyd sonder vedriet geplant*. Amsterdam, 1668.

Koistinen, Olli. 'Spinoza's Proof of Necessitarianism', *Philosophy and Phenomenological Research* 67 (2003), 283–310.

Koivuniemi, Minna. 'L'imagination et les affects chez Spinoza'. *Documents Archives de travail et Arguments*: Spinoza. L'esprit, les passions la politique, No. 52, (2010). Lyon: École Normale Supériure de Lyon—site René Descartes, 25–59.

Kreisel, Howard T. *Prophecy: The History of an Idea in Medieval Jewish Philosophy*. Dordrecht: Kluwer, 2001.

Krop, Henri. 'Spinoza and the Calvinistic Cartesianism of Lambertus Van Velthuysen', *Studia Spinozana* 15 (1999), 107–36.

La Peyrère, Isaac. *Systema theologicum, ex praeadamitarum hypothesi. Pars prima*. N.p., 1655.

—— *A Theological System*. London, 1665.

Lagrée, Jacqueline. 'Louis Meyer et la *Philosophia S. Scripturae Interpretes*. Projet Cartésien, horizon Spinoziste', *Revue des sciences philosophiques et théologiques* 1 (1987), 31–44.

—— 'Sense et Vérité: philosophie et théologie chez L. Meyer et Spinoza', *Studia Spinozana* 4 (1988): 75–81.

—— *La raison ardente: Religion naturelle et raison au xviie siècle*. Paris: Vrin, 1991.

—— and Moreau, Pierre-François. 'La lecture de la Bible dans le cercle de Spinoza'. In *Le grand siècle et la Bible*, edited by Jean-Robert Armogathe. Paris: Beauchesne, 1989, 97–115.

Lapide, C. à. *In Pentateuchum Mosis commentaria*. Paris, 1630.

—— *Commentarius in Esdram, Nehemiam, Tobiam, Judith, Esther, et Machabæos*. Antwerp, 1734.

Lazzeri, Christian. *Droit, pouvoir et liberté: Spinoza critique de Hobbes*. Paris: Presses Universitaires de France, 1998.

Leon, Jacob Judah. *Retrato del Templo de Selomoh*. Middelburg, Va., 1642.

Levene, Nancy. *Spinoza's Revelation: Religion, Democracy, and Reason*. Cambridge: Cambridge University Press, 2004.

Levinas, Emmanuel. 'Le Cas Spinoza'. In *Difficile liberté: Essais sur le Judaisme*. Paris: Albin Michel, 1963, 144–49.

Limborch, Philippus van, and Baltasar Oróbio De Castro. *De veritate religionis Christianæ, amica collatio cum erudito Judæo*. Gouda, 1687.

Lin, Martin. 'Spinoza's Metaphysics of Desire'. *Archiv für Geschichte der Philosophie* 86, no. 1 (2004), 21–55.

—— 'Teleology and Human Action in Spinoza'. *The Philosophical Review* 115, no. 3 (2006).

Livy. *Ab urbe condita*, trans. B. O. Foster et al., 14 vols. *Loeb Classical Library*. London: Heinemann, 1919-59.

Lloyd, Genevieve. *Routledge Philosophy Guidebook to Spinoza and the Ethics*. London: Routledge, 1996.

Locke, John. *Two Treatises of Government*. Edited by Peter Laslett. Cambridge: Cambridge University Press, 1960.

Macherey, Pierre. *Hegel ou Spinoza*. Paris: François Maspero, 1979.

—— 'Louis Meyer, Interprète de l'écriture'. In *Avec Spinoza: Études sur la doctrine et l'histoire du Spinozisme*. Paris: Presses Universitaires de France, 1992, 168–72.

Machiavelli, Niccolò. *The Prince*. Ed. Russell Price and Quentin Skinner. Cambridge: Cambridge University Press, 1988.

—— *The Discourses*. Translated by Leslie J. Walker. Edited by Bernard Crick. Harmondsworth: Penguin Books, 1970.

Maimonides, Moses. *The Guide for the Perplexed*. Translated by Michael Friedländer. 2nd ed. London: Routledge, 1928.

Malcolm, Noel. *Aspects of Hobbes*. Oxford: Clarendon Press, 2002.

—— 'Hobbes and Spinoza'. In *Aspects of Hobbes*. Oxford: Clarendon Press, 2002, 27–52.

Marshall, John. *John Locke, Toleration and Early Enlightenment Culture: Religious Intolerance and Arguments for Religious Toleration in Early Modern And 'Early Enlightenment' Europe*. Cambridge: Cambridge University Press, 2006.

Marshall, Sherrin. *The Dutch Gentry, 1500–1650: Family, Faith and Fortune*. New York: Greenwood, 1987.

Martin, Christopher. 'A New Challenge to the Necessitarian Reading of Spinoza'. In *Oxford Studies in Early Modern Philosophy*, edited by Daniel Garber and Steven Nadler. Oxford: Oxford University Press, 2010, 25–70.

Masius, A. *Iosuæ imperatoris historia illustrata atque explicata*. Antwerp, 1574.

Mason, Richard. *The God of Spinoza: A Philosophical Study*. Cambridge: Cambridge University Press, 1997.

Matheron, Alexandre. *Individu et communauté chez Spinoza*. Paris: Les Éditions de Minuit, 1969.

—— *Le Christ et le salut des ignorants chez Spinoza*. Paris: Aubier Montaigne, 1971.

—— 'Femmes et serviteurs dans le democratie Spinoziste'. In *Speculum Spinozanum*. London: Routledge, 1977, 368–86.

—— 'Spinoza et la problématique juridique de Grotius'. *Philosophie* 4 (1984), 69–89.

—— 'Le "droit du plus fort": Hobbes contra Spinoza'. *Revue Philosophique de la France et de l'Étranger* 110 (1985), 149–76.

—— 'The Theoretical Function of Democracy in Spinoza and Hobbes'. In *The New Spinoza*, edited by Warren Montag and Ted Stolze. Minneapolis, Minn.: University of Minnesota Press, 1997, 207–8.

Matson, Wallace. 'Death and Destruction in Spinoza's Ethics'. *Inquiry* 20 (1977), 403–17.

McKim, Donald E., ed. *Calvin and the Bible*. Cambridge: Cambridge University Press, 2006.

Mechoulan, Henry. 'Morteira et Spinoza au carrefour du Socinianisme'. *Revue des études juives* 135, nos. 1–3 (1976), 51–76.

—— and Gérard Nahon. 'Introduction'. In *The Hope of Israel: The English Translation by Moses Wall, 1652*. Oxford: Oxford University Press, 1987, 1–102.

Meijer, Lodewijk. *Philosophia S. Scripturæ Interpres*. Amsterdam, 1666.

Meinsma, K. O. *Spinoza et son cercle: Étude critique historique sur les hétérodoxes Hollandais*. Translated by S. Roosenberg and J.-P. Osier. Paris: Vrin, 1983.

Melamed, Yitzhak Y. 'The Metaphysics of the *Theologico-Political Treatise*'. In *Spinoza's 'Theologico-Political Treatise'*, edited by Yitzhak Y. Melamed and Michael A. Rosenthal. Cambridge: Cambridge University Press, 2010, 128–42.

Melammed, Renée Levine. *A Question of Identity: Iberian Conversos in Historical Perspective*. Oxford: Oxford University Press, 2004.

Meyer, Louis. *La philosophie interprète de l'écriture sainte*. Translated by Jacqueline Lagrée and Pierre-François Moreau. Paris: Intertextes, 1988.

Miller, Jon. 'Spinoza and the Law of Nature'. *History of Philosophy Quarterly* 20, no. 3 (2003), 257–76.

—— 'Spinoza's Axiology'. In *Oxford Studies in Early Modern Philosophy*, edited by Daniel Garber and Steven Nadler. Oxford: Oxford University Press, 2005, 149–72.

Milton, J. R. 'The Origin and Development of the Concept of the "Law of Nature"', *Archives Européennes de Sociologie*, no. 22 (1981), 173–95.

—— 'Laws of Nature'. In *The Cambridge History of Seventeenth Century Philosophy*, edited by Daniel Garber and Michael Ayers. Cambridge: Cambridge University Press, 1998, 680–701.

Montag, Warren. *Bodies, Masses, Power*. London: Verso, 1999.

Montag, Warren, and Ted Stolze. 'Preface'. In *The New Spinoza*, edited by Warren Montag and Ted Stolze. Minneapolis, Minn.: University of Minnesota Press, 1997, ix–xx.

Moreau, Pierre-François. 'La lecture de la Bible dans le cercle de Spinoza'. In *Le grand siècle et la Bible*, edited by Jean-Robert Armogathe. Paris: Beauchesne, 1989, 97–115.

—— 'Les principes de la lecture de l'écriture sainte dans le *Tractatus Theologico-Politicus*'. In *L'écriture sainte au temps de Spinoza dans le système spinoziste*. Paris: Presse Universitaire de Paris Sorbonne, 1992, 119–31.

—— 'Fortune and the Theory of History'. In *The New Spinoza*, edited by Warren Montag and Ted Stolze. Minneapolis, Minn.: University of Minnesota Press, 1997, 97–108.

Nadler, Steven. 'Spinoza in the Garden of Good and Evil'. In *The Problem of Evil in Early Modern Philosophy*, edited by Elmar Kremer and Michael Latzer. Toronto: University of Toronto Press, 2001, 66–80.

—— Spinoza. *A Life*. Cambridge: Cambridge University Press, 1999.

—— *Spinoza's Heresy: Immortality and the Jewish Mind*. Oxford: Clarendon Press, 2001.

Negri, Antonio. *The Savage Anomaly: The Power of Spinoza's Metaphysics and Politics*. Translated by Michael Hardt. Minneapolis Minn.: University of Minnesota Press, 1991.

—— '*Reliqua Desiderantur*: A Conjecture for a Definition of the Concept of Democracy in the Final Spinoza'. In *The New Spinoza*, edited by Warren Montag and Ted Stolze. Minneapolis, Minn.: University of Minnesota Press, 1997, 219–46.

Nellen, H. J. M., and Edwin Rabbie, eds. *Hugo Grotius Theologian: Essays in Honour of G. H. M. Posthumus Meyjes*. Leiden: Brill, 1994.

Nelson, Eric. *The Hebrew Republic: Jewish Sources and the Transformation of European Political Thought*. Cambridge, Mass.: Harvard University Press, 2010.

Nobbs, Douglas. *Theocracy and Toleration: A Study of the Disputes in Dutch Calvinism from 1600 to 1650*. Cambridge: Cambridge University Press, 1938.

Osler, Margaret J. *Divine Will and the Mechanical Philosophy: Gassendi and Descartes on Contingency and Necessity in the Created World*. Cambridge: Cambridge University Press, 1994.

Pekelharing, Pieter. 'Reflections on Tolerance and Republicanism: The Case of the Dutch Republic'. (Unpublished). 1999.

Pettegree, Andrew. 'The Politics of Toleration in the Free Netherlands 1572–1620'. In *Tolerance and Intolerance in the European Reformation*, edited by Ole Peter Grell and Bob Scribner. Cambridge: Cambridge University Press, 1996.

Pines, Shlomo. 'Spinoza's "Tractatus Theologico-Politicus" and the Jewish Philosophical Tradition'. In *Jewish Thought in the Seventeenth Century*, edited by Isadore Twersky and Bernard Septimus. Cambridge, Mass.: Harvard University Press, 1987, 499–521.

Plutarch. *The Philosophie, Commonly Called, the Morals, Written by the Learned Philosopher, Plutarch of Chæronea*. Translated by Philemon Holland. London, 1603.

—— *Moralia*. Translated by Frank Cole Babbitt, *Loeb Classical Library*. Cambridge, Mass.: Harvard University Press, 1928.

Popkin, Richard H. *Isaac La Peyrère (1596–1676): His Life, Work, and Influence*. Leiden: Brill, 1987.

—— *The Third Force in Seventeenth Century Thought*. Leiden: Brill, 1992.

—— 'Spinoza and Bible Scholarship'. In *The Cambridge Companion to Spinoza*, edited by Don Garrett. Cambridge: Cambridge University Press, 1996, 383–407.

Prak, Maarten Roy. *The Dutch Republic in the Seventeenth Century: The Golden Age*. Translated by Diane Webb. Cambridge: Cambridge University Press, 2005.

Preus, J. Samuel. *Spinoza and the Irrelevance of Biblical Authority*. Cambridge: Cambridge University Press, 2001.

Prokhovnik, Raia. *Spinoza and Republicanism*. Basingstoke: Palgrave Macmillan, 2004.

Puckett, David. *John Calvin's Exegesis of the Old Testament*. Louisville, KY.: Westminster John Knox Press, 1995.

Raei, Joannes de. *Cogitata de interpretatione, quibus natura humani sermonis et illius rectus usus, ab hujus seculi errore et confusione vindicantur*. Amsterdam, 1692.

Ravven, Heidi M., and Lenn E. Goodman, eds. *Jewish Themes in Spinoza's Philosophy*. Albany, NY: SUNY Press, 2002.

Raz-Krakotzkin, Amnon. *The Censor, the Editor and the Text: The Catholic Church and the Shaping of the Jewish Canon in the Sixteenth Century*. Philadelphia: University of Pennsylvania Press, 2007.

Révah, Israël S. *Spinoza Et Le Dr. Juan De Prado*. Paris: La Haye, 1959.

Rijn, Rembrandt van. 'Jan Uytenbogaert, Preacher of the Remonstrants'. Engraving. Cambridge: Fitzwilliam Museum, 1635.

Rooden, Peter T. van. *Theology, Biblical Scholarship and Rabbinical Studies in the Seventeenth Century: Constantijn L'empereur (1591–1648): Professor of Hebrew and Theology at Leiden*. Leiden: Brill, 1989.

—— 'Conceptions of Judaism in the Seventeenth Century Dutch Republic'. In *Christianity and Judaism*, edited by D. Wood. Oxford: Oxford University Press, 1992, 299–308.

Rosenthal, Michael. 'Two Collective Action Problems in Spinoza's Social Contract Theory'. *History of Philosophy Quarterly* 15, no. 4 (1998), 389–409.

—— 'Spinoza's Dogmas of the Universal Faith and the Problem of Religion'. *Philosophy and Theology* 13, no. 1 (2001), 53–82.

—— 'Spinoza, History, and Jewish Modernity'. In *Philosophers and the Hebrew Bible*, edited by Charles H. Manekin and Robert Eisen. Bethseda: University of Maryland Press, 2008, 113–32.

—— 'Spinoza and the Philosophy of History'. In *Interpreting Spinoza: Critical Essays*, edited by Charlie Huenemann. Cambridge: Cambridge University Press, 2008, 111–27.

Rosenthal, Michael. 'Miracles, Wonder and the State'. In *Spinoza's 'Theologico-Political Treatise'*, edited by Yitzhak Y. Melamed and Michael A. Rosenthal. Cambridge: Cambridge University Press, 2010, 231–49.

Rowen, Herbert H. *John De Witt, Grand Pensionary of Holland, 1625–1672*. Princeton: Princeton University Press, 1978.

Ruler, J. A. van. *The Crisis of Causality: Voetius and Descartes on God, Nature, and Change*. Leiden: Brill, 1995.

Rutherford, Donald. 'Spinoza's Conception of Law: Metaphysics and Ethics'. In *Spinoza's 'Theologico-Political Treatise'. A Critical Guide*, edited by Yitzhak Y. Melamed and Michael A. Rosenthal. Cambridge: Cambridge University Press, 2010, 143–67.

Schama, Simon. *The Embarrassment of Riches: An Interpretation of Dutch Culture in the Golden Age*. London: Collins, 1987.

Schookius, Martinus. *Physica Generalis*. Grongingen, 1660.

Scott, Jonathan. 'Classical Republicanism in Seventeenth-Century England and the Netherlands'. In *Republicanism: A Shared European Heritage*, edited by Martin van Gelderen and Quentin Skinner, 2 vols. Cambridge: Cambridge University Press, 2002, vol. 1, 61–84.

Secretan, Catherine. 'La réception de Hobbes aux Pays Bas'. *Studia Spinozana*, no. 3 (1987).

Shabbatai Zevi. In *Encyclopaedia Judaica*. Farmington Hills, Mich.: Macmillan Reference, 2007, 340–59.

Simons, Menno. *The Complete Writings of Menno Simons*. Translated by Leonard Verduin. Edited by J. C. Wenger. Scottdale, Pa.: Herald Press, 1956.

Skinner, Quentin. *The Foundations of Modern Political Thought*. 2 vols. Cambridge: Cambridge University Press, 1978.

—— *Liberty before Liberalism*. Cambridge: Cambridge University Press, 1998.

—— *Hobbes and Republican Liberty*. Cambridge: Cambridge University Press, 2008.

Smith, Steven B. *Spinoza, Liberalism, and the Question of Jewish Identity*. New Haven, Conn.: Yale University Press, 1997.

Spinoza, Benedict de. *Korte Verhandeling Van God, Den Mensch, En Deszelfs Welstand*. Edited by Carl Gebhardt. Vol. I, *Opera*. Heidelberg: Carl Winter, 1924.

—— *Renati Des Cartes Principiorum Philosophiæ Pars I. et II., More Geometrico Demonstratæ Per Benedictum De Spinoza. Accesserunt Ejusdem Cogitata Metaphysica*. Edited by Carl Gebhardt. Vol. I, *Opera*. Heidelberg: Carl Winter, 1924.

—— *Tractatus De Intellectus Emendatione*. Edited by Carl Gebhardt. Vol. II, *Opera*. Heidelberg: Carl Winter, 1924.

—— *Ethica*. Edited by Carl Gebhardt. Vol. II, *Opera*. Heidelberg: Carl Winter, 1924.

—— *Tractatus Theologico-Politicus*. Edited by Carl Gebhardt. Vol. III, *Opera*. Heidelberg: Carl Winter, 1924.

—— *Epistolæ*. Edited by Carl Gebhardt. Vol. IV, *Opera*. Heidelberg: Carl Winter, 1924.

—— *The Emendation of the Intellect*. Translated by Edwin Curley. Vol. 1, *The Collected Works of Spinoza*. Princeton: Princeton University Press, 1985.

—— *Short Treatise on God, Man, and His Well-Being*. Translated by Edwin Curley. Vol. 1, *The Collected Works of Spinoza*. Princeton: Princeton University Press, 1985.

—— *Letters*. Translated by Edwin Curley. Vol. 1, *The Collected Works of Spinoza*. Princeton: Princeton University Press, 1985.

—— *Parts I and II of Descartes' 'Principles* of Philosophy'. Translated by Edwin Curely. Vol. I, *The Collected Works of Spinoza*. Princeton: Princeton University Press, 1985.

—— *Appendix Containing Metaphysical Thoughts*. Translated by Edwin Curley. Vol. 1, *The Collected Works of Spinoza*. Princeton: Princeton University Press, 1985.

—— *Ethics*. Translated by Edwin Curley. Vol. 1, *The Collected Works of Spinoza*. Princeton: Princeton University Press, 1985.

—— *The Correspondence of Spinoza*. Translated and edited by Abraham Wolf. London: Frank Cass, 1966.

—— *Traité Théologico-Politique*. Edited by Fokke Akkerman, Jacqueline Lagrée, and Pierre-François Moreau. Vol. 3 *Œuvres De Spinoza*. Paris: Presses Universitaires de France, 1999.

Steenbakkers, Piet. 'The Text of Spinoza's *Tractatus Theologico-Politicus*'. In *Spinoza's 'Theologico-Political Treatise'*, edited by Yitzhak Y. Melamed and Michael A. Rosenthal. Cambridge: Cambridge University Press, 2010, 29–40.

Steinberg, Justin. 'Benedict Spinoza: Epistemic Democrat'. *History of Philosophy Quarterly* 27, no. 2 (2010), 145–64.

—— 'On Being *Sui Iuris*: Spinoza and the Republican Ideal of Liberty'. *History of European Ideas* 34, no. 3 (2008), 239–49.

—— 'Spinoza on Civil Liberation'. *Journal of the History of Philosophy* 47, no. 1 (2009), 35–58.

—— 'Spinoza's Curious Defense of Toleration'. In *Spinoza's 'Theologico-Political Treatise'*, edited by Yitzhak Y. Melamed and Michael A. Rosenthal. Cambridge: Cambridge University Press, 2010, 210–30.

Strauss, Leo. *Persecution and the Art of Writing*. Glencoe Ill: Free Press, 1952.

—— *Spinoza's Critique of Religion*. New York: Schocken Books, 1965.

—— 'How to Study Spinoza's "Theologico-Political Treatise"'. In *Jewish History and the Crisis of Modernity*. Albany NY.: SUNY Press, 1997, 181–233.

Suárez, Francisco. *De legibus, ac deo legislatore*. Translated and edited by Ammi Brown et al. Oxford: Clarendon Press, 1944.

Sutcliffe, Adam. *Judaism and Enlightenment*. Cambridge: Cambridge University Press, 2003.

Tacitus, Cornelius. *Histories 4–5. Annals 1–3*. Translated by C. H. Moore, *Loeb Classical Library*. Cambridge, Mass.: Harvard University Press, 1931.

Tosel, André. 'Superstition and Reading'. In *The New Spinoza*, edited by Warren Montag and Ted Stolze. Minneapolis, Minn.: University of Minnesota Press, 1997, 147–67.

Tostado, Alonzo. *Opera Omnia*. 23 vols. Venice, 1596.

Triglandius, Jacob. *Dissertatio theologica de civili et ecclesiastica potestate*. Amsterdam, 1642.

Tuck, Richard. 'Grotius and Selden'. In *The Cambridge History of Political Thought 1450–1700*, edited by J. H. Burns and Mark Goldie. Cambridge: Cambridge University Press, 1991.

—— *Philosophy and Government, 1572–1651*. Cambridge: Cambridge University Press, 1993.

Uyl, Douglas den. *Power, State and Freedom: An Interpretation of Spinoza's Political Philosophy*. Assen: Van Gorcum, 1983.

—— 'Sociality and Social Contract: A Spinozistic Perspective'. *Studia Spinozana* 1 (1985), 19–51.

Uytenbogaert, Jan. *Tractaet van t'ampt ende authoriteyt eener hoggher christelicker overheydt, in kerckelicke saecken*. The Hague, 1610.

—— *Remonstrantie van J. Utenbogaert aen de Staten Generael*, Leiden, 1618.

Van den Berg, J. 'Eschatological Expectations Concerning the Conversion of the Jews in the Netherlands During the Seventeenth Century'. In *Puritans, the Millennium and the Future of Israel. Puritan Eschatology from 1600–1660*, edited by P. Toom. London: James Clark, 1970, 137–53.

Van der Wall, Ernestine. 'Petrus Serrarius and Menasseh Ben Israel: Christian and Millenarian Messianism in Seventeenth-Century Amsterdam'. In *Menasseh Ben Israel and His World*, edited by Yosef Kaplan, Henry Méchoulan, and Richard H. Popkin. Leiden: Brill, 1989, 164–90.

Van Leeuwen, Henry G. *The Problem of Certainty in English Thought, 1630–1690*. The Hague: Martinus Nijhoff, 1963.

Velema, Wyger. 'That a Republic Is Better Than a Monarchy': Anti-Monarchism in Early Modern Dutch Political Thought'. In *Republicanism and Constitutionalism in Early Modern Europe*, edited by Martin van Gelderen and Quentin Skinner. 2 vols. Cambridge: Cambridge University Press, 2002, vol. 1, 9–26.

Velthuysen, Lambert van. *Nader bewys, dat noch de leere van de sonne stilstandt en des aertryx beweging, noch de gronden van de philosophie van Renatus Des Cartes strijdig sijn met Godts-woort*. Utrecht, 1656–7.

—— *De initiis primæ philosophiæ juxta fundamenta clarissimi Cartesii, tradita in ipsis meditationibus, necnon de Deo et mente humana*. Utrecht, 1662.

—— *Opera Omnia*. 2 vols. Rotterdam, 1680.

Verbeek, Theo. *Descartes and the Dutch: Early Reactions to Cartesian Philosophy, 1637–1650*. Carbondale, Ill.: Southern Illinois University Press, 1992.

—— 'Tradition and Novelty: Descartes and Some Cartesians'. In *The Rise of Modern Philosophy: The Tension between the New and Traditional Philosophies from Machiavelli to Leibniz*, edited by Tom Sorell. Oxford: Clarendon Press, 1993, 167–96.

—— 'Spinoza and Cartesianism'. In *Judaeo-Christian Intellectual Culture in the Seventeenth Century: A Celebration of the Library of Narcissus Marsh (1638–1713)*, edited by Allison Coudert. Dordrecht: Kluwer, 1999, 173–84.

—— *Spinoza's Theologico-Political Treatise: Exploring 'the Will of God'*. Aldershot: Ashgate, 2003.

Vermij, Rienk. *The Calvinist Copernicans: The Reception of the New Astronomy in the Dutch Republic, 1575–1750*. Amsterdam: Koninklijke Nederlandse Akademie van Wetenschappen, 2002.

Vinciguerra, Lorenzo. *Spinoza et le signe: La Genèse de l'imagination*. Paris: Vrin, 2005.

Voetius, Gisbertus. *Disputationes Theologicae Selectae*. 5 vols. Utrecht, 1648–69.

—— *Politica Ecclesiastica*. Amsterdam, 1663–76.

—— 'Concerning "Precision" in Interpretation of Questions 94, 113, and 115 of the [Heidelberg] Catechism'. In *Reformed Dogmatics: J. Wollebius, G. Voetius, F. Turretin*, edited by John Walter Beardslee. Oxford: Oxford University Press, 1965, 316–34.

—— 'Concerning Practical Theology'. In *Reformed Dogmatics: J. Wollebius, G. Voetius, F. Turretin*, edited by John Walter Beardslee. Oxford: Oxford University Press, 1965, 265–316.

Vossius, Gerardus. *Historia pelagiana sive historiae de controversiis quas Pelagius ejusque reliquiae moverunt*. Amsterdam: Leiden, 1608.

Waarmond, Vraderyck. *'T Nieuw woordenboek der regten, ofte een vertaalinge en uytlegginge van meest alle de Latijnsche woorden en wijse van spreeken, in alle regten en regtsgeleerders boeken en schriften gebruykelijk*. Amsterdam, 1664.

Weststeijn, Arthur. 'The Power of "Pliant Stuff": Fables and Frankness in Seventeenth-Century Dutch Republicanism', *Journal of the History of Ideas* 72, no. 1 (2011), 1–27.

Wittichius, Christophoros. *Dissertationes Duæ*. Amsterdam, 1653.

—— *Consensus veritatis in scriptura divina . . . revelatæ cum veritate philosophica a R. Descartes detecta*. Nejmegen, 1659.

Wolf, Lucien. *Menasseh Ben Israel's Mission to Oliver Cromwell*. London: Jewish Society of England, 1901.

Wolfson, Harry Austryn. *The Philosophy of Spinoza*. New York: Meridian Books, 1958.

Youpa, Andrew. 'Spinozistic Self-Preservation', *Southern Journal of Philosophy* 41, no. 3 (2003), 477–90.

Youpa, Andrew. 'Spinoza's Theory of the Good'. In *The Cambridge Companion to Spinoza's Ethics*, edited by Olli Koistinen. Cambridge: Cambridge University Press, 2009, 242–57.

Yovel, Yirmiyahu. *Spinoza and Other Heretics*. 2 vols. Princeton: Princeton University Press, 1989.

Yovel, Yirmiyahu. ed. *Desire and Affect: Spinoza as Psychologist*. New York: Little Room Press, 1999.

Zac, Sylvain. 'État et nature chez Spinoza', *Revue de métaphysique et de morale* 49 (1964), 14–40.

—— *Spinoza et l'interprétation de l'écriture*. Paris: Presses Universitaires de France, 1965.

—— *Philosophie, théologie, politique dans l'œuvre de Spinoza*. Paris: Vrin, 1979.

—— *Essais spinozistes*. Paris: Vrin, 1985.

Zimmermann, Frank. *The Aramaic Origin of the Four Gospels*. New York: Ktav, 1979.

Index